Alliances

To Mary Furse,

Stephen W. Enderson

Alliances

A Theory of Concerted Human Behavior

STEPHEN W. EUBANK

FIRST EDITION

Catellus Publishing ❖ Houston, Texas

Alliances
A Theory of Concerted Human Behavior
By Stephen W. Eubank

Inquiries should be addressed to:

Catellus Publishing
P.O. Box 550409
Houston, Texas 77255-0409
questions@catelluspublishing.com
www.catelluspublishing.com

First Edition
First Printing 2006

Library of Congress Cataloging-in-Publication Data

Eubank, Stephen W.
Alliances—A Theory of Concerted Human Behavior

    p.   cm.

Includes index.

I. Alliance Theory II. Human Interaction III. Social Interaction
IV. Social Dynamics V. Knowledge, Theory of

ISBN 0-9785421-0-X
ISBN 97809785421-0-8

HM 131 477   302.54

Cover image from Mary Evans Picture Library

Printed in the United States of America
at Morgan Printing in Austin, Texas

Table of Contents

Introduction

This book consists of a theory of alliances. Its thesis is that a large portion of human interactions can be understood as constituting alliances that originate, function, evolve and ultimately end pursuant to certain principles and concepts. This book seeks to identify these underlying principles and concepts and to demonstrate how they might be utilized to understand various human institutions and arrangements that have existed throughout time. This book suggests that alliance theory can be used to understand and analyze ancient organizations such as clans, tribes, villages, and city states as well as newer developments such as kingdoms, empires, and modern nation states. Further, this book proposes that the same alliance theory can be employed to study much more basic associations such as corporations, partnerships, charitable institutions, mutual insurance associations, country clubs, carpools, investments associations, neighborhood-watch programs, and so on. It is hoped that alliance theory will offer the social sciences and the humanities new tools for investigation and study in their respective disciplines.

This book may also offer a new language for contemporary discussions of current events and issues that are of concern to non-academicians. At this juncture in history, it appears that many discussions and debates regarding current events are hampered or thoroughly obstructed by a profound inability to communicate through commonly accepted concepts and principles. If current discussions, debates, and arguments are reviewed for substance, one will usually find that the participants are approaching the central issue from widely varying perspectives or worldviews. The typical result is that the participants are effectively speaking different languages and are unable to comprehend and appreciate the arguments set forward by the other side. As a consequence, it is not uncommon for many discussions and debates to degenerate into acrimony and name calling. It is hoped that this book will supply an analytical framework for persons of widely varying backgrounds, beliefs, worldviews, and dogmas to communicate effectively and identify the true points and issues upon which they disagree.

It should be underscored that this book consists of a *theory* of alliances. The subject matter that it tackles has enormous breadth. As such, no effort is made to prove the theory in a conventional manner. In fact, the principles and concepts identified in the book are not the product of research in a traditional sense. Rather, this book is largely the result of personal experience, observation, and reflection. Because of the novel nature of this work, it is entirely possible that mistakes and errors have been made unwittingly. As a result, debate and criticism regarding the contents of this book are both welcome and encouraged.

ABOUT THE ORGANIZATION AND STRUCTURE OF THE BOOK

This book is organized into six parts with titles that should be self-explanatory. Parts I through III set forward the principles of the book. The chapters within these three parts detail the essential elements and concepts of alliance theory. The chapters within Parts IV through VI apply these principles to various events of the past. Part IV surveys an assortment of historical topics and attempts to analyze them using alliance theory. Part V focuses upon the alliance aspects of the structure of the United States of America and its history. Part VI concludes with speculation regarding the future and offers individual readers questions to consider in their own personal experiences.

The book uses twenty reoccurring examples to illustrate certain points and applications of the theory. Most examples are referenced many times later in the book. For instance, Part I sets forward eight examples of alliances. These eight examples reappear throughout Parts I through III. Other examples originate in Parts II and III and reappear later in the book. When the examples are discussed subsequently, the facts are sometimes modified to explore a new point.

The first six chapters have summaries at the end that recap key points and concepts. These chapter summaries are not used later in the book.

In utilizing indefinite pronouns and other gender specific terminology, the author decided to utilize only the masculine gender. This practice was done to avoid stilted sentences that result when both genders are referenced or the confusion that at times results when the gender is alternated. The reader should be assured that the masculine gender has been used only for purposes of efficiency and uniformity. The absence of references to the feminine gender should not be construed as an indication that alliance principles do not apply to women or that the author holds a discriminatory animus towards women. Any such inferences are false.

Ancient dates are referred to using the following terminology. "Before Christ" or "BC" will be referred to as "Before Common Era" or "BCE." "Anno Domini" or "AD" will be referred to as "Common Era" or "CE." It is the author's understanding that such terminology has become commonplace in the world of academia.

PART I

The Basics of Alliances

CHAPTER 1

Alliance Defined

The principles underlying an alliance are best seen through contemplating examples. Review the following seven examples and consider what they have in common. These seven examples, along with others, will be re-examined throughout this book.

Example 1 "Move the boulder"—A large boulder falls into a pathway frequented by a caveman. The caveman attempts to shove it aside but the boulder is too massive. The caveman finds three other cavemen who frequent the pathway and they agree to push on the boulder together. By combining their efforts, the four move the heavy boulder out of the pathway.

Example 2 "Slay the mammoth"—A prehistoric hunter has long desired to slay a woolly mammoth, but knows that the creature is simply too massive to take down with his wooden spear. After watching a pack of wolves work together to kill a large bison, he concludes that maybe humans can hunt the same way. He assembles twenty others interested in slaying a mammoth. They locate a mammoth, quickly encircle it, and start attacking it from all sides. The mammoth attempts to fight and then flee, but there are too many attackers. The mammoth crashes to the ground riddled with spear holes. The hunters have food for weeks.

Example 3 "Dig the well"—Suffering from a severe drought, ten primitive farmers work together to quickly dig a well. At a depth of 40 feet, they strike the water table. The water is apportioned amongst the ten farmers and their crops are saved.

Example 4 "Wild West"—Somewhere in old "Wild West" of the United States, a small community quickly takes root. As the community grows, it soon attracts a steady fare of thieves and gunfighters. The community members become unsettled by this development and put the money they can spare together to

3

hire a mercenary. The mercenary drives off the criminal elements, bringing order and decency to the community.

Example 5 "Help the needy"—During desperate times, a charitable person strives to give a portion of his modest income to the needy people he comes across on the street, but he senses that his small and sporadic gifts are doing very little. After discussing the matter with his neighbors, he finds that they too give out money on the street and also feel that the gesture is not accomplishing much. The neighbors all agree to combine their gifts and use the large collection to help the needy in a systematic and well-organized manner. Each month, the members meet and a majority vote determines the specific goal that the collection will be used to achieve. After the first collection is taken up, the members vote to set up a soup kitchen. The kitchen is able to feed hundreds of needy people per day.

Example 6 "Carpool"—The children of five parents living in the same neighborhood all play soccer on the other side of town. The parents spend substantial time and gasoline driving their kids back and forth from the soccer practices and matches. One day, a parent proposes a carpool to the other four parents. Each parent agrees to drive all of the children for a given week. Through the carpool, each parent realizes substantial savings in time and gasoline.

Example 7 "Buy the boat"—A parent wants to have a sailboat for his family to use on the weekends. But he has only one-third of the money necessary to buy the boat. He talks to his friends and finds two others that want a boat as well, but cannot afford to purchase one. Together, the three buy the boat with each paying one-third of the price and taking a one-third ownership in the boat. Pursuant to the agreement reached before the boat was purchased, each parent has certain weekends in which he can use the boat with his family and all three have certain calendared cleaning and maintenance duties.

What do these seven examples have in common?

Answer: They are alliances.

In each situation, two or more individuals desired something but realized either:

1) They could not achieve it on their own, or

2) They could achieve it much more effectively or efficiently through a combined effort.

Having made this realization, the individuals then agreed in some manner to contribute resources towards a combined effort at achieving the objective.

THE FOUR ELEMENTS OF AN ALLIANCE

An alliance has four fundamental components:

Objective	Members	Accord	Resource Contribution

Part I of this book discusses each of these components in detail. A chapter is devoted to each one. This chapter provides a brief overview of all four topics.

OBJECTIVE

The essence of an alliance is that it provides some type of advantage or benefit over individual effort. In each example, the individuals identify an objective that they all desire. They then work together to achieve that commonly desired objective. The only reason that they work together is because a combined effort offers more advantages than an individual effort.

Sometimes this advantage or benefit is *absolute* because the individual simply cannot achieve the desired result by his own effort.

Example 1 "**Move the boulder**"—The caveman tries to shove the boulder out of the pathway but is unable to do so. Only by forming an alliance with three other cavemen is the boulder moved.

In other circumstances, the advantage or benefit is *relative*. That is, the individual is able to achieve the desired result but a combined effort is more effective or efficient.

Example 5 "**Help the needy**"—The charitable individual is able to achieve the desired result—helping the needy—simply by handing out a portion of his income on the street. However, he finds that combining his gifts with his neighbors is a much more effective way of achieving his objective.

Example 6 "**Carpool**"—The parents are in fact able to transport their children to and from the soccer events. But, by forming a carpool, they achieve this goal much more efficiently by reducing the amount of time and gasoline spent.

MEMBERS

In addition to an objective, alliances have members. In fact, all alliances have at least two members and potentially many more. These members all desire to achieve the objective of the alliance and they participate in the alliance for that reason.

> **Example 2 "Slay the mammoth"**—All of the members of the hunting party desire to slay a mammoth.

> **Example 3 "Dig the well"**—All of the members digging the well desperately want a water supply to save their crops.

The same holds true for the other examples. All members desire the same objective at which the combined effort is directed.

ACCORD

A third characteristic of alliances is an accord. Accord means some type of agreement between the members to the effect that they will work together to achieve the commonly desired objective. Alliances can take many forms and so can the agreements underlying them. In each of the examples, there is an agreement of some type among all of the members.

> **Example 3 "Dig the well"**—The agreement is fairly simple. All members are to dig at the well until they reach the water table and then they share in the water.

> **Example 7 "Buy the boat"**—The agreement is more complex. The three members have to agree (i) to combine their monies towards the purchase of the boat; (ii) to the times when each parent can use the boat; and (iii) how cleaning and maintenance duties will be apportioned amongst the families.

Some alliances require decisions to be made. In these situations, there might be accords on processes to make the decisions. These decision-making processes can range from the very simple to the extremely complex.

CONTRIBUTION OF RESOURCES

The final characteristic of alliances is contribution of resources. All members must contribute some type of resource towards the achievement of the objective. In the examples, all members contributed something towards achieving the objective.

> **Example 1 "Move the boulder"**—The resource contributed is *labor*, that is, pushing on the boulder.

Example 4 "Wild West"—The resource is *money* that was used to hire the mercenary.

There are no limitations on what can constitute a resource. Anything can be a resource so long as it can be combined with something possessed by other members to achieve the objective of the alliance.

CHAPTER SUMMARY

An alliance exists if the following four characteristics are present.

1. **Objective**—The purpose of the alliance is to accomplish an objective. This objective can be of two types:

   - An objective that cannot be achieved by individual effort but instead only through a combined effort; or

   - An objective that can be achieved more effectively or efficiently through a combined effort, in contrast to individual effort.

2. **Membership**—At least two individuals are members of the alliance and desire the achievement of the objective.

3. **Accord**—There is an agreement of some type between the members regarding the objective and the means to be employed in pursuing the objective.

4. **Contribution**—All members contribute resources towards the achievement of the objective.

CHAPTER 2

The Objective

The first characteristic of an alliance is the objective. The objective is the foundation of the alliance. It is the motivating factor that brings the members together to form the alliance. And, if the alliance is of a long-term nature, the objective is the glue that holds the alliance together.

Objective—The fundamental purpose of an alliance is to attain a certain goal or end result, which will be referred to in this book as an "objective." This objective can be of two types: (i) an objective that cannot be achieved by individual effort but only through a combined effort; or (ii) an objective that can be achieved more effectively or efficiently through a combined effort, in contrast to individual effort.

INDIVIDUAL DESIRE AND OBJECTIVES

All individuals have desires. Although these desires vary substantially from individual to individual, the fact remains that desires exist and all individuals have them. When an individual has a desire, he typically acts upon it. If a person feels thirsty, he gets a glass of water. If he needs to exercise, he goes for a run. If he wants to know the news, he purchases a newspaper. In these situations, the individual has identified *objectives*—thirst, exercise, and curiosity—and attained them through taking action.

The identification of an objective does not guarantee action. An important factor is the ability to achieve the objective. If an individual believes that he is not capable of achieving the objective, no action will be taken.

Example 2 "Slay the mammoth"—The prehistoric hunter wants to slay the mammoth, but concludes that he is not able to do so. He leaves the mammoth alone.

8

Another factor is the cost or effort required to achieve that objective. If the individual perceives that the cost or effort required to achieve the objective is greater than the value he attributes to the objective, no action will be taken.

Example 7 "Buy the boat"—One of the three members is interested in a sailboat and actually has enough money in the bank to buy one. He concludes, however, that the price of the sailboat is greater than any satisfaction that he or his family might get out of sailing it. He does not buy the boat.

INABILITY TO ATTAIN AN OBJECTIVE

At times, an individual's objectives are simply not attainable by individual effort. If individual effort fails, must the objective be abandoned? No. The objective need not be abandoned if it can be attained through a combined effort.

Example 1 "Move the boulder"—The caveman cannot move the boulder by himself, but by enlisting three other cavemen, sufficient strength is mustered and the boulder is moved from the pathway.

One can imagine similar examples where an individual effort fails but a combined effort provides the solution. Overall, many desires of individuals cannot be attained through individual effort. Instead, these desires can be satisfied only through a combined effort.

EFFECTIVENESS OR EFFICIENCY
OF COMBINED EFFORT

Many desires can be attained through individual effort, but a combined effort might be a more effective or more efficient means of achieving the effort.

Example 1 "Move the boulder"—What if the boulder is not as massive and the caveman has the physical capability of moving it off of the pathway? Will the caveman still have a reason to participate in a combined effort to move the boulder? Possibly. Physical exertion can be taxing and moving a boulder can result in injury. Thus, even though the caveman is able to move the boulder, he still might want to enlist the help of others.

Example 3 "Dig the well"—It is possible for each of the primitive farmers to attempt to dig their own wells, but they are desperate to find water and, if they dig separately, they might not locate water in time to save their crops. By combining their efforts, they are able to dig a deep well and quickly locate water.

Example 7 "Buy the boat"—One of the three members has enough money in the bank to buy the sailboat, but he figures that he and his family will not enjoy the boat enough to justify paying the high purchase price. By joining the alliance, however, the member pays much less (that is, one-third of the price) and can use the sailboat as much as he and his family really want (that is, every third week).

There are abundant circumstances where individuals can achieve their desires through their own efforts. But a combined effort is more effective or efficient.

What is the difference between "effectiveness" and "efficiency?" Generally speaking, *effectiveness* means that more quantity or greater quality of the objective can be achieved through combining efforts. Effectiveness can be thought of as a combined effort providing "more bang for the buck," in contrast to individual effort.

Example 5 "Help the needy"—The combined gifts hold the potential to help the needy much more than the gifts given out sporadically on the street.

Efficiency means that the same objective can be achieved through a combined effort but with less expenditure of resources. Efficiency can be thought of as cost savings. Cost savings are not limited to money savings. Instead, they include reductions in labor, time, money, or whatever an individual might utilize to achieve an objective through his own efforts.

Example 6 "Carpool"—The carpool attained the same objective of having the kids transported to soccer events, but at great savings of time and gasoline.

Sometimes a combined effort will produce both effectiveness and efficiency. That is, the combined effort provides more of the objective at less cost.

Example 3 "Dig the well"—Each member could have individually dug his own well, but all were desperate for water to save their crops. By forming an alliance, the objective of digging a well was achieved much more quickly or more *effectively*. In addition, because the digging was spread out over the ten members, the objective was achieved with much less effort from each member or much more *efficiently*.

NATURE OF THE OBJECTIVE

The objective can be literally anything desired by the members of the alliance. There are no boundaries on objectives that an alliance can pursue. An objective is inherently subjective. The defining feature of an objective is simply whether the members of the alliance desire it. If the members desire something and form an alliance to pursue it, that something is the objective. Objectives can appear bizarre or even repulsive to some individuals. An objective can be considered immoral, criminal, or evil yet still form the basis of an alliance.

THE RISE AND FALL
OF OBJECTIVES

As time passes, subjective desires will change. As a result, new objectives will arise while those of the past might fade away. Alliances will adapt to these changes in objectives. Long-standing alliances might disintegrate while new alliances will form, or they might modify themselves to meet the new objectives.

Example 2 "Slay the mammoth"—Mammoths are extinct, so there will be no more alliances to slay mammoths.

Example 7 "Buy the boat"—If sailing boats becomes unfashionable or otherwise undesirable, there will be no more alliances to buy sailboats.

SINGLE-OBJECTIVE
ALLIANCES

In its most simple form, an alliance has a single objective. Individuals identify a mutually desired objective and agree to contribute their resources towards its achievement. When the objective is achieved, the alliance terminates. As new objectives are identified, new alliances are formed. The process of creating a new alliance occurs over and over again for each objective desired.

Example 1 "Move the boulder"—The caveman forms the alliance to move the boulder. After it is moved off the pathway, the alliance is over and the cavemen go their separate ways. If a large tree falls on a water spring frequented by the caveman the next day, the caveman might enlist ten other cavemen to work together to drag the tree out of the spring. If another boulder blocks another favored pathway a week later, the caveman might put another alliance of cavemen together to push it out of the way. Each alliance is formed to pursue a single objective. When the objective is achieved, the alliance is disbanded. When a new objective arises, a new alliance is put together to address that single objective.

In all seven examples, the alliances have a single objective. Although the nature of the objectives varies from alliance to alliance, all are formed to pursue a single goal.

Example	Objective
One	Move the boulder
Two	Slay the mammoth
Three	Dig the well
Four	Regain order and decency
Five	Help the needy
Six	Transport the kids to soccer
Seven	Acquire a boat to sail

MULTI-OBJECTIVE ALLIANCES

Not all alliances are limited to a single objective. In fact, many alliances have more than one objective. Why is this? The answer lies in the difficulties associated with forming and maintaining separate alliances for each objective.

Multiple-objective alliances arise because of the efficiencies associated with their structure. The formation of, and the participation in, numerous alliances with single objectives can be time consuming and otherwise burdensome. Time is limited and, if an individual has many objectives that are well suited for achievement by an alliance, that individual will be very busy constantly forming and participating in separate alliances for each objective he desires.

Example 2 "Slay the Mammoth"—Twenty prehistoric hunters form an alliance to slay a mammoth. At the time they initially meet to agree on the alliance, one hunter complains that some marauders recently raided his camp and took most of his stored food and tools. Several other hunters speak up and complain of the same thing happening to them. All are now concerned about the marauders coming into their camp. Around the same time, another hunter speaks of a large tree of very hard wood that he located in the forest. He would like to cut it down and make many spears of it, but the tree is too large. After conferring, the twenty hunters agree to three objectives for their alliance: (i) to slay a mammoth, (ii) to hunt down and kill the marauders, and (iii) to cut down the large tree and use its hard wood to make many spears for everyone. This new alliance is the same as the original one, except that it has three objectives instead of one.

Forming an alliance that can tackle multiple objectives has the potential for reducing the time, attention, and other commitments that would be required if separate alliances were formed for each objective. A multi-objective alliance can "kill two birds with one stone."

IDENTIFICATION AND DESCRIPTION OF OBJECTIVES

The manner in which members describe or identify an objective can have a profound influence upon the nature of the alliance. This topic falls into three categories.

Specific Objective	Indefinite Objective	Open Objective

SPECIFIC OBJECTIVES

The simplest alliances are ones with specific and set objectives. Generally, these alliances are short lived. These are the types of alliances that are formed to address particular issues that arise from time. When the objectives are achieved, the alliances terminate. As new objectives arise, new alliances are formed to address them.

> **Example 2 "Slay the mammoth"**—The alliance is formed to achieve a specific objective—slaying a mammoth. After the mammoth is slain, the alliance terminates. In the modification of this example just discussed, the alliance has three specific objectives—(i) to slay a woolly mammoth; (ii) to hunt down and kill the marauders; and (iii) to cut down the large tree. After these are achieved, the alliance terminates.

Features associated with specific objective alliances will be discussed in greater detail subsequently.

INDEFINITE OBJECTIVES

The objectives of some alliances are indefinite or vague. Consider the objectives of the seven examples. Most of them are quite specific. It is evident what the purposes of the alliances are and it will be easy to determine if the objectives have been achieved. If the boulder in Example 1 is moved, the objective has been attained. Similarly, if the boat is acquired and sailed in Example 7, that objective has been attained as well.

Example	Objective
One	Move the boulder
Two	Slay the mammoth
Three	Dig the well
Four	Regain order and decency
Five	Help the needy
Six	Transport the kids to soccer
Seven	Acquire boat to sail

But two of the objectives are somewhat vague and imprecise. "Help the needy" of Example 5 is certainly not very clear. There are many different conceptions of "help." How can one determine if this objective has been achieved? Is any help sufficient or are only particular types of help acceptable? Are certain types of help (for example, food and shelter) to be preferred over others (for example, education)? Similarly, the objective of "order and decency" of Example 4 is not completely clear either. There are different types and degrees of "order." And "decency" has many subjective aspects. How is one to be sure what this objective means?

Objectives such as these are indefinite. Although all the members have a fairly good grasp of what the objectives mean, there are some gray areas. For example, in Example 4, all members would agree that "order and decency" includes putting an end to theft and gun fighting. But what else does it include? Does it encompass prostitution, adultery, alcohol consumption, lewd attire, or tobacco use?

Alliances that have indefinite objectives typically require a *decision-making process* to resolve these uncertainties. That is, part of the agreement initially struck will include some type of procedure or means for filling in the gray areas of the objective.

Example 5 "Help the needy"—The members agree to meet to vote on the specific measure the alliance will undertake to help the needy for a given month.

Example 4 "Wild West"—The members agree to elect a council of five community members to advise the mercenary on what "order and decency" means and does not mean.

Decision-making processes are a part of Chapter 4, which covers the accord. Decision-making processes are very important to the functioning of many alliances and are discussed throughout the book.

As a general rule, alliances with indefinite objectives tend to have two traits. First, they are likely to be long lasting, having been established to achieve the indefinite objective over an extended period of time. Second, they tend to require some type of decision-making process to define the objective in greater detail (that is, determining what falls within, and outside of, the objective).

OPEN OBJECTIVES

Sometimes alliances exist that really have no articulated objective. These alliances tend to be rather informal and are not common. In these situations, the alliance is formed and ready to act. But the questions are, "Act upon what? What is the objective?" Consider the following example.

> **Example 8 "Council of elders"**—Imagine a prehistoric tribal community. The tribe members live near each other and travel together. It is up to each tribe member to provide for his own food and shelter, except for children who are taken care of by parents. From time to time, various small alliances will form between certain individuals. These will be short lived and constitute single-objective alliances, such as to kill a sizeable animal, cut down a large tree, or move a heavy rock. When these objectives are completed, the alliances end. If another objective arises, another alliance will be formed. Observing the tribe, there appears to be no overall alliance between the tribe members as a whole. They behave like separate and distinct individuals that happen to live right near each other.
>
> One day, the oldest members of the tribe meet in private and talk. The next day, the tribe members pack up and move away to a new location where there is more food and water. A few weeks later there is talk of a band of thieves in the vicinity. The oldest members meet again. The next day, a war party of tribe members goes out, tracks down, and kills the thieves. A few weeks pass without rain. The oldest members meet again. The next day, all tribe members begin storing up as much food and water as they can in the tribe's storage bins.

What is going on here? There is an alliance, but it is very different from every alliance discussed so far. The difference is that the objective is open ended. In effect, the objective is to have a procedure in place to take advantage of circumstances where a combined action is advantageous to the members. That is, the tribe members have implicitly recognized that, while they are pretty much on their own, there are advantages to combined action from time to time. The problem is recognizing that the combined action is advantageous and acting upon it. To achieve this objective, there is an unspoken recognition that a council of elders will identify the objectives and decide how to achieve them.

As discussed in the example, the first thing the council did was observe that the community was using up all of the food and water in the area and then moved the tribe to a new location. The second was identification of a threat from the thieves and then organization of a hunting party to stamp the thieves out. The third was recognition of a coming food shortage and coordination of stores of food upon which tribe members can draw. In all circumstances, the council identified objectives that it believed all tribe members desired—abundant food, safety and security, food storages—and then devised solutions that employed a combined effort.

Like alliances with indefinite objectives, alliances with open objectives typically have certain characteristics. First, the alliances usually last a very long period of time. Second, the alliances typically rely heavily upon a decision-making process to identify both the objective and the means to achieve the objective. It is helpful to see the real objective as being the decision-making process. That is, the goal of the alliance is not a specific objective, but rather to have in place and ready for action, a long-standing (or permanent) process for identifying commonly desired objectives that are suitable for combined action. This arrangement is particularly appealing if the objectives require quick action or if it is otherwise difficult to continually form new single-objective alliances for each objective that might arise.

CHAPTER SUMMARY

1. The objective is an end, result, aim, or goal.

2. The objective is the motivating factor that brings members together to form an alliance. All members desire the achievement of the objective and form the alliance for that purpose.

3. Objectives that underlie alliances can be classified into two categories: (i) objectives that cannot be achieved by individual effort; and (ii) objectives that can be achieved more efficiently or effectively through a combined effort. The former pertains to objectives where individuals simply are not capable of achieving the objective by individual effort. The latter relates to situations where individuals are able to achieve an objective but combining efforts with others provides one or more advantages over individual effort. These advantages include gains in efficiency, effectiveness, or both.

4. Objectives can be anything, including matters found disgusting, outrageous, or criminal by some individuals.

5. Objectives rise and fall over time. There is no permanency to objectives.

6. A single-objective alliance is one that seeks to achieve a single objective.

7. A multi-objective alliance is one that seeks to achieve two or more objectives. Multi-objective alliances are motivated by efficiency concerns.

8. The description of objectives can fall into three categories: (i) specific, (ii) indefinite, and (iii) open. Alliances with specific objectives are typically simple and short lived. Alliances with indefinite objectives are usually more long term and typically require some type of decision-making process to define and/or limit the meaning of the vaguely described objective. Finally, alliances with open objectives are rare and require a decision-making process to select objectives. In this situation, the objective in reality is to have a decision-making process in place to select for the members objectives that are in their interest and that are well suited for combined effort.

CHAPTER 3

The Members

The second characteristic of an alliance is membership. Members are individuals who comprise the alliance and participate in it by contributing resources towards the achievement of a mutually desired objective.

Membership—At least two individuals are members of the alliance and desire the achievement of the objective.

MEMBERS ARE INDIVIDUALS

In Chapter 2, it was emphasized that the purpose of the alliance is to achieve the objective. That is a true statement, but it is not the entire picture. The ultimate purpose of an alliance is to satisfy the common desire of the individual members. The members are the force behind the creation of the alliance. It is their desire to achieve the objective that creates the alliance in the first place. And it is this same desire that keeps the alliance together until the objective is achieved.

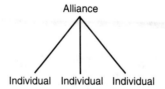

MEMBERS CAN BE ALLIANCES

Two or more alliances can form an alliance. In this situation, there is an *alliance of alliances*. The member alliances are individual members in the same manner as if

18

two or more humans formed an alliance. It is sometimes helpful to refer to the alliance formed by two or more alliances as an *arch-alliance*.

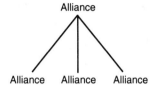

The relationships can be spun even further, with alliances of alliances of alliances, and so on.

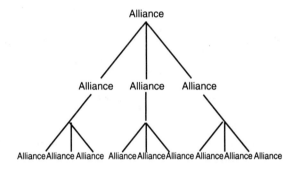

In referring to these entities as "alliances of alliances," it is important to note that the members of an arch-alliance can consist of both individual persons and alliances. That is, one or more individual persons can work together with one or more alliances towards a common end, resulting in a larger alliance of both individuals and alliances.

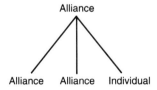

As time progresses, alliances of alliances tend to become one large alliance. In this regard, the smaller-member alliances effectively dissolve over time and merge into the arch-alliance. This result is especially likely to occur if the benefits associated with the smaller alliances dissipate and all functions are being served by the arch-alliance.

When an alliance of alliances is formed, it is sometimes necessary to refer to the individual members of the member alliances. These references can be confusing as it might be difficult to ascertain which members and which alliances are being referenced. To eliminate confusion, it is useful to refer to these individuals as *derivative members* of the alliance of alliances. In this regard, the derivative members of the arch-alliance are members of the alliances that form the arch-alliance. Often, the derivative members will consider themselves to be members of both the arch-alliances and a member alliance.

MEMBERSHIP STATUS

Members hold the status of "membership" in the alliance. This status can be achieved by participating in the formation of a new alliance. The status also might be garnered by entering an existing alliance and being accepted as a member. At times, membership status is not clear, especially for informal alliances. In such situations, many or all members might not even realize that they are members of an alliance or that an alliance even exists.

MEMBERS CONTRIBUTE RESOURCES

Members contribute resources to the achievement of the objective. As discussed in greater detail in Chapter 5, the resources and the manner in which they are contributed can take many forms.

MEMBERS DESIRE THE ACHIEVEMENT
OF THE OBJECTIVE

Members all mutually desire the achievement of the alliance's objective. The members form the alliance for the purpose of achieving the objective. The individual subjective desires of the members to see the objective achieved need not be equal. They can vary substantially in some situations.

MINIMUMS AND MAXIMUMS OF MEMBERSHIP

Critical Mass

Critical mass is a minimum amount of members necessary to achieve the objective. Many, but not all, alliances have a critical mass of members. In such situations, the members will strive to attract sufficient members to achieve this critical mass. If insufficient members are not attracted, the alliance cannot succeed.

> Example 1 "Move the boulder"—The caveman had to locate at least three other cavemen to generate enough force to move the boulder. If the

caveman was able to locate only two others, the boulder would not have been moved.

Positive Aspects of More Members

Some existing alliances will benefit from increased membership. In these situations, the addition of members will reduce the amount of resources that must be contributed by each member. Accordingly, an alliance will tend to increase its membership so long as this benefit is achieved.

> Example 4 "Wild West"—The more members that can be attracted to contribute money to cover the mercenary's wages, the less each member will have to pay.

Negative Aspects of More Members

Other alliances might be impaired from increased membership. In this regard, increasing members can result in a dilution of the benefit of the alliance. As a result, the alliance will seek to limit membership.

> Example 3 "Dig the well"—The ten members agreed to share the water produced by the well that they dug. But if they added additional members, they would have to share water with them and then there might not be enough water to go around.

Positive and Negative Effects at the Same Time

In some situations, increasing membership can both reduce the contribution of resources of individual members and also dilute the benefit received by the individual members. Membership will be increased so long as the value attributed to the reduction in resource contribution outweighs the dilution of the benefit. New members will not be allowed where a net dilution of benefit results.

> Example 7 "Buy the boat"—There are only three co-owners of the boat. Had they included three more members, the money contributed to the purchase would have declined substantially. Each member would have contributed one-sixth of the purchase price, instead of one-third. But there would also be much less time for the co-owners to use the boats with their families. These factors will have to be balanced in deciding whether to add more members.

IDENTIFYING MEMBERS

Identification of individuals holding member status can be confusing at times. One might tend to mistake non-members as members or question why an alliance appears to be harming the interests of its apparent members. These perceptions might result from errors in identifying the members of the alliance. This confusion typically results in three situations.

Aiding Non-Members

The objective of an alliance might be to assist, or provide some benefit to, other individuals. That is, members have formed an alliance to pool their resources for the purpose of assisting non-members. In such situations, it is important to recognize that the recipients of this benefit are not members. The members are the individuals who are contributing resources towards achieving the objective (that is, the provision of some benefit to non-members).

> Example 5 "Help the needy"—The members of the alliance are not the needy. The members are the ones contributing the money to satisfy their desires to help the needy. These members have a subjective desire to help the needy and have formed an alliance to benefit these non-members.

Hurting Non-Members

Some alliances are formed for the purpose of causing harm to other individuals. Thus, if certain individuals are harmed by an alliance, it is important to recognize that these individuals are not members of the alliance, although sometimes they might appear to be at first consideration.

> Example 4 "Wild West"—The members of the new community form an alliance to hire a mercenary. Recently, thieves and gunmen have shown up in the town and the members want the mercenary to bring "order and decency" to the community. The targets of the mercenary's actions are non-members (that is, the thieves and gunmen). These individuals did not participate in forming the alliance and are not members.

Forced Membership

In some situations, individuals are compelled by circumstance into becoming members and, as a result, are not true members of the alliance. Although the individuals might appear to be members and might contribute resources, such individuals either do not desire the achievement of the objective or are not in accord with the agreement struck to achieve the objective. Due to other factors compelling membership, these individuals will nevertheless participate in the alliance to some degree. However, their participation is not willing and such forced members will tend to avoid contributing resources and will depart the alliance when circumstances allow it.

Example 4 "Wild West"—The local hotelier was profiting greatly from the traffic of gunmen and did not want "order and decency." However, to fit into the community and not cause trouble for himself, he went along with the alliance and contributed money towards hiring the mercenary. But he longs for a return of the old days.

———————•———————

CHAPTER SUMMARY

1. The members are the force behind the creation of an alliance. It is their desire to achieve the objective that forms the alliance and that holds it together.

2. Members are typically individuals. However, alliances can be members of a larger alliance (that is, an "arch-alliance"). And alliances can be members of other alliances that are members of other alliances and so on. "Derivative members" are the individual members of an alliance that is a member to the arch-alliance.

3. Members all desire the achievement of the objective, hold the status of being "members," and contribute resources towards the achievement of the objective.

4. Some alliances require a "critical mass" of members to achieve the objective. If the membership rolls are not sufficient, the alliance will not form or will fail.

5. Many alliances benefit from increasing membership. Others do not. For some alliances, increased membership provides advantages and disadvantages. In these situations, the alliance will tend to increase membership until there is no net advantage to having more members (that is, where the negatives outweigh the positives).

6. The status of membership can be confusing at times. The objective of some alliances is to aid or benefit other individuals. In these situations, it is important to keep in mind that the individuals benefiting from the alliance are not members of the alliance. The members are the individuals who form the alliance and contribute resources towards the aid of the others. The objective of other alliances might be to harm the interests of other individuals. In these situations, the individuals being harmed by the alliance are not members.

7. At times, individuals are forced by circumstances to become members of an alliance against their will. These individuals are members in name only and

usually do not desire the attainment of the objective or are not willing to contribute the necessary resources towards the effort. If these individuals are forced into becoming members, they will tend to avoid contributing resources when possible. Further, they will be likely to abandon the alliance when possible.

CHAPTER 4

The Accord

The third characteristic of an alliance is an accord. An accord is an essential part of an alliance and represents an agreement between the members. The subject matters of this agreement include at least the objective of the alliance and the basic means to be used in achieving that objective. Other topics can be included in the accord as well.

> *Accord—An agreement of some type among the membership regarding the objective and the means to be employed in pursuing the objective.*

Why "accord?" The term "accord" is used to emphasize the breadth and flexibility of the concept. Many types of agreements can underlie alliances and "accord" best reflects this variety.

THE DIFFICULTY OF IDENTIFYING
CERTAIN ACCORDS

A basic characteristic of any alliance is an accord pertaining to both the objective of the alliance and the means to be used in achieving that objective. This accord represents a concurrence of all members that (i) they agree upon both the objective and the means; and (ii) their willingness to participate in the alliance and contribute resources towards its efforts.

Many times, the accord underlying an alliance is easy to spot. In the initial seven examples, the accords reached among the members were fairly obvious, but a particular accord might not always be that easy to identify. The reason is the rather narrow conception of an "agreement" present in today's world. In this regard, agreements are typically regarded as formal matters where both sides negotiate, shake hands, and then sign a written document representing the agreement. While this serves as a good example, it is certainly not the only situation where an agreement can arise. Agreements, and consequently accords, can come in all types and forms.

To better spot the variety of accords that can exist, it is useful to classify them into two categories. The first category is the one with which most readers are familiar. It is *express* accords. The second category will be curious to most readers. It is *implied* accords.

EXPRESS ACCORDS

Express accords are characterized by the fact that the parties "express" their agreement in some identifiable manner. That is, the parties confirm the existence of an accord through articulating it or otherwise verbalizing it.

Such expressions come in two forms—written words and spoken words. A written accord occurs when the parties memorialize the agreement in a written document. The document is often formally drawn up and is usually signed by all parties.

Example 7 "Buy the boat"—To memorialize the accord on purchasing the sailboat, the members prepare a typewritten document embodying all of the agreements and then sign it.

On the other hand, a spoken accord occurs when the parties strike a deal solely through spoken words. Although not necessarily required, a spoken accord is usually marked by handshakes, embraces, or expressions such as, "It's a deal." It goes without saying that a spoken accord is not reduced to writing.

Example 6 "Carpool"—One of the five parents approaches the other four about the carpool. Each parent expresses in words an agreement to participate in the carpool.

Often, express accords do not cover all relevant details. Any accord underlying an alliance will have some type of agreement on the objective and means, but the agreement can be quite vague and unformulated. In these situations, the deal is struck, an alliance exists, but a number of issues remain unresolved.

Example 2 "Slay the mammoth"—The accord is only that (i) the objective is killing a mammoth, and (ii) the means are attacking like a "wolf pack."

Example 5 "Help the needy"—The accord is only that (i) the objective is to help the needy, and (ii) the means consist of the members meeting monthly and a majority vote decides how the month's collection will be expended to achieve this objective.

Example 3 "Dig the well"—The accord is fairly specific. The objective is to have a well quickly and the means are digging. But the accord does not spell out what happens when they find water. Who gets to draw water first? How much?

IMPLIED ACCORDS

In contrast to express agreements, implied accords are not expressed in words. Instead, these accords are "implied" from *the circumstances and the conduct* of the parties.

It is important to emphasize that implied accords are genuine, bona-fide agreements. There is an actual understanding between the parties. However, unlike an express accord, the parties do not formalize the existence of the accord. An implied accord is neither reduced to writing nor acknowledged through spoken words. Instead, it is the surrounding circumstances that imply the agreement. That is, consideration of the situation overall yields a conclusion that the parties have an accord. One of the most important of these circumstances is the manner in which the parties behave. If their actions reflect a combined effort, an implied accord almost always exists.

Example 1 "Move the boulder"—The caveman seeks out three other cavemen and convinces them to enter an alliance to move the boulder from the path. Such an accord is express because the four acknowledge the agreement in words. But now assume that the four cavemen are standing near the pathway when the boulder suddenly rolls into it. These four, desiring a clear pathway, immediately approach the boulder and then work together shoving the boulder out of the way. In this instance, the four say nothing to each other about combining forces or working together. But the simple fact is that they are working together and it is upon an objective desired by all four. In this situation, a consideration of the circumstances reveals an implied accord.

Because implied accords are not spoken or put into words, their terms are quite nebulous. Generally, implied accords exist only in situations where (i) the circumstances make express acknowledgement of the accord unnecessary due to the obviousness of the coordinated effort, or (ii) there is a long-standing practice or course of performance such that there is no need to express the accord. With regard to the latter situation, the formation of the alliance is a natural and normal response to an objective that has arisen in the minds of the members.

Example 2 "Slay the mammoth"—The prehistoric hunters have never teamed up before to slay a mammoth. The alliance is formed because one hunter infers that a large group of humans can kill a mammoth in the same way a wolf pack takes down a huge bison. Because the hunters have never hunted like a wolf pack before, the concept is new to them. As a result, the hunter with the idea must explain the concept to them. As a part of this process, all of the hunters express their agreement to participate in the alliance. But as teaming up to hunt mammoths becomes more common, there will be less of a need to actually express the accord between the members. Instead, when the hunters want mammoth meat, they will typically head out to hunt together with little or no discussion. This implied accord occurs because the process of hunting together has become natural and commonplace. There is no need to express it.

Because implied accords often arise as natural events, members might not be consciously aware that such accords exist. That is, although the parties combine their resources towards a mutually desired objective, they might not be fully aware that they are acting in coordination with fellow members to an alliance. However, if the parties are confronted with the issue and ponder it, they might acknowledge that they have an "unspoken agreement" regarding the matter. Overall, the subtler the nature of the implied accord, the less likely the parties are to consciously recognize its existence.

"MEANS" EXPLAINED

As noted in Chapter One, all alliances have some type of an accord on both (i) the *objective* of the alliance, and (ii) the *means* to be used in achieving that objective. The previous chapter discussed the objective. But there has been no discussion of means yet.

"Means" are the manners in which individually possessed resources are to be combined and utilized to attain the objective. Means can be a way, method, technique, or procedure for achieving an objective.

Means is a very broad term and can encompass a variety of matters. Perhaps the best way to look at means is as a *tool* that the alliance is using to achieve the objective. In essence, that tool is either the combination of the resources of the members or another tool acquired through such combined resources. There are no set or predetermined categories of means. Anything can be the means so long as it achieves the objective.

The agreement on the means has two parts. The first is an express or implied concurrence that the alliance will use a way, method, manner, technique, or procedure to achieve the objective. The second is an express or implied promise that all members will contribute individually possessed resources towards the achievement of the objective. The specificity of these agreements can vary substantially.

Example	Objective	Means
One	Move the boulder	Shoving together
Two	Slay the mammoth	Attacking in unison
Three	Dig the well	Digging together
Four	Regain order and decency	Pooling money to hire a mercenary
Five	Help the needy	Pooling money to fund a new endeavor each month
Six	Transport the kids to soccer	Apportion the driving time amongst the members
Seven	Acquire a boat to sail	Pooling their money

THE ESSENTIAL ACCORD ON THE OBJECTIVE AND THE MEANS

An alliance has some type of an accord on both (i) the objective of the alliance, and (ii) the means to be used in achieving that objective. These accords come in many variations and forms. To facilitate seeing this variation, it is useful to classify accords into four categories.

1) *Specific Express Accords*—The accord is express and it is fairly specific, identifying the objective and means with particularity.

   Example 1 "Move the boulder"—The cavemen all expressly agree that they desire to move the boulder from the pathway and that shoving the boulder in unison will be the means employed.

   Example 7 "Buy the boat"—The three members agree that the objective is to buy a sailboat, and there is a specific agreement on the means (that is, each member contributes one-third of the purchase price).

2) *Specific Implied Accords*—The alliance members have a specific agreement on the objective and means to be used, although they never express it in words.

   Example 1 "Move the boulder"—Consider the modification of this example where the boulder suddenly falls into the pathway while the four cavemen are standing nearby. Desiring the pathway cleared, the four approach the boulder and shove in unison to move the boulder out of the path. In this modified example, the agreement is implied from the circumstances. And this agreement includes the means to be used. That is, by approaching the boulder and shoving in unison, there is an implied agreement between the four to use combined pushing to move the boulder. Again, this type of an accord usually arises in alliances with specific objectives.

Example 2 "Slay the mammoth"—After slaying mammoths through a joint effort becomes commonplace, there is no need for the alliance members to express the accord on the objective or means. Instead, members coalesce on the hunting plains until the membership reaches a critical mass and then they attack a mammoth in unison. Here, the objective and the means are fairly specific, despite the fact that they were never expressed by the members.

3) *Indefinite Express Accords*—The members have an express agreement. However, the objective, the means, or both are described with vague or broad terminology. As a result, it is not altogether clear what the objective or the means actually are. This level of vagueness can be insignificant or quite considerable. Where it is substantial, the alliance will typically have a decision-making process in place to decide what the objective includes or what means can be undertaken.

Example 4 "Wild West"—The means consist of hiring a mercenary to bring order and decency as he sees fit. In this situation, the accord on the means is limited to the hiring of a mercenary. The specific means that the mercenary will use though are not identified. Instead, it is up to the mercenary to determine what he will utilize to achieve the objective of order and decency.

4) *Indefinite Implied Accords*—The accord underlying the alliance is implied. As is common with most implied accords, the terms are not well specified. As a result, *both* the objective and the means are not specific. Alliances with such vague accords must have some type of a decision-making process to address these uncertainties.

Example 8 "Council of elders"—The members of the prehistoric tribe have never expressly agreed to the accord underlying the alliance. That implied accord provides that the oldest members of the tribe will meet when they see fit and make decisions in the interest of all tribe members and where a combined effort is advantageous. In this situation, the council decides what objectives will be undertaken. And the council picks the means to be used to achieve those objectives.

In many, but certainly not all, alliances, there will be a need for some type of decision-making process. This need varies with the specificity of the accord. If the accord is unambiguous, there is less need for a decision maker. If the accord on the means is indefinite or open ended, some type of decision-making process is essential. The topic of decision-making processes will be discussed in greater detail subsequently.

ACCORDS ON NON-ESSENTIAL TOPICS

As this chapter makes clear, all alliances have some type of accord on both the objective underlying the alliance and the means to be used in achieving that objective. These matters are essential to any accord.

An accord, though, need not be limited to these two matters. When alliances are formed, the members can choose to have accords on other topics as well. The following includes discussions of typical examples of accords on non-essential topics.

Contribution

As noted earlier, an essential part of an accord is an agreement regarding the means. This agreement includes some type of promise by all members to contribute individually possessed resources and combine them to achieve the objective.

Some alliances might choose to elaborate upon the topic of contribution in the accord underlying the alliance. This might occur because members foresee that certain issues relating to contribution will arise in the future. Therefore, the members conclude that it would be prudent to have an accord on these issues before they arise.

As a result, aside from having an accord on the objective and means, some alliances might also have an accord on contribution. Topics typically addressed in such contribution accords include the following:

Type of contribution—The concern here is identifying the characteristic or nature of the contribution. Are a variety of types of contribution acceptable or is the contribution limited to one type?

Example 3 "Dig the well"—All ten members are to contribute labor (that is, digging and moving dirt) in making the well. Contribution of a shovel, expertise, or food is not acceptable.

Example 4 "Wild West"—Community members might contribute money, food, goods, or valuable services towards the retention of the mercenary.

Amount of contribution—The concern is specifying the amount of contribution that must be provided. Can some members contribute more or less?

Example 5 "Help the needy"—All members can contribute as much or as little as they desire to the neighborhood fund to help the needy.

Example 7 "Buy the boat"—The three members must each contribute exactly one-third of the purchase price of the boat.

Quality of the contribution—If the contribution is not fungible (for example, money), are there certain parameters placed on the quality of the contribution?

Example 1 "Move the boulder"—All that is required is that the four members shove on the boulder as hard as they can.

Example 6 "Carpool"—All parents are to use a safe, reliable car in transporting the children.

When is the contribution to be provided?—Sometimes it is not clear when contribution must be provided.

Example 5 "Help the needy"—All members are to contribute money to the neighborhood collection once per month.

Example 6 "Carpool"—A parent is to provide contribution (that is, driving) only during certain weeks.

Example 7 "Buy the boat"—Each member has a specific schedule for when he is to clean and maintain the boat.

Consequences for not contributing—What happens if contribution is not provided?

Example 2 "Slay the mammoth"—If members fail to show up to slay the mammoth (or show up but do nothing), they get no mammoth meat.

Example 4 "Wild West"—If members fail to contribute to the mercenary's pay, such members will spend a week in jail or their property will be seized and sold at public auction to make up for the unpaid contribution.

Example 5 "Help the needy"—If members do not make a monthly contribution to the neighborhood fund, they cannot vote in the monthly decision on how to use the collection.

Modification or Amendment of the Accord

At the time the accord underlying the alliance is entered, the members might be concerned that the accord will need to be modified in the future. The potential reasons for such amendments are numerous. The members might foresee a need to adapt the accord to changing or new circumstances, to correct any operational problems associated with the accord, to pursue new objectives, or to utilize means not authorized in the accord.

If these concerns are present, some accords include an agreement specifying how the accord can be modified or amended. Such accords are more likely in alliances that are contemplated to be long term. If there is an accord on modification or amendment, it will usually specify some type of decision-making process for determining how the accord in question can be modified.

Example 5 "Help the needy"—Instead of agreeing upon a flexible accord with a rather vague objective and means, the alliance enters an accord with very specific provisions. The objective is limited to providing food to the needy. The means are limited to providing potato soup. At the time this accord is entered, many members question why the alliance cannot pursue other topics of aid, such as providing clothing, shelter, and medical care to the needy. Other members express doubts on limiting the means to providing potato soup and suggest also providing bread, fruit, and vegetables. The alliance members compromise and agree that the accord will be limited to an objective of food to the needy and the means of potato soup. But the accord will also include a modification provision. Under this provision, the members can vote to amend the accord and add new objectives and means. It is decided that sixty percent (60%) of the members must vote for a proposal for it to be included in the accord.

Withdrawal from the Alliance

Members might be concerned about entering an alliance and then not being able to get out of it. If this concern is present, the accord will address the withdrawal of members from the alliance.

Example 7 "Buy the boat"—One of the members might be concerned that his employer will move him to another state where he cannot enjoy the boat. Thus, the accord might provide that, if a member is moved to another state by his employer, he may leave the alliance but the other two must reimburse his earlier monetary contribution towards the boat purchase (that is, "buy him out").

Some alliances might prohibit or penalize withdrawal from an alliance. Generally, a concern with having adequate amounts of contribution motivates the implementation of such provisions.

Example 4 "Wild West"—The alliance hires a mercenary and guarantees him a salary. To make sure that the mercenary is paid, there is an accord specifying that no one can leave the alliance. The only exception is if a member moves away from the community permanently.

New Members

Members might foresee the likelihood of new members joining the alliance in the future. As a result, there might be an accord on this subject. The accord will usually specify the terms and conditions on which new members may join the alliance. This accord can be intended to encourage new members to join. Conversely, the accord can be designed to limit or prevent new members from joining.

Example 3 "Dig the well"—If more members are added, there will likely be less water to go around. Thus, there is an accord prohibiting new members from joining.

Example 5 "Help the needy"—The more members there are, the more money there is to spend on projects. Thus, there is a provision in the accord that anyone may join the alliance provided that they contribute resources.

Termination of the Alliance

Alliances can also specify in accord how the alliance can terminate. This termination can be linked to certain events, such as achievement of the objective, a decline in the membership to a certain point, and so on. Or a decision-making process can trigger the termination.

Example 4 "Wild West"—As previously noted, the accord prohibits withdrawal of members and has strict contribution requirements to insure that the mercenary is paid. Many members are concerned about committing to such onerous obligations. The members agree that the solution is to allow for the termination of the alliance. If 65% of the members vote to terminate the alliance, it will terminate and all members will be free of its obligations.

Sharing in the Benefits of the Alliance

If the objective of the alliance is to provide some type of tangible benefit to the members, there is usually an accord regarding how such a benefit is to be apportioned.

Example 3 "Dig the well"—The members foresee disputes over distribution of the water including how much water each member may draw from the well and when each member may access the well. As a result, there is an accord specifying when each member may draw water and how much may be drawn.

Example 7 "Buy the boat"—To insure equal access to the boat, the members enter a detailed accord on the specific dates for each member to have use of the boat.

Restrictions or Prohibition on Means

Why would alliance members desire an accord regulating means? As noted earlier, some accords will specify the means to be used while others will identify them imprecisely or leave them entirely open. With regard to the latter situation, the potential for the alliance using any and all types of means can cause concern at times. As a result, accords often place some type of restrictions on the means that can be used.

Example 4 "Wild West"—The objective is order and decency and this will be attained by running off thieves and gunmen. The means are to hire a mercenary to achieve this objective. Since the mercenary will be dealing with many violent individuals, the members recognize that the mercenary often will use violent methods to achieve this objective. But the members are concerned with what the mercenary might do to both members *and* non-members. As a result, the accord includes specific restrictions on the mercenary's activities (the "means"). But these restrictions vary depending upon whether the targeted person is a member or non-member of the alliance.

Non-members: The mercenary may kill non-members in his discretion and judgment. The mercenary, however, may never use torture on non-members as a means of bringing about order and decency.

Members: If the mercenary feels it is necessary to take action towards a member of the alliance, the mercenary must take the member into custody and immediately arrange for a committee of alliance members to meet. This committee will listen to the mercenary's recommendation and then decide what to do to the alliance member.

The restrictions on means do not have to address grave issues. Instead, the restrictions can be rather mundane.

Example 5 "Help the Needy"—There might be a concern that unhealthy food would be purchased to feed the needy. Thus, there might be an accord that only food meeting some type of nutritional criteria may be purchased.

Example 7 "Buy the Boat"—There might be a concern that members will damage the boat's paint in maintaining it. Thus, there might be a specific accord on how to go about cleaning the boat.

Restrictions or Prohibitions on Objectives

Many alliances regulate the objectives through the accord. In these situations, there are usually three different reasons for the regulation. First, the members might have aversion for a particular objective and desire to prevent the alliance from ever pursuing it. Second, the members might be concerned with the alliance growing out of control and pursuing too many objectives. Third, the members might be troubled by some combination of these two concerns. As a result, the members might desire to place restrictions on the objectives.

Not all alliances will have accords regulating or restricting objectives. Chapter 2 included a discussion of three categories of objectives: (i) specific, set objectives, (ii) indefinite objectives, and (iii) open objectives. An accord regulating the objective is unlikely in the first category. And it is very likely in the third category. Why? There are several reasons.

Specific objectives—If the objective of an alliance is quite specific, there usually will be no accord placing limitations on the objective. The reason is that, because the objective has such specificity, there is no need to prohibit the alliance from undertaking other objectives.

Example 1 "Move the boulder"—The objective is to move the boulder from the pathway. Because the identification of the objective is precise, there is no need for an accord prohibiting the objective from being something else, such as moving a large tree. That would not make sense.

Second, alliances with specific objectives are typically short lived and are usually formed to address a single matter. When the matter has been addressed, the alliance usually terminates. This is especially so with single-objective alliances. In these situations, because the alliance is contemplated to be of short duration, there is usually no concern with limiting the objective.

Example 2 "Slay the mammoth"—When the mammoth is slain and its meat has been divided up, the objective has been achieved and the alliance terminates. Again, it would make no sense to have an accord prohibiting something else, such as the slaying of bison.

Finally, alliances with specific objectives typically have no accord restricting the withdrawal of members from an alliance. As a result, there usually is no concern with limiting the objective. If the alliance undertakes an objective not desired by certain members, such members can simply withdraw from the alliance.

Example 5 "Help the needy"—No member is required to stay in the alliance. If the alliance undertakes an objective (for example, education of the needy) that is not desired by certain members, the member can simply quit the alliance. This member can resume giving sporadic gifts to the needy on the street or can seek to form a new alliance that pursues objectives in line with that member's interests.

Indefinite objectives—An alliance with an indefinite objective typically has some type of an accord regulating the specific endeavors that the alliance may undertake. In this situation, the objective is usually a topic that is difficult to define with precision. The members typically know in their minds what the objective means but have difficulty articulating what it includes. To solve this problem, the indefiniteness of the objective will be clarified to some extent with an accord allowing flexibility in the matters that may be undertaken but flatly prohibiting certain specific areas.

Example 4 "Wild West"—The alliance members have a good grasp of what order and decency means, although they have difficulty putting it into words. They might say, "We cannot define order and decency, but we know it when we see it." Thus, instead of listing out specific topics (for example, no gun-fighting, no theft, no brawls, and so on), the members use the indefinite term—order and decency—to identify the objective. This indefiniteness is useful and allows flexibility in the operation of the alliance. But it also has its risks. Its vagueness creates the potential for non-desirable objectives to creep into the alliance and to be pursued. For example, as noted earlier, order and decency undoubtedly means ending gunfights and theft. But does it also encompass prostitution, adultery, alcohol consumption, lewd attire, or tobacco use? If the members are concerned with these topics creeping into the objective, they might strike a balance between indefiniteness and specificity. The accord on the objective will be indefinite (that is, order and decency). But at the same time, there will also be an accord prohibiting order and decency from including certain matters (that is, adultery, alcohol consumption, lewd attire, or to-bacco use). Thus, the overall accord is that the objective is order and decency but this term cannot include adultery, alcohol consumption, lewd attire, or tobacco use.

Open objectives—Similarly, alliances with open-ended objectives are likely to have some type of regulation of the objectives that the alliance may undertake. Recall that the true objective of an alliance with open-ended objectives is to have a structure in place to act on matters that benefit all members and where a combined effort is advantageous. Thus, whenever the decision-making process selects an objective to pursue, the selected objective should be one that benefits all members and is one particularly suited for a combined effort. If members are concerned with the decision-making process straying from this purpose, there can be an accord limiting the objectives that may be pursued.

OVERVIEW OF THE DECISION-MAKING PROCESS

A decision-making process is the method or procedure by which an alliance makes any necessary decisions. Decision-making processes come in all forms and types, including express and implied processes. The particular decision-making process used by an alliance can be the determinative factor in whether the alliance achieves its objective. A successful alliance will take great care to insure that its decision-making process is best suited for the particular circumstances present in the alliance. Factors to consider in selecting the appropriate decision-making process are numerous and vary with the circumstances. These factors are discussed in Chapter 7.

It is important to keep in mind that there is no set format for the making of decisions. The decision-making processes used by alliances will vary from alliance to alliance. Each alliance will attempt to select a decision-making process that appears best suited for the circumstances presented.

WHEN IS A DECISION-MAKING PROCESS NECESSARY?

Not all alliances have use for a decision-making process. In fact, if there is a specific accord on both the objective and the means, often no decisions need to be made.

> **Example 1 "Move the boulder"**—The objective (that is, clear the boulder from the path) and the means (that is, push in unison) are quite specific. Thus, when an accord is reached on these matters, there are no decisions to be made.

However, many alliances have at least some need for a decision-making process. And this need can vary considerably from alliance to alliance. There are three areas where a decision-making process might be needed:

Means	Objective	Organizational

Means

Whenever the means are not specified in an accord, a decision-making process will be present in some form. The process will make decisions on the means to be used in achieving the objective.

The issues that are decided depend upon the amount of discretion afforded to the process in the accord. If the accord provides little specifics on the means, the decision-making process is often unrestrained in selecting from a range of means. The more the means are specified, the less discretion the process has in selecting the means.

Example 6 "Carpool"—The accord is fairly specific on the means. Each parent is to transport the children on specified weeks. The transportation is to be the parents' automobiles and the children are to arrive at the soccer event on time and be brought home promptly after the event ends. Although this is specific, there is still some discretion. For example, the parents are allowed to decide the routes that they will take to and from the events.

Example 4 "Wild West"—Here, the community's accord on the means consists of nothing more than hiring a mercenary. The community then vests in the mercenary's essentially unfettered discretion to decide the specific means that he will utilize in achieving the objective of bringing order and decency to the community. This mercenary is a decision maker and he has been granted authority to determine the means. For example, to bring order and decency, the means available to the mercenary include cajoling, reasoning, warnings, fines, threats, public beatings, imprisonment, torture, and execution.

Example 5 "Help the needy"—The accord does not specify the means whatsoever. Instead, the accord on the means is that the members will vote each month and the majority shall decide what to do with the collection for that month. Thus, in this alliance, the decision-making process holds complete discretion to select any means to achieve the objective of helping the needy.

Objective

If the objective of the alliance is either indefinite or open, there must be a decision-making process. If the objective is *indefinite*, the decision-making process will make decisions on whether a particular desire falls within the parameters of the objective.

Example 4 "Wild West"—The objective is bringing order and decency to the community. This objective is rather nebulous. Obviously, order and decency means ending gunfights and prostitution, but does it also encompass adultery, alcohol consumption, lewd attire, or tobacco use? It is not clear. To address these concerns, the alliance has two options: (i) it can place specific restrictions in the accord as discussed earlier in this chapter; or (ii) it can set up an on-going decision-making process to determine what matters fall within the agreed-upon objective of order and decency. With this latter option, a range of alternatives is possible. They include vesting the discretion to determine this issue in the mercenary, having a membership vote on the topic, or establishing a council to resolve the matters as they arise.

Example 5 "Help the needy"—In this alliance, a decision-making process is necessary. The objective of "helping the needy" is imprecise and the accord does not regulate it. Thus, the question exists as to whether helping the needy is limited to providing the bare necessities, such as food and water, or does it include other concerns, such as educational or spiritual development? To address these issues, the alliance has a decision-making process. Specifically, the members meet monthly to decide what to do with the month's collections. At these meetings, the vote of members decides what falls within the objective of helping the needy.

If the objective is *open*, the alliance must have a decision-making process. This process will select the objective to be pursued by the alliance.

Example 8 "Council of elders"—In this alliance, there is an implied accord that the alliance may pursue any objective in the interests of all community members, provided that a combined effort would be advantageous. Because this alliance had no fixed objectives, a decision-making process is vital. The council of elders serves as the decision maker and decides what objectives the tribe will pursue.

At times, it can be confusing as to whether a decision relates to the means or the objective. If the objective is vaguely identified, it is very likely that this confusion will result. For example, if the objective of the alliance is "to promote the welfare" of the members, a decision to undertake a certain action could be seen as (i) a decision on the means to be used to achieve the promotion of member welfare, or (ii) a decision on what the objective of "promote the welfare" includes.

Focusing on the reasoning process used by the decision maker can usually clear up this confusion. The decision pertains to the *objective* if the decision maker attempts to determine whether a proposal is something that is suited for combined action. For example, the decision maker inquires whether the proposal is (i) one that cannot be obtained by individual action, or (ii) can be achieved more efficiently or effectively through a combined effort. On the other hand, the decision pertains to the *means* if the decision maker focuses more on the manner or method to obtain a predetermined goal. Nonetheless, it is likely that the confusion will result where the objective is vaguely articulated. The problems posed by this confusion are explored later.

Organizational Matters

If an alliance has certain organizational issues, there might be a decision-making process to address this subject. It is important to not confuse organizational issues with decision-making processes for objectives and means. *Processes for objectives* pertain to determining whether the objective is one suited for combined action by the membership. *Processes for means* focus on selecting the most suitable method for achieving the objective.

Processes for organizational matters pertain to ancillary issues. These matters include determining the amount of contribution, collecting contribution, allowing in new members, allowing members to withdraw, apportionment of the benefits of the alliance, resolution of disputes between members, terminating the alliance, and overseeing or regulating the decision-making process. If these organizational issues are prevalent, the alliance will likely have a decision-making process to address them.

Example 3 "**Dig the well**"—This alliance has an accord on how to share and distribute the water. Confusion or conflict might arise over the specifics of this arrangement. As a result, the alliance has a decision-making process in place to resolve these disputes and apportion the water pursuant to the accord.

Example 4 "**Wild West**"—This alliance has an accord on what happens if a member fails to contribute to the mercenary's salary: ten days of prison or a public auction of the member's property. As a result, the alliance has a decision-making process, both to assess which members have not contributed, and to impose the punishment.

TYPES OF DECISION-MAKING PROCESSES

Decision-making processes come in all types. It is important to recall that the purpose of the process is to make any necessary decisions. Thus, if the topics of the decisions are simple, the process might be simple. Conversely, if the topics are complex, it is likely that the process will be complex as well.

The following discussion will subdivide the topic of decision-making process into two categories.

Formal Decision Making	Nebulous Decision Making

FORMAL DECISION-MAKING PROCESSES

A *formal decision-making process* is one that has structure and recognition by the members as a decision-making process. Formal decision-making processes are present only in alliances formed by express accords. Formal decision-making processes come in two general areas: (i) a vote by all members, and (ii) a delegation of the decision-making authority to a person or group of people.

Membership	Delegation of Decision
Vote	Making Authority

A *membership vote* is a process where all members participate in the decision-making process. The proposal receiving a predetermined amount of votes (for example, plurality, simple majority, and so on) becomes the decision of the alliance. The members directly make this decision for the alliance.

Any process other than a full vote of members constitutes a *delegation of decision-making authority*. In this situation, another person, entity, process, or thing makes the decision on behalf of the alliance. In effect, the alliance has delegated the decision to this person or group of people.

MEMBERSHIP VOTE

A membership vote is some type of vote by all members. Basically, if a certain number of votes are cast in favor of an option, that option is selected. The number of votes cast can range from a plurality (the option receiving the most votes), a simple majority (the option receiving more than 50% of the votes), or a super majority (the option must receive a predetermined percentage exceeding a simple majority, such as 60% of the votes).

> **Example 5 "Help the needy"**—The accord provides for decisions on the objective and means to be decided by a vote of the membership. Every month the members contributing for that month assemble and vote on what the alliance should do with the monthly collection. A majority vote constitutes the decision of the alliance.

DELEGATION OF AUTHORITY

Delegation of decision-making authority can be subdivided into three forms of delegation: (i) executive, (ii) committee, and (iii) non-standard.

Executive	Committee	Non-Standard

Executive

An executive decision-making process is a determination by one individual. In this situation, a single individual is charged with making the necessary decisions for the alliance. This individual is usually a member, but sometimes an alliance will retain a non-member to serve as the decision maker.

> **Example 4 "Wild West"**—The alliance delegates to the mercenary the discretion to use whatever means he sees fit in achieving order and decency. The mercenary is the decision maker. He decides what means to use, subject to any restrictions imposed upon him in the accord (for example, he cannot use torture).

Committees

Committees range widely in their structure, but their defining characteristic is that decisions are made by more than one individual but less than the entire membership. Committees can consist of just two participants or thousands of participants.

Committees share traits with both (i) a membership vote, and (ii) an executive decision maker. Committees are similar to a membership vote in that more than one person participates in the decision-making process. Committees are similar to an executive decision maker in that a decision has been delegated to the committee. Other similarities and differences will be discussed subsequently.

Non-Standard

The category of non-standard decision-making processes is a catchall for all other methods of making decisions. Examples include processes that are of a random nature, extraordinary complexity, or complete rigidity. The common feature is that the alliance has delegated decision-making authority to these non-standard processes. They will be discussed in greater detail in Chapter 7.

NEBULOUS DECISION-MAKING PROCESSES

Some decision-making processes are entirely unstructured and nebulous. These types of processes usually arise in (i) alliances formed through an implied accord, or (ii) alliances formed through express accords, but which are nevertheless very informal. The best way to describe this type of decision-making process is as an informal group consensus. An informal consensus reaches a decision when, from a review of the overall circumstances, it is evident that the alliance has made a decision, although there is no vote or anything similar.

> **Example 2 "Slay the mammoth"**—The alliance meets to head out on the mammoth hunt, but there are five potential hunting areas, and therefore, a decision must be made as to the area in which they will hunt. There is some vague discussion and then the group just heads off to a hunting area. In this

situation, there was no formal vote and there was no clear executive or committee decision maker. Nevertheless, it is evident that a decision was made. The process by which that decision was made was an informal group consensus.

THE SIGNIFICANCE OF THE ACCORD

This chapter has covered multiple issues that relate to the accord. The importance of the accord to an alliance cannot be understated. The accord is the structure of the alliance and serves to define its parameters.

The accord can make or break the alliance. If the accord fails to address certain matters that are likely to arise, the alliance will probably fail to achieve the objective. More importantly, the alliance might not even get off the ground, with the members soon quitting the alliance or the alliance becoming paralyzed by squabbles over small topics or serious battles over important issues that were ignored in the accord.

Many members will often refuse to join an alliance unless the accord is sufficiently specific on certain issues. These issues are "deal breakers" and can prevent the formation of the alliance if not addressed. For example, certain members might be concerned with objective creep and refuse to enter the alliance unless there are specific restrictions on the objectives that might be pursued. Similarly, many members might be concerned with the means that might be used. They will refuse to enter the alliance unless the accord prohibits the use of certain means. Other members might be concerned with other issues discussed earlier, such as contribution, withdrawal of members, termination of the alliance, and so on. These members will refuse to join unless the accord has explicit provisions addressing these concerns.

CHAPTER SUMMARY

1. The accord is a broad term used to describe the variety of types of agreements that underlie alliances.

2. Accords can be express or implied. Express accords are articulated in words and are written, spoken, or a combination of both methods. In contrast, implied accords are not articulated. Instead, such accords are "implied" from the circumstances and conduct of the parties. Implied accords constitute real, bona-fide agreements. Implied accords generally arise only in situations where there

is a long-standing practice or course of conduct such that there is no need to actually express the accord.

3. All alliances have an accord on the objective of the alliance and the means to be used in achieving the objective. Means is the manner in which the individually possessed resources of members will be combined to achieve the objective of the alliance.

4. Accords can come in many degrees of specificity. Some are quite specific while others can be rather nebulous.

5. There can be accords on a multitude of other subjects. These non-essential topics often include contribution, modification or amendment of the accord, withdrawal from the alliance, new members, termination of the alliance, sharing in the benefits of the alliance, and regulation of the means or objectives.

6. A decision-making process is a method or procedure by which an alliance makes any necessary decisions. Decision-making processes can come in all forms.

7. Not all alliances have decision-making processes. Many alliances have no need for making any decisions.

8. Decision-making processes typically address three areas: (i) means, (ii) objective, and (iii) organizational. A decision-making process for means makes decisions about means to be used in achieving the objective. A decision-making process for the objective resolves questions raised by indefinite and open objectives. If the objective is indefinitely described, the decision-making process can determine what falls within and outside of the description. If the objective is open, the decision-making process has a free hand at deciding what the objective of the alliance will be. Finally, a decision-making process relating to organizational matters makes decisions about issues relating to the operation of the alliance. These areas do not include means or objectives, but can pertain to contribution, membership, apportionment of the benefits of the alliance, resolution of disputes amongst members, termination of the alliance, and related matters.

9. Decision-making processes fall into two broad categories: (i) formal decision making and (ii) nebulous decision making. The former process has structure and is typical of alliances with express accords. The latter lacks structure or definition and is typical of alliances with implied accords.

10. Formal decision-making processes can be divided into two sub-categories: (i) membership vote, and (ii) delegation of decision-making authority. The former consists of the decision being made by a vote of all members. The latter occurs

when the alliance has delegated the decision to a person, a committee, or a non-standard method.

11. Delegation of decision-making authority can fall into three areas: (i) executive, (ii) committee, and (iii) non-standard. An executive decision maker is a single individual charged with making one or more decisions. A committee is a group of two or more individuals charged with making one or more decisions. Finally, a non-standard decision maker is a catch-all for all other types of delegated processes whereby someone or something other than a membership vote is responsible for making the decision.

CHAPTER 5

The Contribution

The fourth and final characteristic of an alliance is the contribution of resources. These resources can consist of literally anything. They can include both tangible and intangible items.

Contribution—All members contribute resources towards the achievement of the objective.

RESOURCE EXPLAINED

The term "resources" encompasses anything that can be used to achieve the objective. Typically, contributed resources consist of labor, material, time, liberty, life and limb, or money. This list is not exhaustive as the contributed resources can be anything. That is, anything that can be effectively combined with other similar items for the purpose of achieving the objective can constitute a "resource."

The character of the resource is determined by the nature of the objective (and the means). For instance, if the objective involves building something, such as a bridge, the contributed resources will be material and labor. If the objective involves a watch, such as a look out for invaders or burglars, the resource will be time. If the objective pertains to a code of conduct to which all members agree to adhere and therefore forego certain acts, the resource is liberty (that is, foregoing the freedom to take some act). If the objective pertains to engaging in dangerous conduct, such as defending against an aggressor, the resource is life and limb. Finally, in today's world, the contribution of choice is money, which is discussed in greater detail subsequently.

THE AMOUNT OF CONTRIBUTION IS USUALLY THE SAME

Must each member contribute the same amount of resources? In most situations, the amount of resources contributed by each member will be the same. Each member will contribute an equal share of resource towards the achievement of the mutually desired objective.

Why is this? There appears to be a fundamental and common belief among humans that everyone should contribute the same amount, especially if they all receive the same benefit. Any proposals to have differing amounts of contribution are typically met with very strong and negative reactions from most or all members. This is usually a sticking point in the formation of any alliance. As a general rule, a proposed alliance with disparate levels of contribution is likely to never form.

This concept reflects what appears to be a core belief of humans. The primary rationale underlying it seems to be a belief that all humans are equal, and therefore, should contribute an equal share. However, because the concept is so fundamental, it is difficult to identify with specificity the reasons supporting its widespread acceptance. It falls in the area commonly known as "fairness." In arguing against a proposal for disparate levels of contribution, the typical position would boil down to a contention that "it is unfair."

SITUATIONS WHERE CONTRIBUTION AMOUNTS ARE UNEQUAL

Are there situations where alliances can have disparate levels of contribution? Certainly. There are many such situations. The following includes a discussion of the more prominent examples.

Objectives of Great Value

A member might place such a great value on the achievement of an objective that the typically strong, emotional reaction favoring equal levels of contribution will be overcome. In this situation, a member with such a valuation will be willing to contribute more to the alliance than other members.

> **Example 4 "Wild West"**—The potential members place substantially different values on achieving the objective of order and decency. The thieves and the gunmen hit the storekeepers the hardest in comparison to other potential members. Thus, while all members of the community are willing to contribute to hiring the mercenary, the storekeepers are willing to contribute substantially more than most members.

The fact that a member is willing to contribute more does not necessarily mean that the member will in fact contribute more. In most circumstances, a potential member will conceal his willingness to pay more. However, if the alliance requires a certain minimum threshold of combined contribution to get off the ground, potential members will tend to disclose their willingness to pay more.

> **Example 4 "Wild West"**—The potential members discover that the mercenary's salary requirements are quite high and that their combined contribution is a little bit short to cover it. The potential members are all asked to contribute more, but there is substantial balking at this proposal. It appears that the alliance will not be formed. The storekeepers are willing to contribute substantially more than most people. Fearing that the alliance will not be formed, the storekeepers speak up and indicate a willingness to make up the difference to insure payment to the mercenary.

Of course, a member contributing more resources also could require that he receive more of the objective attained.

> **Example 7 "Buy the boat"**—One member agrees to contribute money for half of the price of the boat while the other two members agree to each contribute one-quarter of the price. The members agree in the accord that the member contributing more may use the boat for two weeks per month while the other two members may use it only one week per month.

Members with Ulterior Motives

Sometimes, a potential member will agree to pay a disproportionate amount due to an ulterior motive. This motive is independent of the value the member places upon the achievement of the objective of the alliance.

> **Example 4 "Wild West"**—When the storekeepers agree to pay more contribution, the cobbler also agrees to contribute a greater amount as well. The cobbler, however, has a different motivation for taking this act. Because the thieves and gunmen do not bother the cobbler often, the cobbler's willingness to pay more is not motivated by a higher value that he might place on the objective. Instead, the cobbler believes that contributing more will generate goodwill towards him and his cobbler business will increase as a result. This desire for increased business is the cobbler's ulterior motive.

Promotion of Other Objectives

Aside from achieving the objective, the alliance might have a secondary objective that will result in disparate levels of contribution. Examples of these secondary objectives include fairness or inclusiveness.

In such a situation, the primary goal of the alliance is to achieve an objective that benefits all members. But a secondary goal is to advance another concern relating to the members. If the alliance has one of these secondary objectives, it will tend to allow in members who contribute less than other members.

Fairness—As discussed earlier, conceptions of fairness often prevent disparate amounts of contribution. Potential members will insist that everyone contribute the same because it is "fair." This same concept of fairness, however, can result in an opposite outcome, with certain members contributing less. Why? The concept of fairness discussed earlier pertains to situations where the potential members all possess roughly the same amount of resources. As a result, most potential members find it reasonable to expect all members to contribute the same amount. But an important exception is that such an expectation is not applicable to potential members with substantially less resources. Such potential members obviously have less total resources to expend and a contribution equal to that of other members will tend to be much harder on them, in comparison to the other members. Accordingly, if an alliance embraces a secondary objective of fairness, it will tend to allow members with fewer resources to contribute less.

Example 4 "Wild West"—During the formation of the alliance, a potential member reveals that the gunmen just robbed him of all his money. Another potential member points out that he has ten children and is barely scraping by. Another states that he is disabled and has trouble finding paying work. The potential members conclude that it would be unfair to expect these three to pay the same as everyone else. As a result, an accord is reached allowing these three to contribute less.

Inclusion—Concerns for inclusiveness will often result in an accord allowing disparate levels of contribution.

Example 5 "Help the needy"—In forming the alliance, the potential members desire in part to foster a community spirit of unity and overall participation. As a result, it is agreed that members may contribute as much or as little as they desire. This accord promoting membership does result in marginal increases in contribution. But more importantly, it results in sizeable increases in the membership and notable enthusiasm and harmony in the community.

Importantly, fairness and inclusion are typically pursued only if a sufficient portion of the membership has a large enough desire for the objective to justify contributing more than other members. This concept was just previously discussed. As such, a prerequisite for fairness or inclusion is an objective valued highly by the members with sizeable resources.

Miscellaneous—A variety of other factors might result in members providing disparate levels of contribution. One factor might be a desire to prevent turmoil or envy in non-members. In this situation, members might fear the possibility of non-members becoming envious of the alliance or otherwise angry at being excluded. These negative sentiments could jeopardize the alliance. As such, to guard against this possibility, these non-members may be allowed to join the alliance, even though their contribution of resources will be substantially lower than that of most other members. This factor and similar ones will be discussed subsequently.

THE NATURE OF THE CONTRIBUTION IS USUALLY THE SAME

A different issue from the amount of contribution is the class or nature of the contribution. Do the members all contribute the same resource or do they contribute a variety of resources?

As a general rule, the class or nature of the contribution is the same. All members contribute the same resource, whether it is labor, material, time, liberty, and so on.

Example 3 "Dig the well"—All members contribute labor towards digging the well. Other forms of contribution, such as food or shovels are not acceptable.

Example 7 "Buy the boat"—One of the potential members is in the business of manufacturing brooms. His business is not doing well and he is short of cash. In the place of contributing one-third of the purchase price of the boat, this potential member offers to contribute 1,000 brooms. The two other potential members find this to be unacceptable and he is not allowed into the alliance. The two seek out and finally locate a potential member possessing cash to pay his share of the purchase price.

Of course, exceptions to this generalization are common. Many alliances allow members to contribute a variety of forms of resources.

Example 3 "Dig the well"—The alliance could reach an opposite accord on contribution. The members could agree that a member did not have to contribute labor. Instead, he could contribute something else, such as valuable digging tools or food to feed the other members while they dig the well.

Example 4 "Wild West"—The alliance had to accumulate sufficient contribution to pay the mercenary's salary. Assuming that the mercenary was agreeable, a portion of his salary could be something other than money. This portion could consist of non-monetary contribution from various members, such as food, goods and wares, complementary services, or lodging.

THE SIGNIFICANCE OF THE ACCORD
TO CONTRIBUTION ISSUES

In a simple alliance, the provision of contribution is usually straightforward and there is no need for the agreement to address the topic in any detail. More complex alliances, especially those that are formed to last long periods of time or address a variety of objectives, can experience a wide variety of problems with contribution. From the beginning, a successful alliance will strive to have a firm and clear accord upon the topic of contribution. These comprehensive accords will address all of the matters that were covered earlier in this chapter.

MONEY AS CONTRIBUTION

The development of money has had an important effect upon the nature and growth of alliances. Before money, most organizations could arise only if a sufficient number of members were able to contribute very specific types of resources towards achievement of the objective. Potential members that were not able to contribute the obligatory resource typically would not be allowed into the alliance.

> Example 2 "Slay the mammoth"—As the alliance is forming to slay the mammoth, several aged and disabled individuals lobby to be included in the alliance. Because these individuals are unable to strike the mammoth with a spear, they are not allowed into the alliance.

> Example 4 "Wild West"—Assume that money is very rare in this frontier community and most commerce consists of bartering goods and services. For instance, if a farmer needs shoes, he will give the cobbler some produce; if the cobbler needs medical attention, he will give the doctor shoes. When the potential members meet to confer on the mercenary's salary, each potential member offers some type of good or service as contribution. Immediately, some potential members attack others' proposed contribution as being insufficient. The blacksmith, who has offered to contribute eight horseshoes, argues that the barber's offer of a free shave and a haircut is far too small. The hotelier, who has offered room and board, contends that the farmer's contribution of a sack of potatoes is ridiculously insignificant. Heated debates develop but there is no resolution. The alliance is not formed because of such substantial disputes over the values of the proposed contributions.

Money serves as a highly effective means of bridging the gap between individuals possessing differing types of resources. Money allows potential members lacking the requisite resource to instead contribute an acceptable amount of money in its place.

As noted in the examples, the formation of alliances can be hampered by disputes over the relative values of resources contributed. For example, if several members proposed contributing a variety of resources (for example, labor, several different types of material, and so on), the members might be unable to agree that each member is making an appropriate contribution and the alliance will never get off of the ground. Money solves this problem by providing a uniform means of identifying the contribution required by each member.

In today's world, money is the most common resource contributed towards the achievement of an objective. The growth and development of alliances over the course of history can likely be correlated with the spread and usage of money.

"FREE-RIDER" ISSUES

At times, individuals desiring the achievement of an objective and willing in principle to contribute the required resources will nonetheless fail to join an alliance. Why? It is because of the *free-rider effect*. This effect occurs when the nature of the objective is such that non-members can benefit from it without joining an alliance or undertaking any effort to achieve the objective.

In this situation, the individuals refusing to join the alliance understand that other individuals will form the alliance, contribute the resources, achieve the objective, and that the achievement of the objective will benefit the non-members as if they were a part of the alliance. Accordingly, these individuals will not participate in the alliance or contribute resources, recognizing that they can "ride for free" upon the efforts undertaken by the alliance. It goes without saying that such individuals receiving the free-rider benefit are not members of the alliance.

> **Example 1 "Move the boulder"**—When the alliance is forming, a potential member refuses to participate despite the fact that he very much desires having the boulder removed from the pathway. Why? It is because he knows that the other potential members will form the alliance and move the boulder, regardless of whether he participates in the alliance. He can benefit from the alliance without joining it.

To combat this situation, some alliances will compel beneficiaries of the free-rider effect to join the alliance and contribute resources. This is a situation of "forced membership" discussed earlier. As noted, forced members are not really members because they have not willingly entered the alliance.

> **Example 4 "Wild West"**—When the alliance is forming, several potential members indicate that they will not participate. Why? It is for the same reason as in the caveman example. These potential members know that the alliance

will be formed, the mercenary will be hired, and order and decency will be brought to the community. To address this situation, the alliance reaches an accord that everyone in the community must join the alliance and contribute resources. There is no choice. If certain members do not want to participate, they will be compelled to do so.

SPOTTING THE CONTRIBUTED RESOURCES IS NOT ALWAYS EASY

As noted at the outset, the resources comprising contribution can come in all types and forms. In analyzing an alliance, there will be a tendency to identify only tangible resources—material, labor, money, and so on—as the contribution provided. Care, however, should be taken to carefully examine the objective of the alliance to insure that all resources contributed have been correctly identified.

For example, if one were to examine the prestigious social clubs of the past, one would tend to identify the dues as the only resource contributed by the members. But this analysis would fail to take note of the most important resource contributed—the perceived prestige of the individual members. To be allowed into the club, one would have had to possess a certain level of social status that would contribute to the overall prestige of the club. While the annual dues constituted a portion of the resources contributed by the membership, the most important resource was the social status of the members. And, should members lose their status through some type of scandal, they likely would be asked to leave the club as their contribution would have dried up or actually taken on a negative value.

Other examples can serve to underscore the often subtle nature of the resources contributed.

Alliance	Evident Resources	Subtle Resources
Labor Union	Dues and time spent picketing	*Liberty*—Foregoing the ability to work for an employer except under the terms and conditions negotiated through the chosen decision-making process
Intellectual Club	Dues	*Brainpower*—The intellect, knowledge, reasoning, and other capabilities possessed by the members
Posse Comitatus	Time and labor spent chasing the criminal	*Life and Limb*—Chasing criminals is dangerous and can result in serious injury or death
Psychic Club	Time spent participating in séances	*Psychic Power*—The perceived ability to conjure up spirits
Alliance to Enforce Criminal Laws	Taxes to pay for the courts, police, prosecutors, and jails	*Liberty*—Foregoing the option of committing the conduct prohibited by the law and acceptance of the penalty for violating the law

This chart is intended to collect a few less obvious examples of contribution underlying alliances. As noted at the beginning, contribution can be anything so long as it can be combined effectively to achieve the objective of the alliance.

CHAPTER SUMMARY

1. Resources are contributed by all members towards the achievement of the mutually desired objective.

2. Resources can consist of literally anything although they are usually labor, material, time, liberty, life and limb, or money.

3. Members usually contribute equal amounts of contribution, although many exceptions exist.

4. Contribution is typically of the same class or nature, but exceptions do exist.

5. If the contribution issues are complex, there is usually an accord addressing the matters.

6. The growth and expansion of money has greatly facilitated the development of alliances by allowing individuals with diverse resources to have an easy mechanism for measuring their respective contributions.

7. A "free rider" is one who benefits from the achievement of the objective of the alliance without joining the alliance or contributing resources. At times, an alliance will strive to force potential free riders to join the alliance to combat this situation.

8. The contributed resources are often difficult to spot. Analysis of the objective of an alliance will provide insight into the contribution.

CHAPTER 6

Putting it Together

Why are alliances formed? The answer is simple. Alliances are formed when they offer perceived advantages over individual effort.

All individuals have desires. In this book, these desires are termed "objectives." If an individual decides to act upon a particular objective, that individual might find that he is incapable of achieving it. The reason can be anything including lack of strength, time, or material. If an individual cannot attain an objective, that individual might explore entering an alliance with one or more other members to achieve the unattainable objective. In this situation, the advantage of the alliance is that it allows the individual to achieve what he cannot accomplish on his own.

In other circumstances, the individual might be able to attain the objective by himself. However, an alliance can offer an advantage over this individual effort. One advantage is effectiveness where a combined effort of an alliance achieves the objective but in more quantity or a higher quality, when compared to individual effort. The other advantage is one of efficiency where the combined effort achieves the same result as individual effort but with less exertion. Or the advantage might be a combination of these two concepts—effectiveness plus efficiency at the same time.

Overall, alliances are formed because they offer advantages over individual effort. In the situation where the individual cannot attain the objective alone, the advantage is absolute. In the situation where the individual can attain the objective, the advantage is relative to the burden of individual effort.

HOW DOES THE INDIVIDUAL EVALUATE ALTERNATIVES?

In deciding whether to enter an alliance, an individual goes through a certain mental process. Understanding how this mental process works is very important to understanding why alliances are entered.

57

Before describing the mental process, it is important to observe that the process is not unique to alliances. Instead, this mental process underlies the making of all decisions by anyone.

This mental process is best described as "cost-benefit analysis." This concept is well known in today's world. The idea is that an action will not be taken unless the perceived benefits outweigh the perceived costs. It is quite a simple idea and comports with common sense. Before acting, every individual weighs what he considers to be the benefits and costs of the action. The action will be taken if there are more perceived benefits than costs.

The best image of this reasoning process is the scales. In an old-fashioned marketplace, scales were used to judge the relative weights of two items. In deciding to act, it is as if the individual mentally places the benefits in one scale and the costs in the other scale. Whichever scale is heavier controls the decision. If the scale with the benefits is heavier, the action is taken. If the scale with the costs is heavier, the action is not taken.

This cost-benefit reasoning process is employed in making all decisions. It is even used in deciding whether to enter an alliance. An individual will put the perceived benefits on one side and the perceived costs on the other. Whichever side is heavier controls the decision.

IN COMPARING THE ALTERNATIVES, WHAT IS CONSIDERED?

It depends. If the individual cannot attain the objective by himself, the analysis is fairly straightforward. Because the only way to accomplish the objective is through an alliance, the individual will not consider the relative advantages of attaining the objective himself. Instead, the individual will consider the perceived value of the attained objective in comparison to the perceived value of the resource contribution the individual must make to the alliance. If the perceived value of the attained objective is greater than the perceived value of the resource contribution, the individual will enter the alliance. If it is less, the individual will not enter the alliance. If it is equal, the individual will be indifferent to joining the alliance.

Value of objective >	Value of resource	Alliance is entered
Value of objective <	Value of resource	Alliance is not entered
Value of objective =	Value of resource	Indifference

In this situation, the individual is essentially inquiring into whether entering the alliance and attaining the objective is worth the resources that must be contributed. If the individual concludes that the alliance will provide more to him than he puts into it, the individual will join the alliance.

Example 1 "Move the boulder"—A caveman is approached about joining an alliance to move the boulder. He greatly values the pathway that has been blocked and sees no real costs associated with pushing the boulder aside. He joins the alliance. Another caveman is approached. He cares only a little about the pathway, but is very concerned about become injured in moving the boulder. He does not join the alliance. Another caveman values the pathway to some degree but is also somewhat concerned about injury. He is indifferent to joining the alliance.

If the individual can achieve the objective by himself, the comparisons become more complex as the individual must compare individual effort versus combined effort. Using the mental scale analogy, the individual is no longer weighing costs and benefits. Instead, he is weighing only net benefits. In one scale is the net benefit of individual effort. In the other scale is the net benefit of an alliance effort. Whichever is greater is selected.

THE MENTAL ANALYSIS CAN BE BROKEN DOWN INTO STEPS

STEP ONE: **Determine the value of the individual effort**—The individual will determine the net perceived value he places on achieving the objective through individual effort. "Net value" is the perceived value of the objective less the perceived value placed on the resources required to achieve the objective individually. This could result in positive, zero, or negative value.

Valuation of Objective	$-$	Valuation of Resource	$=$	Net Value of *Individual* Effort

STEP TWO: **Determine the value of the alliance effort**—The individual will determine the net perceived value he places on achieving the objective through the alliance. To do this, the individual will determine the perceived value of the objective. He will then offset this by the perceived value of the resources that must be contributed to the alliance. This could result in positive, zero, or negative value as well.[1]

---

[1] Note that the perceived values (that is, the values given to both objective and the resources) associated with an alliance effort might be different from those associated with an individual effort. Why? If the alliance can achieve the objective more *effectively*, it will provide more value. Similarly, if the alliance can achieve the objective more *efficiently*, fewer resources will be contributed in comparison to an individual effort.

| Valuation of Objective | − | Valuation of Resource | = | Net Value of *Combined* Effort |

STEP THREE: **Weigh individual effort versus alliance effort**—The individual will then compare the relative net perceived values of individual effort versus collective effort. The individual will select the one with the higher net perceived value. If both values are negative, the individual will select neither option and the objective will not be attained. If the two net values are equal, the individual will be indifferent to joining the alliance.

Net value of individual effort	<	Net value of alliance effort	Alliance is entered
Net value of individual effort	>	Net value of alliance effort	Alliance is not entered
Net value of individual effort	=	Net value of alliance effort	Indifference

Example 3 "Dig the well"—Two primitive farmers are contemplating entering the alliance. Both are able to dig their own wells, but to do so will be very labor intensive and they might not strike water early enough to save their crops. One farmer sees a higher net value to the alliance effort and joins it. Another farmer feels that he will be able to dig the well on his own very quickly and obtain sufficient water to save his crops. In addition, he does not like the idea of sharing the well water with others. This farmer sees a higher net value to an individual effort. He does not join the alliance.

WHAT IS THE SIGNIFICANCE OF "PERCEIVED" VALUE?

The word "perceived" is significant. The point is that each individual determines what advantages and disadvantages are considered relevant and worthy of consideration. This concept is commonly referred to as "subjective" valuation and is to be contrasted with "objective" valuation.

Note that the concept of objective valuation is distinct from the "objective" that underlies an alliance. The former is an adjective while the latter is a noun. Analysis of *subjective* values focuses solely upon the inner mind of the individual. Value judgments of others are not relevant. In fact, efforts must be undertaken to avoid the values of others from straying into the analysis of subjective valuation.

Subjective valuation can be best summed up with the expression, "Beauty is in the eye of the beholder."

In contrast, *objective* valuation is considered to be a detached valuation independent of the individual thoughts of particular individuals. Objective valuation attempts to utilize a semi-scientific method to determine the valuation of an item. Many different methods can be utilized. Some argue that objective valuation is not possible. In any event, the best example of objective valuation in today's world is a marketplace price determined through extensive bidding of buyers and sellers. The price resulting from this process would be thought to be the product of an objective valuation process.

The focus of "perceived" value is subjective, with an emphasis upon the inner mind of the individual. In weighing the relative costs and benefits in the scale analogy, the individual is placing his subjective valuations in the respective scales.

If two or more individuals are contemplating an issue, will they focus upon the same criteria? Often they will, but not always. In most circumstances, the advantages and disadvantages considered relevant by the individuals will be substantially similar. However, the possibility still remains that the different individuals will identify different factors to consider in deciding whether to enter an alliance.

Example 2 "Slay the mammoth"—In deciding to enter the alliance, all of the prehistoric hunters balance the perceived value of the mammoth meat versus the dangers associated with attacking a mammoth. Aside from these two considerations, certain hunters have some unique considerations of their own. One hunter values the mammoth's hide. Another values its tusks. Another fears angering animal spirits by attacking the mammoth and balances this fear against the value of the mammoth's meat.

Even if individuals identify the same advantages and disadvantages to consider in entering an alliance, different individuals can attribute different values to these matters. As a result, it is possible that two individuals facing identical circumstances can place different weights on the values of individual and collective efforts.

Example 2 "Slay the mammoth"—Several primitive hunters refuse to join the alliance. These hunters do value the mammoth's meat. Unlike the twenty hunters that join the alliance, however, these hunters attribute great significance to the dangers associated with attacking the mammoth and find that it outweighs the value of the meat.

Importantly, individuals can make errors or miscalculations in attributing values to the objective or the costs. Remember that the focus is upon the *perceived* values. Accordingly, an individual can compare various values, conclude that an alliance is advantageous, enter the alliance, and then re-evaluate the situation. In re-evaluating, the individual might conclude that too much weight was given to the objective or too little weight was given to the costs, or both. This individual will not be happy about entering the alliance. Similarly, another individual might find that he did the opposite by under-weighing the value of the objective, overweighing the value of the costs, or both. This individual will be very happy about joining the alliance.

Example 7 "Buy the boat"—One of the members concludes that sailing is boring and wishes that he never joined the alliance. Another finds it exhilarating and is joyful about entering the alliance.

ARE INDIVIDUALS REALLY THINKING LIKE THIS?

Yes. Individuals always compare the relative costs and benefits in acting. The only exception is action by immediate impulse where no thought occurs. Otherwise, if any contemplation is involved, the individual is weighing costs and benefits.

It must be underscored, however, that this thought process can take many forms. On one extreme is an individual who carefully evaluates every aspect, deliberates extensively, and then makes a painstaking decision between the options. On the other extreme, the mental process will be subconscious with the individual making a "snap" decision. In between are many variations.

To generalize, alliances formed by express accords are likely to entail long, drawn-out ponderings over entering an alliance. Alliances formed by implied accords are more likely to involve subconscious, almost spontaneous decisions. Regardless of the nature of the deliberative process, the individual will compare the relative perceived values of the available options.

HOW DOES INDIVIDUAL OUTSOURCING FIT INTO THE ANALYSIS?

So far, the discussion has focused on two alternatives: (i) individual effort, and (ii) an alliance effort. In an individual effort, a single individual achieves the objective by himself. In an alliance effort, two or more members achieve the objective through a combined effort. But what happens if an individual retains another to attain the objective for him? That is, what happens if the individual outsources the effort to another person or group of persons?

Individual Outsourcing is a form of individual effort. The individual uses his own resources to hire another to attain the objective. No alliance is involved in this situation. There is no accord. There are no members. And there are no combinations of resources to attain a mutually desired objective. Instead, the individual is attaining the objective individually except that he outsources the effort to another.

> **Example 1 "Move the boulder"**—Instead of forming an alliance of four members to move the boulder, the caveman hires four persons to push the boulder out of the way. In exchange for their efforts, the caveman gives each some food. The caveman has achieved the objective through an outsourced individual effort.

Individual outsourced efforts can resemble alliances. This perception arises because of the involvement of several persons working towards a common goal. However, because these working individuals are being paid for their efforts, no alliance exists. Instead, the objective is being attained by an individually outsourced effort.

An individually outsourced effort should not be equated with an alliance outsourced effort. An *alliance outsourced* effort occurs when an alliance retains someone other than an alliance member to attain the objective of the alliance.

> **Example 4 "Wild West"**—The alliance members pool monetary resources and then use this collection of money to hire a mercenary to attain the objective of order and decency. This is not an individually outsourced effort because an alliance exists. But it can be considered an "outsourcing," because the alliance is retaining a third party to attain the objective instead of accomplishing the objective through efforts and labors of the members.

Individual outsourcing is relevant to alliance analysis because it offers another option for an individual to consider in attaining an objective. An individual can weigh the costs and benefits associated with: (i) a purely individual effort, (ii) an individually outsourced effort, or (iii) an alliance effort.

WHY ARE ALLIANCES NOT FORMED?

The answer is simple. Alliances are not formed when they *do not offer perceived advantages* over individual effort.

Whenever an individual is confronted with a proposed alliance, he will inquire as to how it benefits him and his own subjective desires. If there is no perceived value to the alliance, or if the perceived costs of the contribution exceed any value, the individual will not join it. Note that a bystander might be perplexed by an individual's decision to enter or to not enter an alliance. But remember that the concern is with subjective value. The bystander might attribute different values to the benefits and costs and therefore achieve a different outcome. There is nothing out of place in this situation. It is the nature of subjective valuations that two or more individuals might value something differently.

Even if the elements necessary for the formation of an alliance are present, the alliance nevertheless might not form due to outside factors. These outside factors are discussed subsequently.

DO ALLIANCES HAVE LIVES?

Yes. All alliances have a beginning, middle, and end.

The *beginning* is the time period when the alliance is formed. Typically, the first step is where one individual realizes that a combined effort might be useful in achieving an objective. This individual solicits other individuals to join the alliance. If other potential members are located, they then form some type of an accord confirming the objective and means of the alliance. Accords on other, nonessential topics might be entered into as well. When the accord is struck, the alliance has formed. (Note that alliances formed by implied accords are much less structured with the alliance forming through unspoken agreements.)

The *middle* is the time period when the alliance strives to achieve the objective. During this stage, the contributed resources are assembled. The alliance utilizes the selected means to attempt to attain the objective. If the alliance requires that decisions be made, a decision-making process of some form will be employed. These decisions can pertain to choosing between two or more means. Or, if the objective is indefinite or open, the decisions can include defining or selecting the objective for the alliance to undertake. And, if the alliance has organizational issues (for example, allowing in new members, collecting contribution, dividing up the benefit of the objective, and so on), the decisions can relate to these matters as well. The middle is also the time when the alliance might change or transform itself into a different alliance or into an illusory alliance. This topic of transformation will be discussed in greater detail shortly.

The *end* is the time period when the alliance comes to a conclusion. The end of an alliance can come about for various reasons. If the alliance achieves the objective, the members might formally disband it. If members no longer possess sufficient resources to contribute towards the achievement of the objective, the alliance might fall apart. As time passes, members might become less and less interested in the objective of the alliance and the alliance will end. Or the members might conclude that the means utilized by the alliance are not effective or are actually harming the interests of the members. It might be determined that another alliance exists that is more effective at achieving the objective. Or it could be found that attainment of the objective by individual effort is preferable to a combined, alliance effort. Finally, several or even all of these factors might work together to contribute to the end of an alliance.

DO ALLIANCES CHANGE?

It depends on the alliance. Before discussing this topic, the subject matter of "change" must be clarified. An alliance can undergo two types of changes: (i) contemplated change, and (ii) fundamental change.

In a *contemplated change*, an alliance is altered pursuant to a mechanism agreed upon in the underlying alliance. At the time the accord is struck, it is contemplated that such a change might be instituted somewhere down the road. Types of contemplated changes were discussed in Chapter 4 relating to decision-making processes. That chapter identified three areas where decisions might have to be made: (i) the means, (ii) the objective, and (iii) organizational issues. If the accord provides for a decision-making process on one or more of these areas, then any change made pursuant to such a provision is a contemplated change.

> Example 5 "Help the needy"—The accord underlying the alliance provides for a monthly meeting of all members. At this meeting, a majority vote determines the specific endeavor that the alliance will undertake with that month's collection of contribution. At the first meeting, the alliance decides to set up a soup kitchen. Then, for five straight months, the alliance votes to continue the soup kitchen. After the end of these six months, the alliance votes to use the contribution to build housing for the needy. There has been a change in the means used by the alliance. But this change is a "contemplated change" because the accord provided for it.

Note that contemplated changes can be undertaken in unstructured, informal manners. In Chapter 4, "nebulous" decision-making processes were briefly discussed. If an alliance utilizes such a process, then the contemplated change will be made in a hazy, unformulated manner.

In contrast, a *fundamental change* pertains to an alteration of the accord underlying the alliance. If an alliance is in the middle of its life and its accord is then altered, there has been a fundamental change to the alliance. Note that the focus is on the accord and whether its substance is different upon what was originally agreed.

> Example 4 "Wild West"—The community is founded near a small stream that the inhabitants often cross by rowboats or crude, unsteady bridges. A

member of the alliance has the idea of building a large, sturdy bridge over the river. He suggests the idea to the alliance and an agreement is struck that all members will increase their contribution to fund the building and maintaining of a bridge over the river. In this situation, the accord has been fundamentally changed. Originally, the accord was limited to hiring the mercenary. Now it includes building a bridge.

Often, a fundamental change to an alliance can be viewed as a termination of the original alliance and the formation of an entirely new alliance. This topic has fuzzy parameters so it is not possible to delineate clear-cut principles. But if a new accord largely replaces the substance of the original accord, it is more accurate to say that the original alliance has terminated and a new alliance has formed.

Example 7 "Buy the boat"—The members become bored with the sailboat. They confer and agree to sell the sailboat and jointly invest the proceeds in the stock market. This can be described as a "fundamental change" in the alliance. However, because the original accord and the new accord are so different, it might be better to say that an entirely new alliance has been formed.

As a final matter, alliances can change by transforming into an *illusory alliance*. What is an "illusory alliance?" It is an entity that utilizes combined resources of individuals and resembles an alliance, but it lacks one or more of the essential elements of an alliance. For instance, the individuals contributing resources might not hold true membership status. The purported members might not desire the objective. The objective might not be one where a combined effort is advantageous. Or there might not be any accord—express or implied—underlying the alliance. This topic will be discussed in greater detail subsequently.

THE RELEVANCE OF THE ACCORD TO CHANGE

As the foregoing discussion has made abundantly clear, the significance of the accord to the issue of change cannot be understated. The propensity for an alliance to change is directly related to the accord and its provisions.

If the accord is quite specific on what the alliance constitutes (and does not constitute), there is very little propensity for change in the alliance. Of course, the alliance can still change notwithstanding, but such a change would be fundamental. Fundamental changes are more difficult to effectuate and are likely to result in the effective termination of the original alliance and a birth of a new alliance.

Conversely, if the members have foreseen the need for change and provided for it in the accord, there is much more propensity for change. Similarly, the vaguer the underlying accord is (especially with alliances formed by implied accords), the more propensities for change exist.

It must be observed that a propensity for change is not always desirable. In Chapter 4, it was noted in great length that members are often concerned with the alliance transforming itself into something unpredictable or contrary to the desires of the members. As a result, members will often impose severe restrictions limiting the propensity of an alliance to change.

The potential undesirability of change can be elaborated upon. Recall that the purpose of an alliance is to take advantage of a combined effort to achieve an objective desired by all members. If the alliance has a high propensity for change, there is a corresponding high propensity for the alliance to be transformed into what was described as an illusory alliance. Recall that an illusory alliance is something that resembles an alliance. It utilizes combined resources of individuals but lacks one or more of the essential elements of an alliance. If the accord allows for change, the potential for an unfavorable change exists.

Example 5 "Help the needy"—The accord underlying this alliance has a high propensity for change. There is a monthly meeting where a majority vote decides the endeavor the alliance will undertake for that month. For six months, the alliance decides to run a soup kitchen. For the seventh month, the alliance decides to build housing for the needy. On the eight month, the alliance decides by a bare majority (51% of the votes) to provide the needy with volumes of Shakespeare to improve their culture and sophistication. Many members are upset. They believe that there are many more effective means to employ in helping the needy than teaching them about Shakespeare.

Example 4 "Wild West"—To bring order and decency to the community, the alliance delegated the mercenary with broad authority to determine what "order and decency" comprises and what means should be used to achieve this objective. To check this delegation of authority, the alliance's accord instituted a five-member panel for the mercenary to consult. The mercenary has great success running off the gunfighters and thieves. Without much to do, the mercenary concludes that the alliance's objective of "order and decency" includes insuring that the women of the community wear dresses completely covering their legs. The mercenary consults with the five-member panel. The panel agrees with his decision, and the mercenary begins fining women whose dresses are too short. This is so despite the fact that most members of the alliance do not care about the issue. The alliance's decision-making process has defined the indefinite objective of "order and decency" to include a goal that is not desired by its members.

Example 8 "Council of elders"—The council concludes that their spouses and children should not have to collect their own food. As a result, the council orders the tribe to provide the council's family with food everyday. The council has instituted a change in the alliance, but this change is in the interests of only the council members and not the membership as a whole.

What will be the consequences of these changes? Are alliances still present? Or is an illusory alliance now in effect? What will happen? These issues and others will be discussed subsequently.

Overall, change in an alliance is a thorny topic. Alliances that are formed to address a single discrete matter are typically short-lived and do not change. Such alliances are formed, achieve the objective, and then terminate. But most alliances have a need for some degree of change. The accord can address this situation by identifying specific mechanisms for effecting change. But this mechanism allowing for change has its drawbacks as just touched upon. Thus, in forming accords, members often will have to make difficult compromises between allowing for positive change on the one hand and guarding against a negative change on the other.

WHY DO ALLIANCES TERMINATE?

To understand the termination of an alliance, it is best to analyze the reasoning of the individual members of the alliance. By focusing on the individuals, the explanation for the termination of an alliance becomes evident.

Earlier in this chapter, the life of an alliance was discussed including the beginning, middle, and end. The discussion of end identified various situations that might prompt the termination of an alliance. These factors include:

The objective is achieved	**The contributed resources become more valued**
The objective is not achieved	**A new alliance offers more advantages**
The objective is no longer desired	**Individual effort is found preferable**

A combination of these factors

All of these factors relate to the "net perceived value" concept discussed earlier in this chapter. Recall that an individual enters an alliance only if it provides a net perceived value to him. For instance, if the individual cannot achieve the objective by himself, the perceived value of the objective must be greater than the perceived costs of the contributed resources. If the individual can achieve the objective by himself, the net perceived value of the alliance must be greater than the net perceived value of the individual effort. Overall, the important point is that an individual enters an alliance if it provides a net perceived value to him.

The same concept pertains to a decision of an individual to leave an alliance. If the individual concludes that the alliance is not providing a net perceived value to him, he will terminate his membership and leave the alliance.

What can make an individual conclude that the alliance does not offer to him a net perceived value? The answer is the list of factors just identified. Each one of these has the potential to reduce the net perceived value of the alliance. For example, if the objective is obtained, the alliance is no longer providing a benefit to the individual. As a result, he has no reason to stay in the alliance. Similarly, no benefit is provided to the individual if the alliance fails to achieve the objective or if the individual determines that he no longer desires the objective. Or if the perceived value of the objective to the individual lessens (for example, the alliance achieves the objective in part, or the individual's tastes change and he no longer values the objective to the same degree), the perceived value of the objective will be lessened instead of being eliminated.

Even if the perceived value of the objective stays the same, other factors can reduce the net perceived value. For instance, if the contributed resources increase in perceived value, this increase will offset the perceived value of the alliance. If the increase is particularly large, it could eliminate the net perceived benefit of the alliance. Similarly, if other alliances or even individual efforts are subsequently perceived to offer more advantages over the existing alliance, the advantage of the existing alliance is eliminated.

Finally, a combination of these factors can work to eliminate the net perceived benefit of an existing alliance. For instance, if the perceived value of the objective declines somewhat while the perceived value of the contributed resources increases somewhat, the changes might be sufficient to result in no net benefit being offered by the alliance. As a consequence, the individual will terminate membership in the alliance.

Overall, the guiding concept is that, if the alliance is no longer perceived to be providing a net benefit, the individual will leave it. This reduction in net perceived benefit can be caused by a single factor or a host of factors.

Significantly, the departure of one member will not necessarily result in the termination of the alliance, but the departure of increasing numbers of members can cause the termination of alliance. This result can occur in two situations.

The first situation relates to the concept of critical mass. In Chapter 3, it was observed that some alliances must have a certain number of members to be able to achieve the objective. In that discussion, critical mass was thought of as a precondition to the formation of an alliance, but critical mass also can be a condition to the continuation of an alliance. If the membership levels drop below this critical mass, the alliance will not be able to achieve the objective and it will terminate out of necessity. Thus, if sufficient members depart an alliance, the alliance might terminate as a direct consequence.

> **Example 2 "Slay the mammoth"**—As the twenty prehistoric hunters approach the mammoth, twelve become terrified and run away. The remaining eight hunters conclude that they do not have the numbers to slay the mammoth. At least twenty hunters are thought to be needed. The alliance terminates.

The second situation is similar to the concept of critical mass, but it pertains to the indirect consequences of membership losses. Many alliances do not have a critical mass of members required to achieve the objective. Instead, many alliances are more effective, efficient, or both when they have more members. For example, more members might increase the quantity or quality of the objective (that is, effectiveness). Or more members might reduce the amount of contribution by spreading it over many members (that is, efficiency). If members begin to leave the alliance, its effectiveness, efficiency, or both might decline. If the declines are substantial enough, the net perceived values of the remaining members might decline to a point where the values are eliminated. As a consequence, the alliance will terminate.

> **Example 3 "Dig the well"**—Five members of the alliance quickly drop out. As a result, each remaining member has to dig much more. Further, the progress of the digging becomes slower, reducing the alliance's benefit of quickly finding water for the members' crops. Each remaining member re-evaluates his membership and decides to quit the alliance. In light of the reduced effectiveness and efficiencies caused by the departures or members, the remaining members conclude that digging wells by themselves offers more advantages over the diminished alliance.

HOW DOES CHANGE RELATE TO TERMINATION?

The topic of change can have a substantial impact on the life of an alliance. A change in an alliance can prolong its life, or bring about the quick termination of the alliance.

The first topic to discuss is change that prolongs the life of an alliance. Recall that the members are in the alliance because it provides a net perceived value to them. As time passes, this net perceived value might decline for a variety of reasons.

The value given to the objective might drop. The means used by the alliance might be seen as ineffective. The resources contributed might increase in perceived value. Competing alliances offering more attractive net perceived values might appear. Organizational issues might become a large burden to the members and offset the value attributed to attaining the objective. More effective or efficient individual methods of attaining the objective might be discovered. For whatever reason, it is likely that the net perceived value of an alliance will diminish over time.

The alliance can adapt to these changing circumstances by changing itself. As noted earlier in this chapter, one change is a contemplated change. Recall that a contemplated change is one that is provided for in the original accord. Contemplated changes are usually effectuated through a decision-making process. Thus, if an alliance desires to avoid termination, it must use its designated decision-making process to change. If these changes are done properly, they will maintain or increase the net perceived benefit of the alliance. For instance, the decision-making process might find new or improved means to obtain the objective in a more effective manner, a more efficient manner, or both. Or it might find a way of reducing the contribution of the members. Or it might change to eliminate any organizational issues that are causing burdens or annoyances to the members. Or, if the alliance allows the decision-making process to define an indefinite objective or even pick the objective, the decision-making process will have to do a better job of defining or selecting objectives that are desired by the members. This latter situation is particularly necessary where tastes have changed and the original objective of the alliance might have become disfavored.

If the accord does not have a mechanism for change, the alliance might undergo a fundamental change. Recall that a fundamental change is one that is not provided for in an accord. Fundamental changes are typically difficult to effectuate and often can be viewed as a termination of the original alliance and the creation of a new alliance. The changes implemented in a fundamental change will be the same in substance as in contemplated change, with the focus being on increasing the net perceived value of the alliance.

Regardless of whether the change is contemplated or fundamental, alliances can prevent termination by changing. And, in all circumstances, the change is implemented to increase the net perceived value of the alliance. If the change does not increase this net perceived value or increase it sufficiently, the alliance will be prone to termination.

The second topic on change and termination is change that causes termination. Just as change can increase net perceived value, it can decrease it as well. For instance, the alliance could employ a different means that fail to achieve the objective as efficiently or effectively. Or an objective could be pursued that is not desired by most members. Or the required contribution could be increased. Or new means could be used that are distasteful or otherwise undesirable to members. Or the benefit of the objective could be apportioned in an undesirable manner. Or the membership could be increased where the benefit of the objective became substantially diluted. A multitude of other possibilities exist that could reduce the net perceived value. But the point is that a change in an alliance can reduce the net perceived value and jeopardize the existence of the alliance.

When will a member leave the alliance? If the alliance fails to change to meet new circumstances, will a particular member leave? If the alliance changes and adopts something undesirable to the member, will he leave? The answers depend on analysis of the net perceived value to that member. If the net perceived value of the alliance is eliminated by either a failure to change or a negative change, the individual will leave the alliance. Accordingly, a failure to change will not necessarily cause an individual to leave, provided that there is still a net perceived value to the alliance. Similarly, a change that reduces the perceived value will not cause an individual to leave, unless the change eliminates the net perceived value.

Example 4 "Wild West"—The mercenary demands more wages and the required contribution of all members is increased substantially. The members are not happy with the change and begin to question whether the alliance is worth the heavy price. Furthermore, the members question why the mercenary is regulating the lengths of women's dresses when basically no one cares about the issue. Nevertheless, the members stay in the alliance. Although the net perceived value of the alliance has been reduced, the members still find it to be positive.

Example 5 "Help the needy"—After the alliance votes to distribute volumes of Shakespeare to improve the culture and sophistication of the needy, about one half of the members quit the alliance. They conclude that they derive little satisfaction from tending to the culture and sophistication of the needy when they remain hungry, sick, and cold. Some of these former members resort to their prior practice of handing money out sporadically on the street. Others, however, form a new alliance and provide in the accord that the means of the alliance will be limited to providing food, medicine, and shelter to the needy.

Example 8 "Council of elders"—After the council decrees that the tribe members shall provide their family with food, the tribe members question the benefits of the alliance. They ask how they benefit from having a council of elders order them around and require them to feed the family members of the council. The tribe members become so angry that they refuse to obey the council on any issue. The alliance terminates and the council disbands. But a week later, a large raiding party is spotted on the horizon. The tribe members confer and then agree to allow the council to reconstitute itself and come up with plan to deal with the new threat.

IS TERMINATION BAD?

It must be observed that the termination of an alliance is not necessary an unwelcome result. Recall that the ultimate purpose of an alliance is to satisfy the desires of its members. If the members no longer desire the alliance and it terminates as a consequence, that is not necessarily an undesirable outcome. This is so especially if the alliance has achieved its objective or if the objective has become outdated, with new alliances or individual efforts providing more advantages.

But the termination of an alliance can be an undesirable result if the termination is the product of an unreasonable failure to adapt to changing circumstances. For instance, if the members desire the continuation of the alliance, but a relatively obvious change is not implemented and the alliance terminates as a consequence, this outcome is not desirable. By failing to change, the beneficial alliance has let itself perish needlessly.

Similarly, if a change causes a beneficial alliance to terminate, that result is not desirable either. For instance, the alliance institutes a change that reduces the net perceived value of the alliance to the point that the members all leave and the alliance ends. In effect, by implementing the wrong change, the alliance has effectively committed suicide.

At times, alliances lose sight of the objective in an effort to preserve the alliance. In this situation, the objective of the alliance becomes the preservation of the alliance, instead of achieving the objective. This peculiar situation is prevalent in many long-term alliances. Such alliances strive to undertake change for the sake of preserving the alliance, rather than to achieve the objective and satisfy the desires of the alliance members. Because there is no fundamental objective common to all members holding the alliance together, these efforts generally fail in the long run and the alliance ends as a consequence.

CHAPTER SUMMARY

1. Alliances are formed for one simple reason. They offered perceived advantages over individual effort.

2. In deciding whether to enter an alliance, an individual engages in a mental process best described as "cost-benefit analysis," where the benefits of a proposed course of action are weighed against the costs. The concept of marketplace scales is an effective image.

3. If an individual cannot obtain an objective individually, he will weigh the perceived value of the attained objective against the perceived value of the contributed resource. If the value is greater than the cost, the individual will enter the alliance.

4. If an individual can obtain an objective individually, he will weigh the net value of the individual effort against the net value of an alliance effort. These net values are determined by deducting the costs of attaining the objectives through the respective efforts (individual and alliance) less values attributed towards obtaining the objective. The effort with the greater value will be selected.

5. The focus of the analysis is on the value in fact perceived by the individual. As such, there is no effort to provide a detached, universally accepted value. Instead, the subjective feelings and impressions of the individual are controlling.

6. The subjective values attributed to various items can vary from individual to individual. Further, individuals might miscalculate the values they attribute to items and regret having made, or not made, certain decisions.

7. Outsourcing is a form of individual effort, whereby an individual uses his own resources to hire another to attain the objective. Outsourcing arrangements often resemble alliance efforts, but they are not alliances.

8. Outsourcing offers another option for an individual to consider in attaining an objective. An individual can weigh the costs and benefits associated with: (i) a purely individual effort, (ii) an outsourced individual effort, or (iii) an alliance effort.

9. Every alliance has a life characterized by a beginning, middle, and end.

10. During the middle of the lives of an alliance, change is possible. A contemplated change is alteration of the alliance through a mechanism implemented when the alliance is first formed. A fundamental change is an alteration of the accord underlying alliance in a manner not agreed upon at the formation of the alliance.

11. The accord can have a large impact on the propensity of an alliance to change. If the accord provides for a mechanism for altering the alliance, then a contemplated change is possible. Conversely, if the accord is specific and does not provide for change, change is unlikely.

12. The occurrence of a change in an alliance can serve to preserve the alliance. Conversely, a change can also cause an alliance to terminate.

13. An alliance will terminate when it presents no net perceived value. Net perceived value can be the product of changing valuations, defects in the operation of the alliance, the arrival of a new, more effective alliance, the development of individual abilities to attain the objective, or a combination of these factors.

14. The termination of an alliance is not necessarily a bad outcome.

Part II

Advanced Issues

CHAPTER 7

Decision-Making Processes

The topic of decision-making processes was raised in Chapter 4. This chapter will address decision-making processes in much greater detail.

INTRODUCTION

Recall that all alliances have some type of an accord addressing at least two matters: (i) the objective of the alliance, and (ii) the means to be employed in achieving that objective. This accord can be express or implied. If the accord is express, its provisions can be specific, indefinite, or somewhere in between these two extremes. If the accord is implied, its provisions are ascertained from the underlying circumstances and conduct of the members.

Also recall that the subject matter of any accord is not necessarily limited to the objective and means. It can also address any other topic of concern to the members. These issues might include contribution, distribution of the benefits of the alliance, membership, procedures for amending the accord, limitations on means or objectives, and termination. Sometimes the accord includes a decision-making process.

A decision-making process is a method or procedure by which an alliance makes any necessary decisions. Not all alliances have decision-making processes, but many alliances have at least a few decisions to be made and therefore require some type of a decision-making process.

There are three areas where decisions are made. The three are: (i) decisions relating to the *means* to be used to achieve the objective, (ii) decisions regarding what *objective* to pursue, and (iii) decisions pertaining to *organizational* issues underlying the alliance.

Decision-making processes can be divided into two categories: (i) formal processes and (ii) nebulous processes. A formal process has structure and some degree of recognition by the members as a method or procedure for making decisions. In contrast, a nebulous process has no structure and no real recognition by the members as decision-making process. Nevertheless, the nebulous process will make decisions.

This chapter will largely pertain to formal decision-making processes. The operations of the various processes will be explored. Nebulous processes will not be raised in detail, as they are fairly straightforward. In addition, the strengths and weaknesses of certain types of processes will be considered.

FORMAL DECISION-MAKING PROCESSES

A *formal decision-making process* is any method or procedure that has some degree of structure and is acknowledged by the members as a mechanism for making decisions. Formal decision-making processes can be divided into two areas: (i) decisions made by all members through a *membership vote*, and (ii) decisions that are *delegated* by the alliance to a person or entity.

Membership Vote	Delegation of Decision-Making Authority

These two areas will be discussed separately.

MEMBERSHIP VOTE

A decision-making process by membership vote is exactly what the description implies (that is, the decision is made through a vote of all members). Importantly, *all* members must participate in the vote, or at the very least, all members must be given the opportunity to vote, an option which they may decline to exercise by not casting a vote.

Before any membership vote can occur, there must be an agreement on what number or percentage of votes must be cast in favor of an option for that option to be the decision of the alliance. This agreement is a part of the accord. As such, any alliance with a membership vote must have some type of an accord on the minimum number of votes (or a minimum percentage of the votes) that an option must receive to constitute the decision.

By far, the favorite minimum number or percentage is a simple majority, where the option receiving greater than fifty percent of the votes becomes the decision of the alliance. A simple majority, however, is one of many variations for setting the minimum number of votes. A few of the more common possibilities include:

Option	Description	Examples
Plurality	The option with the most votes constitutes the decision. If there are numerous options receiving votes, it is possible that the prevailing option might have only marginally more votes than the option coming in second place.	There are five options—A, B, C, D, and E—and 100 votes are cast. The votes are distributed as follows: A (22), B (24), C (21), D (8), and E (25). The decision is option E, even though it receives only one more vote that option B.
Majority	The option with over 50% of the votes (for example, 50.0001%) constitutes the decision. If there are three or more options, it is possible that no option will receive a majority, resulting in no decision being made.	In the preceding example, no decision is reached as no option received a majority of the votes (that is, at least 51 out of 100). The solution to this impasse is usually a runoff between the two options receiving the highest vote totals (that is, B and E).
Super Majority	The option with a predetermined percentage in excess of 50% constitutes the option. It is up to the alliance to determine this percentage. The percentage might range from a figure over 50% but less than 100% (for example, 57%, 65%, 89%).	The super majority threshold is 75% of the votes cast and there are two options—A and B. A receives 73% of the votes and B receives 27%. No decision is reached.
Unanimity	The option must receive all votes to constitute the decision.	There are two options—A and B—and 10 members. Option A receives 9 votes and B receives 1 vote. No decision is made.

Aside from having an accord on the minimum number of votes necessary for an option to become the decision of the alliance, there might be a need for agreements on many other subjects. These will vary with the circumstances and the concerns of various alliance members.

A common concern is the quorum required for a vote to be effective. A *quorum* is a device intended to insure that a substantial portion, if not all, of the membership participates in the voting. Usually, the quorum requires that a minimum number of members participate in a vote on a decision. If the minimum does not participate, any vote taken is ineffective.

Example 5 "Help the needy"—Recall that the alliance meets every month to vote on the specific task to be undertaken for that month to help the needy. The alliance currently has 100 members. The accord provides for a simple majority decision-making process, and sets the quorum at 80. Thus, for an option to become the decision of the alliance, at least 80 votes must be cast to satisfy the quorum. And for an option to become the decision, it must receive a simple majority (that is, greater than 50%) of the votes cast. For example, if 80 members participate in the vote, an option must receive at least 41 votes to be the decision (41 divided by 80 is 51.25% of the votes). If 90 participate, the option must receive 46 votes (46 divided by 90 is 51.11%). If all 100 participate, the option must receive 51 votes (51 divided by 100 is 51%).

Without the quorum, the focus is upon only the percentage of votes cast. At times, this can produce undesirable results. For example, if there are 100 members and only 9 show up to vote, it will take only 5 votes for an option to become the decision of the alliance. By requiring that at least 80 members vote, the quorum insures that at least 41 votes must be cast in favor of an option for it to become the decision.

A different tact is to specify the number of votes that must be cast in favor of an option, instead of identifying a specific quorum.

Example 5 "Help the needy"—One month, 73 members show up to vote. The quorum is not met and no vote can be taken. A few months later, 78 members appear and no vote can be taken. In both situations, non-binding votes are taken and options receive more than 51 votes. A member points out that the goal should not be to make sure that 80 members vote. Instead, the member suggests, it should be only that at least 51% of the members vote in favor of an option. This reasoning is persuasive. The alliance amends its accord to provide that an option must receive 51 votes to become the decision and that the number of votes cast is not relevant. Essentially, this alternative procedure guarantees that at least 51 members vote on any decision since that is the minimum amount of votes necessary for an effective vote.

Overall, the purpose of a high quorum is to insure that no decision is made without a substantial portion of the membership voting upon it. And the quorum can be set at any level that an alliance sees fit. Some alliances might not be concerned with the issue and have no quorum. Other alliances might require participation by all members and set the quorum at all members.

An additional factor that some alliances address is the procedure for *notifying* members of upcoming votes. These procedures are enacted to see that all members have an opportunity to participate in the decision-making process. In addition, these procedures might be necessary to guard against intentional efforts to exclude certain members from participating in votes.

Example 5 "Help the needy"—Bob is a member of the alliance, and Bob wants the alliance to decide upon a particular option. Bob believes that he has 51 votes, the minimum amount necessary for the option to pass. But Bob recognizes that several of the members voting in favor of the option have no firm convictions and could easily change their minds. Further, Bob recognizes that Sam opposes the option and is a very persuasive communicator. Bob is concerned that Sam might appear at the vote and convince at least one member currently favoring the option to change his mind. If this happens, the option will not have a majority and will not become the decision. As a result, Bob convenes a secret meeting where only members favoring the option are invited. Bob specifically sees that Sam is not notified of the vote so that Sam will not show up. The vote is held and Sam does not appear. Bob's favored option receives 51 votes and becomes the decision. Subsequently, Sam learns of the vote and complains about how he was excluded from the voting process. The alliance then amends the accord to institute specific mechanisms for notifying all members of all votes.

In summary, a membership-vote process is fairly straightforward. A decision is made through the vote of all members. Before the vote, there must be an accord identifying the minimum number of votes that an option must receive to constitute the decision of the alliance. If an option receives this minimum and all other procedural prerequisites are satisfied (for example, quorum, notification), the option is the decision of the alliance.

DELEGATION OF DECISION-MAKING AUTHORITY

What if the membership does not want to make a decision? Can some other person or thing make the decision? Certainly. A decision can always be entrusted to another person or entity.

The opposite of a membership vote is for a decision to be made by a decision maker other than the membership. In this situation, the decision is *delegated* to another person, group of persons, or some other process. This delegated decision maker holds the authority to make the decision on behalf of the alliance and to bind the members with the decision.

There are three types of delegated decision makers: (i) executive, (ii) committee, or (iii) non-standard. Each will be discussed separately.

Executive	Committee	Non-Standard

EXECUTIVE DECISION MAKERS

An executive decision maker is a single individual. This individual is granted a certain *scope of authority* in which to make decisions for the alliance. The scope of authority granted can vary substantially. The scope can be limited to a single, insubstantial area. Or the scope can include all decisions to be made by the alliance. Or the scope can be somewhere in between these two areas. Whatever the scope of authority might be, the executive is to use his discretion in making the decision.

> Example 2 "Slay the mammoth"—To slay the mammoth, the alliance members must first encircle it and then attack at the same time. The alliance authorizes one member to coordinate these actions. He is vested with authority to decide both where each member should line up and when the attack should begin. This individual is an executive decision maker with authority to make decisions in two limited areas.

> Example 4 "Wild West"—The mercenary is an executive decision maker. His scope of authority includes selecting and using whatever means he sees fit in achieving the objective of order and decency.

> Example 6 "Carpool"—Each parent has a designated week to drive the carpool. During their week, the parents are to use their discretion in determining which route to take to and from the soccer event. Each parent is a decision maker with authority limited to making decisions on the appropriate route.

> Example 8 "Council of elders"—Recall that the Council sends out a war party to track down and kill a band of thieves that was recently observed. When the Council assembles this war party, it names one member as the commander. This commander leads the war party and all members follow the

decisions that he makes. This commander is an executive decision maker with the authority to make decisions relating to the eradication of the thieves.

The decision maker is usually chosen from the ranks of the members, but alliances at times might select non-members to serve as executive decision makers. Selection of non-members is likely where the non-member has specialized knowledge or skills relevant to the decisions to be made. The topic of selecting both executive *and* committee decision makers is addressed subsequently.

COMMITTEE DECISION MAKERS

A committee decision maker is similar to an executive, except that a *group* makes the decision instead of one person. A committee is simply two or more individuals that have been granted authority to make a decision on a certain topic. There must be at least two committee members and there could be hundreds or thousands of committee members.

As with the executive, the scope of decision-making authority granted to a committee can vary from very little to unlimited authority. Furthermore, regardless of the scope of authority granted, the committee is to use its discretion in making the decision.

Example 4 "Wild West"—The objective of the alliance is to bring order and decency. The means are to hire a mercenary and make him a decision maker with full authority to decide how to achieve this objective. As noted earlier, the objective—"order and decency"—is indefinite. Everyone knows that it means ending murder and theft, but does it also include adultery, alcohol consumption, lewd attire, or tobacco use? To address this issue whenever it might arise, the accord provides for a five-member assembly to meet as needed and decide what "order and decency" means. This five-member assembly is a committee decision maker vested with limited authority to resolve uncertainty over the meaning of the objective.

Example 8 "Council of elders"—The Council is authorized by an implied accord to decide both what objectives the tribe should pursue *and* what means should be used in achieving the chosen objectives. This Council is a committee decision maker with unlimited decision-making authority.

By what manner do committees make decisions? In almost all circumstances, committees make decisions in a *formal* process. Recall that a formal decision-making process has structure and is recognized by the alliance as a decision-making process. As such, a committee, which itself is a formal decision-making process, will use formal methods to make decisions.

What are these formal methods? They are the same, basic types of procedures employed when a membership is the decision maker. Because a committee has two or more members, there is a potential for disagreement among the committee members over the appropriate decision. If there are five committee members and three vote for an option and two vote against it, what is the decision of the committee? The committee must have some type of an agreed-upon method for resolving this issue. This is the same issue that was discussed earlier in relation to a membership vote (that is, what number of votes by committee members is needed to constitute the decision of the committee?). As with a membership vote, there are many variations including a plurality, simple majority, super majority, or unanimity. Regardless of which scheme is selected, an option receiving the requisite number of votes becomes the decision of the committee, and therefore, the decision of the alliance.

> **Example 4 "Wild West"**—The accord provides for a five-member assembly to serve a committee decision maker vested with limited authority to resolve uncertainty over the meaning of the objective. The accord further provides that a super majority—four of the five members (that is, 80%)—must vote in favor of an option for it to constitute a decision.

The opposite of a formal decision-making process is a *nebulous* one. This situation is peculiar since a committee is a formal process. (Recall the alliance has formally delegated decision maker authority to the committee.) Nonetheless, some formally created committees might use a nebulous decision-making process. In this situation, there will not be a formal vote. The committee will make a decision, but it will be made through an informal consensus or something similar. Typically, this results either in alliances with implied accords or in alliances with express accords that do not specify how a committee is to make decisions.

> **Example 8 "Council of elders"**—Whenever the Council makes a decision, there is no formal vote. Typically, the Council members meet and discuss the matter. Sometimes all Council members are in agreement. At other times, sharp debates arise. At the end of the deliberations, an informal consensus emerges. Specifically, after all the various arguments have been put forward, the committee members gauge the sentiments of their fellow members. It soon becomes evident which option has the prevailing support. The option holding this informal consensus becomes the decision and is announced to the tribe.

NON-STANDARD DECISION MAKERS

A non-standard decision maker is a catchall category. It encompasses all other situations (that is, other than an executive or a committee) where a decision has been delegated.

There are three subcategories to the non-standard category: (i) random, (ii) rational chaos, and (iii) programmed.

Random	Rational Chaos	Programmed

In each of these situations, the decision-making authority has been delegated to these processes.

Random

A random process is any mechanism used for making a decision which has an essentially arbitrary nature. Common examples include a coin toss, drawing straws, or playing "rock/paper/scissors."

Although these processes might appear absurd at first consideration, it is undisputed that decisions are made in such manners from time to time. In fact, using a random decision-making process appears to be the preferred method where there is no reasoned basis for making a decision.

> **Example 2 "Slay the mammoth"**—The alliance decides to lure the mammoth into a ravine where it will be more easily trapped. The problem is that one member will have to serve as the bait (that is, enticing the mammoth to chase him into the ravine). This task is very dangerous. To pick the unlucky one, the alliance agrees to draw straws. The member drawing the shortest straw will serve as the bait. The drawing of straws is the decision-making process.

> **Example 3 "Dig the well"**—There is a controversy over which member gets to use the first water drawn from the well. The members play an ancient version of "rock/paper/scissors" to resolve the dispute. The "rock/paper/scissors" is the decision-making process.

Rational Chaos

A rational-chaos process is any method for making decisions where a seemingly chaotic concept or process is used which ultimately results in a sensible and sound decision, or what is at least to be perceived as a sensible and sound decision. In this regard, another could view these types of decision-making processes as being essentially random, but the mindset of the alliance members is the important consideration (that is, whether they perceive the method as constituting a legitimate means of making the correct decision).

Example 8 "Council of elders"—It has not rained in weeks and the Council fears a severe drought and famine. But the Council knows that requiring all tribe members to save and contribute food and water to a tribal supply will be controversial. As such, the Council asks the tribe's religious guide if there will be a drought. The religious guide kills a chicken and casts its entrails upon the ground. He studies the entrails and responds that there will be a very severe drought. The decision has been made (albeit through what is considered today to be an unusual or irrational process). The Council orders the tribe members to begin saving food.

Programmed

A programmed process is any situation where decision-making authority has been delegated, but in such a fashion that the decision maker has only nominal discretion or no discretion at all in reaching a decision. That is, the decisions have been effectively predetermined. The decision maker's role is essentially to look at the circumstances presented and determine which predetermined decision is to be implemented. In effect, there is a specific program for the decision maker to follow and deviations from the program are not permissible.

Example 8 "Council of elders"—After raiders attacked the tribe one night, the Council institutes a watch system whereby five tribe members will stand watch at all times during the night. The five-member group has a commander. The Council gives the commander specific instructions. If someone approaches in the dark, the commander is to ask for the password. If the password is given, the person is to be allowed to enter the camp. If the password is not given, the commander is to order the group to fire arrows at and kill the person. No exceptions or deviations are permissible. This commander is a decision maker. However, because he holds no discretion and all decisions are predetermined, he is a programmed decision maker.

Many alliances have programmed decision makers. This type of process is especially prevalent in complex alliances that have multiple levels of decision making. Typically, another delegated decision maker holding discretion gives the programmed decision maker the specific instructions. In other situations, the accord underlying the alliance might be quite specific and might limit both the decision maker's scope of authority *and* discretion. In this regard, the members have effectively agreed that there will be a delegated decision maker, but that it shall hold no discretion to make decisions.

A programmed decision maker might at times resemble an executive or a committee in many regards. However, the distinguishing factor is the extent of discretion afforded to the decision maker. If most or all of the decisions have been predetermined and the decision maker's role is more or less the implementation of these instructions, the decision maker is programmed.

The recent development of computers and complex software raises interesting questions in this area. It is certainly possible to have a computer serving as a programmed decision maker. In this situation, the alliance delegates authority to the computer to make a decision. However, the computer is bound to follow the programming code and therefore has no discretion. It is a programmed decision maker.

SELECTION OF DELEGATED DECISION MAKERS

An executive decision maker is a person. A committee decision maker is a group of persons. How are these roles filled? How does an alliance select these persons to be decision makers?

The selection of a decision maker is a decision itself. Accordingly, the same concepts discussed earlier are applicable. Namely, the decision can be made through (i) a formal process, or (ii) a nebulous process.

Formal

As noted earlier, a formal decision-making process has structure and is recognized by the alliance as constituting a mechanism for making decisions. Express-accord alliances typically have formal procedures for selecting decision makers. In most circumstances, alliances will pick decision makers through a membership vote. Because the entire membership is making the decision, the same concepts discussed earlier are applicable in this situation. There must be agreed-upon numbers (or percentages) of votes that a candidate must receive to become a decision maker. This is true regardless of whether the alliance is selecting one executive or a group of committee members.

> **Example 5 "Help the needy"**—The alliance is very successful and attracts a large number of members and contributions of money. There are so many alliance members that membership votes become difficult. It is simply too cumbersome to have all members show up and vote on every issue. Further, many members are bored with the details of running the alliance and its charitable efforts and would rather not be involved in the particulars.

The alliance votes to amend its accord to create an executive decision maker charged with making all decisions necessary to fulfill the task selected for a given month. The alliance will still meet monthly and a membership vote will select the task to be performed to help the needy, but the executive will be charged with organizing and managing the effort to fulfill that task. How is this executive to be selected? The accord provides that the executive will be selected by a majority vote of all members.

The executive decision maker is a success. The alliance continues to grow. It is soon determined that one executive does not have the time to make all of the decisions. The alliance votes to amend its accord to create two more executive positions and a seven-member committee, each charged with specific decisions to make. The accord further provides that the three executive positions are to be elected through a majority vote of all members. The seven members of the committee are to be chosen through a plurality vote of all members.

There is no universal requirement that a delegated decision maker be selected by a membership vote. A wide variety of delegated decision makers can select a particular decision maker. Common examples include decision makers being selected by other executives or committees, or by even random processes.

Example 4 "Wild West"—Recall the situation in Chapter 6 where the alliance decides to fundamentally alter the accord by selecting an additional objective—the building of a large bridge. The alliance concludes that a single executive should be made the decision maker on aspects of the bridge building. Instead of having a membership vote to select this executive, the alliance delegates the decision to the five-member committee that oversees the mercenary. This committee then votes and chooses a decision maker for the bridge construction. After the bridge is completed, the alliance decides that there should be a three-member committee to make decisions on the maintenance and upkeep of the bridge. The original five-member committee votes and picks the three members of this committee. In both situations, delegated decision makers—one executive and one committee—have been selected by other delegated decision makers.

Example 3 "Dig the well"—The alliance decides that it needs a single decision maker to coordinate the digging and related work. Rather than have a membership vote, the alliance draws straws to pick the executive. The alliance has delegated the decision to a random process—drawing straws.

Due to certain weaknesses associated with membership votes, delegating the selection of decision makers is often imperative in complex alliances. There is often insufficient time, interest, or expertise for a membership vote to adequately select a decision maker.

Nebulous

Alliances at times select decision makers through nebulous processes. This is true for express-accord alliances and implied-accord alliances. A common situation is that of the so-called "natural born" leader who rises to positions of decision-making authority without any formal selection by the members.

> **Example 1 "Move the boulder"**—The four cavemen work together shoving the boulder out of the pathway. One of the members begins issuing directives on where to push, when to push, and so on. The other members obey. This individual has become an executive decision maker through a nebulous selection process.

> **Example 3 "Dig the well"**—Three of the ten members begin conferring on where to dig, techniques for digging, work shifts, and related matters. They then tell the other members of the alliance of their proposals. The others listen and follow the proposals. As the three members issue new proposals relating to the digging effort, the other seven members continue to listen and follow. The three members have been chosen as committee members through a nebulous selection process.

In other situations, custom or tradition might serve to select the decision maker.

> **Example 8 "Council of elders"**—The Council members are not selected through a vote or any formal process. The Council consists of the oldest person in each family. Thus, when one member of the Council dies, the next oldest member of the family assumes the open position in the Council.

Sometimes, a decision maker might be selected solely due to the date of his birth.

> **Example 2 "Slay the mammoth"**—As noted earlier, the alliance has a leader that coordinates and leads the attack on the mammoth. As the alliance continues over time, this becomes a hereditary position. Whenever the leader dies, his eldest son replaces him.

MULTIPLE TIERS OF DECISION MAKING PROCESSES

Recall that the concept of decision making can be divided first into two areas: (i) decision making by membership vote, and (ii) delegated decision making. The second area—delegated decision making—can be subdivided into three categories: (i) executive, (ii) committee, and (iii) non-standard. These three all pertain to situations where someone or something other than the full membership makes a decision. Authority for the decision has been delegated to the selected process.

Can decision makers "re-delegate" their authority to decision makers that report to them? That is, can there be multiple levels, or tiers, or decision makers? Yes, this is a common occurrence, provided that the accord does not prohibit it and the alliance members otherwise permit it.

Example 4 "Wild West"—The mercenary feels that he is stretched too thinly in his position. With a portion of the salary the alliance is paying him, the mercenary hires a deputy mercenary to serve under him. The mercenary instructs the deputy on achieving the objective of order and decency. And the mercenary authorizes the deputy to use whatever means he sees fit to achieve this objective. If the deputy has any questions, he is to report to the mercenary for answers. The deputy is a decision maker beneath the mercenary.

The accords of alliances might expressly create tiers of decision makers. The more complex that an alliance is, the more likely it is that such a tiered system in place.

Example 5 "Help the needy"—The alliance continues to grow and attract new members. Because of the complexities associated with the growth, the alliance amends its accord and sets up a new decision-making structure. At the top is a nine-member committee where the members are selected by plurality vote. Beneath this committee are five separate committees with seven members each selected by plurality vote. Each of these five committees is charged with a specific area in which to make decisions. Each of these five committees then has executive decision makers underneath them making decisions on specific issues within the committee's area. These executives are selected by a simple majority vote of the committee. Many of these executives have sub-executives that make decisions on more specific areas. The executives select these sub-executives. The accord provides that a decision maker in a higher tier can overrule any decision made by lower-tier decision maker. Thus, an executive can overrule the decision of a sub-executive. The area-specific committee can overrule a decision of an executive. The nine-member committee can overrule a decision of any area-specific committee.

This intricate arrangement of decision making is not unusual in large, long-term alliances tackling multiple objectives. In fact, it is quite common. And, if the alliance is sufficiently complex, this arrangement can be essential to the success of the alliance. Large alliances typically have an intricate web of decision-making structures and relationships.

In the previous example, all decision-making authority ultimately rests in the nine-member committee. In effect, the lower-level decision makers did make decisions, but the approval of all decisions was funneled upward to the next decision maker. There is no requirement, however, that all decisions be channeled upwards to a single decision maker. Different alliances might structure the tiers in different manners. Instead of having one centralized authority, an alliance could have several decision makers on the highest level that are authorized to overrule only those decisions made below them. In this instance, the highest level of decision makers would have ultimate decision-making authority only in their limited areas.

INTERWOVEN DECISION MAKERS

Can two different types of decision-making processes work together in some fashion? For example, can an executive and a committee participate in the making of a decision jointly? Can the membership also take part in the process? Can one of the non-standard decision-making processes be involved as well?

The answer to all of these questions is, "yes." Alliances structure their decision-making processes as they see fit. An alliance can establish a variety of different decision makers and then require that each of them participate in the making of a decision. The alliance can require that the various processes work directly together. Or it can have a decision move step-by-step from one decision maker to another, with each decision maker holding the authority to decide against, or "block," the proposal; or a variety of other alternatives are possible. The point is that the presence of one type of decision maker (for example, "executive") does not prohibit this type from working with a decision maker of a different type (for example, "committee"). An alliance might interweave various types of decision makers together into a combined decision-making process.

> **Example 5 "Help the needy"**—As noted earlier, the membership meets each month to select a specific project within the objective of helping the needy. Chaos and confusion begin to develop at these meetings as the members propose a variety of projects in a haphazard fashion. To streamline the process, the alliance amends the accord to create two decision makers: one executive and one five-member committee. Each month, the executive will decide in his discretion ten proposals that fall within the alliance's objective of helping the needy. The executive will present these ten proposals to the committee. The committee will deliberate and then select two using a plurality vote. The two proposals decided upon by the committee will then be presented to the membership for a vote. The proposal receiving a simple majority of votes will become the project of the alliance for the month. Thus, the final decision is reached through a combination of three decision-making processes—executive then committee then membership vote.

Why would an alliance desire a structure of interwoven decision makers? There is no universal answer. However, one reason could be to slow down the decision-making process by requiring that several independent decision makers approve any decision. Another reason could be to check the authority of one decision maker to bind the alliance by having a decision reviewed by one or more decision makers. A third reason could be to profit from the combined experiences, knowledge, and skills of the various interwoven decision makers.

CAN THERE BE A SINGLE EXECUTIVE DECISION MAKER FOR AN ALLIANCE?

Absolutely. To some, the idea of having an alliance where a single executive decision maker makes all decisions might sound peculiar if not absolutely unacceptable. In fact, the concentration of absolute authority and power in one individual might be found appalling to many.

However, an alliance is free to delegate any and all decisions to a single individual if it so chooses. This is true even if it means excluding the membership from participating in any decision whatsoever. From an analytical perspective, the crucial issue is whether the members have consented in the form of an express or implied accord to this concentration of absolute authority and power in one individual. If the consent exists, an alliance is present.

Example 8 "Council of elders"—A horde of raiders appear on the horizon one day. It appears clear that there will be many attacks on the tribe and that it could even be wiped out. The Council immediately confers on the topic and how to respond to the impending attacks. The Council recognizes that its decisions are slow in coming and that the Council is not well suited to respond quickly to the urgent situation. The Council agrees to disband and appoint one member to serve as the Chief.

The Chief is authorized to order, in his complete discretion, any tribe member to do anything, including preparing and coordinating a defense against the impending attack. The Council announces its decision to the tribe. The tribe does not object, seeing the need for one decision maker with absolute authority. In effect, the tribe impliedly accepts the new Chief (that is, through a nebulous decision-making process).

The Chief coordinates a large defensive effort against the attacks. He issues many orders and they are obeyed. When circumstances change quickly, the Chief makes an immediate decision in response. Through concentrating absolute power in the Chief, the tribe repels the attacks and survives.

Importantly, the mere fact that an alliance can have a single executive vested with absolute authority does not mean that every situation where such a single decision maker is present constitutes an alliance. Earlier, the concept of *illusory alliances* was raised. Recall that an illusory alliance is an entity that utilizes combined resources of individuals and resembles an alliance, but it lacks one or more of the essential elements of an alliance. Accordingly, it is possible to have something resembling an alliance (that is, an illusory alliance) with a single executive decision maker. Despite these appearances, the entity in reality is not an alliance.

CONSIDERATIONS IN SELECTING DECISION-MAKING PROCESSES

Recall that the decision-making processes can be initially divided into two areas: (i) membership vote, and (ii) delegated decision making. The second area can then be subdivided into three categories: (i) executive, (ii) committee, and (iii) nonstandard. Alliances can structure and interweave these various decision-making processes as they see fit.

Are certain advantages and disadvantages associated with the various processes? Certainly. While there are no inflexible rules in this area, each process has relative strengths and weaknesses. Some processes are valuable for certain matters and ineffective for others topics.

The following chart compares and contrasts the relative advantages of a membership vote to those of a delegated decision maker. This chart does not include a comparison of the non-standard decision-making processes as there is a substantial variation within them. The non-standard processes will be discussed subsequently.

Membership Vote as Decision Maker	Delegate as Decision Maker (Committees and Executives)
Accuracy—An alliance is formed to effectuate the desires of its members. Thus, a vote by the membership holds the potential to most accurately reflect these desires. *Contrast*: Delegates' decisions attempt to correspond with the members' desires, but very well might not.	*Ability to act quickly*—A delegate can quickly decide a pressing issue and act. *Contrast*: The deliberative nature of memberships as well as the logistics associated with assembling a membership vote often precludes the making of speedy decisions.
Legitimacy—A decision reached by a membership tends to have substantial acceptance including by those on the losing side. *Contrast*: Decisions made by delegates are often subject to much debate, criticism, and disapproval.	*Micromanagement capabilities*—If the nature of the alliance requires extensive administration, a delegate is much better suited to micromanage the issue. *Contrast*: Due to the slowness of most votes, a membership is not able to

Diversity of viewpoints—The participation in the decision-making process by all members tends to increase the perspectives, analyses, and opinions on a particular topic. This brainstorming might ultimately result in the making of better decisions. *Contrast*: Delegates tend to consult with no one.

Deliberative process—Membership votes usually involve long and multiple debates with substantial reflection and analysis, tending to yield better decision making. *Contrast*: Delegates tend to make quick or even hasty decisions.

Strengthens the alliance—The participation by all members in decision-making encourages involvement and interest in the alliance. *Contrast*: Decisions made by a delegate tends to decrease the interest of members in the alliance.

address multiple issues. If the membership size is large, frequent votes usually are not feasible.

Expertise—Delegates might possess valuable skills, knowledge, and prior experiences that they can utilize in making decisions. *Contrast*: Most members voting on an issue typically will have little or no expertise in the area.

Dispassionate—Delegates are thought to be more calm, detached, and reasoned in their decision making. *Contrast*: Membership votes are thought to be influenced by undue passions and prejudices, not reflective of the rational interests of the membership. This is sometimes termed "demagoguery" and the person stirring up the passions and prejudices is referred to as a "demagogue."

As this table makes clear, the various decision-making processes have many respective strengths and weaknesses. In structuring decision-making processes, alliances will consider these relative advantages and weaknesses. For example, if the decision in question can be made over an extended period of time and does not involve a high degree of expertise, the tendency is for a membership vote to make the decision. On the other hand, if the decision must be made quickly or requires intensive micromanagement, the decision will be typically delegated to an executive or committee decision maker.

The preceding table lumped executives and committees together and compared them to a membership vote. Observe, however, that the committee and executive processes have their relative strengths and weaknesses as well. If an alliance determines that a delegated decision maker is better than a membership vote, the analysis is not complete. The alliance will then have to determine whether a committee or executive is a more appropriate decision maker for the situation at hand. Because a committee involves a vote of at least two committee members, it shares many traits with a membership vote. However, a committee also shares many traits with an executive decision maker as well. Accordingly, a committee decision maker sits between the two extremes of (i) a membership vote and (ii) an executive. A committee also tends to maximize the strengths of each of these extremes, but not their weaknesses.

Overall, the types of decision-making process will vary with each alliance. Some alliances will use only one process. Other alliances might use multiple tiers of decision makers, which constitute an interweaving of all three processes or a combination of tiers and interweaving. In all of these situations, the alliance will be attempting to choose the decision-making process that is best suited to achieve the objective at hand.

THE LIMITATIONS OF DELEGATED DECISION MAKERS

Delegated decision makers are entrusted with the power and discretion to make decisions within a certain scope of authority. This scope of authority might be limited to a single, discreet matter. At other times, the scope might be quite broad or even unlimited in some situations.

Two types of delegated decision makers—executive and committee—have certain unique limitations uncommon to membership votes or non-standard decision-making processes. These limitations are best understood by examining the assumptions underlying the delegation of decision-making authority to executives or committees.

The grant of authority to the delegated decision maker is based upon confidence and trust. In deciding to forego a membership vote and instead delegating a decision to another, the alliance *assumes*:

- *Motivation*—The selected decision maker has sufficient motivation and interest to seek out and make the best decision.

- *Ability*—The selected decision maker is both able to make the best decision *and* is more capable of making the correct decision in comparison to a membership vote or forms of delegated decision making.

- *Fidelity*—The selected decision maker will act only in the interests of the overall alliance and will not favor the interests of (i) the decision maker, (ii) certain members of the alliance, or (iii) non-members of the alliance.

At times, one or more of these assumptions will be unfounded with regard to a particular decision maker. As a consequence, negative or even catastrophic consequences will result. Problems that can stem from these three assumptions are discussed in the following three sections.

MOTIVATIONAL LIMITATIONS

Motivational limitations pertain to the potential for a delegated decision maker to lack sufficient interest in making the proper decisions. In theory, one would expect a delegated decision maker to invest substantial time and interest in making the best decisions for the alliance. After all, that is why the alliance has delegated decision-making authority to this executive or committee. One would envision this delegate investigating all options, considering all angles, probing potential consequences, and scrutinizing the entire situation before making a decision.

In reality, this theoretical ideal is often not met. Generally speaking, most delegated decision makers will invest only moderate amounts of time and effort in formulating a decision. Also, many decision makers will spend insufficient time and effort on a decision. In some circumstances, decision makers might abdicate all responsibilities and make a haphazard, ill-conceived decision simply because they have no motivation at all.

Example 4 "Wild West"—The mercenary becomes bored with enforcing the objective of law and order. He frequently sleeps on the job, takes vacations, ignores many transgressions, and avoids any risks. Basically, he does just enough to get by and avoid getting fired.

Example 8 "Council of elders"—The council is composed of the oldest members of the tribe. As a result, they are often tired and sickly and have little interest in focusing on the welfare of the tribe.

The net result of the motivational limitation is that the decision-making process might not be as thorough and as rigorous as the members of an alliance expected when they chose it. The alliance can attempt to counteract this problem with compensation, perquisites, fame, or anything other factor that tends to increase motivation. Alternatively, if the problem of motivation seems insurmountable, the alliance might have to reconsider viability of the entire alliance.

CAPABILITY LIMITATIONS

Capability limitations relate to the tendency of alliance members to overestimate the cleverness, intellect, acumen, available time, brainpower, and overall productivity of the delegated decision maker. In delegating a decision to a decision maker with capability limitations, the alliance has essentially miscalculated and charged the decision maker with responsibilities that are impractical or simply unattainable.

This problem typically does not pertain to the individual failings of a particular executive or committee member. Instead, the problem is often associated with the fact that all humans are imperfect and have limitations. In delegating the decision, however, the alliance ignores or discounts this fundamental fact.

To put it another way, the problem arises when an alliance expects too much from a decision maker and charges this delegate with making decisions that are either impossible or too difficult to be made reliably and accurately. At times, the alliance might appear to believe that the delegated decision maker is so talented that it in effect possesses a "magic wand" that need only be waived at a problem and it will go away. The outcome is that a delegated decision maker will typically fail to achieve, or at least fully achieve, the objective of the alliance.

Example 8 "Council of elders"—Food becomes scarce and the council meets to find a solution. The council finds that the scarcity is occurring because the tribe members are hunting and gathering food in a disorganized and haphazard manner that causes much of the food to be wasted. For example, a tribe member will typically slay a deer, cut out the choice parts of meat, eat them, and leave the rest of the deer to rot in the field. Other tribe members are destroying food-bearing vegetation with destructive foraging techniques.

The council concludes the food-gathering practices of the members must be regulated. The council delegates the decision of the means—the specific regulations—to a three-person committee. This committee meets and formulates specific rules for the hunting and gathering of food. However, the tribe members ignore the rules and hunt as they always have. The three committee members attempt to catch rule violators, but there are hundreds of tribe members and it is very difficult. Further, the tribe members warn each other of when a committee member is approaching. The committee fails because it simply does not have the ability to enforce its regulations. The council erred in assuming that the committee was able to regulate the tribe members.

Example 4 "Wild West"—From time to time, the community is hit with epidemics of serious illnesses. The alliance members meet and conclude that ending the epidemics should be an additional objective of the alliance. The alliance selects the resident doctor to serve as an executive decision maker to achieve this objective. Despite his best efforts, the doctor achieves nothing. He has no idea what is causing the disease and has no way of preventing the epidemics. In short, the objective is simply not achievable. The alliance members were mistaken in assuming that a doctor could eliminate the epidemics.

The result of ability limitations is that the objective is achieved only in part *or* not at all. The problem of ability limitations can be addressed in two ways. First, in selecting a decision-making process, successful alliances will recognize the ability limitations associated with each type of process. Such alliances will then pick the process that is the least prone to ability limitations. Second, successful alliances will always undertake a reality check and assess whether the objective is in fact achievable. These alliances will often find that the objective is simply not attainable due to ability limitations and that any effort to achieve it will fail. As a result, these alliances will never attempt to pursue such an objective.

FIDELITY LIMITATIONS

Fidelity limitations are best described as the potentials for dishonesty, deceit, fraud, and corruption that are inherent in all persons. Technically speaking, the limitations can be summed up as the undue favoring of an interest over that of the alliance members.

Fidelity limitations are often a prevalent problem in delegated decision-making processes. The topic can be subdivided into three sub-categories, from the most benign to the most base: (i) position protection, (ii) favoring the interest of a minority of alliance members or of an outsider to the alliance, and (iii) pure, unadulterated corruption.

Position Protection

The first form of fidelity limitation is protection of the position of the delegated decision maker. Recall that the alliance has entrusted the decision maker to make the best decision in the interests of the alliance members. If a fidelity limitation is present, however, the decision maker will place a higher priority, if not an overriding priority, upon maintaining its position as decision maker. Because of this concern with position protection, the decision maker will make decisions that are, at the very least, not the best decisions for the alliance. At the worst, the decisions will be contrary to the interests of the alliance.

For instance, a delegated decision maker might know that a particular decision is in the interests of the alliance members. However, the implementation of that decision entails certain risks that could jeopardize the delegate's position. These risks vary, but the common element is that, if the risks become realities, there is a substantial possibility that the decision maker will lose his position. As such, the decision maker will undertake a less-risky, and therefore less-appropriate, decision to safeguard his position. In this situation, the decision maker has placed its interest over that of the alliance members.

Example 5 "Help the needy"—As discussed earlier, the alliance grows and creates an executive position to make decisions on various issues. The executive is selected each month by membership vote. One month, Harold is selected to be the executive. Harold comes up with a novel course of action, and he is convinced that it is the best decision for the alliance. However, there is a remote possibility it could fail miserably. This concerns Harold greatly as he loves the position as well the power and prestige that comes with it. If the correct course of action fails, Harold fears that he will be voted out of the position. Placing an overriding concern on protecting his position, Harold selects the decision that is much less appropriate, but much safer for his position.

A more egregious situation is where a decision maker will undertake imprudent endeavors, or engage in intentional wrongdoing, to artificially demonstrate the decision maker's value or worth. For example, a decision maker might conclude that the objective of the alliance has been achieved or is not worth pursuing. In theory, a decision maker would then advise that the alliance be terminated. However, if the decision maker enjoys its position, a termination of the alliance is very undesirable as the decision maker will soon be out of work.

So what might a decision maker do to preserve its position? If the decision maker values its position and fears that the alliance might be terminated, the decision maker might undertake countermeasures to prevent this result. For instance, the decision maker might carry out some action to manufacture a false impression in the membership that the alliance's objective has not been achieved or remains an important issue. The creation of this false impression will tend to preserve the decision maker's position.

Example 5 "Help the needy"—Recall that Harold is the executive decision maker for the alliance and greatly enjoys his position. Over time, poverty is drastically reduced in the area. Harold fears that the alliance might terminate as a consequence and that he will lose his treasured position. As such, Harold continually generates false data on the extent of poverty in the community and broadcasts this fabricated information to the alliance members.

Example 4 "Wild West"—As time passes, order and decency is established in the community. This result is due, in part, to the efforts of the mercenary, as well as demographic changes. With regard to the latter, the community has matured and the undesirable elements have either changed their ways or moved on. The mercenary fears that he might lose his position (and salary) due to these changes. As a result, the mercenary repeatedly asserts the threat posed by outlaws is still very real and dangerous, even though the mercenary knows his statements are false. Periodically, the mercenary secretly sets random buildings on fire at night and then blames the arsons upon an alleged lawless element that still plagues the community. Overall, the mercenary is lying to the membership regarding the threats and engaging in serious misconduct to create a false perception of a threat. The reason for these actions is that the mercenary is attempting to protect his position.

Overall, the problem with position protection is that the decision maker is not making the best decision. In the more benign situations, the decision maker is avoiding reasonable risks to protect his position. In the more harmful scenarios, the decision maker is engaging in deception and inflicting injuries to protect his position.

The favoring of another interest over the interest of all alliance members

The second category of fidelity limitation pertains to the favoring of another interest over that of the interest of all alliance members. This other interest consists of either (i) the interest of a small group of members or (ii) the interest of an outsider to the alliance.

The first subcategory is the favoring of an interest of a small group of members. Why is this problematic? Recall that a delegated decision maker has been entrusted with making decisions in the furtherance of an objective that is desired by *all* alliance members. If the decision maker instead furthers the interest of a small group of members, the objective underlying the alliance is not being advanced.

Why would a decision maker favor the interests of a minority of members? The reasons vary with the situation. However, one reason might be that the decision maker is a part of the minority interest.

Example 3 "Dig the well"—The alliance delegates the specifics of digging the well to an executive who is also one of the ten members of the alliance. The first decision to be made is the location of the well. This is an important issue as the members each desire for the well to be as close to their property as possible. From reviewing the situation, it is apparent that there are three possible well locations. Three members live near one, three live near the second, and four live near the third. The decision maker picks the well location nearest to where he lives. Here, the decision maker has favored a minority interest because he is part of it.

The decision maker might also favor the interests of an outsider to the alliance. This outsider is not a member, does not contribute resources, and is not part of the accord. Again, this is problematic as the decision maker has been entrusted with making decisions only in the interests of the alliance members. Why would this happen? Again, the reasons vary with the situation. Yet a common reason is that the decision maker has some type of friendly relationship with this outsider.

Example 5 "Help the needy"—The alliance sets up a committee of three members to decide which supplies to purchase. Two of the committee members are good friends with an owner of a retail store. These two committee members always vote to purchase supplies from this store. Thus, instead of picking the best store for supplies, the committee members are favoring the interest of their friend.

At other times, a decision maker might favor an outsider because of the expectation of receiving some small reward either in the present or in the future.

Example 5 "Help the needy"—The alliance sets up another committee of three members to decide which supplies to purchase for another matter. A store frequently sends boxed candies and small gifts to one of the committee members. This committee member is afraid that the gifts will stop if he does not vote for purchasing the supplies from this store. Another committee is very interested in getting a job with the store and feels that voting for the store will further his chances of landing a job there. As a result, these two committee members vote to purchase supplies from this store to receive small gifts or the possibility of employment.

Observe that this second category of fidelity limitation—favoring another interest—goes by another name in this day and age. It is the problem of "special interests." As these examples make clear, the decision maker is not necessarily making the best decision in the interests of all alliance members. Instead, the decision maker is furthering a special interest either because (i) the decision maker is part of that interest, or (ii) the decision maker is receiving, or expects to receive, some type of reward or benefit.

Corruption

The third category of fidelity limitations is pure corruption. Although this category is similar to the second category (that is, favoring of another interest), it differs because it pertains to the most dishonest and sordid of circumstances.

In this category, the decision maker has no concern for making the proper decision or achieving the objective of the alliance. Instead, the decision maker has one purpose and that is the furtherance of his own interest. In this situation, the delegated decision maker completely abuses the authority granted to further his own interests and with complete disregard for his responsibilities. A few illustrations are:

- Embezzlement of alliance funds

- Theft of alliance property

- Use of alliance property or services for personal ends

- Engenderment of personal fame and glory, at the expense of the members' interests

- Outright bribery (that is, opposed to minor gifts or expectations of future rewards)

- Utilizing the alliance structure to fundamentally harm the interests of alliance members

- Destroying the alliance structure and seizing control

A few examples include:

Example 4 "Wild West"—The mercenary has been charged with enforcing order and decency in the community as a whole. However, the mercenary is frequently "not available" when a particular band of thieves comes to town. In reality, the mercenary has been bribed by the thieves to be absent when they come to town.

Example 5 "Help the needy"—The alliance picks a decision maker to serve as the treasurer of the alliance. This decision maker diverts a portion of the monthly contributions from alliance members and pockets it.

Example 8 "Council of elders"—The council orders that the tribe build elaborate accommodations for the council members and provide them with the best food.

Example 4 "Wild West"—The mercenary grows weary of his job. He schemes to take over the town. The mercenary slowly begins arresting outspoken alliance members on false, trumped-up charges. The mercenary has these members run out of town, jailed, and sometimes executed. Soon, the mercenary is in control of the community and runs it with an iron fist for his exclusive benefit.

Overall, the category of corruption requires little discussion. The problem of corruption of decision makers is known to all.

SUMMARY OF LIMITATIONS

Limitations of committee and executive decision makers pose problems for alliances. If a decision maker is subject to one or more of these limitations, less-than-perfect and often completely flawed decisions will be made. Further, if fidelity limitations are present, there is strong potential for the decisions to actually harm the interests of alliance members. As such, successful alliances will scrutinize the desirability of committee and executive decision makers. Alliances that do not focus on this topic are often doomed to failure, or worse.

THE PROBLEM OF THE SWING VOTE

The preceding discussion of limitations focused only on problems associated with executive and committee decision makers. The problem of the "swing vote," however, pertains to the membership-vote process and its close relative, the committee decision maker.

The swing-vote describes the ability of a minority of members to exert substantial influence on the decision-making process of the alliance. The problem is most prevalent in a membership vote.

Example 5 "Help the needy"—Recall that the membership meets every month to select the project to be undertaken for the month. At this time, there are 100 members participating in the vote. Forty-five (45) members favor one option, 45 members favor another option, and the remaining 10 members favor yet another option. Because a majority of 51 votes is required, the vote of this group of 10 members will determine the outcome. That is, the outcome "swings" with whichever way this group votes. And, if given the opportunity to negotiate prior to the vote, this group can bargain with the two groups of 45 to structure an option that heavily favors the desires of this small, 10 member group. As a result, if the group of 10 strikes a deal with one of the groups of 45, it is likely that the outcome will give weight to the desires of these 10 that is substantially out of portion to their numerical standing of only 10% of the membership.

Why is this swing vote problematic? It depends. If the accord is premised on an assumption that the vote of each member will count equally in the decision-making process, a swing vote is contrary to this premise and undermines the accord. However, if the accord is not concerned with this situation, or in fact presumes that a swing vote might develop from time to time, it is not problematic.[1]

The swing-vote situation can arise in committees as well. Recall that a committee usually involves voting, and therefore, shares many attributes of a membership

---

[1] Under certain circumstances, a swing vote may be the product of the creation of sub-alliances within an alliance. The members of the swing vote, in effect, constitute an alliance seeking to pursue a specific matter desired by them.

vote. As such, a minority of committee members could control the outcome of a vote and therefore constitute a "swing vote."

The swing-vote problem can affect an executive decision maker as well, but the effect is different from the way the swing vote affects membership votes or committees. If an executive is selected by a membership vote or even a committee, the executive might tend to favor the swing vote to be selected, or reselected, for the position. This is sometimes called "pandering."

> **Example 4 "Wild West"**—The mercenary is up for reappointment. All alliance members will vote on whether to renew his contract. A majority vote constitutes the decision. The mercenary knows that about 40 percent of the members support him unconditionally and 40 percent despise him. As a result, to win the election, the mercenary will focus all his efforts on pleasing the remaining 20 percent, (that is, the "swing vote"). In the days preceding the vote, the mercenary spends all his time in the areas inhabited by the swing-vote members and makes specific promises to protect them. Further, with regard to the 40 percent of members that despise the mercenary, the mercenary ignores their neighborhoods and allows disorder and indecency to reign there.

A swing-vote can be a problem, but not always. It is problematic if it undermines the accord by diluting the net benefit to alliance members. Further, if the decision in question relates to objectives, a swing vote can result in the alliance undertaking an objective not favored by a substantial portion of the alliance. This situation can be quite destabilizing to the alliance as discussed earlier. Finally, if an executive decision maker is pandering to a swing vote, it can result in less-than-perfect decisions being made and many alliance members receiving no benefit at all.

THE ROLE OF THE ACCORD IN DECISION-MAKING

This chapter has focused upon decision-making processes. It has explored the need for making decisions, the various types of decision-making processes, and the strengths and weaknesses of each.

It is really not possible to overstate the role of the accord in the decision-making processes. There are several reasons for this fact. First, the accord is the fundamental basis of the decision-making process. An alliance makes a decision only because the accord permits it to do so. No decision will be recognized or implemented unless there is an express or implied agreement amongst the members endorsing the decision-making process.

Second, the accord determines the type of decision-making process. As noted in the chapter, there are a wide variety of processes available. Each of these processes exists only because there is accord (express or implied) adopting or recognizing that specific type of process. In selecting a decision-making process, the alliance can study the situation presented and then pick the advantageous process.

Third, the accord controls the arrangement of two or more decision-making processes used within the alliance. As discussed earlier, decision-making processes might be structured into tiers such that a decision flows through various types of decision makers. Additionally, the processes might be interwoven so that two or more decision makers must approve a selection before it becomes the decision of the alliance. The accord determines whether these tiers or interwoven structures exist.

Fourth, the accord dictates the scope of authority and discretion held by the decision maker. Most alliances do not desire a decision maker with authority and discretion to make any and all decisions. The accord typically places limitations on the areas upon which the decision maker is authorized to make decisions. Further, the accord at times provides the decision maker with certain criteria or restrictions that must be followed in making any decisions, thus limiting its discretion.

Finally, the accord can diminish, or even eliminate at times, the weaknesses of the various decision-making processes. In this regard, if the alliance is aware of a drawback associated with a certain process, the alliance can address this concern with a specific provision in the accord. A few illustrations include:

- *Membership vote*—The members are concerned with demagoguery (that is, the potential for an individual to manipulate the members into making irrational decisions based on emotional provocations). To counter this problem, the members might identify specific topics prone to demagoguery. The accord can then institute procedures or limitations for making decisions on such topics that are designed to guard against demagoguery.

- *Motivational limitations*—If the alliance fears this limitation, it might counter it with a provision in the accord giving the decision maker additional compensation, perquisites, fame, or anything other factor that tends to increase motivation.

- *Fidelity limitations*—To counter the problems of fidelity, the accord might have rigid rules and penalties to punish a decision maker who lacks fidelity. Further, the accord could institute other procedures to guard against or to root out instances of infidelity.

CHAPTER 8

Internal Objectives

P art I covered various topics relating to objectives. This chapter as well as Chapters 9 and 10 will attempt to categorize various purposes underlying objectives pursued by alliances. These three categories of purposes are: (i) internal objectives, (ii) external objectives, and (iii) open objectives. To place this analysis in its proper perspective, it is useful to review the various ways in which objectives can be categorized.

The first manner of analysis relates to the *number* of objectives pursued by an alliance. Chapter 2 identified two types of alliances which were defined based on the number of objectives of the alliance. The first is *single objective alliances*. These are the simplest form of alliances and are generally short lived. The second is *multiple objective alliances*. These alliances encompass any that have two or more objectives. They are generally complex and last long periods of time.

The second manner of classification pertains to the accord's identification of the objective. There are three general ways in which the accord can identify an objective: (i) specific, (ii) indefinite, and (iii) open. A *specific description* is a clear-cut identification of the objective that leaves no uncertainty as its meaning. Examples of specific accords include moving a boulder off a pathway, slaying a mammoth, or digging a well. An *indefinite description* is a loose identification of the objective where the core concept is usually evident but the parameters are not well-defined. Examples of indefinite objectives include "order and decency" and "helping the needy." Alliances with indefinite objectives usually have a decision-making process determine what falls within the objective. An *open description* is essentially a boundless objective. The alliance is unfettered in its ability to undertake any objective. An example of an open objective is the tribal council of elders that pursues any objective perceived to be of value to the tribe. Alliances with open objectives always have some type of decision-making process.

The third manner of classification relates to the *purpose* underlying the objective. This analysis seeks to identify rationales or aims forming the foundations of different objectives and then to create classes of objectives. The ultimate end is to place identified objectives into one or more categories and sub-categories. The three basic categories are: (i) internal objectives, (ii) external objectives, and (iii) open objectives. These three categories are discussed separately in Chapters 8, 9, and 10, respectively.

SUBJECTIVITY

Before addressing the topic of internal objectives, it would be useful to revisit the concept of subjectivity. Recall from Chapter 2 that the objective of an alliance is derived from the *subjective* desires of the members. What does "subjective" mean in this context? It means that there are no universally accepted criteria for determining or evaluating an objective pursued by an alliance. An objective is simply whatever the members of the alliance want. It can be anything, so long as it is desired by the members. Objectives might seem bizarre or even repulsive to some. An objective might even be considered immoral, criminal, or evil yet still form the basis of an alliance.

In *analyzing* alliances, the issue of whether particular objectives are worthy, valuable, or otherwise proper is not a consideration. Instead, the focus is on identifying the objective underlying an alliance and analyzing how the alliance strives to achieve it.

Example 2 "Slay the mammoth"—A reader of this book is considering this example. As noted earlier, the objective is to kill a mammoth and eat its flesh. This carnivorous concept is repugnant to the reader as he is a strict vegetarian. The reader concludes that the example cannot be valid as the so-called "alliance" is pursuing a wholly invalid, if not morally wrong, objective.

Example 7 "Buy the boat"—In this example, the objective is to buy a sailboat. Another reader of the book wonders why anyone would want to buy a sailboat. In this reader's mind, it would be much preferable to purchase a motorboat.

In these two examples, the readers have erred by substituting into the analysis either their own personal, subjective views or some form of perceived, universally accepted criteria (that is, "objective" analysis). Thus, by questioning the legitimacy of the objectives, the readers have strayed from analysis of alliances and entered a normative world of universal judgment.[1]

---

[1]The "normative world of universal judgment" is a difficult concept to define. A person espousing this concept would assert that there are absolute realities and truths, and would hold that there are universal classes of legitimate objectives and illegitimate

It should be observed that the evaluation and judgment of the legitimacy of objectives is an issue of extraordinary significance. However, in *analyzing and studying* alliances, the objective must be accepted for it is–a reflection of the personal desires of the members. The study of the legitimacy of objectives is not within the scope of this book.

ASCERTAINING THE TRUE OBJECTIVE

Although an objective should be accepted without judging it, care should be taken to insure that the objective has been properly identified. The concern here is with accuracy. The true objective is sometimes difficult to identify and double-checking might be warranted.

> **Example 5 "Help the needy"**—The professed objective of the alliance is to help the needy, but if one looks under the surface, one will see a different picture. Recall that the alliance has monthly meetings where the members are to vote on the project of the month. The votes usually take a minute or less and few, if any, members seem to pay much attention to the issue. Instead, most of the attention is focused upon what happens after the vote. Specifically, after the vote is taken, a lengthy and lavish party is held with mountains of food, music, dancing, and revelry. As such, the true objective of the alliance is to have a colossal party each month.

CATEGORIZING AND CLASSIFYING OBJECTIVES

The next two chapters will discuss rough categories of objectives commonly pursued by alliances. It must be emphasized that these discussions are intended only to loosely identify classes of objectives. Because objectives can be literally anything, it is not possible to describe firm, rigid categories in which various types of objectives fit. Moreover, alliances will often seek to achieve two or more objectives with one undertaking, a fact which further complicates the analysis.

When this book references an objective category, the first letters of the objective category will usually be capitalized. Examples include "Law-Compelled Objective" or "Conservation" or "Paternalism." The book will adhere to this format to denote that a generalized, rough objective category is being discussed. As the discussion of objective categories proceeds, it is hoped that the reader will see patterns and relationships associated with the various objective categories.

---

objectives. Such an approach conflicts with analysis of alliances to the extent that the objectives are evaluated for their normative worth. In analyzing alliances and their objectives, the inquiry should be limited to identifying the true objective underlying the alliance.

As its title suggests, this chapter focuses on *internal* objectives. The following chapter will focus on *external* objectives. Observe that the categories of objectives discussed in these chapters are not set in stone and are highly imprecise due to the inherent flexibility underlying objectives. However, after the reader completes these chapters, he should have a flavor of the nature of objectives and their wide varieties.

LOOKING AT OBJECTIVES AND MEANS TOGETHER

Once an alliance has identified an objective that is well suited for a combined effort, the alliance must determine the appropriate *means* for achievement of the objective. Means typically focus in one of two directions. One direction is outward, or *external*. External means concentrate on something outside of the membership, including persons, animals, inanimate objects, forces, ideas, and so on. The other direction is *internal*. Internal means focus on the members themselves, instead of on something outside of the alliance. Internal means typically seek to achieve some end through controlling or otherwise affecting the actions or circumstances of the members themselves.

What happens if you look at objectives along with their selected means? You will typically find that a given objective can be achieved by either an internal means or an external means but not both. As such, objectives can usually be classified as either:

• Internal objectives

• External objectives.

THE TWO CLASSES OF OBJECTIVES

As just discussed, objectives can be divided into two classes—external and internal. The external class focuses on something (for example, persons, objects, forces, concepts, and so on) outside of the membership. The internal class concentrates upon the members of the alliance themselves.

So far, this book has set forward eight examples of alliances. The objectives of the first seven examples are all *external*.[1] That is, all of the objectives are tied to achieving some result outside of, or external to, the members. For instance, the first three examples focus on outside forces or animals—a boulder, a mammoth, and the earth. The fourth and fifth pertain to non-member persons—the lawless and the needy. The sixth example relates to a need to transport children to and from a soccer event. The seventh concerns a boat. In all of these examples, the

---

[1] The eighth example is unusual and will be discussed later.

members' resources are being combined to focus on something external to the members. The overriding concept is that this outside issue can be best attained through a combined effort.

Internal objectives are a little bit more subtle and difficult to recognize. An internal objective focuses on the members of the alliance and strives to achieve some end through controlling or otherwise affecting the actions or circumstances of the members themselves. Internal objectives typically relate to some type of agreed-upon course of conduct that members are to exhibit. This course of conduct is usually, but not always, exhibited towards fellow members. Here, the overriding concept is that, if the specified course of conduct is followed by all members, all members will benefit.

THE CLASS OF INTERNAL OBJECTIVES

Consider the following examples:

Example 9 "No killing"—Several hundred cavemen live in close proximity to each other. From time to time, the cavemen come to blows over various issues. In many of the fights, one caveman kills another. The cavemen become troubled by these killings and hold a meeting attended by all. At this meeting, it is agreed that the killing must stop. Fighting is tolerable, but killing is not. If one caveman kills another, the cavemen will band together and kill the killer.

Example 10 "No theft"—Hundreds of prehistoric hunters live on the same plain. Each hunter has various possessions including primitive spears, knives, needles, and awls. These items are fairly light and the hunters have little trouble carrying them around. Each hunter, however, has camp materials such as hides and other camping items. These items are bulky and are difficult to carry around when hunting, but if a hunter leaves the camp possessions at his camp, there is sizeable risk that another hunter will take them. This problem is a source of constant frustration for the hunters. A meeting is called of all hunters on the plain. It is agreed that no one can take the camp possessions of another hunter. If a hunter's camp possessions have been taken, all other hunters will search for the thief. When caught, the thief will be severely beaten and kicked off of the plain. If he ever returns, he will be killed.

Example 11 "Enforce promises"—A throng of primitive farmers reside in the same valley. One farmer asks another farmer to spend a day at his farm helping to dig stones out of his field. In return, the requesting farmer promises to return the favor upon demand. Unfortunately, when the demand is made, the promising farmer reneges on his promise and refuses to return the favor. This situation is not uncommon. Farmers often break promises such as these. Soon, few if any farmers will help out other farmers because there is little faith that the favor will be returned. As a result, the farmers meet and it is agreed that, when a farmer makes a promise, the farmer may not later refuse to carry it out. A promise made must be performed. If a farmer reneges on his promise, the other farmer can call a meeting of all farmers and demand a remedy.

Example 12 "Conservation"—In a small community, the residents hunt and kill the nearby deer for food. Soon, the deer population is wiped out. The community residents realize that they have over hunted the deer and that all have suffered as a consequence. Antelopes are still nearby for hunting. The residents agree that each member can kill no more than one antelope per month. If a member violates this rule, he will be expelled from the community.

Example 13 "Moral obligations"—In a village, the residents follow the same religion. This religion entails a number of ritual practices that must be followed including certain requirements for food, dress, and prayer. If the rituals are not followed, it is feared that the community might suffer dire consequences from the deity. As a result, it is agreed that all members are to follow all rituals. Further, all members agree to keep watch over the conduct of their neighbors and insure that they are following the rituals. If a lapse is observed, it must be reported to the community. The offending person will be subject to reprimand, beating, imprisonment, banishment, or worse.

Example 14 "Human weaknesses"—A small community hears rumors of mysterious liquid being brought into the area. This liquid inebriates those who drink it and they lose control of themselves. They engage in acts of stupidity, clumsiness, or violence and usually harm themselves or others. The community also hears that this liquid is addictive and those who drink it usually become enslaved to it. The members become very concerned about these rumors. It is agreed that no member can consume this liquid. Any member who attempts to consume it will be restrained including being imprisoned to keep him away from the liquid.

Example 15 "Leveling"—Individuals in a community conclude that excess is wrong and that no member should have more than a certain amount of possessions. As a result, the members form an alliance that imposes strict rules on the quantity and nature of items that can be possessed. If members exceed the limits, their excess possessions will be taken away.

Example 16 "Customs"—A small town is situated in a cold, windy area. The buildings are very sturdy. To keep out the cold and the wind, the doors are huge and heavy. Opening one of these great doors is fatiguing. Because of this great effort, a tradition of holding an opened door for others to pass through develops. Most residents in the town follow this tradition. However, a few residents do not observe the tradition and let the door slam shut in the faces of the others. The residents take note of this practice and refuse to hold the door open for these individuals. Furthermore, if a stranger visits the town, the residents typically fail to hold doors open for them.

What do these eight examples have in common?

Answer: The means for achieving the objectives focus on the members themselves. The objectives are *internal*.

Before discussing the internal nature of the objectives, it is useful to confirm that these six examples represent actual alliances. Recall that an alliance has four fundamental components.

Objective	Members	Accord	Resource Contribution

The six examples have objectives. They have members. And the six have accords as well. (Note that the accord underlying the alliance in Example 16 "Customs" is an implied accord.) Do the examples have resource contribution? After all, the members are not contributing labor, material, or money towards the alliance. So what is the resource underlying the alliance? Is contribution present? What is going on here?

Yes, resource contribution is present. Bear in mind that contributed resources are sometimes difficult to spot. As was noted in Chapter 5, resources can take many different forms. One resource that can be contributed is liberty. That is, the members promise to take a specified action, or to forego taking a specified action. In so making this promise, the members diminish their overall liberty and freedom to do as they please. To put it another way, before entering these alliances with internal objectives, the members possess a certain level of freedom. After entering the alliances, this level of freedom has been reduced by at least a marginal degree, if not a substantial amount.

Consider the examples again and the contribution underlying them:

EXAMPLE	CONTRIBUTION—AN AGREEMENT TO . . .
Example 9 "No killing"	. . . not kill another member
Example 10 "No theft"	. . . not take another member's possessions
Example 11 "Enforce promises"	. . . not break promises made to a member
Example 12 "Conservation"	. . . use a resource only in a certain manner
Example 13 "Moral obligations"	. . . follow the religious rituals
Example 14 "Human weaknesses"	. . . not consume the prohibited liquid
Example 15 "Leveling"	. . . place limits on the material items that might be possessed
Example 16 "Customs"	. . . hold open a door for other members

As this table makes clear, the members are contributing their liberty towards the alliance. Before entering the alliance, the members were free to kill others, steal, break promises, not hold open door, and so on. After entering the alliance, these freedoms are no more. They have been relinquished.

Why are the members contributing these freedoms? The answer is that the relinquishment of the freedoms will yield greater benefits to the members. Recall that all members desire achievement of the objective. The contribution of freedom is necessary to achieve the objective. It is a tradeoff. The members agree to follow a certain course of conduct in exchange for the attainment of the objective.

Example 9 "No killing"—Before the alliance, a caveman was free to kill anyone, but anyone was free to kill the caveman. After the alliance, the caveman may not kill a member of the alliance, and no member of the alliance may kill the caveman. The members may still kill non-members if they want, but now members are protected from other members.

By contributing freedom, the members all further their interests. They are all bound to not kill fellow members and, in return, they hope to not be killed themselves.

What happens if a member fails to follow the prescribed course of conduct? What if a member makes a promise to do, or not do something, but then fails to fulfill this obligation?

Example 10 "No theft"—A prehistoric hunter returns to his camp and finds that his possessions have been stolen. The other hunters quickly gather and follow the thief's footprints, locating him a few miles a way. The thief is a fellow hunter and a member of the alliance. The alliance members beat the thief, take away all his possessions, and kick him off the hunting plains. The alliance tells him he will be killed if he ever comes back.

Example 11 "Enforce promises"—A farmer refuses to return a favor and help out in another farmer's fields. He is brought before the alliance membership. They find that he owes the other farm a day's labor. The alliance takes away a bushel of wheat from the reneging farmer and gives it to the other farmer.

Example 15 "Customs"—One townsperson fails to hold a door open for another. All townspeople hear of this omission through the rumor mill and subsequently fail to hold the door open for this offending townsperson.

These examples make clear that, for alliances with internal objectives, the promise of a contribution of liberty is usually not enough. Instead, these alliances require some mechanism for extracting compliance from members. These mechanisms can be pretty much anything and might include tit-for-tat slights, compensatory remedies, beatings, or death.

All internal objectives share a common element—a focus on the conduct of the members to the alliance. Regardless of what the objective might be, the unifying concept is that the members are supposed to behave in a certain manner. Because an internal objective can be anything, it is not possible to list out or categorize them in a comprehensive manner. However, it is useful to identify common types of internal objectives.

LAW-COMPELLED OBJECTIVES

Law-Compelled Objectives are the most basic form of internal objectives. Law-Compelled Objectives are based on very specific rules of conduct to which members must adhere. If members fail to follow the prescribed conduct, the alliance will impose consequences on the non-complying members.

Law-Compelled Objectives consist of both the objective and the means. The desired conduct can be seen as the objective and law as the means for achieving it. From this perspective, law is not an end. Instead, law is a tool used to compel a certain course of conduct. Other means might be available for achieving the conduct, but law is selected because it is seen as being the most efficient or effective instrument for attainment of the objective. Thus, the law forces, or *compels*, the conduct and the objective underlying the alliance is a "Law-Compelled Objective."

It is important to observe that the term "law" has a very narrow meaning as used in the context of Law-Compelled Objective. Specifically, law means rules of conduct for all members to follow which usually have consequences for noncompliance. Law in this context does not include rules governing or regulating decision makers. And law does not include other rules relating to the administration and running of alliances. In this situation, law is limited to those rules intended to compel members to behave in a certain manner.[1]

Law-Compelled Objectives can be placed into three broad categories:

- Protection of the Person

- Protection of Property

- Enforcement of Promises

These three categories will be discussed subsequently.

Protection of the Person

Alliances often pursue Law-Compelled Objectives relating to protection of members. The concern here is with the person and protecting him from injury from others.

Sometimes, individuals strive to protect themselves through their own defensive mechanisms. At other times, they might find that an alliance offers more advantages than individual effort. In this latter situation, the alliance structure is used to guard against death, physical harm, or other personal injury at the hands of fellow members.

---

[1]For instance, numerous institutions referred to as "laws" do not constitute law-compelled objectives. Examples include "bankruptcy laws," "welfare laws," or "tax laws." These institutions relate to other considerations.

Example 9 "No killing"—By establishing an alliance prohibiting the killing of other members, the cavemen have created a very basic form of law. The objective is simply to avoid being killed by another member of the alliance. All members have made a contribution of liberty in the form a promise to not kill another member. And this contribution of liberty—the ability to kill—is enforced by death if one member kills another.

This internal objective of Protecting the Person can encompass numerous other areas. The key concept is that the members identify a perceived harm inflicted by other members. They then agree to not inflict such harm on each other and usually institute some means to insure compliance. The perceived harm can be anything that concerns members. A few examples include:

Perceived Harm	An agreement to not. . .
Death	. . . kill other members
Physical harm	. . . assault other members
Defamation	. . . make false statements about other members
Accidental harm	. . . act negligently in manner that would cause harm to other members
Privacy	. . . invade another member's privacy
Obscenity	. . . publicize or display items found offensive by the community of members
Discrimination	. . . treat a person differently from others because of some trait associated with that person
Mental health	. . . cause another to suffer mental anguish or emotional distress
Mistreatment in warfare	. . . kill or torture prisoners of war.

This table shows only potential examples of internal objectives that alliances might strive to pursue through law. It is important to keep in mind that not all alliances will seek to pursue these objectives. For instance, potential alliance members might not be concerned with one or more of these perceived harms. As such, the members will have no interest in the objective and the alliance will not be formed.

In addition, even if potential alliance members desire achievement of one of these objectives, they might find that an alliance is not preferable to individual effort. That is, the individual members might believe that they can achieve the objective more efficiently or effectively on their own.

> **Example 9 "No killing"**—The cavemen all consider themselves to be excellent fighters and more than capable of defending themselves. As such, they see no reason to form an alliance to guard against being killed by fellow members. The alliance is not formed.

What about the enforcement issue? If a member fails to supply the promised form of contribution, how is it extracted from him? Typically, an alliance will utilize some type of a decision-making process to achieve this end. The process will determine whether the law has been violated and what the consequence should be.

The simplest decision-making process is a nebulous process essentially consisting of group action.

> **Example 9 "No killing"**—A caveman kills a fellow caveman in violation of the rule against killing members. The alliance members gather together and kill the offending member.

As laws become more numerous and complex, the decision-making process is usually delegated to a decision maker. In these situations, the delegate typically undertakes two aims. One is to *detect* violations of the prohibited conduct. This type of process attempts to determine if members have complied with the prescribed conduct. The other aim is to *enforce* the prohibition. This type of decision-making process strives to implement the consequences of non-compliance when a member engages in the prohibited conduct. In today's modern world, these roles are often fulfilled by the police, prosecutors, courts, and prisons.

Do Personal-Protection laws concentrate only on conduct directly and proximately causing harm to persons? Or is it possible for such laws to also forbid conduct that has a *potential*, but not a certainty, to cause harm to members? Certainly. Alliances will often institute Personal-Protection laws to prevent conduct that has a tendency, rather than a certainty, of causing harm to members.

> **Example 9 "No killing"**—Many caveman hunt animals by setting forests on fire. The fire drives the animals out where they can be killed easily. These fires, though, often kill one or more unsuspecting cavemen by accident. The alliance agrees to ban the lighting of forest fires. Anyone who lights a forest fire will be put to death, even if no member is hurt by the fire.

In this situation, the perceived harm is the same as in the original example—death, but the situation is different because the caveman lighting the fire does not desire to cause death to another member. The alliance is not prohibiting the act of killing another. Instead, it is prohibiting the burning of fires. So what is going on here?

The answer is the alliance has identified conduct believed to cause a substantial risk of death to other members. The risky practice is the lighting of fires. It is risky because it is likely to kill other members. As such, to protect members from death, the alliance prohibits an action that can indirectly cause the deaths. It is not the action itself that is considered undesirable. Instead, it is the consequences indirectly caused by the action. By banning the conduct, the expectation is that the consequence will not occur.

A few examples of this concept might be instructive:

Action Prohibited	Indirect Consequence of Action
Firing weapons in a neighborhood	Ricochet of a bullet into a member
Driving a car over the designated speed limit	Car wreck that might then injure pedestrians or other drivers
Shooting off fireworks	Fire which could result in deaths
Consumption of alcohol while driving	Reckless driving that could injure pedestrians or other drivers

All of these examples underscore that the concern is not with the action itself. Instead, the concern is with the potential for the action to indirectly cause harm to members. For this reason, the action is prohibited.

Aside from prohibiting the action, the Law-Compelled Objective might also focus on *remedying* the harm caused by the action. In this regard, alliances might set up a wide variety of means for compensating members who are damaged by the failures of other members to adhere to the applicable standards of conduct.

Protection of Property

Alliances often pursue Law-Compelled Objectives relating to Protection of Property interests. The concept is that individuals from time to time come into possession of certain tangible and intangible items. If the individuals value these items and fear them being taken away by others, the individuals might find that an alliance is a useful mechanism for protecting the items.

Property Protections are usually motivated by two interrelated factors. The first reason is driven by the immediate circumstances. Typically, individuals have come into possession of property and they desire to protect and maintain that possession. They often see an alliance effort as a useful mechanism for safeguarding the possession of that property. The second reason is more long-term and pertains to property that requires effort to bring about. In these situations, individuals come to the realization that a certain type of property exists only because persons are motivated to spend effort on crafting or acquiring the property. This motivation is driven by a desire to posses and use the property after the effort has been expended. If individuals are not allowed to possess the property, however, they will not expend the effort on crafting or acquiring the property. The result is that the property will never come into existence. Thus, in this situation, members of the alliance recognize that Property Protection is a necessary condition to the creation of additional property, and therefore, pursue it as an objective.

Usually, the concern is with defining property and then protecting it from members. What is property? There is no universal conception or definition of property. Instead, the meaning of property is relative to the alliance. Just as anything can be an objective of an alliance, basically anything can be defined as property. In this regard, the alliance members desire something to be property and it becomes a Law-Compelled Objective.

Example 10 "No theft"—All of the prehistoric hunters have various possessions that are of value to them. These include small items like spears and knives that can be carried around with ease, but the camp materials are heavy and cannot be carried around while hunting. If the camp materials are left unattended, there is a substantial risk that another hunter will take them. Thus, while the hunters can protect the small items by carrying them around, they cannot adequately protect the large camp items. The solution is an alliance with a Law-Compelled Objective. All members agree that another member's camp materials are to be left alone. If a member violates this course of conduct, he will be punished.

Protection-of-Property objectives usually have several components. The first is *defining* property. As just observed in the example, property is defined when the members conclude that something has value and should be designated as property. Thus, it is the desires of the members that ultimately determine what constitutes property in a given alliance.

Example 10 "No theft"—The small items are not defined as property. Spears and knives are light and can be carried around with ease. As such, each individual hunter can adequately protect these items by himself. A combined effort through an alliance affords no advantage, but an alliance does provide a substantial advantage to protecting camp materials. As a result, camp materials are defined as property.

The second component is identifying *exceptions*, if any, to the definition of property. The members might not desire for something to always constitute property, or they might want something to be property but others will be allowed to share in the property under certain circumstances, or the members might institute some other type of exception.

Example 10 "No theft"—The members agree that camp materials can be borrowed in an emergency. For example, if a member is severely injured, he can use another member's camp materials (for example, rope, rags, healing herbs, and so on) until he can get back to his own camp materials. Further, the members agree that there will be no punishment if a member damages or destroys another member's materials by accident. Finally, the members agree that, if these exceptions are applicable, the member using or causing harm to another member's property must make amends and compensate the member for the lost or damaged property.

The third component pertains to the *transfer* of property. Some alliances will agree upon rules for how property can be exchanged between members.

Example 10 "No theft"—The members agree that camp materials can be exchanged between members. Further, it is agreed that, if members manufacture camp materials (for example, tan hides, twist ropes, and so on), they can trade these items to other members. If these exchanges occur, it is agreed that the items will become the property of the member receiving them.

The final component relates to enforcement of the property rules. The enforcement measures typically take two different approaches: (i) punitive, and (ii) compensatory. *Punitive measures* seek to punish the non-complying member and deter others from engaging the wrongful conduct.

Example 10 "No theft"—If a member takes another member's camp possessions, he will be severely beaten and expelled from the plains.

Compensatory measures focus on the loss to the member and attempt to make the member whole. Compensatory measures are usually selected when the property loss was not caused by intentional misconduct by another member.

Example 10 "No theft"—One member accidentally starts a large fire that burns up another member's camp materials. The victim is awarded the camp materials of the other member to compensate him for the loss.

Punitive and compensatory measures can be combined as well.

Example 10 "No theft"—If a member takes the camp possessions of another, two things will happen. First, the member will be severely beaten and expelled from the plains. Second, before he is expelled, all his camp possessions will be given to the victim.

Property-Protection objectives often involve numerous decisions. Examples include:

- Is the item in fact property that can be owned?

- Who owns the property?

- Was the property transferred to another?

- Did a member take the property in violation of the rules?

- Should a member be punished for violating the rules?

- Should the victim be compensated and in what manner?

These decisions can be made through a membership vote, or they can be made through the various delegated decision-making processes discussed earlier.

Enforcement of Promises

Individuals from time to time may strike agreements with others relating to a host of matters. In entering agreements, there is always a danger that the other side will break his word. Liars, cheats, and swindlers are commonplace.

An individual has several mechanisms to guard against such scoundrels. A primary method is the reputation of the other in the community. If the person has a reputation for cheating others (that is, he is "disreputable"), the individual should not do business with him. Alternatively, the individual might demand that another's promise be backed up by some form of collateral or security, or the individual could try to use force or violence to compel the individual to perform as promised.

These mechanisms are not always available or suitable. To address these inadequacies, individuals might see value in forming an alliance to address the matter of broken promises. In this situation, members agree to adhere to certain standards of conduct in making and performing promises. If these promises are not complied with, consequences will follow.

> **Example 11 "Enforcement of promises"**—In the valley where the farmers live, it was necessary from time to time for farmers to help each other out with large tasks such as digging stones out of fields. To induce others to help out, a farmer would promise to return the assistance later. However, so many farmers reneged on their promises that farmers refused to help other farmers. No farmer trusted the other farmer's promise to return the favor. As a result, all farmers' fields languished since they could not induce other farmers to help out. The solution to this malaise was an alliance whereby promises were to be enforced. If a member broke a promise, he would face consequences.

As the example demonstrates, the Promise-Enforcement objection is in the interests of all members. With a system in place for enforcing promises, the farmers are much more willing to help out other farmers. If a farmer helps out and the favor is not returned, he knows that he will receive compensation for the broken promise. Thus, the farmer is much more likely to help out. And, in return, the farmer is much more likely to attract others to help him on his farm.

The rules relating to enforcement of promises can range from very simplistic concepts to incredibly detailed rules. The degree of complexity rests upon the desires of the members. As for the consequences of promise breaking, a typical alliance would choose a compensatory remedy. This type of remedy could compel the wrongdoer to perform the promised act, or it could force the wrongdoer to give the victim something representing the rough value of the promised, but unfulfilled, act. Punitive measures, however, are not unheard of and many alliances find them to be appropriate as well.

Of course, Promise-Enforcement objectives usually require some type of decision-making process. This process can be a straightforward membership vote or a delegation to a multifaceted, interwoven decision-making process. The decisions that are typically made relate to (i) whether an enforceable promise was in fact made, and (ii) what the remedy for the broken promise should be.

An alliance with a Promise-Enforcement objective can have a profound effect upon the development of other, smaller alliances. And such an objective can also greatly further the ability of individuals to achieve objectives without the need to form alliances. These topics are explored in Chapter 12.

In summary, the three Law-Compelled Objectives are internal, with the focus on influencing, manipulating, or controlling the conduct of the members. Further,

Law-Compelled Objectives typically utilize specific rules or regulations to achieve the desired conduct. The three most common forms of Law-Compelled Objectives are: (i) Personal Protection, (ii) Property Protection, and (iii) Enforcement of Promises. Finally, the conduct brought about by the rules and regulations is desired by, and of benefit to, the members.

CONSERVATION

Conservation is an internal objective. It focuses on the conduct of the members and their relationship to a limited-quantity item. The objective is founded upon a recognition that all members to an alliance will benefit if their use of, or access to, the item is restrained in some fashion.

> **Example 13 "Conservation"**—The members realize that they unintentionally destroyed the deer population to the detriment of all members. The antelope population is still around, but could be devastated in a similar manner. To guard against this result, the members agree to regulate the hunting of antelope.

Conservation objectives are quite similar to Law-Compelled Objectives. They strive to impose a certain conduct upon the members. They are enforced by rules or regulations. And the conduct imposed is believed to be of benefit to all members.

So what is the difference between Conservation and Law-Compelled Objectives? The difference lies in the relationship between the prescribed conduct and its effect on the members.

With Law-Compelled Objectives, the focus is on conduct and its direct effect upon members. The rules and regulations of Law-Compelled Objectives pertain to how one member is to act towards another member. For example, a member cannot kill another member; a member cannot take another's possessions; a member cannot break a promise to another member; and so on. In these instances, the prescribed conduct directly benefits fellow members.

With Conservation objectives, the prescribed conduct is not directed at interactions with other members. Instead it relates to the usage of, or access to, a limited item by members. That is, the rules direct the members to behave in a certain manner with regard to something other than members themselves.

Conservation objectives typically relate to living items like animals or fish, but the items can include natural conditions, such as plants, forests, plains, oceans or substances such as minerals, oil, and air, or even intangibles, such as solitude and tranquility. In reality, a Conservation objective can be anything so long as the members benefit from the item being conserved. Conservation objectives can even include products sold by alliance members, as demonstrated in the following example.

> **Example 13 "Conservation"**—The alliance to conserve the antelope is a success. The residents of the community soon see a parallel in another area. The residents all build unique cuckoo clocks that they sell to residents of other communities. Recently, the competition for sale of cuckoo clocks has been fierce and the price has steadily eroded to where the profits are marginal. Having succeeded with the antelopes, the community residents apply a similar reasoning to the cuckoo-clock sales. All residents agree to limit their sale of cuckoo clocks to one per month. As a result, the supply of cuckoo clocks on the market will drop sharply, but the price will rise substantially. With this rise, the profits to the residents will be great. Thus, by agreeing to "conserve" the sales of cuckoo clocks, the members of this alliance all benefit.

MORALITY

Like Conservation objectives, Morality objectives are similar to Law-Compelled Objectives. Moral objectives are internal. They strive to impose a certain conduct upon the members. They are enforced by rules or regulations. And the conduct imposed is believed to be of benefit to all members.

Moral objectives differ from Law-Compelled Objectives because of their focus. Just like Conservation objectives, Moral objectives strive to have members act in a certain manner *towards something other than other members.*

The category of Moral objectives is expansive, but it typically appears in two broad sub-categories: (i) Religious Concerns, and (ii) Bolstering Concerns. These two are united by a common thread—all members are to behave in a certain way towards something other than members.

Religious Concerns

This Moral objective typically relates to the appeasement or gratification of a religious deity. Specific rules of conduct are identified that are thought to please, or not offend, a deity. If these rules are adhered to by all members of an alliance, it is believed that the members will benefit.

> **Example 13 "Moral obligations"**—The religious rules require all members to adhere to specific conduct regarding food, dress, and prayer. The focus of this required conduct is not on the members themselves. No member will directly benefit if another member says his prayers or wears the correct clothing. Instead, the focus of the conduct is on the deities worshiped by the members. The

members believe that adhering to the prescribed conduct will please, or at least placate, their deities. In return, the deities will either aid the members, or at least not cause them to suffer harm. As such, the members benefit indirectly.

The concern is usually that a religious deity will impose hardship on all alliance members if members stray from the proper religious conduct. The Biblical account of the destruction of Sodom and Gomorrah constitutes a famous example. The towns were obliterated with fire and brimstone due to the community's decadent and immoral life styles. Ancient civilizations are replete with other examples of beliefs that large communities were penalized or destroyed by a religious force due to a failure of the members to adhere to prescribed religious conduct.

It should be observed that not all religions support the pursuit of such an objective. Some religions do not support a collective-action rationale. In these religions, it is up to the individual to live the proper life. A failure of an individual to adhere to a set course of conduct will impact only that individual, and not his neighbors. This situation could be termed *"private morality."* If a concept of private morality prevails, there will be no alliance effort to pursue the objective of Morality—Religious Concerns.

Overall, if a religious objective is pursued, the overriding concern is that something undesirable will happen to all members if even a few members fail to adhere to the proper code of conduct. To guard against the feared punishment, the alliance agrees that all members must follow certain conduct or consequences will be imposed.

Bolstering Concerns

This Moral objective is present only in long-term, multi-objective alliances and has no direct connection to a religion or a deity. In this situation, an alliance seeks to compel its members to behave in a certain manner because such conduct is believed to strengthen the ability of the members to achieve some other objective pursued by the alliance.

Example 8 "Council of elders"—The tribe experiences a time of prosperity. Many members lounge around and become quite obese. Further, many members begin wasting food. The council meets and orders the members to stop their slothful ways and gluttony. The council is well aware that the current prosperous times will not last. Soon, the members will have to contribute towards objectives of the alliance, such as fighting attackers and conserving in times of famine, but if the members develop bad habits, they will be unable to meet these challenges.

Bolstering concerns relate to beliefs that certain ways of life and even world views are undesirable and can ultimately be of detriment to an existing alliance. The focus is on the relationship between potential conduct of members and the long-term consequences of such conduct. By pursuing the bolstering objective, the alliance sees itself as strengthening the ability of the alliance to pursue the other objectives. Examples of Bolstering Concerns that might be pursued by an alliance include:

Physical Health	Education	Courage
Moderation	Wisdom	Honesty
	Honor	

If an alliance strives to inculcate these traits into members, the reason is usually that the alliance is striving to strengthen, or bolster, its ability to attain other objectives of the alliance.

PATERNALISM

Paternalism is an internal objective that strives to guard against some defect in the members. Paternalism is founded on a notion that members desire a certain course of conduct but that a personal shortcoming will prevent the members from attaining this course of conduct.

> **Example No. "Human weaknesses"**—Alcohol has been introduced into this community and members, by their own apparent choice, are consuming it. The alliance, however, bans the consumption of alcohol. It is believed that, although members seemingly want to consume alcohol, the members in reality do not desire this consumption. Instead, the members are drawn to consuming alcohol because of some defect or flaw within themselves.

A paternalistic objective differs from the preceding internal objectives, because the benefit of the objective is not derived from some type of common conduct by other members. For instance, Law-Compelled Objectives and Moral objectives can be attained only if all the members engaged in the required conduct. Paternalism, however, focuses on each individual and his following of the prescribed conduct for his own personal benefit. There is no benefit to the individual if others follow the conduct. Instead, the benefit is to the member and is attained only if he follows the prescribed conduct.

What is the defect or weakness that an alliance seeks to guard against? They are numerous but all relate to a common concept—irrationality. The gist is that the alliance is trying to prevent the member from engaging in some act that the member knows to not be in his interest. Examples of possible paternalistic objectives include:

Irrational Propensity	Paternalistic Measure in Response
Ignoring safety	Requiring motorcyclists to wear helmets
Dangerous leisure pursuit	Prohibiting bungee jumping
Addictive substances	Regulating consumption of narcotics, alcohol, tobacco
Personal degradation	Outlawing prostitution
Risky financial conduct	Forbidding gambling
Hopelessness/depression	Banning suicide

The underlying theme of these examples is that humans are not perfect and are prone to not act in their best interests at times. To combat these flaws and defects, members agree to paternalistic objectives.

Paternalistic objectives range widely in the intent to limit human conduct to a standard that is seen as rational and in the members interests. The simplest version of Paternalism is an agreement between members that a certain act is not desirable, but that most members, if unchecked, will be prone to engage in it. In this situation, the undesirable conduct is specifically identified and the accord reached pertains directly towards achieving that goal.

> **Example 14 "Human weakness"**—The members believe that consumption of alcohol is undesirable, but that all members have a propensity to consume it. As such, the members agree to band to together to try to keep each other from drinking.

The more complex versions of Paternalism relate to delegated decision makers. In these situations, alliances have delegated authority to determine what constitutes a paternalistic objective and the proper means for achieving it. The delegated decision makers then are charged with deciding what is truly in the best interests of the members.

LEVELING

This internal objective focuses on restraining or limiting something associated with the members. The idea is that members might be prone to accumulating an item in excess and that this result is undesirable. As a result, the alliance imposes rules on the members setting some type of limits on what can be accumulated.

Example 15 "Leveling"—In this case, the members subjectively desire to limit what other members can possess. As a result, an alliance is formed to limit, or "level" the possessions held by all members.

The Leveling objective is not common but it does appear from time to time. The key concept is that excess accumulation is undesirable and that all members benefit if the alliance limits their accumulations.[1] The objective can include things other than material wealth, such as pride and prestige.

CUSTOMS

A subtle type of internal objective is Customs. Although it might not be apparent at first glance, many day-to-day traditions adhered to by communities can be seen as internal objectives underlying an implied-accord alliance. These Customs constitute a phenomenon often termed "common courtesy." Common courtesy is often summed up by the Golden Rule, which provides:

Act towards others as you would have them act towards you.

Examples of these Customs include:

- Holding open doors for others

- Not sneezing or coughing on others

- Not interrupting another when he is speaking

- Automatically forming and standing lines

- Not making loud noises or creating disturbances at night

- A willingness to feed and house travelers

- Exhibiting the utmost respect to a host who has fed you or provided you with lodging

---

[1] As observed earlier, objectives can overlap. Leveling provides a potential example of this overlap. For instance, leveling can be seen as having a moral component in that it might bolster values necessary for a strong alliance. For instance, leveling might be seen as promoting moderation and prudence in the members which in turn strengthens the ability of these members to contribute resources to other objectives of the alliance. Additionally, leveling might be seen as a paternalistic objective in that it counteracts a perceived irrational and harmful tendency of members to over accumulate material possessions to their personal detriment.

Underlying each of these Customs are implied alliances. The individuals in the community following the Customs are the *members*. The *objectives* are social practices that all of the members are interested in:

Custom	Objective
Holding open doors for others	Not having to always open heavy doors
Not sneezing or coughing on others	Reduction of germ infection and disease transmission
Not interrupting another when he is speaking	Maintaining functional conversations without ill will or ego bruising
Automatically forming and standing in lines	Orderly and efficient receipt of whatever is at the beginning of the line
Not making loud noises at night	Peaceful sleep
A willingness to feed and house travelers	A place to stay whenever traveling
Always showing a host the utmost respect	Security in allowing a traveler to lodge in your residence

The *accords* are all implied. Obviously, there is no formal agreement between the members to act in a certain manner or observe a certain practice, but there is an implied understanding that all members are to conduct themselves in a certain manner with regard to other members. The *resource contribution* is freedom. By impliedly agreeing to conduct themselves in a certain manner, the members have limited their liberty to do as they please.

There are other interesting characteristics of common courtesy. One is that common courtesy is required to be shown only to members of the community. If a non-member appears, there is usually no requirement that the Custom be exhibited.

Example 16 "Customs"—A stranger visits the town and approaches a public building with a heavy door. A townsperson has just entered but allows the door to slam in the stranger's face.

Why is the townsperson not exhibiting common courtesy towards the stranger? Is it because he despises strangers? Is it because he wants to offend the stranger? The answer can vary with each individual but the most common reason is that the stranger is not perceived to be a member of the alliance. If a member of an alliance perceives another as being a non-member, the member has nothing to gain from exhibiting the courtesy towards to the non-member. As such, he will tend to not exhibit the courtesy.

Of course, it is still possible that a member will exhibit a Custom towards a non-member.

> Example 16 "Customs"—Later in the day, the stranger approaches another building with a heavy door. This time, a townsperson holds the door open for him.

Why was the courtesy extended? Many reasons are possible. The townsperson could have been exhibiting charity—that is, granting a favor with no expectation of reward. The townsperson could have mistaken the stranger for a member or been unsure of his status, or the townsperson might have liked strangers and was trying to entice the stranger to stay. Overall, the point is that Customs will at times be exhibited to non-members. This is especially so when the cost associated with performing the courtesy is negligible.

> Example 16 "Customs"—The townspeople are usually willing to hold open doors for strangers since there is little effort associated with it. However, townspeople rarely if ever feed or lodge strangers. The price of such courtesies is too steep.

What happens if a member does not exhibit the proper conduct—that is, the courtesy—towards other members? Typically, this member will become a non-member and will be impliedly excluded from the alliance. Members will be inclined to not show him courtesy. This member has failed to provide the requisite contribution and therefore is not entitled to receive the benefits of the implied alliance. Nonetheless, some members may continue to extend courtesies to a former member for the reasons just discussed regarding the stranger (for example, charity, confusion, an attempt to entice the non-member back into the alliance).

Are these alliances grounded in Customs limited to small communities? No, these types of alliances can be huge. In fact, certain Customs arguably can encompass everyone in the world. Why? Customs typically arise because they make evident sense. For instance, once someone has gone through the trouble of opening a door, it makes sense that he should hold it open for others that are nearby. As such, he will be inclined to hold the door open for others, provided that he expects them to return the favor to him. There is no reason why only a small community might notice the benefit associated with all members engaging in this practice. Instead, because the benefit is obvious, most anyone would tend to follow the prescribed conduct. As such, certain Customs can be seen around the world. Other Customs, such as taking one's shoes off when entering a house, might be limited to areas of the world where streets are typically filthy and shoes therefore should not be worn inside. In an area of the world where the streets are relatively clean, this Custom might not make sense.

In general though, common courtesy is the most evident in small communities. Why? Small communities have small memberships. As a result, the concept of mutual contribution and benefit is convincingly reinforced. If one member holds a door open for another, it is likely that the same member will return the favor to him fairly soon. This reciprocal conduct highlights the benefit of the alliance. Similarly, if a member fails to engage in the Custom in a small community, he can expect other members to readily notice and deny him the Custom in turn.

In large communities, common courtesy is much less common. Why? It is because the sense of membership and expectation of return favors is much less. A large community has thousands or even millions of members. If an individual grants a Custom towards a person he meets on the street, he cannot realistically expect to obtain the return favor from that same individual. In all likelihood, he will never see the individual again. Similarly, if an individual fails to grant a favor to a person he meets on the street, he cannot realistically expect to have that individual reciprocate and deny him a favor at a later date. Overall, in a large community, common courtesy is much less prevalent because individuals see little benefit to it. Most practitioners of common courtesy in large communities do so only for charitable reasons. They expect nothing in return.[1]

---

[1]This analysis regarding Customs does not entail a proposition that any and all traditions are derived from alliance concepts. However, it appears that many traditions are grounded in alliance theory. Further, it is likely all traditions at least originally served some type of purpose. Overtime, the purpose underlying these practices faded and they became seemingly meaningless social acts. For example, shaking hands was probably a mechanism for two individuals formerly suspicious of each other to convey their mutual trust and respect. If the trust was not present, allowing another to approach one and clasp one's hand could be quite dangerous. Today, shaking hands is seen as a mere formality without much meaning. Similarly, the practice of lying prostrate before a king or other leader is seen today as some technique for imposing notions of inferiority. In the past, though, it probably served an important safety mechanism in that it would be much easier to detect an attack upon the king, and guard against it, if everyone in the King's presence was always required to lie flat upon the ground.

OVERLORD

The last type of internal objective covered in this chapter is that of the Overlord. The concepts underlying an Overlord alliance are similar to the other internal objectives just discussed. The central difference pertains to membership. Specifically, the Overlord objective can be pursued only by alliances whose membership is comprised of alliances.

Before discussing the Overlord objective, it will useful to review "alliances of alliances." Recall from Chapter 3 that alliances can form alliances. In this situation, smaller alliances are members of a greater alliance and all of conditions for the formation of an alliance are satisfied.

Example 4 "Wild West"—The alliance retains the mercenary to end violence in the community. On occasions, large bands of ruffians appear in the community and the mercenary is outnumbered and powerless. The alliance approaches four other alliance/communities within about 50 miles. These five reach an accord. If any alliance/community is overwhelmed by ruffians, the other alliances/communities will loan out their mercenaries. The five mercenaries will combine their efforts to run out the ruffians.

Example 5 "Help the Needy"—The alliance has a long-term plan to build a free medical clinic for the needy. But this is an incredibly expensive undertaking and the alliance cannot come up with the funding. The alliance approaches nine other charitable alliances in the area. The ten alliances agree to pool their resources and build the medical clinic together.

As these two examples make clear, an alliance of alliances is the same as an alliance of individual human beings. The only difference is that the members of the larger alliance are smaller alliances instead of individuals. And the same conditions are present in alliances of alliances. Namely, there are members, objectives, accords, and contribution.

Having reviewed alliances of alliances, the internal objective of an Overlord can be discussed. What is an Overlord objective? It is an internal objective that focuses upon the conduct of the member alliances. The alliance of alliances is the "Overlord." The Overlord alliance watches over the member alliances and imposes a prescribed course of conduct upon them. Just as an alliance of individuals will pursue internal objectives that strive to impose a prescribed course of conduct on the individual members, an Overlord alliance seeks to compel the members to follow a certain course of conduct.

The prescribed course of conduct is not just any type of internal objective.

This factor makes the Overlord objective unusual. The course of conduct must relate to the manner in which the member alliances act towards their individual members. That is, the Overlord objective seeks to protect the interests of the individual members of the alliances, or the Overlord objective strives to insure that the member alliances operate and function as intended.

Example 4 "Wild West"—The alliance begins to run into trouble with its mercenary. He is very powerful and he at times abuses his power, and there is little the townspeople can do about it. They have to accept his abuses to get the benefit of running the ruffians out. As discussed earlier, the five alliance/ communities form an alliance of alliances relating to loaning mercenaries when a member is overrun by ruffians. Subsequently, they decide to expand this alliance of alliances to include an Overlord objective. The five alliances will police each other to check the mercenaries. If a mercenary abuses his power, the members of his alliance can petition the Overlord alliance for relief. The Overlord alliance will then combine its mercenaries to intervene into a member's situation and insure that renegade mercenary adheres to basic operating standards and does not engage in abuse.

Example 5 "Help the needy"—The alliance makes decisions through a variety of membership votes. Some of these decisions relate to specific objectives to tackle for a given month. Others pertain to electing decision makers. After a while, numerous complaints arise relating to these votes. The complaints relate to allegations of errors, confusion, and corruption in the voting process. The alliance decides to solve this problem by allying with the nine other charitable alliances in the area. This Overlord alliance agrees to specific voting procedures for all alliances to follow. Further, it creates a committee comprised of ten members (one from each alliance) to oversee all elections and insure that they do not suffer from the problems experienced earlier.

As these examples demonstrate, the Overlord objective seeks to protect the individual members of smaller alliances from abuse. By creating an alliance, the members have granted the alliance power. This power is to be used for the benefit of the members. However, because power has a tendency to corrupt, an Overlord alliance might be necessary to protect the members from their alliance.

Is an Overlord alliance always necessary? Can the member alliances protect themselves against potential abuses? Yes, they certainly can by, for instance, using certain provisions in their accords or by implementing delegated decision-making bodies designed to police the alliance, and so on. Keep in mind the rationale underlying the objective of an alliance. It is the same concept discussed extensively in Chapter 2. Recall that an individual will seek to attain something by himself unless (i) a combined effort is the only way to achieve it, or (ii) a combined effort is a more effective or efficient means of achieving it. This concept is equally applicable with regard to Overlord objectives. Alliances will form an Overlord alliance to protect them if (i) they are unable protect themselves, or (ii) an Overlord alliance is a more effective or efficient way of protecting themselves. Accordingly, alliances always have the option of guarding against abuse through an individual effort, but at times, an Overlord alliance may be a more desirable means of achieving this goal.

In terms of the internal objectives discussed earlier, the Overlord objective is most akin to the Paternalism objective. The Paternalism objective is founded on a belief that individual members will, at times, decide to do things that are not in their best interests. This decision to do undesirable things is due to some inherent defect or flaw in the individual. The alliance provides the solution to this defect or flaw by imposing a prescribed course of conduct upon the individual member.

Similarly, the Overlord alliance is premised upon a notion that an alliance has a potential to fail and either not fulfill the objective or actually harm the interests of the members. The Overlord alliance provides the solution by imposing a standard of conduct upon the member alliance. In most circumstances, the members of Overlord alliances are complex long-term alliances where there is a history of abuse of power. Usually, this abuse arises from a delegation of authority to one or more decision makers, but the abuse can also arise from membership votes where minority interests are targeted.

CHAPTER 9

External Objectives

As just discussed, internal objectives focus on the membership and strive to have the members behave in a certain manner thought to be of benefit to the members. In contrast, external objectives focus on something outside of the alliance. The principal concept is that this external matter can be best attained through a combined effort. This chapter will attempt to categorize the various external types of objectives.

THE EXTERNAL CLASS OF OBJECTIVE

The first seven examples demonstrate the concept of external objectives. In each, the alliance focuses its efforts on something outside of the membership. These subjects vary widely:

- Moving a boulder

- Slaying a mammoth

- Digging a well

- Controlling ruffians

- Helping the needy

- Transporting children

- Acquiring a sailboat

In each of these, the objective does not focus on the conduct of the members. Although these alliances typically utilize means that focus on the members' actions (for example, pushing on the boulder, attacking the mammoth, and so on), the objective is to attain some result extrinsic to the membership. For this reason, these objectives are external.[1]

Consistent with the overall concept of objectives, an external objective can be anything. Even so, external objectives can be classified into commonly appearing categories, just as internal objectives were earlier. The following discussion will address the more common forms of external objectives. It should be kept in mind that these classes of objectives are not precise due to the flexible nature of objectives.

UNITING AGAINST NATURAL OBSTACLES

Nature presents many obstacles. Often, humans find that individual effort offers the best way of addressing the problems that nature creates. But this is not always the case. In many circumstances, humans find that a combined effort offers advantages over an individual effort in tackling natural objectives. A few representative examples include:

Moving a boulder	**Slaying a mammoth**	**Digging a well**
Building a bridge	**Laying a road**	**Tunneling through a mountain**
Operating a ferry	**Exploring a foreign land**	**Researching a disease**

All of these are examples of objectives where a combined effort *might* offer advantages over an individual effort.

These objectives are not always suitable for pursuit by alliances. In some

---

[1] Observe that external Example No. 4 "Wild West" has the potential for internal objectives. Recall that the alliance is established to target the transgressions of the thieves and robbers. This objective is described as bringing "order and decency" to the community. Because the thieves and robbers are not members of the alliance, the objective of "order and decency" is external. Subsequently, it was observed that "order and decency" is an indefinite objective and arguably can also include prostitution, adultery, alcohol consumption, lewd attire, or tobacco use. These objectives are internal in nature, because they focus upon the conduct of the members to the alliance. As such, in pursuing "order and decency," the nature of the alliance could be altered fundamentally, with the objective transforming from an external objective into an internal objective. This result reinforces the fluid nature of alliances with indefinite accords. If alliances desire to avoid such fluidity, the accord should identify the objective with greater specificity.

situations, individuals might be able to achieve these objectives through their own pure individual effort or through an outsourced individual effort. As discussed earlier in Chapter 6, *pure individual efforts* are where individuals achieve objectives solely by themselves. In contrast, an *outsourced individual effort* involves individuals retaining others to attain the objective for them in exchange for some form of compensation.

In other situations, individuals might find that an alliance offers advantages over both pure individual efforts and outsourced efforts. The following table summarizes generalizations about when Natural Obstacle objectives are suitable for pure individual effort, individual outsourced effort, or an alliance effort. Some objectives can be attained by all three forms of efforts while others are typically suited for achievement by an alliance effort only.

Natural Obstacle Objective	Individually Pure	Individually Outsourced	Alliance
Moving a boulder	•	•	•
Digging a well	•	•	•
Building a bridge	•	•	•
Slaying a mammoth		•	•
Operating a ferry		•	•
Laying a road			•
Tunneling through a mountain			•
Exploring a foreign land			•
Research into a disease			•

This table contains only generalizations about the objectives. For example, there are certainly situations where an individual might be able to tunnel through a mountain by pure individual effort alone, but such circumstances would be rare. Similarly, an individual might be able to retain others to tunnel on his behalf. But this is unlikely as well due to the great expense associated with such an effort. Accordingly, as a general rule, tunneling through a mountain is an objective suited only for attainment by an alliance.

Similarly, an individual can explore a foreign land by himself or he can research into the cause and cure of a disease, or he can outsource these efforts to others. But these are typically extraordinary efforts and usually can be attained only by an alliance. Consider modern examples of these objectives.

Exploration of foreign lands	• Investigation of the ocean floor • Travel to other planets and stars
Research into diseases	• Cancer • Heart disease • Viruses, such as HIV or influenza

An extraordinarily wealthy individual might be able to achieve these objectives by an outsourced individual effort. As a general rule, however, individuals cannot achieve such results and must resort to an alliance.

DEFENSE AGAINST AGGRESSORS

A second common example of an external objective is Defending against Aaggressors. In this situation, the members combine their resources to defend against a threat posed by another individual or group of individuals. The defense is typically against a physical menace, but not always.

Example 4 "Wild West"—In this situation, gunfighters and thieves are plaguing the vicinity. To deal with these aggressors, the individuals in the vicinity form an alliance. The objective is to stop the threat posed by the aggressors by combining resources to retain a mercenary.

This type of external objective is common. Some real world examples include:

Militia   Army   Navy

Surveillance   Espionage

Diplomacy   Appeasement   Pacification

The common factor underlying these examples is the protection of members from aggression posed by others.

Note that two internal objectives are substantially similar to this objective. These internal objectives are Law-Compelled Objectives. Recall that there are three sub-categories of Law-Compelled Objectives: (i) Protection of the Person, (ii) Protection of Property, and (iii) Enforcement of Promises. The first two, which relate to protection of the person and property, overlap with Defending against Aggressors. They seek to protect the lives and property of members.

| **Internal Law** | | **External Defense** |
| **Compelled Objective** | ≈ | **against Aggressor Objective** |

The difference between the two types of objectives is that the former is internal and the latter is external. Law-Compelled Objectives are *internal,* and focus upon establishing mutually beneficiary rules mandating how members conduct themselves with regard to their fellow members. The objective of Defending against Aggressors is *external* and focuses on defensive measures against *non-members* of the alliance.

The distinction is subtle, but significant. With the internal objective, the members have willingly entered into an alliance and agreed to abide by certain standards of conduct to benefit from all other members exhibiting the same conduct towards them. With the external objective, the aggressors are not members of the alliance and have not agreed to conduct themselves in a certain manner.

Example 9 "No killing"—The alliance prohibits members from killing other members and is largely successful. One day, a band of raiders appears in the area inhabited by the cavemen. This band slaughters several members of the alliance and flees. The alliance has failed to prevent these deaths.

Why has the alliance failed? Because the raiders are not members of the alliance. They have not agreed to follow the prescribed course of conduct and probably are not even aware of it. Moreover, the Law-Compelled Objective is founded on an assumption that the punishment for noncompliance can be effectively administered. In this example, however, the raiders are not going to linger around to receive the punishment of death. As such, the alliance can have no expectation of a Law-Compelled Objective protecting members from the raiders. It serves to protect members from only other members. To summarize, the law-compelled internal objectives focus on members and setting codes of conduct that members are to exhibit towards each other. In contrast, the external objectives of Defending against Aggressors concentrate upon non-members and using the combined resources of the members to fend off or otherwise defend against.

Another difference between the two pertains to the manner and degree with which the offenders are dealt. In the case of an internal Law-Compelled Objective, recall that the penalty for non-compliance is applicable to all members. As such, members will tend to select penalties that are not considered unduly cruel or vengeful. This tendency is usually not present in the case of an external objective of Defending against Aggressors. Because the aggressors are non-members, the alliance will tend to defend against them using the harshest (and most deadly) measures available. Further, if the aggressors are caught, they will usually receive much harsher penalties.

OFFENSE AGAINST NON-MEMBERS

Remember that an objective can be anything, including matters that many consider to be immoral, criminal, or evil. Sometimes, members might form an alliance to conduct an offensive against non-member humans. A few representative examples include:

Gang of robbers	Conspiracy to murder	Collusion of businesses against another
Repression of non-members	Organized crime	Laborers picketing a disfavored employer
Conquest of another land	Genocide	Leveling[1]

In each example, the objective focuses on imposing some result upon non-members. Sometimes, the result is rather innocuous, like the picketing of an employer by laborers. Other times, the result can be quite consequential, such as genocide. The common factor is that the members see the alliance as an effective means of attaining the result against non-members.

A somewhat symbiotic relationship exists between offensive and defensive objectives. If an alliance is created to pursue an offensive objective, it will be targeting

---

[1] Note that "leveling" was earlier identified as an internal objective. But leveling can also be an external objective. In both internal and external situations, the desired result is parity in something that can be accumulated or possessed. Leveling is an internal objective if the members to an alliance agree upon the level of parity and therefore consent, at least initially, to having the accumulated items taken away. Leveling is an external objective if the focus is upon the accumulations of non-members. In this situation, the members target non-members and reduce their accumulations, usually against their will, to a level of parity desired by the members.

certain non-members. These non-members then will typically create their own alliance to pursue a defensive objective (that is, defending against the offensive objective of the other alliance).

COOPERATIVES

A Cooperative is a broad concept and is difficult to define. The difficulty lies partially in the fact that the word "cooperative" is closely related in meaning to the definition of the word "alliance." The distinction between the two is that an alliance is a very expansive concept while a Cooperative is a subset of an alliance. That is, all Cooperatives are alliances but not all alliances are Cooperatives. Examples of Cooperatives include:

Carpool	Library	Park
Museum	Mail System	Playground
Meeting Hall	Swimming Pool	Golf Course
Student Bookstore	Fraternity or Sorority	School
Credit Union	Commune	Kibbutz

As with any objective underlying an alliance, the trait that these examples share is that a combined effort is often more efficient or effective than an individual effort. The alliance members commonly desire certain objectives and they then pool their resources to efficiently and/or effectively achieve it. For example, some individuals desire to have a large number of books available to read. They could attempt to achieve this objective individually by purchasing the books themselves. However, this effort is quite expensive. As such, the alliance members form a cooperative alliance known as a "library" to achieve this objective. This same concept is applicable to the other examples previously identified.

MITIGATION OF CATASTROPHE

Catastrophes present a classic external objective. By their very nature, catastrophes cannot be addressed by individual behavior. Instead, a combined effort is usually essential to mitigate their consequences. The focus of the combined effort is usually to reduce or alleviate the suffering and damage wrought by the catastrophe.

Group Catastrophe

Catastrophes are usually natural disasters, like earthquakes, floods, epidemics, and the like. These types of catastrophes are *Group Catastrophes* because they tend to strike across wide swaths of individuals. As a result, these potentially wide ranging groups of people usually have an interest in forming a combined effort to help lessen the consequences of a catastrophe. In these situations, the objective is mitigating the pain and suffering that arises after a disaster strikes. Examples of measures that such alliances might take include:

Rescue squads	**Emergency relief services**	**Evacuation**
Fire departments	**Shelter & food**	**Medical care**

Personal Catastrophe

In contrast to a group catastrophe, a disaster that typically afflicts only one individual at a time is a *Personal Catastrophe*. Examples of Personal Catastrophes include a house burning down, a disabling injury or illness, or financial bad luck. Individuals can often deal with these situations themselves. For example, they can reduce the chances of the catastrophe from occurring by eliminating risks, or they can save money or resources for when catastrophe strikes (that is, the proverbial "rainy day"). Nonetheless, individuals will often find that a combined effort is more advantageous and will form alliances to guard against certain Personal Catastrophes.

A classic alliance to guard against Personal Catastrophes is insurance. In today's world, most insurance is offered by for-profit insurance companies. An individual who purchases insurance from one of these companies is individually attaining the objective of insurance but through an *outsourced* effort. Specifically, he is individually guarding against the risk by paying another to insure him.

Insurance was not always this way. In the past, most insurance was acquired through alliances. Members would pool their monies in various manners to guard against catastrophes.

Example 17 "Insurance"—100 individuals each own houses worth $10,000 and they are concerned about their destruction in house fires. In the recent past, 1 out of every 100 houses has burned down in a given year. The individuals realize that they could each set aside $10,000 to rebuild their houses in the event of fire, but that is a lot of money. Instead, they decide to pool their resources together by forming an alliance. It works this way. Because there is likelihood of one house per year being destroyed (that is, 100 houses and a 1% chance of fire per hundred equals one house per year), the alliance needs $10,000 on hand. Where will the alliance get the $10,000? It will come from the members as a form of resource contribution. There are 100 members so each will have to contribute $100 ($10,000 divided by 100 members equals $100 per member). As a consequence of the alliance, each member can feel safe that, if his house burns down, the $10,000 will be on hand to rebuild it. And the price of this security is only $100 per year (opposed to keeping $10,000 in the bank).[1]

Alliances like this example were called "mutual insurance companies." Many mutual insurance companies are still around today, although they are on the decline. Similar examples include multi-objective alliances such as fraternal benefits societies and other associations that provided various benefits to members including insurance.

Virtually anything can be insured. Some common examples of things that are insured against include:

Property   **Liability**
                              Disability
Life   **Health**

These types of insurance can be offered through a variety of alliances. In today's world, insurance typically constitutes providing the stricken member with monetary payments to offset the financial consequences of the Personal Catastrophe.

Monetary payments are not the only form of insuring against a Personal Catastrophe. For example, benefits associated with disability do not have to be monetary. Disability benefits can constitute revising accommodations to enable disabled individuals to move more freely, or they can consist of rules forbidding others from treating individuals with disabilities differently. These instances are less-obvious examples of insurance against Personal Catastrophes. The basic concept is that one who becomes disabled will not have to bear the costs of the disability alone. Instead, the costs will be spread amongst all alliance members through various accommodations of the disability. And because everyone holds the potential to become disabled at some point in their lives, all members of the alliance benefit from this form of insurance.

Another subtle form of insurance pertains to economic catastrophe. From time to time, individuals might be concerned with plunging into poverty. This

---

[1]This example is a very simplified explanation of insurance but it gets the general idea across. For the insurance to really work, the calculation of the premium (that is, the $100 per year) would be more complicated and would involve consideration of additional factors. Nonetheless, the example conveys the gist of how an alliance provides insurance benefits to its members.

predicament can result from a person's stupidity, negligence, risk taking, or simple bad luck. To address this situation, an alliance might be formed to guard against this risk. For example, if a member falls on hard times, the alliance will provide them with sustenance until they can get back on their feet. Or, if a member incurs a number of obligations that they cannot satisfy, the alliance may allow for some or all of these obligations to be negated or restructured (for example, "bankruptcy"). Of course, this form of insurance can be abused by undeserving members, a fact which tends to weigh against an alliance adopting it as an objective.

As a final matter, it should be noted that *guarding against* catastrophe does not fall within this objective of *mitigating the consequences* of catastrophe. Guarding against a catastrophe pertains to two different types of objectives. The first is Uniting Against a Natural Obstacle where the members join forces to stop the catastrophe (for example, building a sea wall to stop a tidal wave). This topic was discussed earlier in this chapter. The second consists of internal objectives discussed in Chapter 8, where the alliance imposes some type of mutually beneficial conduct upon the members for the purpose of preventing a catastrophe. Examples include mandated directives regarding:

- Decreasing emissions by members of "green house" gases believe to alter the Earth's climate and foster cataclysmic weather changes

- Quarantining members who are victims of a communicable, deadly disease to prevent its spread

- Reducing deforestation by members to avert a feared ecological collapse of all species

These are all examples of internal objectives intended to prevent a catastrophe from occurring.

GENERATION OF PROSPERITY

Individuals often desire material prosperity and see it as an objective to be attained. Although individuals commonly utilize individual efforts towards maximizing their material prosperity, alliances will be formed from time to time to pursue this objective. In this situation, the members believe that some type of coordinated or united activity can result, usually indirectly, in increasing material prosperity to all members. The various means utilized to achieve this objective vary considerably.

Example 18 "Prosperity"—A group of ten businessmen are trying to sell a starchy food called "poi." The dish is not selling well. Although they are competitors, the ten businessmen form an alliance to advertise and promote the good taste and health benefits of poi. All ten contribute resources and these are used to advertise poi. Because the contributions total a large sum, the advertisements hit a large market and sales of poi skyrocket. All ten businessmen profit greatly.

This example demonstrates how a combined, alliance effort can increase prosperity for all members.

This objective is commonplace in extraordinarily large and complex alliances, such as the governments of modern days. A few representative examples include:

Mercantilism	**Socialism/Communism**	**Industrial planning**
Stimulus spending	**Subsidies to select industries**	**Targeted contribution (or tax reductions)**

These examples will be discussed in greater detail subsequently. The point, though, is that they all constitute examples of alliances undertaking certain measures for the purpose of generating overall material prosperity for the membership.

PROMOTION OF CHARITY & JUSTICE

Alliances typically pursue objectives that benefit the members in a direct, tangible manner. This, however, is not always the case.

Recall that an objective can be anything. At times, individuals desire to attain objectives that do not directly benefit them in any evident manner. These objectives often relate to the wellbeing, happiness, or security of other individuals. Sometimes they can relate to animals or nature. For a lack of a better terminology, objectives that do not directly benefit individuals will be termed "Charity & Justice." The individual pursuing Charity & Justice typically thinks that it is the "right" thing to do and he is willing to contribute resources towards its attainment.

In these situations, the individual desires Charity & Justice for one simple reason. He desires them. This tautological reasoning underscores the subjective nature of objectives. There is no need to scrutinize the situation and attempt to find some way in which the individual is tangibly rewarded for the achievement of Charity & Justice. To the individual, the attainment of Charity & Justice is a sufficient reward.

Often, individuals can achieve Charity & Justice through their own individual efforts. At times, a combined effort may offer a more effective or efficient means of achieving Charity & Justice. As such, an alliance will be formed and the objective will be attainment of the Charity & Justice objective.

Example 5 "Help the Needy"—The members all desire to aid the less fortunate in their community. This objective pertains to Charity & Justice. To achieve Charity & Justice more efficiently and effectively than individual effort, the members form the alliance.

It is important to observe that the objective underlying these alliances does not include aiding members. Other objectives pertain to that situation. The aim of the alliance is to achieve charity or justice by focusing on *non-members, animals, or whatever else that may be desired.* Examples of this include aiding non-members through:

- Shipping food to avert starvation

- Donation of necessities such as clothes or shelter

- Provision of money, technology, and so on

- Support in fighting against a tyranny

Or the objective can focus on non-members such as children with initiatives like:

- Protection from abusive parents

- Training and education

Or the objective can relate to non-humans such as:

- Protection of animals from cruelty

- Preservation of far-away environments or animals that one will never see.

In all of these situations, certain individuals desire these Charity & Justice objectives simply because they desire them. The achievement of the objectives is a sufficient reward for the contribution of resources.

As a final note, it must be observed that these initiatives can fall within other objectives, depending on the motivation underlying the action. If members undertake one of these actions for a purpose other than its perceived "rightness," the objective is no longer in the category of charitable and justice objectives. Instead, it falls within another objective.[1]

---

[1] For example, one external objective is Defense against Aggressors and one means of achieving this objective is diplomacy. An alliance may engage in a diplomatic effort by providing food and clothing to another alliance. Because this effort is being taken for diplomatic reasons, the objective is not in the category of Charity & Justice.

CHAPTER 10

Open Objectives

Chapter 8 pertains to internal objectives where the focus is on the conduct of the members. That is, the purpose of the objective is to cause the membership to do or not do one or more acts. This category of internal objective can be divided into numerous sub-categories.

Chapter 9 concerns external objectives where the focus is upon something outside of the membership. Instead of concentrating on the members, an external objective targets a matter external to the membership such as persons or nature. Like internal objectives, this category can be divided into numerous sub-categories.

This chapter will cover the final category of purpose-based analysis of objectives. It is the category of open objectives.

EXAMPLE 8 RE-EXAMINED

Recall Example 8:

Example 8 "Council of elders"—Imagine a prehistoric tribal community. The tribe members live near each other and travel together. It is up to each tribe member to provide for his own food and shelter, except for children who are taken care of by parents. From time to time, various small alliances will form between certain individuals. These will be short lived and constitute single objective alliances, such as to kill a sizeable animal, cut down a large tree, or move a heavy rock. When these objectives are completed, the alliances end. If another objective arises, another alliance will be formed. Observing the tribe, there appears to be no overall alliance between the tribe members as a whole. They behave like separate and distinct individuals that happen to live right near each other.

One day, the oldest members of the tribe meet in private and talk. The next day, the tribe members pack up and move away to a new location where there is more food and water. A few weeks later, there is talk of a band of thieves in the vicinity. The old members meet. The next day, a war party of tribe members goes out and tracks down and kills the thieves. A few weeks pass but with no rain. The old members meet. The next day, all tribe members begin storing up as much food and water as they can in the tribe's storage bins. What is going on here?

As discussed in Chapters 2 and 4, an alliance is undoubtedly present. But the alliance is unusual because its accord does not restrict the alliance to pursuing a single objective or a group of specific objectives. Instead, the accord underlying the alliance essentially authorizes the alliance to undertake anything. The objective is open.

THE NEED FOR A DECISION-MAKING PROCESS

Recall also that any alliance with an open objective must have a decision-making process in place. Why? Because the alliance must decide what objectives to pursue. The decision-making process is therefore fundamental to the making of these determinations. These decision-making processes can take all forms including membership vote processes, delegated processes (committee or executive), non-standard processes (random, rational chaos, or programmed), tiers of various processes, and interwoven processes.

WHAT IS THE PURPOSE OF AN OPEN OBJECTIVE?

The aim of this chapter, as well as the two preceding chapters, is to identify the purposes underlying various objectives and show how they fit into the conceptual framework of alliances. In the case of an open objective, there is a single purpose associated with the category.

The purpose of an open objective is the decision-making process. The alliance members see value in having in place and ready for action a long-standing (or permanent) process for identifying commonly desired objectives that are suitable for combined action. Having such an arrangement in place can offer advantages. A primary advantage is that there is no need to form new alliances for each objective that might arise. An alliance is already in place and all it must do, in theory, is act on those objectives. This arrangement is particularly appealing if the objectives are ones that require quick action.

As Example 8 demonstrated, the Council of Elders constitutes the decision-making process. This Council is vested with authority to both (i) determine objectives that are suited for a combined effort, and (ii) decide on the means to achieve these objectives. This Council is in place because it is of value to the membership. The members have agreed in an implied accord to follow the Council's mandates and to contribute resources as it dictates. In return, the members expect to benefit from the combined efforts selected by the Council, in comparison to living and surviving on their own. Overall, the members perceive that the open-objective alliance offers a greater net benefit over both individual efforts and repeatedly forming single-objective alliances.

DRAWBACKS

Open objectives have their drawbacks. Recall that all decision-making processes have their weaknesses. These limitations include:

- A potential to make mistakes

- Lack of motivation

- Capability limitations

- Fidelity limitations including position protection, favoring special interests, and corruption.

These limitations are significantly amplified in an open-objective alliance. Why? Because such an alliance typically grants substantial, if not absolute, authority to the decision-making process. As such, if the selected process is prone to decision-making limitations, there is much greater opportunity for the failings of decision-making processes to manifest themselves.

Example 8 "Council of elders"—Although the Council often selects objectives which are suitable for combined effort and otherwise in the interests of the tribe members, the Council from time to time deviates from the authority delegated to it. For example, the Council pays insufficient attention to the fact that food supplies in the area are declining and the tribe narrowly escapes famine (that is, lack of motivation). Also, the Council fails to recognize that the tribe is encamped in a gully where it will be subject to flooding in a rain storm (that is, lack of capability). And the Council frequently undertakes objectives that seem to only benefit the Council members and their families (that is, special interests). Finally, the Council members at times take food out of the tribal storage bins that are meant to be touched only in times of famine (that is, corruption).

TOLERATION OF DECISION MAKER LIMITATIONS

Although decision makers in open alliances might make mistakes and engage in corruption from time to time, many alliances will tolerate this conduct. Why? The reason is that the alliance provides a net benefit to the alliance members notwithstanding the negligence or misconduct of the decision maker.

Recall that an alliance is entered into because its perceived net benefits are greater than those offered by either individual effort or another form of alliance. Thus, even if the decision-making process is not performing properly, members will stay in the alliance so long as they perceive the alliance to be better than the alternatives.

Example 8 "Council of elders"—Many of the tribe members are outraged by the mistakes of the Council and its corruption in stealing food from the storage bins. Nonetheless, these tribe members recall the various benefits offered by the alliance including their triumph over numerous raiding parties and the general availability of food. Because these advantages are substantial, the failings of the Council are overlooked.

OBJECTIVES NOT IN THE INTERESTS OF CERTAIN MEMBERS

The accord underlying an open-objective alliance does not restrict the objectives that the alliance can pursue. Thus, such an alliance is free to pursue any objective chosen by the decision-making process. Because of this unfettered ability, open-objective alliances will tend to undertake objectives that are not desired by all members.

This result appears to conflict with a fundamental aspect of alliances. Namely, it seems contrary to the principle that an alliance will undertake only objectives desired by *all members* of the alliance. As discussed in Part I, the members' mutual desire for achievement of a certain objective is the force that creates the alliance in the first place and is the glue that subsequently holds it together. If an alliance undertakes an objective not desired by certain members, this result conflicts with this principle underlying all alliances. As such, the glue bonding the members to the alliance should dissolve, contribution will be withheld, members will leave, and the alliance will seem doomed to terminate. Notwithstanding these tendencies, alliances can survive for two reasons.

The first is the net-benefit concept just discussed. If the members who are not interested in the objectives nonetheless perceive a net benefit from the existence of the alliance, they will grudgingly remain members.

The second reason relates to the accord underlying the alliance. Some alliances either expressly or impliedly authorize the alliance to undertake objectives that are not in the interests of all members. As noted earlier in the chapter, the purpose underlying open-objective alliances is to benefit from having a decision-making process in place and ready to act. In the formation of such an alliance, the members might recognize that the alliance, due to its structure and decision-making process, will be likely to undertake objectives from time to time with which they disagree or even strongly oppose. Nonetheless, the members see a net benefit in having the open-objective alliance in place. As such, they agree in the accord, expressly or impliedly, that such objectives can be pursued, provided that they are selected by the decision-making process. Such members are more prone to accept this situation where they believe that it will benefit them. For instance, if they perceive that the alliance will pursue objectives that they desire (but are not necessarily desired by other members), they are more likely to support the situation, in contrast to always being on the losing end of objective selection.

INSTABILITY OF OPEN-OBJECTIVE ALLIANCES

Open-objective alliances tend to not be particularly stable. This tendency results from the inclination of members to see more suitable alternative alliances offering greater net benefits.

In theory, an open-objective alliance appears to be an outstanding concept. If it is able to pursue only objectives that are suitable for a combined effort, it should be very rewarding for its members. These rewards will tend to make the alliance long-standing or even permanent.

The real world is often very different from theory, however. In this regard, the propensity of open-ended alliances to suffer from decision-making process draw-backs and to pursue objectives not in the interests of many members tends to reduce the perceived net benefit of such alliances. If other alliances are available, members will often see these as offering more advantages. These advantages include having a specific or at least indefinite objective which will offer more of a safeguard against the alliance pursuing undesired objectives. Another important advantage may be greater protections against mistakes and abuses by the decision-making process. Finally, if the alternative is pursuing fewer objectives, the contribution will likely be less. As a result of these factors, members of open-objective alliances will often see alternative alliances as being superior and will leave the open-objective alliance.

PART III

———•———

SPECIAL TOPICS

CHAPTER 11

Illusory Issues

Things are not always as they seem. Things that appear to be alliances might really not be alliances. And things that seem to be the farthest thing from alliances might actually constitute alliances. This chapter explores these concepts.

ILLUSORY ALLIANCES

An illusory alliance appears to be a valid functioning alliance that pursues objectives desired by all its members. In reality, an illusory alliance furthers objectives of only one individual or a small group of individuals, rather than those of the apparent members.

The illusion is that an alliance exists. The purported members of the illusory alliance perceive that a valid alliance is present and that it is acting to further their interests. However, the purported members are in reality not members. Instead, one of the objectives of the illusory alliance is to create this perception in the minds of the purported members that they are in fact members of a valid alliance. But in the end, the alliance serves only the interests of the actual members.

Example 19 "The Alleged Army"— A region has approximately 100,000 individuals living in it. From time to time, cruel and brutal raiders terrorize the region. In a time of peace, a power-hungry person named Rex decides to seize upon the residents' justified fears of these periodic invasions. Rex contends that the solution to the invasions is to form a standing army and he will be its leader (that is, decision maker). Rex claims that all residents of this region will be protected by the army, provided that they make contributions of money in the form of an annual tax.

Rex's arguments are persuasive and the apparent alliance is formed. All 100,000 residents contribute resources (that is, the tax). Rex receives the resources and uses a small portion to put together a large but poorly organized and poorly equipped army. Rex uses the remaining resources to build lavish castles and retain numerous servants. Rex frequently orders his army to travel around the region and to put on marches and drills for the residents. Rex proclaims to the residents that they are now safe from the raiders.

After a few years, the raiders come again. The army marches out to do battle with the raiders but it is quickly trounced. During the army's short existence, its main purpose had been to engage in pomp and circumstance in order to delude the residents into thinking it is a real, functioning instrument of war. In reality, the generals and soldiers know nothing about battle or warfare. The army is worthless and the raiders terrorize the region again.

What has happened here? The ostensible alliance is a sham. To a casual observer, there appears to be an alliance because there are apparent members, an objective, means, an accord, contribution, and so on. However, there is no alliance. The purpose of Rex's creation is to personally enrich himself through deception. Rex tricks the residents into thinking that they are members of an alliance through his words and through forming a sham army and then constantly displaying the army to them. This conduct creates, and then reinforces, a perception in the minds of the members that a bona fide alliance exists and that it is well worth their contribution of resources. In reality, the army is worthless and the only result of the entire enterprise is to make Rex very wealthy.

Illusory alliances rarely have a single controlling individual such as Rex. Instead, illusory alliances usually have actual, functioning alliances within the structures of the illusory alliances. The memberships of these actual, internal alliances will be comprised of small groups of individuals who foster the deceptions of the illusory alliances and reap the benefits of the resulting illusions. The accords underlying these actual alliances will identify objectives such as (i) to take as much of the contribution for their own personal enrichment as possible, and (ii) to trick the purported members into believing that there is a large alliance in effect and working for their benefit. The types of resources contributed by the members will vary but typically constitute the time, effort, and know-how necessary to achieve the objectives.

Example 19 "The Alleged Army"—Rex finds that the job of maintaining the illusory alliance is far too great for him to handle by himself. As a result, Rex enlists 100 individuals to assist him in maintaining the illusion and provides them with a share of resources contributed by the illusory members. The 100 individuals plus Rex constitute the membership of the actual, internal alliance. The objective is to profit from exploiting the contribution supplied by the illusory members. The accord is a spoken agreement to combine resources to maintain the illusion. The contribution supplied is the time, labor, and effort required to maintain the illusion. The decision-making process is a delegated executive decision maker, with Rex being the decision maker.

In today's world, illusory alliances are commonly seen in fraudulent business enterprises such as pyramid schemes or other fake business ventures. In these situations, a swindler, or a group of swindlers, deceive individuals into thinking they are entering some type of investment alliance where members will all contribute resources (that is, usually money) and all will reap benefits in the form of profits. Instead, the actual purpose of the entire endeavor is to steal the purported members' money.

THE SLIDE INTO ILLUSORY ALLIANCES

Unlike Example 19, most illusory alliances do not begin as illusory alliances. Instead, they begin as real, true alliances. Over time, these alliances are transformed into illusory alliances.

Example 4 "Wild West"—As time passes, order and decency are established in the community. This result is due in part to the efforts of the mercenary as well as demographic changes. With regard to the latter, the community has matured and the thieves and robbers have either changed their ways or moved on. Because of these improvements, there is no need for the mercenary or the alliance. Nonetheless, the alliance persists. Why? It is because the mercenary transforms the alliance into an illusory alliance to preserve his position. For instance, the mercenary repeatedly asserts the threat posed by outlaws is still very real and dangerous, even though the mercenary knows his statements are false. Periodically, the mercenary secretly sets random buildings on fire at night and then blames the arsons upon an alleged lawless element that still plagues the community. Here, the mercenary is lying to the membership regarding the threat and engaging in serious misconduct to create a false perception of a threat. The mercenary is maintaining an illusion that there is a continuing need for the alliance and that its existence is of benefit to the members.[1]

In this example, a real alliance exists at the beginning and acts to benefit the interests of all members. However, after the objective is attained and there is no need for the alliance, the alliance is transformed into an illusory alliance.

---

[1] This same issue was discussed in Chapter 7 relating to the fidelity limitations of decision makers. There, it was observed that a decision maker will tend to protect his position by creating a false perception of a continuing need for an alliance. This limitation of decision makers therefore can create and perpetuate an illusory alliance.

As discussed in Part I, once a true alliance attains its objective, it will terminate, at least in theory. In reality, however, the alliance structure often remains intact. Sometimes, the membership uses this structure to undertake new objectives suited to combined effort. In this situation, a prior true alliance is transformed into a new true alliance pursuing a new objective.

Alternatively, the alliance structure can be used to form illusory alliances as just shown in the example. A primary factor in the transformation of a one-time authentic alliance into an illusory alliance is the decision maker's desire to protect and entrench his position.

Decision maker improprieties are not the only cause of a transformation to illusory alliances. Another factor is the presence of indefinite or open objectives in the alliance. This subject will be discussed in the next section.

THE ROLE OF INDEFINITE AND OPEN OBJECTIVES

A frequent factor in the slide from a true alliance into an illusory alliance is the presence of indefinite or open objectives. In Chapter 6, the subject of "change" in alliances was raised. There, it was observed that the propensity for an alliance to change is related to the accord and its provisions. If the accord is quite specific on what the objective of the alliance constitutes (and does not constitute), there is very little propensity for change in the alliance.[1] Conversely, if the members foresee the need for change and provide for it in the accord, there is much more propensity for change. Similarly, the vaguer the underlying accord is (especially with alliances formed by implied accords), the more likely a propensity for a change will exist.

This potential for change can be a positive factor. Flexibility in pursuit of objectives might be fundamentally necessary to the purpose sought to be furthered by the alliance. As such, indefinite or open objectives can be very useful in satisfying the desires of the membership.

But the propensity for change is not always a positive factor. This potential constitutes a readily available catalyst for the transformation of a true alliance into an illusory alliance. Why? Recall that alliances with indefinite or open objectives require decision-making processes. In the case of indefinite objectives, the meaning

---

[1] Of course, the alliance can still change notwithstanding such specificity in the accord, but such a change would be fundamental. Fundamental changes are more difficult to effectuate and are likely to result in the effective termination of the original alliance and a birth of a new alliance.

and parameters of the objective (for example, "order and decency") must be clarified or defined from time to time. With open objectives, the alliance is free to pursue any objective and a decision-making process is necessary to determine the specific objective to pursue. In both of these situations, the alliance grants the decision-making process substantial (if not complete) authority to determine the objective to be pursued. This grant of authority can be abused and utilized to transform a true alliance into an illusory alliance.

How can the authority be abused? Recall that there are two broad categories of decision-making processes:

1) Membership vote, and

2) Delegated decision making.

Abuse by Membership Vote

If a membership-vote process requires less than unanimity in defining indefinite objectives or selecting open objectives, the potential for abuse exists.

> **Example 5** "Help the needy"—The objective is indefinite (that is, "help the needy") and therefore requires a decision-making process to define its parameters. The decision-making process is a membership vote in a monthly meeting with a majority vote. For six months, the alliance decides to run a soup kitchen. For the seventh month, the alliance decides to build housing for the needy. On the eight month, the alliance decides by a slim majority (51% of the votes) to provide the needy with new mattresses to insure that the needy sleep well. Month after month, the alliance votes to provide mattresses to the needy by the slim 51% majority. As it turns out, the members voting for the mattress initiative have an ulterior motive. All of them secretly own stock in the local mattress factory. The monthly purchases of mattresses by the alliance are providing substantial profits to the mattress factory and large dividends to the voting members.

In this example, the alliance appears to be fulfilling its objective—helping the needy—and therefore satisfying the charitable desires of the members. In reality, however, it is no longer an authentic alliance. What started out as a true alliance is now an illusory alliance. The illusion is that the alliance is helping the needy by providing them with mattresses to insure healthy sleep. The reality is that the bare majority of members (that is, the fifty-one percent) are the true members of the alliance and its objectives are to (i) insure that the mattress proposal is always selected by the illusory alliance, and (ii) to conceal their profiting from the alliance and to make it appear that the original alliance is still present and functioning. The minority members (that is, the forty-nine percent) are no longer real members of the alliance. Instead, they are saps and suckers, contributing resources to an alliance that in reality does not serve their interest of helping the needy. They are unwittingly lining the pockets of the fifty-one percent.

Abuse by Delegated Decision Makers

The other broad category of decision making is the delegated decision maker.[1] As discussed in Chapter 7, committee and executive decision makers are subject to many potential fidelity limitations. If an alliance has a large potential for change and the delegated decision maker is subject to a fidelity limitation, the likelihood of transformation into an illusory alliance is substantial.

> **Example 4 "Wild West"**—To bring order and decency to the community, the alliance delegates the mercenary with broad authority to determine what "order and decency" comprises and what means should be used to achieve this objective. The mercenary determines that the community should build a huge, expensive wooden wall around the community. The mercenary explains that the wall will keep out thieves and robbers. In reality, the mercenary has been bribed by a local lumberyard that will profit greatly from supplying lumber for the wall's construction. The alliance is now an illusory alliance. It appears to benefit all of the members. But it actually is a tool to benefit the lumberyard and the mercenary.

> **Example 13 "Moral obligations"**—In a village, the residents follow the same religion. This religion entails a number of ritual practices that must be followed including certain requirements for food, dress, and prayer. If the rituals are not followed, it is feared that the community might suffer dire consequences from the deity. As a result, it is agreed that all members are to follow all rituals. A committee of religious leaders is charged with discerning the rituals and religious tenets to be followed. Over time, the committee becomes jaded and realizes the immense power that it holds to control the village. Instead of divining the true religious concepts, the committee begins devising rules and practices that increase both the wealth and prosperity of the committee members and the sole authority of the committee to determine applicable religious rituals and tenets. The alliance has become an illusory alliance. The membership is limited to the committee members and the

---

[1] Recall that the category of delegated decision making can be subdivided into three processes: executive, committee, and non-standard. The first two—executive and committee—are prone to motivational, ability, and fidelity limitations. The fidelity limitation manifests itself in three ways: (i) position protection, (ii) special interests, and (iii) corruption.

objective is to use the illusory alliance to increase the committee's wealth and power.

In both of these examples, true alliances have died and been replaced with illusory alliances.

ILLUSORY BENEFITS

Illusory benefits are alliance undertakings that appear proper and legitimate but actually are inconsistent with the objective(s) underlying an alliance. Illusory benefits constitute the ruse that allows illusory alliances to exist.

How does this work? Recall that the purpose of an alliance is to attain an objective desired by all of the members. In most alliances, the objective is oriented towards benefiting the members in some manner (for example, increasing the members' food, safety, well-being, and so on). As such, the alliance will undertake endeavors that attempt to achieve, further, or maintain the objective.

In fabricating an illusory benefit, the perpetrator will hone in upon the benefit sought to be provided by the alliance. This perpetrator will attempt to demonstrate that his proposal is consistent with and furthers the alliance objective, when in fact it does not. Instead, the proposal benefits the perpetrator, and any other individuals with whom he is conspiring. Nonetheless, the perpetrator will strive to cover up this fact and to convince alliance members that the proposal is legitimate.

Example 4 "Wild West"—Recall the variation of this example just discussed wherein the mercenary determines that the community should build a huge, expensive wooden wall around the community. The mercenary explains that the wall will keep out thieves and robbers. In reality, the mercenary has been bribed by a local lumberyard that will profit greatly from supplying lumber for the wall's construction. The illusory benefit, however, is that the wall will help reduce theft and robbery.

The same concept is applicable for charitable and justice objectives, notwithstanding the fact that there is no direct benefit to the members of the alliance. In this situation, the ruse is that the proposal furthers the well-being of the non-member individuals sought to be aided by the alliance.

Example 5 "Help the needy"—The proposal is to provide the needy with new mattresses to insure that they sleep well. This alleged furtherance of the healthy sleep of the non-members is the illusory benefit. The true reason underlying proposal, however, is to profit the members of the alliance holding stock in the mattress factory.

The concept of illusory benefits encompasses several different situations which are sometimes interrelated. In these situations, the proposal is perceived as furthering the alliance objective but in reality the proposal:

- Does not further the objective;

- Harms or otherwise impairs the objective; or

- Furthers the objective only marginally (such that any actual value associated with it is outweighed by the value placed on the contribution necessary to achieve it).

In these situations, the alliance members do not realize the real nature and purpose of the proposal. They have been duped and perceive the illusory benefit as constituting reality.

TYRANNY AND ILLUSORY ALLIANCES

A *tyranny* is a structure resembling an alliance in many respects except that there are no members and no accord. Instead, the purpose of a tyranny is the furtherance of the interests of the tyrant.

Tyrannies typically involve numerous individuals being compelled into contributing their resources into a combined effort. These individuals have not agreed to this contribution. There is no accord. There is no objective that they mutually desire. Instead, the tyrant has one or more objectives that he desires and he uses force to coerce individuals under his power to achieve his objectives using their resources.

Example 20 "Slavery"—Five individuals live in a tribal setting similar to the one described in Example 8 "Council of Elders." One day, raiders abduct these five individuals and take them to a far away land. They are then sold into slavery to an owner. Daily, the owner has the slaves combine their labor towards achieving objectives desired by him, including moving boulders, digging wells, and so on. These are objectives that can be achieved only by combined efforts. As such, the efforts resemble an alliance in some respects. However, the slaves never agreed to contribute their labors and do not desire the attainment of the objectives that they daily pursue. A tyranny is present.

Tyrannies are typically pictured as centering around one individual known as the "tyrant." This is not always the case. An alliance can constitute a tyranny towards other individuals. In this regard, the objective of the alliance is to create a tyranny towards non-members. The members of the alliance desire to exploit the resources possessed by these non-members and form an alliance to further and maintain this exploitation.

Example 20 "Slavery"—The owner of the five slaves is concerned that the slaves might attempt to escape. The owner forms an alliance with other slaveholders in the area to form search parties to hunt down any escaped slaves.[1]

Few individuals want to be known as tyrants. Tyrants never proclaim themselves to be "tyrants." Why is this? One reason seems to be a psychological tendency of most people to view their own actions as being justified and legitimate. For instance, even the most horrendous monsters of history seem to have somehow believed that they were good and decent persons. Another reason is revolution. The existence of a tyranny provides an excellent foundation for the creation of an opposing alliance. The members of this prospective revolutionary alliance would be the individuals exploited by the tyranny. The objective would be to destroy the tyranny and liberate exploited members. The resources contributed would typically be the life and limb risked in fighting the tyranny.

Because of these reasons, tyrannies often utilize illusory benefits to create the perception of an illusory alliance. In creating such an impression in the minds of the exploited individuals, the chances of a revolution are reduced and the tyrant's reign becomes more stable and productive.

Example 20 "Slavery"—The owner of the five slaves constantly explains to them how inferior and ignorant they are, mocks their prior hard and tough tribal life on the plains, and shows how fortunate they are to have been captured and brought to his civilized world as slaves. Further, the owner explains that, if the slaves are good, he might grant them their freedom and they can then acquire their own slaves. In articulating this position, the owner feels better about himself. Further, the slaves see partial truths in what he says and begin to feel that they are actually benefiting from the enslavement.

If the tyranny convinces the exploited individuals of the existence of the illusory benefits, the exploited individuals might become *illusory members* of an illusory alliance under some circumstances. These illusory members perceive themselves as being bona-fide members of an alliance that furthers objectives desired by them. In reality, these illusory members are the target of another alliance that is combining

---

[1]Note that this is an external objective under the sub-category of "Offense against Non-Members." The owners are combining their resources to target non-members with a combined effort.

the resources of its members to entrench the exploitation and deception of the illusory members.

THE TOOLS OF TYRANNY

It is probably rare that a tyranny succeeds in deluding the exploited individuals into actually believing that they are members of a mutually beneficial alliance. Nonetheless, the illusory benefits provided by a tyranny can tend to dilute revolutionary fervor. This is one of the many tools of tyranny.

Why do illusory benefits tend to dilute revolutionary fervor? The answer relates back to the reasons why alliances are formed. Any revolution against the tyranny will be brought by a revolutionary alliance consisting of the exploited individuals. For these individuals to enter the alliance, they must perceive the revolutionary alliance as providing a net benefit greater than the net benefit offered by the tyranny. In determining the perceived benefit of the revolutionary alliance, the potential members must consider many factors including the value of being free of the tyranny, the likelihood of success, and the value of the contribution such as risking life and limb. This perceived benefit, if positive, will then be compared to the perceived benefit of living under a tyranny. If the perceived benefit of the revolutionary alliance exceeds that of living under a tyranny, the individuals with such perceptions will join the alliance and revolt against the tyrant. However, the more the tyranny is perceived as providing benefits, the less individuals will be inclined to find that the revolutionary alliance offers a net benefit. In this situation, the individuals are likely to conclude that, although the tyranny is not particularly desirable, the net perceived benefit of a revolutionary alliance does not justify action. As such, these individuals would conclude that living in the tyranny is unfortunately the best option for them.[1]

Aside from issuing propaganda regarding illusory benefits allegedly provided by the tyranny, other tools available to tyrannies include:

- Suppressing information or knowledge tending to show that alternatives to the tyranny exist

- Issuing misinformation regarding the alleged limitations and failures of known alternatives to the tyranny

---

[1] If the tyrant's position is particularly weak and he is fearful of a revolution, life for the subjugated individuals might be fairly pleasant.

- Prohibiting any communications tending to expose the illusory nature of the benefits offered by the tyranny

- Forbidding any meetings or assemblies of exploited individuals whereby they might form a revolutionary alliance

- Preventing the illusory members from departing the illusory alliance or otherwise terminating their illusory membership

The common thread in all of these tools is the prevention of the exploited individuals from seeing a viable alternative to the tyranny. As part of these efforts, the tyranny will seek to suppress any knowledge of better alternatives and to raise the costs of forming a revolutionary alliance to the point where such an endeavor is not within contemplation. In most circumstances, the most effective tool of tyranny consists of restricting free communication and expression.

TYRANNICAL ALLIANCES

Occasionally, an actual, true alliance will exist but will nevertheless resemble a tyranny. This is a *tyrannical alliance*. In this situation, the members form an alliance and select a decision maker that behaves in many regards like a tyrant. Why would an alliance ever select such a decision maker? The reason is that the alliance perceives the decision maker as offering the only means of achieving the objective. Under this reasoning, the tyrannical aspects of the decision maker must be accepted in order to obtain the objective.

> **Example 8 "Council of elders"**—The tribe is repeatedly hit by the raiders and its future is in jeopardy. In desperation, the tribe retains a band of ten ruffians to protect the tribe from the raiders. These ruffians are expert fighters and are very effective at running off the raiders. But the price is quite steep. In retaining the ruffians, the tribe agrees to provide the raiders with substantial food and other material goods. Nonetheless, the ruffians demand more, frequently stealing things from and otherwise abusing tribe members. Although the tribe members despise these acts, they tolerate the situation because the ruffians provide the only means of fending off the raiders.

What is the difference between a tyrannical alliance and a tyranny? In a tyrannical alliance, individuals consent to the tyrannical aspects in order to receive a benefit of a combined effort. Although the individuals usually do not relish the situation, they have willingly agreed to submit to the tyrannical aspects in order to attain a desired objective. The sacrifices made to the tyrant constitute a form of contribution. In the preceding example, the combined material items furnished to the ruffians, as well as the toleration of the ruffians' improprieties, constitute the contribution submitted to attain the objective.

A tyrannical alliance can be best understood by considering it to be a caged monster of the alliance. When an enemy of the alliance approaches, the alliance opens the cage door and releases the monster upon the enemy. Because the creature is a monster, however, it cannot be controlled and it easily can turn upon the alliance members and harm them. This risk, though, is considered by the members to be worth it.[1]

COMBINED-EFFORT ENTITIES AND SEMI-ALLIANCES

The topics of illusory alliances, illusory benefits, and illusory members can substantially cloud analysis of alliances. Why? Because it is always possible that a seemingly true alliance is in reality an illusory alliance providing illusory members with illusory benefits.

To effectively discuss this subject, a description is required that encompasses both true alliances and apparent alliances. This term is "combined-effort entity." A *combined-effort entity* includes alliances and all other efforts that use combined efforts (or resources) of individuals to achieve certain objectives. All alliances are combined-effort entities, but not all combined-effort entities are alliances.

Combined-effort entities can be placed upon a spectrum that might make identification of their nature a little less difficult. On one end of the spectrum are true alliances while tyrannies are on the other end. In between these extremes are *semi-alliances* and illusory alliances.

True Alliance	Semi-Alliance	Illusory Alliance	Tyranny

True Alliance

A true alliance has the four essential elements: (i) members, (ii) an accord, (iii) contribution of resources, and (iv) an objective. The preceding chapters have discussed this concept extensively. One unusual true alliance is the tyrannical alliance discussed earlier in this chapter. Another curious alliance is the open-objective alliance that pursues objectives that are not desired by all members.

Semi-Alliance

A semi-alliance is an entity that stands between a true alliance and an illusory

---

[1] See Thomas Hobbs, Leviathan (1651).

alliance. It shares traits of both and therefore is difficult to place in either category. A semi-alliance is typically a long-standing, complex entity that pursues many objectives. At first glance, it appears to be a true alliance. Upon further scrutiny, however, it might appear that the entity is not pursuing objectives desired by all members. Instead, it might seem that the alliance is either (i) controlled by a decision maker subject to serious fidelity limitations, or (ii) the decision-making process is a majority vote and a slim majority is controlling the alliance and the objectives that it pursues. At the same time, however, the alliance might look as if it is acting in the interests of all members, at least to a certain extent. Overall, a semi-alliance will share traits of both a true alliance and an illusory alliance. If it is unclear as to whether an entity is a true alliance or an illusory alliance, it falls within a category of a semi-alliance.

Illusory Alliance

An illusory alliance is an entity that appears to be an alliance but is not in reality. Sham alliances founded to deceive the gullible and steal their contributions are illusory alliances. Also, true alliances might slide into illusory alliances when the decision makers become subject to fidelity limitations or when a majority vote takes control of a decision-making process to the detriment of minority members. Finally, tyrannies will often try to cloak themselves as illusory alliances by attempting to demonstrate that they provide valuable benefits to the individuals that they exploit.

Tyranny

A tyranny is a structure resembling an alliance in many respects except that there are no members and no accord. Instead, the purpose of a tyranny is the furtherance of the interests of the tyrant. The tyrant can be a single individual or a group of individuals constituting an alliance to impose a tyranny upon non-members. A tyranny typically fears the formation of revolutionary alliances whose purpose is to throw down the tyranny. A tyranny will use many tools to stifle the development of revolutionary alliances.

THE RELATIVE NATURE OF THE ANALYSIS

The analysis and categorization of combined-effort entities is a relative process. A particular entity, for instance, can constitute a true alliance to certain individuals and a tyranny to others. Other permutations are possible. For instance, an entity can represent a true alliance for some individuals and an illusory alliance for others.

> *Illustration*—Ten-thousand individuals reside on an island. One thousand of the individuals form an alliance with a primary purpose of enslaving the other

nine-thousand individuals. The one-thousand members combine their resources and efforts, enslave the other nine-thousand individuals, and profit as a result. A true alliance exists with regard to the one-thousand individuals. But this entity is a tyranny to the remaining nine-thousand individuals.

Illustration—Ten-thousand individuals reside on an island. One-thousand of the individuals form an alliance with a primary purpose of exploiting the other nine-thousand individuals. The one-thousand combine their efforts into creating an illusory alliance that dupes the other nine-thousand into believing that a true alliance exists. As a result of this arrangement, the one thousand manipulate the illusory alliance to covertly exploit the nine thousand and profit as a result. Again, a true alliance exists with regard to the one-thousand individuals. But this entity is an illusory alliance to the remaining nine-thousand individuals.

SECOND-CLASS MEMBERS

Second-Class Members (sometimes called "second-class citizens") are apparent members that are provided with less than the full range of benefits offered by a multi-objective alliance. For instance, an alliance might pursue objectives A, B, and C but certain members will be eligible to receive the benefits of only objective A. Why is this? There are several different answers.

In some situations, there is not a true alliance in place. Instead, the entity is either a semi-alliance or an illusory alliance. The decision-making process has been commandeered by a decision maker subject to a fidelity limitation or by a majority voting process. As a result of this seizure of the decision-making process, the alliance is undertaking objectives not in the interest of all members and is instead focusing upon the interests of another individual or group (for example, the decision maker(s), a special interest, and so on). But the entity is not a tyranny. It is acting somewhat like an alliance by pursuing objective A, which the second-class members desire.

In other situations, a combined-effort entity such as a semi-alliance or an illusory alliance might not be present. Instead, a true alliance might be present, but it consists of only the first-class members who receive the benefits of objectives A, B, C, and a fourth, subtle objective of D. Objective D is uniting against aggressors, where the second-class citizens are the aggressors. That is, the first-class, true members are concerned with some form of aggression (broadly defined) from the illusory, second-class members. As a result, the alliance pursues objective D which in effect is an effort to appease the second-class members. This appeasement is achieved by providing a benefit of the alliance, such as objective A, to the second-class members. Such an arrangement might be present if a ruling class feared an uprising of the non-member masses and therefore sought to appease the masses by guaranteeing them free bread. In this situation, the masses might perceive themselves as being members of the alliance.

Alternatively, the apparent alliance might actually be an alliance of two (or more) smaller alliances. In this case, there is an alliance of the first-class members and it pursues objectives B and C. It also forms an alliance with the second-class member alliance to pursue objective A. As a result, the second-class members receive only objective A and are excluded from participating in objectives B and C.

A related situation is present where an alliance of first class members will temporarily open its membership ranks to include other individuals to attain a particular objective. When the objective is achieved, the new members will be ejected from the membership. For instance, if an alliance requires additional manpower to defend against aggressors, it might temporarily allow additional individuals to join the alliance to fight off the attack (that is, generate a "critical mass" of members). When the attack is repulsed, the new members will be kicked out and denied other benefits of the alliance.

The apparent distinction between first and second class members might be artificial. Instead of a bifurcated membership, the alliance might have numerous decision makers. These decision makers might be afforded substantial privileges and perquisites as incentives and rewards for their service as decision makers. These items are not made available to the members (that is, the apparent second-class members). In this situation, a true alliance exists and it seeks to attain objectives for the benefit of all members. The additional benefits (that is, the privileges and perquisites) are not objectives of the alliance but instead constitute inducements to decision makers to perform their duties.

Often second-class membership is interwoven with class structure. If the social structure stratifies individuals into one or more classes, it is likely that each class will receive different benefits. It is also likely that each class will contribute different levels of contribution. If the contribution level for a particular class is less than the benefits received by that class, it is probable that an alliance is not present.

Overall, if second-class members are present, it is a sign that a true, single alliance is probably not in existence. Instead, something else is present. The situation must then be examined carefully to determine the true nature of the arrangement.

THE TRANSFORMATIONS OF COMBINED-EFFORT ENTITIES

When it comes to alliances and all four types of combined-effort entities, nothing is set in stone. Everything can change with the passage of time. This is not a new concept. Chapter 6 explored the beginnings, middles, and ends of alliances as well as the manners in which alliances evolve over time. It was shown that many alliances change as time passes, pursuing new objectives or adopting new operational strategies.

This concept of change is applicable to all four combined-effort entities. An entity in one category can be transformed into another entity. For instance, earlier it was noted how a true alliance might slide into an illusory alliance. Similarly, it was observed that a tyranny might attempt to portray itself as an illusory alliance. These types of transformations can occur among all of the categories of combined-effort entities.

True Alliance

A true alliance can easily transmute into a semi-alliance, an illusory alliance, or a tyranny. This transformation is usually the result of a decision-making process not functioning as intended. In more extreme examples, such as a tyranny, the transformation is often the result of a seizure of power by a very powerful delegated decision maker.

Semi-Alliance

A semi-alliance sits between a true alliance and an illusory alliance. The entity can shift towards a true alliance if it begins acting in the interests of all members. Or it can swing towards an illusory alliance, if the decision maker attempts to delude the members into thinking that objectives undertaken benefit them, when they in fact do not. As with a true alliance, a semi-alliance can transform into a tyranny if a decision maker seizes control of the alliance and runs it for his benefit.

Illusory Alliance

An illusory alliance can move towards a semi-alliance if the decision makers reduce efforts to delude members and begin pursuing objectives in the interests of all members. If the decision makers drop such efforts altogether, the illusory alliance might move all the way to a true alliance. Alternatively, if the decision makers decide to drop the ruse of an alliance and openly seize the alliance structure to boldly pursue their own interests, the illusory alliance will become a tyranny.

Tyranny

A tyranny can fear a counter alliance and attempt to stem revolutionary sentiment by cloaking itself as an illusory alliance. If revolutionary alliances grow powerful, a tyranny might actually transform itself into a semi-alliance to provide benefits to the purported members and therefore attempt to show that a revolution is unwarranted. Or, if the tyranny faces a threat from the outside, it might find that it can combat that threat only by transforming itself into a semi-alliance. In this situation, the reasoning would be that exploited individuals will not generate a sufficient combined effort to defeat the threat but that members of an alliance would. As such, the tyranny compromises by transforming into a semi-alliance, with the hope and expectation that it can transform back into a tyranny after the threat dissipates. If the outside threat is sufficiently substantial, a tyranny might conclude that it must become a tyrannical alliance in order to defeat the force. Finally, if the tyranny is faced with a revolutionary alliance and loses the fight, the revolutionary alliance could choose to retain the tyrant as its decision maker subject to the alliance structure, thus transforming the tyranny into a true alliance.

The concept of transformation of combined-effort entities is complex and can be bewildering. There will always be a tendency to view combined-effort entities as fixed, immutable structures. However, the reality is that such entities both change and transform themselves over time. Some go through this process very slowly and over thousands of years. Others go through the process in an instant. Yet the fact remains that transformation occurs.

CHAPTER 12

Loose Ends

This chapter contains a number of topics that do not properly fit into other chapters. As a result, there will not be a significant degree of concept progression in this chapter. Nonetheless, the topics discussed in the chapter are significant and assist in understanding alliances.

LIBERTY AND ITS DEPRIVATION

Liberty, also know as freedom, is the ability to act and do as one pleases. Liberty can be willingly surrendered to a combined-effort entity or liberty can be taken away by a combined-effort entity.

When willingly surrendered, liberty constitutes a resource that members of an alliance contribute towards achieving a mutually desired objective. For instance, Chapter 8 discusses the concept of law-compelled objectives. A law-compelled objective is an internal objective that is achieved by focusing upon the conduct of the members. In achieving a law-compelled objective, the members typically agree in the accord to perform, or not perform, an action. If all of the members behave as agreed, the objective will be achieved. By agreeing to behave in this way, members have contributed liberty. Specifically, the range of actions available to the members has been constrained (at least to some degree) and the members therefore have less freedom to do as they please.

When any resource including liberty is seized (that is, without the consent of members), a tyranny is present. As discussed in Chapter 11, a tyranny resembles an alliance in many respects except that there are no members and no accord. Instead, the purpose of a tyranny is the furtherance of the interests of the tyrant. Tyrannies typically compel individuals into contributing their resources (for example, labor, materials, money, and so on) towards a combined effort.

Tyrannies rarely seize liberty in order to attain an objective resembling a law-compelled objective. Instead, tyrannies take liberty only as protection against a revolutionary alliance. Appropriation of liberty is a very effective tool of tyranny because it can result in both (i) suppression of knowledge of better alternatives to the tyranny and (ii) raising the costs of forming a revolutionary alliance to the point where such an endeavor is not within contemplation.

In the case of a tyrannical alliance, a true alliance is present although it might not appear so at first. Recall that, in a tyrannical alliance, the decision maker is a tyrant that has been vested with substantial power and authority out of necessity. This occurs because the objective is of such a nature that it can be attained only by utilizing the tyrant as a means to an end (that is, usually something relating to defense against horrific attackers). In this situation, members grudgingly contribute liberty to the tyrannical alliance. This contribution is made only because the members see it as offering the only means of achieving a much desired objective.

COMPLAINTS ABOUT COMBINED-EFFORT ENTITIES

Complaints regarding a combined-effort entity can be revealing. These complaints can include:

- The objective is not desired

- The objective is not worth the contribution required to achieve it

- Better means exist to achieve the objective

- Another alliance is better suited for achievement of the objective

- Individual effort is better suited for achievement of the objective

If apparent "members" of alliances make such complaints, it is often a sign that a true alliance is not present. Instead, a combined-effort entity might be present such as a semi-alliance, illusory alliance, or a tyranny.

Importantly, the existence of such complaints should not be automatically equated with the non-existence of an alliance. Members of a true alliance might complain about deprivations of liberty without calling into question the validity of an alliance. In these situations, the members are usually questioning whether the value they place on the contributed liberty is in fact worth the benefit that they are receiving from the alliance. Such questions often constitute a call for a change or modification in the alliance rather than a condemnation of the alliance itself. Further, if complaining members are free to leave the alliance but do not leave, such a situation indicates a true alliance is present.

REVOLUTIONS

There are two kinds of revolutions: those from the inside and those from the outside.

Outside Revolutions

An *outside revolution* occurs when members form an alliance to challenge another alliance, or tyranny, that exploits or otherwise directly harms them. The members of an outside revolutionary alliance are typically enslaved or oppressed in some fashion. These members conclude that, if they combine their efforts in an alliance, they will be able to end their enslavement or oppression. The objective is external and falls within the category of "Offense against Non-Members." If an outside revolutionary alliance succeeds, the exploitative alliance or tyranny is usually destroyed.

> *Illustration*: An island is populated by hundreds of thousands of slaves. Weary of the bondage, the slaves form an outside revolutionary alliance that unites into a large force consisting of almost all slaves on the island. After multiple battles and a lengthy struggle, the alliance of slaves kills or drives off all slave owners. The slaves are now free.

> *Illustration*: A computer company develops an operating system that is present on most personal computers. Many programmers see the operating system as constituting a tyranny that restricts their programming freedoms. As a result, these programmers unite into various alliances to formulate competing operating systems and applications, with the objective being to liberate programming from the dominant operating system.

Inside Revolutions

An *inside revolution* occurs within an alliance and is in reality a sudden and drastic change in the alliance's accord. Recall that Chapter 6 addresses the two types of change in an alliance: contemplated change and fundamental change. In a *contemplated change*, an alliance is altered pursuant to a mechanism agreed upon in the underlying alliance. The alliance changes through a manner the members envisaged at the alliance's founding. On the other hand, a *fundamental change* pertains to an alteration of the accord underlying the alliance in a manner that was not planned or contemplated when the alliance was created. For instance, if an alliance is in the middle of its life and its accord is then substantially altered, there has been a fundamental change to the alliance.

An *inside revolution* is a form of a fundamental change, because it results in a sizeable change in the accord but the overall alliance structure remains substantially the same. What makes an inside revolution different from a run-of-the-mill change is that it is sudden and drastic. This distinction can be blurry at times. But, when an accord is changed swiftly and in a significant manner, a revolution has occurred.[1]

> *Illustration*: A new executive decision maker is selected to lead a large overarching governmental alliance of multiple alliances. The accord underlying the overarching alliance severely limits the objectives and means that might be undertaken. Due to the persuasive skills of the executive, the accord is reinterpreted to authorize the overarching alliance to undertake numerous objectives, and utilize various means, that were previously off limits. This change in the accord is so quick and extensive that it can be viewed as an inside revolution.

Sometimes, the distinction between an inside and outside revolution is difficult to ascertain. In these situations, the confusion arises because it is unclear whether the group demanding change is operating on the inside of the alliance, on the outside, or on both sides. For instance, the group might attempt to effect a sudden and drastic change to the accord underlying the existing alliance by lobbying within the existing decision-making process. At the same time, the group might form a competing alliance that attacks the existing alliance. The objective of this competing alliance is external and falls within the subcategory of "offense against non-members."

> *Illustration*: A very large, governmental alliance exists. A political party (that is, a separate alliance) seeks to institute fundamental changes in the overarching alliance structure of the alliance through *both* inside and outside revolutionary efforts. The inside efforts consist of fielding candidates for the elected offices. The goal is to have sufficient delegated decision makers in offices to effect a substantial change in the governmental alliance. The outside efforts include instituting guerilla attacks on the government alliance and blaming them on an opposition party. Using these attacks as a pretext for drastic change, the party institutes draconian measures on all members for the ostensible purpose of protecting the alliance and its members. The real reason for these measures, however, is to increase the power of the political power. Overall, through engaging in revolutionary activity both inside and outside of the alliance structure, the party has seized control of the alliance and is able to institute revolutionary changes to the alliance.

---

[1]Perhaps the best rule of thumb is to consider whether circumstances effectively have been turned upside down by the change. The expression "revolution" is reportedly derived from the concept of a change so drastic that the world has been turned, or "revolved," upon its head. Thus, if circumstances have only been modified, a run-of-the-mill fundamental change has occurred. On the other hand, if the state of affairs has been radically altered, there has been a revolution.

FORCED MEMBERSHIP

The concept of forced membership was touched upon in Chapter 3. Forced membership occurs when individuals are *compelled by circumstance* into becoming nominal members of an alliance. Although the individuals might appear to be members and might contribute resources, such individuals either do not desire the achievement of the objective or have substantial disagreements with the accord struck to achieve the objective. Nevertheless, due to other factors compelling membership, these individuals will nevertheless participate in the alliance to some degree.

Forced members should not be confused with victims of a tyranny. In a tyranny, the subjugated individuals really have no choice and must contribute resources to the tyrant. In contrast, a forced member has a choice to not participate in the alliance. By definition, a forced member does not really desire the objective but chooses to enter and stay in the alliance because of some other reason.

Forced members will tend to leave the alliance whenever possible. In addition, forced members will reluctantly contribute resources and will often undertake measures to avoid contribution. Finally, forced members are particularly likely to engage in revolutionary activities (inside and outside) against the alliance that they have been compelled to join.

ESPRIT DE CORPS

Esprit de corps is a mood or atmosphere pervading through the members of an alliance. The concept is generally associated with high morale, a sense of belonging, and a comradeship among the members. In addition, the presence of esprit de corps often results in enthusiastic contribution of resources to the alliance.

At times, the esprit de corps might be so great that members will donate a level of contribution that exceeds the value of what they receive from the alliance. Recall from Chapter 6 that members join an alliance only if the value they place on the contribution is less than the perceived value received from the attainment of the objective. As such, the perceived value of the contribution should always be less than the perceived value of the attained objective. If esprit de corps is present, however, members might contribute an amount over the perceived value of the attained objective. This excess amount is the value the members place in their esprit de corps sentiments for the alliance.

| Perceived Value of Contribution | − | Perceived Value of Attained Objective | = | Perceived Value of Esprit de Corps |

Esprit de corps is often but not always present in alliances. When it is present, it can come in two different forms:

1) an *effect* of the alliance, or

2) an *objective* of the alliance.

These two forms will be discussed separately.

ESPRIT DE CORPS AS AN EFFECT

When alliances are successful at attaining their objective(s), esprit de corps sentiments typically arise. This occurs because the members see the objective as being achieved and they are satisfied with the alliance. Further, the members might derive emotional enjoyment from participating in an effective, well-functioning alliance. And the members might develop strong bonds with their fellow members, especially if an intense effort or struggle is required to attain the objective. These factors add up to esprit de corps sentiments developing in many, but not all, successful alliances.

> **Example 5 "Help the needy"**—The members create the alliance to attain one objective (that is, helping the needy). The alliance is remarkably successful in achieving this objective and greatly improves the lives of many needy people. The members become very proud of the alliance and its achievements and derive gratification from participating in the alliance itself. Further, many close friendships develop among the members as they work together in the alliance. Over time, the members develop a feeling of unity and fondness towards fellow members and the alliance itself. The alliance is no longer a mere mechanism for attainment of a desired objective. It is now an important part of each member's life and self image.

> **Example 6 "Carpool"**—This alliance functions well and the children are efficiently and effectively transported to and from the soccer events. Due to the nature of the alliance, the member parents rarely see each other and have little interaction. Moreover, the members view the alliance as being rather mundane and of little consequence. For these reasons, no esprit de corps sentiments develop in the alliance.

Effect-based esprit de corps tends to reinforce itself. In this regard, the more successful an alliance is, the greater the esprit de corps is. When the esprit de corps increases, the effectiveness of the alliance tends to increase. This increase in effectiveness tends to increase esprit de corps. The number of self-reinforcing cycles that an alliance might experience depends upon the nature of the alliance.

Example 3 "Dig the well"—The ten primitive farmers are united in an alliance solely to achieve the objective of quickly digging a well. But, as they work together and make great progress on the digging, a feeling of brotherhood slowly overcomes the members. They regard each other highly and are excited to be working together. This esprit de corps makes the members work more quickly and effectively. As a result, the well is completed in a time no member thought was possible.

ESPRIT DE CORPS AS AN OBJECTIVE

At times, esprit de corps can be an objective of an alliance. In this situation, the members actively desire camaraderie and participate in the alliance to obtain this sentiment. These members tend to profess deep affection for the alliance and are often willing to contribute resources valued far more than what they receive from the original objective.

It is rare that members create an alliance for the express purpose of pursuing esprit de corps as an objective. When such alliances are created, they usually take the form of a club or society of persons with a common social or emotion-based interest. Examples might include fraternities, sororities, or social clubs.[1]

Typically, esprit de corps objectives tend to develop over time in an established alliance. In this common situation, members initially form an alliance to pursue one or more objectives that have nothing to do with esprit de corps. As the alliance works towards attainment of the objectives, esprit de corps will develop if the alliance is successful, if the members enjoy working together, and so on. These are the same reasons just discussed in effects-based esprit de corps.

As time passes, however, the esprit de corps becomes an actual objective of the alliance. Recall the earlier discussions of how alliances change over time and can expressly or impliedly undertake new objectives. In the case of esprit de corps, this

---

[1] An argument could be made that alliances are never formed to pursue esprit de corps as an objective. Even college fraternities and sororities, which by definition have a strong esprit de corps aspect, were initially formed to attain an objective other than esprit de corps. For instance, it appears that college fraternities developed to provide housing and food to all members while they attended college. As such, the original objective was to combine members' money to pay for common housing and food and therefore benefit from a combined effort. As the fraternity became successful at attaining this objective, fraternal sentiments, or an esprit de corps, developed and became an objective of the alliance. Today, this esprit de corps prevails and is usually the primary objective underlying college fraternities and sororities.

objective is usually undertaken impliedly and without much fanfare. Typically, an esprit de corps objective will be so ingrained in an alliance that members might not recognize its presence. Once esprit de corps becomes an objective, the alliance will undertake efforts to preserve or even further it.

> **Example 5 "Help the needy"**—The members originally create the alliance to attain one objective (that is, helping the needy). The alliance is very successful at achieving this objective and esprit de corps develops. The members take pleasure in the camaraderie and fellowship associated with the esprit de corps and attempt to further these sentiments by avoiding disharmony and conflict. In addition, the alliance institutes membership luncheons, parties, and other activities whereby members of the alliance can continue and expand upon their friendships and the overall esprit de corps. Moreover, the alliance adopts slogans and produces tee-shirts, hats, and other gadgets with the alliance's name upon them. These efforts are undertaken to emphasize, reinforce and further the esprit de corps associated with the alliance. Thus, without formally acknowledging it, the alliance has adopted esprit de corps as an objective, along with the original objective of helping the needy.

ASSOCIATION GLORY

Association glory is similar to esprit de corps but not the same. Esprit de corps is a sense of community or fellowship amongst the membership. In contrast, *association glory* is a pride-base emotion felt by members of the alliance. It is a feeling of honor or esteem stemming from a member's association with the alliance. It can take the forms of self-esteem flowing from being a member, public esteem by non-members towards members, and a combination of both types of esteem.

> **Example 5 "Help the needy"**—As time passes, the alliance develops a proud reputation and history of great achievements in helping the needy. The members derive self-esteem and satisfaction from their association with the alliance. Further, the members find that non-members regard them with honor due to their alliance memberships.

At times, association glory can be a small side effect of a successful alliance. At other times, association glory can actually become an objective of the alliance.

> **Example 5 "Help the needy"**—The alliance continues to develop a proud reputation and history of great achievements. As time passes, the alliance undertakes efforts to maintain and advance this reputation and history. For instance, when selecting endeavors to aid the needy, the alliance is predisposed towards selecting the most glamorous and high profile projects. The result is that the alliance usually undertakes efforts to help the needy that are not the

most effective measures. Although the alliance is attaining the objective of helping the needy, this objective has become secondary to achieving the objective of association glory.

Under certain circumstances, association glory can entirely eclipse the original objective. In this situation, the original objective typically remains in name only and the only true objective is to further association glory.

Example 5 "Help the needy"—The alliance continues to undertake endeavors for the professed purpose of helping the needy. However, the only true objective of the alliance is to increase its reputation. As such, the alliance decision-making process always selects the proposal that is most likely to increase the prestige of the alliance. At times, the process selects projects that do very little or nothing to actually help the needy but do greatly augment the alliance's reputation.

The dominance of association glory can be difficult to ascertain in most circumstances. This difficulty results because the alliance appears to pursue one or more of the original objectives, while it is actually pursuing association glory. Moreover, the members of the alliance will typically not realize that they are in fact pursuing association glory and that it is the controlling objective of the alliance. Instead, members will usually insist that the alliance is pursuing one or more of the original objectives.

In many circumstances, the dominance of an association-glory objective waxes and wanes over time. In these situations, association glory will dominate for a certain period of time and then recede into the background as the alliance resumes the pursuit of its original objectives. At some point in the future, the association-glory objective will then reassume its dominant role in the alliance.

Association glory sometimes dominates an alliance in the context of membership issues. As discussed in Chapter 3, alliances often require a critical mass of members to generate sufficient combined contribution to obtain the objective. Further, alliances often, but not always, benefit from additional members as a larger membership tends to reduce the contribution necessary to achieve the objective. As such, if an alliance is concerned with preserving or increasing its membership, it will tend to emphasize association glory in order to draw in and retain members. These potential members are attracted to the esteem that they will automatically acquire as consequence of joining the alliance.

THE BOOST EFFECT

The presence of either esprit de corps or association glory can significantly increase the performance of an alliance. Both of these phenomena act as a boost to an alliance's achievement of an objective. But this boost effect comes about in different ways.

With esprit de corps, the camaraderie typically results in more efficient interaction and more willing contribution of resources which in turn result in a more effective alliance. On the other hand, a concern with association glory will often cause members to strive to achieve an objective more effectively in order to increase the prestige and reputation of the alliance. When esprit de corps and association glory are both present in an alliance, the resulting boost can be quite substantial.

At times, esprit de corps or association glory can be so powerful as to result in surprising contributions of resources from members. As noted earlier, if a member contributes resources of a perceived value in excess of the perceived value of the attained objective, the excess is the degree to which the member values the esprit de corps associated with the alliance. The same holds true for association glory. The excess contribution represents the value placed upon the association-glory objective. Under certain circumstances, members will place such a high value on these phenomena—esprit de corps, association glory, or both—that they will contribute extraordinary resources to preserve or further them. These exceptional actions are sometimes seen as "sacrifices."

> **Example 5 "Help the needy"**—The alliance undertakes a major endeavor to bolster its prestige (and to help the needy). However, the alliance has miscalculated the resources needed to achieve the endeavor. If the effort fails, the alliance will suffer shame and humiliation. A member who particularly values the association glory of the alliance is very concerned with this failure and its consequences. As such, he provides the alliance with a massive contribution in part to make up for the shortfall, but also to preserve the alliance's reputation.

> **Example 8 "Council of elders"**—A band of raiders suddenly appears on the tribe's prairie. The Council of Elders meets and decides to move the tribe to a far away plain to escape. As the tribe is moving out of the prairie into a safe area, the raiders strike and begin to inflict heavy losses. Ten of the strongest members of the tribe stay behind to fight the raiders, knowing that they are overmatched and will have no chance of victory. These ten are killed by the raiders but the diversion they cause allows the rest of the tribe to survive. These ten were strong and agile and were able to flee ahead of the other tribe members to escape into the safe area. However, because of their love for the tribe and its long and proud history, these ten decided to contribute their lives to the alliance and stay behind.

The boost effect can also cause alliances that normally would have terminated to continue on longer than expected. In these situations, circumstances changed such that the alliance no longer offers a net perceived value to its members (that is, in terms of the original objectives) and a termination is therefore imminent. However, the presence of either esprit de corps or association glory will provide the added value to members justifying the continued existence of the alliance.

> **Example 2 "Slay the mammoth"**—The alliance originally forms because only a combined effort of twenty individuals could kill a mammoth. As time passes, new and more powerful weapons are developed that allow smaller groups or even individuals to slay mammoths. As such, it would seem that the original alliance of twenty individuals would provide no net perceived value and the alliance would terminate. However, a very strong esprit de corps has developed within the alliance. As a result, the twenty individuals continue to hunt together because they enjoy the camaraderie associated with the alliance.

COMBINED-EFFORT ENTITIES AND THE BOOST EFFECT

The phenomena of esprit de corps and association glory are not limited to alliances. Both are effects of group dynamics and therefore can develop whenever humans interact in a coordinated manner. Because all combined-effort entities (that is, true alliance, semi-alliance, illusory alliance, and tyranny) utilize group interactions, esprit de corps or association glory can occur in all of these entities, including a tyranny.

> **Example 20 "Slavery"**—The owner of the five slaves usually has them work together in a coordinated effort. Over time, an esprit de corps develops from the five working together. Furthermore, the slaves are very successful at achieving the tasks given to them. As a result, they develop a reputation for their ingenuity and devotion to work. The five slaves are very proud of this reputation and strive to maintain it.

Because of the boost effect, combined-effort entities other than true alliances will often strive to create or further both esprit de corps and association glory. The combined-effort entities by and large recognize that the presence of these phenomena can make the exploited individuals work more efficiently and effectively. Furthermore, the presence of esprit de corps and association glory can serve to reduce the attraction of a revolutionary alliance. This result occurs because the perceived value associated with either esprit de corps or association glory will offset the negatives associated with the combined-effort entity.

> **Example 20 "Slavery"**—The owner of the five slaves observes the presence of both esprit de corps and association glory in the slaves. The owner encourages these sentiments because they tend to make the slaves forget their prior lives and to actually enjoy their new, enslaved life.

Illusory alliances will often attempt to create esprit de corps or association glory in the illusory members. Recall that an illusory alliance appears to be a valid functioning alliance that pursues objectives desired by all its members. In reality, an illusory alliance furthers objectives of only one individual or a small group of individuals, rather than those of the illusory members. Sometimes, esprit de corps and association glory can constitute illusory benefits for the illusory members.

Example 19 "The Alleged Army"—The unscrupulous Rex creates an illusory alliance of 100,000 illusory members to contribute money towards an apparently competent, but actually worthless, army to defend them. Aside from parading the army around for the members to see, Rex begins publicizing the alleged power and capabilities of the army. Rex declares to the illusory members that the army is the finest instrument of war ever created. The illusory members derive esteem and honor from being associated with this allegedly amazing army. Furthermore, Rex asserts that the members of the alliance are "comrades" and insists that they refer to each other as "comrades." Rex does this to develop camaraderie amongst the members. Because the members contribute only money to the alliance (to fund the army), there is no real interaction between members and therefore not much potential for esprit de corps to develop. As such, Rex's effort to artificially create esprit de corps fails.

RATING THE COMBINED-EFFORT ENTITIES

As noted earlier, there are four combined-effort entities: (i) true alliance, (ii) semi-alliance, (iii) illusory alliance, and (iv) tyranny. What generalizations can be drawn about their relative performances?

As a general rule, a true alliance tends to be more effective and efficient at achieving an objective, in comparison to the other combined-effort entities. One reason lies in the fact that the members have purposefully joined the alliance to attain the objective and willingly contribute resources to its achievement. Another factor is that true alliances are more prone to developing esprit de corps and association glory which tend to boost performance of the alliance.

In contrast, a tyranny is usually the least effective and efficient at achieving an objective. Individuals exploited by tyrannies do not willingly contribute resources. Instead, the tyranny must expend resources upon seizing resources from the exploited individuals and otherwise coercing them either directly or indirectly into participating in the tyranny's effort. In addition, a tyranny is not likely to generate much esprit de corps or association glory and therefore will not have the boost typically associated with true alliances.

In the middle of these two extremes are semi-alliances and illusory alliances. The relative performances of these vary with the circumstances. They are usually better than tyrannies, but not as good as true alliances.

The notion that a true alliance is the most effective and efficient is only a generalization. Numerous other factors including the decision-making processes used in each combined-effort entity and good (or bad) luck can affect whether a particular true alliance will perform better than another combined-effort entity.

ALLIANCES *WITHIN* AN ALLIANCE STRUCTURE

Chapter 3 identified the concept of an alliance of alliances. In this situation, two or more alliances form a larger alliance. The alliances that form the larger alliance constitute members and the same concepts of alliances are applicable to this arrangement. For instance, Alliances A, B, and C might determine that a mutually desired objective can be attained more efficiently or effectively through a combined effort. As such, the three alliances form an arch-alliance whereby Alliances A, B, and C are all members. These three members combine their resources to achieve the objective in the same manner that individual humans might operate.

A different concept is alliances *within* an alliance. In this situation, small alliances form within the framework of a larger alliance. An essential aspect of this larger alliance is that it pursues and enforces a Law-Compelled Objective pertaining to Enforcement of Promises. It is this Law-Compelled Objective that allows smaller alliances to flourish. Recall that a core element of an alliance is an accord. An accord is an agreement between the members which typically consists of mutual promises. If promises cannot be enforced, accords are largely meaningless and alliances will either fail or not be entered into in the first place.

What is the significance of this point? It is that a promise-enforcement mechanism is crucial to the creation of many alliances. It provides an environment in which smaller alliances between members might originate, develop, and thrive.

Example 11 "Enforcement of promises"—The alliance is created whereby broken promises will be remedied. Several thousand farmers in the valley are members of the alliance. Although the primary purpose of the alliance is to enforce work-sharing agreements among farmers, the alliance is soon adjudicating promise-breaking disputes pertaining to smaller alliances formed within the greater alliance. For example, ten farmers form an alliance to dig a well. Three of the farmers do not contribute to the digging as promised. The decision-making process of the alliance finds that these three failed to supply the required contribution and awards the other members compensation. The other thousands of farmers in the valley see how the alliance can make forming smaller alliances possible. Specifically, the accords underlying the alliances can actually be enforced. As a result, all types of small alliances begin forming in the valley. And the farmers all benefit greatly from the combined efforts.

Not all alliances require an overarching promise-enforcement mechanism in order to start and flourish. However, the effect that such an environment can have on the birth and successful development of alliances cannot be overstated. As observed in Chapter 6, individuals choose alliances when the net value of a combined effort exceeds that of an individual effort. Often, alliances offer superior value in theory. The problem is reality. Although an alliance might make perfect conceptual sense, it is worthless if the members cannot be held to their promises and commitments. As a result, in the absence of an effective enforcement mechanism, members stick with individual efforts because the real-world value of an alliance with an unenforceable accord is negligible.

An arch-alliance that enforces promises changes the entire situation. It makes the theoretical value associated with an alliance a reality. As such, individuals are much more likely to create, and maintain, alliances in an environment where promises are enforced.

OUTSOURCING AND THE ENFORCEMENT OF PROMISES

Chapter 6 raised the subject of outsourcing. Recall that outsourcing is a form of individual effort. But, instead of achieving the objective through one's own effort, an individual retains another to attain the objective (or to aid the individual in attaining the objective). The individual then compensates this individual in some fashion with resources. Importantly, no alliance is involved in this situation. There are no members and there is no combination of resources to attain a mutually desired objective. Instead, the individual attains the objective individually except that he outsources the effort to another. Outsourcing is relevant to alliance analysis because it offers another option for an individual to consider in attaining an objective. An individual can weigh the costs and benefits associated with: (i) a purely individual effort, (ii) an outsourced individual effort, or (iii) an alliance effort.

An alliance with a promise-enforcement mechanism can have a profound effect upon the ability of individuals to outsource efforts. In the absence of such a mechanism, individuals have few tools to enforce promises. These devices are generally limited to avoiding disreputable persons, requiring collateral or some type of security, and self-enforcement in the form of force or violence. These tools have many limitations and, for this reason, outsourcing is often not available.

A promise-enforcement mechanism supplements these tools immensely and allows much more outsourcing of effort. With a promise-enforcement mechanism, individuals can retain others to attain objectives for them with many more expectations of a successful relationship. The knowledge that one can enforce a promise made or otherwise attain a remedy against a promise-breaker will make outsourced efforts much more viable. Further, because a promise can be enforced against the outsourcing individual, those retained to attain the objectives will be much more willing to enter into the transaction. In the absence of a promise-enforcing mechanism, these individuals doing the outsourced work would be much less likely to take on the work.

OUTSOURCING AND MONEY

Chapter 5 discussed the concept of money as a resource and its effect upon alliances. The development of money has had an important effect upon the nature and growth of alliances. Before money, most organizations could arise only if a sufficient number of members were able to contribute very specific types of resources towards achievement of the objective. The appearance of money has served as a highly effective means of bridging the gap between individuals possessing differing types of resources. Money allows potential members lacking the requisite resource to instead contribute an acceptable amount of money in its place.

Money has had similar effects upon the ability of individuals to outsource efforts. Without money, an individual can outsource an effort only if he possesses a resource desired by the person performing the effort. For instance, if a person's only resource is corn, he can outsource an effort only if he can locate a person willing to work for corn. Money, on the other hand, is accepted by everyone. A person possessing nothing but corn can sell it and obtain money. The person can then use the money to outsource an effort to another at a price the two agree upon. As such, along with promise-enforcement mechanisms, money has a substantial effect upon one's ability to outsource efforts.

OBJECTIVE CREEP

The concept of objective creep was touched upon in Chapter 5 in discussing the significance of the accord. Objective creep is the adoption by an alliance of a new objective without a clear recognition that a new objective has been in fact adopted. The objectives that creep in are usually either ones (i) that are not desired by all or most members, or (ii) where there is no net benefit to a combined-effort and individual action is preferable. As the term "creep" implies, the new objectives slip into the alliance without fanfare or notice of their true nature.

Example 4 "Wild West"—To bring order and decency to the community, the alliance delegates broad authority to the mercenary to determine what "order and decency" comprises and what means should be used to achieve this objective. At the outset, the means selected by the mercenary are fairly straightforward and include violence, prison, and executions.

Over time, though, the mercenary begins undertaking new means which he asserts are intended to achieve this objective. One means is free education. The mercenary claims that free education will provide moral instruction to potential criminals that will keep them out of a life of crime. Another means is banning the consumption of alcohol. The mercenary alleges that alcohol consumption often results in violence and banning it will decrease crime.

Are these two new endeavors means to achieve the objective of order and decency? Or are the new endeavors really entirely new objectives that have crept into the alliance? It is not clear. But a strong case can be made that new objectives of Morality/Bolstering (that is, the education program) and Paternalism (that is, banning of alcohol consumption) have been unofficially adopted by the alliance.

Single-objective alliances are not likely to exhibit objective creep. Single objective alliances are usually short-lived and terminate immediately after the objective has been attained. Further, objective creep rarely appears in alliances with specific accords. As discussed in Chapter 4, specificity usually prevents new objectives from creeping in.

Alliances with indefinite accords are particularly prone to objective creep. As addressed in Chapter 4, the accords underlying these types of alliances are either indefinite express accords or indefinite implied accords. The common factor is the indefiniteness in the objective. This lack of clear parameters allows new objectives to slowly creep into the alliance without much notice.[1]

Objective creep can serve to lengthen the life of alliances. As discussed earlier, alliances often have to change in order to adapt to new circumstances. Objective creep offers a mechanism for an alliance to slowly adjust to these new situations. This feature serves to preserve alliances and often to fulfill the desires of the members.

Objective creep can also serve to shorten the lives of alliances by increasing the contribution required of the members, decreasing the perceived value of the alliance, or both. In this regard, an alliance generally requires more contribution for

---

[1]Alliances with open objectives do not have objective creep. This is because the accord in an open alliance places no limitations upon the objectives that might be pursued.

each objective that it undertakes. As new objectives slowly creep into an alliance, the requisite contribution typically increases as well. After a while, the perceived value of the contribution can exceed the perceived value of the alliance and termination becomes likely. In addition, the objective creep can cause displeasure in many members. This displeasure might stem from the undertaking of objectives that appeal to only a portion of members and are opposed by another portion of members. This situation can serve to decrease the perceived value of the alliance to the point that termination is imminent. The combination of these two factors is particularly likely to result in termination.

Aside from typically appearing in alliances with indefinite objectives, objective creep is often present in alliances with poorly functioning decision-making processes. As noted in Chapter 7, decision-making processes suffer from three broad types of limitations:

- Motivational limitations

- Capability limitations

- Fidelity limitations with three sub-areas of: (i) position protection, (ii) favoring a special interest, and (iii) corruption.

Objective creep will often occur if one of these limitations is present. For instance, if a decision maker is lacking in motivation or capability, the decision maker might allow in an objective that does not properly fit in the alliance. Or, if a decision maker is lacking in fidelity, the decision maker might select an objective to protect its position, reward a special interest, or derive a corrupt benefit.

Chapter 7 also raised the issue of the swing vote. The presence of a powerful swing vote can cause objectives to creep into the alliance that appear inconsistent with its original conception. In this situation, the power of the swing vote causes the decision maker to undertake an objective favorable to the swing voters, but not necessarily to other members.

Because objective creep in most often associated with indefinite or open objectives, it can be avoided by explicit identification of the objective in the underlying accord or by prohibiting the alliance from undertaking new objectives. Another useful manner to avoid objective creep is to prohibit the alliance from using certain means in achieving objectives. If an alliance does implement these limitations in its accord, it will have to exhibit diligence to enforce the accord and its limitations.

Such specificity, however, does have consequences. An alliance with such a rigid accord will be static and unable to address new situations or circumstances.

OBJECTIVE DISGUISE

How do objectives "creep" into alliances? What allows them to slip in without much notice? The answer is that creeping objectives are often in a disguise. Objective disguise occurs when a new objective undertaken by an alliance is disguised as a means to achieve an existing objective.

> **Example 5 "Help the needy"**—The alliance begins an annual tradition of having an extravagant party at year's end. The rationale for the party is that it will draw more members to the alliance and therefore increase the total contribution that can be used to help needy. In reality, the proponents of the party merely desire to have an elaborate party paid with membership contributions. But these proponents disguise the new objective as a means to achieve the original objective of helping the needy.

> **Example 4 "Wild West"**—The mercenary begins addressing broken promises. If one member breaks a promise to another, the mercenary will hear out each side. If the mercenary agrees that a promise has been broken, he will order the promise breaker to make amends. When asked why he is adjudicating broken promises, the mercenary asserts that it is crucial to preserving order and decency. In reality, the alliance has undertaken an entirely new objective. The original objective of order and decency was an external objective targeting thieves and murders. The new objective is an internal objective focusing upon the conduct of the members. Nonetheless, the novelty of this objective is disguised by the contention that it is means of achieving order and decency.

In these examples, the alliances have effectively undertaken entirely new objectives. But the novelty of these new objectives is not recognized. Instead, circumstances have made it appear that the alliances selected only a new means to achieve well-established objectives.

Objective disguise can be intentional or it can be accidental. If a delegated decision-making process has been compromised by fidelity limitations, objective disguise is a very valuable tool for masking the true nature of the decision maker's actions. For instance, if a decision maker is corrupt, he might select a proposal that personally enriches him. But he will conceal this personal profit by asserting that the proposal is a mere means to achieve an existing objective. Similarly, if a decision-making process of any kind is subject to a powerful lobby, objective disguise will provide an equally powerful tool to obscure the reality of a proposal. For instance, if an alliance makes decisions by a 51% majority vote of members, objective disguise can be used to trick swing voters into seeing a new objective as only a means to achieve an existing objective.

Objective disguise that develops accidentally is probably less common. In general, it will develop unintentionally if the decision-making process is sloppy and fails to recognize that the alliance is in fact adopting an entirely new objective.

What are the consequences of objective disguise? The primary consequence is that an alliance will tend to become unstable and prone to termination. The reasons for this likely development are the same as those discussed with respect to objective creep. As objective disguise allows more objectives to enter the alliance, the members question the perceived value of the alliance and the alliance tends to become unstable. If the members determine that the perceived value of the contribution is exceeded by the perceived value of the alliance, termination is imminent. An additional consequence is that objective disguise tends to thwart the efficient functioning of an alliance. Alliances are formed either expressly or impliedly upon a notion that only certain objectives will be pursued by the alliance. Members desire these objectives and therefore contribute resources towards their attainment. If new objectives are proposed, they should be recognized as such and the members should be given the opportunity to determine whether they are willing to contribute resources towards their attainment. But, if new objectives are disguised as means, this process breaks down and the alliance will tend to not function as efficiently.

As a final matter, a distinction should be drawn between objective disguise and illusory benefit. These concepts are similar in that they both pertain to deceptive situations. But they are not the same. An illusory benefit is present only in non-alliances such as a tyranny or an illusory alliance. The purpose of an illusory benefit is to trick individuals into thinking that they are in an alliance or to otherwise dissuade individuals from revolting against a tyranny. In contrast, objective disguise is present in true alliances (and semi-alliances) and constitutes a mechanism for concealing the true nature of an undertaking.

INDIRECT ATTAINMENT

A concept closely related to objective disguise is indirect attainment. Indirect attainment is achievement of an objective through a circuitous or roundabout method. At times, indirect attainment can constitute a bona fide method of actually achieving an objective. At other times, indirect attainment is used as a smokescreen to disguise the true objective being pursued. In this latter situation, indirect attainment is a part of an objective-disguise effort.

All alliances use means to achieve their objectives. In most circumstances, alliances will employ means that *directly* accomplish the objectives.

Example 4 "Wild West"—The mercenary uses direct means of force and imprisonment to attain the objective of order and decency. If a marauder appears in the community, the mercenary either runs him off using weapons or imprisons him.

Example 5 "Help the needy"—The direct means are the food and shelter provided to the needy. Provision of these items aids the needy to overcome their circumstances.

At times, though, alliances will use means that *indirectly* attain the objective.

Example 4 "Wild West"—The mercenary dictates that all employers in the community must pay a minimum wage to laborers. The mercenary contends that higher wages will draw individuals into the workforce and away from a life of theft and murder. And, as a consequence, order and decency will be indirectly attained.

Example 5 "Help the needy"—The alliance provides job-skill training to the needy. It is thought that the training will allow the needy to find good employment and therefore raise themselves out of their circumstances. Although the training does not alleviate the plight of the needy, it is hoped that the training will indirectly result in improvement of their situation.

Although indirect attainment is often a logical means of attaining a given objective, it can be manipulated to serve as camouflage disguising the true objective. In this situation, indirect attainment is a part of objective disguise.

Example 5 "Help the needy"—The alliance undertakes the annual extravagant party as ostensible means of increasing contribution that will then have the effect of aiding the needy. In reality, the members advocating the party merely desire a party, regardless of the effect that it might have on contribution. But these members have disguised this objective by pointing to the indirect effects of the party (that is, allegedly helping the needy in a roundabout fashion through purported increased contribution).

Example 7 "Buy the boat"—One of the members advocates the alliance purchasing expensive scuba diving equipment. In support of this proposal, the member contends that the equipment will serve an important means of maintaining the boat. Specifically, he argues that members can use the scuba equipment to inspect and clean the underside of the boat. In reality, this member desires for the alliance to undertake a new objective (that is, pooling resources towards the purchase of expensive scuba equipment to be used exploring reefs and other underwater sights). But the member conceals this true objective by asserting that the equipment is a legitimate means for maintaining the boat.

Indirect attainment is a tool typically used by compromised delegated decision makers to mask their fidelity limitations. Why is this? It is rare, if not impossible, for delegated decision makers to actually admit that they are subject to fidelity limitations. As such, delegated decision makers usually employ an indirect-attainment rationale to validate improper undertakings.

Example 4 "Wild West"—The mercenary retains a company to build a large, expensive wall around the community. The company has secretly bribed the mercenary handsomely. When asked about the need for such an expensive wall, the mercenary explains that he expects it will keep the thieves and criminals out and therefore will indirectly result in order and decency within the community. The mercenary is concealing his corruption by citing to an alleged indirect attainment of the objective.

Example 8 "Council of elders"—The council orders the tribe members to provide them with food, clothing, and shelter. The elders assert that they are too busy serving and that having these items provided to them will increase the effectiveness of the council. In reality, the elders have plenty of time to find their own food, clothing, and shelter. They are just lazy but hide this fact with an indirect-attainment contention.

Example 12 "Conservation"—The alliance has a delegated decision maker that decides what items are to be conserved. The decision maker decrees that no more farmland in the community might be developed. The purported rationale is to reduce the consumption of water. In reality, the decision maker owns a number of farms. By putting a hold on farming developments, the decision maker limits the supply of produce and increases the profitability of his farming operations. But the decision maker obscures his own profit by contending that he is attaining the objective of conserving water through limiting farming.

Example 13 "Moral obligations"—The religious alliance has a delegated decision maker who is charged with seeing that the members follow the proper rituals. If these rituals are followed, it is contemplated that the deity will be pleased and the members will benefit. The decision maker institutes a rule that all members must contribute a large portion of their earnings to the alliance each week in order to fund the construction of temples and shrines. In reality, the decision maker intends to steal large portions of the contribution for his own enrichment.

Example 15 "Leveling"—A delegated decision maker is charged with possessing all material wealth of members over the determined threshold. This decision maker announces that, instead of holding the material wealth, he will destroy it. This is necessary, the decision maker states, because it has become too difficult to store the various items and that he can do a better job of leveling if he destroys the excess property. In reality, the decision maker is not destroying the wealth. Although he asserts to everyone that he is destroying it, he is really hiding it away for his own profit.

Overall, an indirect-attainment strategy can be a valuable means of achieving a selected objective. However, the concept can also be used to camouflage the undertaking of new objectives or to conceal the fidelity limitations of delegated decision makers.

ONE MEANS FOR MULTIPLE OBJECTIVES

As the foregoing discussion of indirect attainment demonstrated, the relationship between means and objectives can become cloudy at times. In particular, analysis of an alliance might reveal numerous questions regarding the identity of the true objective underlying the alliance and whether the selected means is actually furthering another, unstated objective. Care should be taken, however, in equating a cloudy means/objective relationship with situations of either objective disguise or a compromised decision maker. Another source of the murkiness might be the fact that the means in question is intended to attain two or more objectives.

Often, an alliance will use a single means to attain multiple, independent objectives. If one fails to take this possibility into account, one might be tempted to conclude that the true objective has somehow been disguised. By recognizing that multiple objectives can be addressed by the same means, the actual situation is much clearer.

Consider, for instance, an alliance that provides free education to anyone (that is, including members and non-members). Is education the objective? Or is it the means to attaining some other objective? There is no universal answer. But, most likely, education is the means to achieving several typical categories of objectives discussed in Chapters 8 and 9, including both internal and external objectives. Consider the following table:

Objective	Internal or External?	Explanation
Cooperative	Internal	Pool resources to provide for education of children of all members
Charity and Justice	External	Satisfy the desire of members to educate non-members
Morality-Bolstering	Internal	Education has the effect of improving the ability of alliance members to contribute resources to other alliance endeavors
Paternalism	Internal	Compelling members to do what is in their best interests
Defense Against Aggressors	External	Providing education to non-members will tend to enlighten them and reduce the likelihood of violence and theft from non-members
Generation of Prosperity	Internal and External	Educated members (as well as non-members) will be more productive workers which will increase the prosperity of all

Situations such as this one will occur in longstanding, complex alliances. Sorting out the objectives sought to be furthered by a particular means can be bewildering at times. Nonetheless, after careful examination of the circumstances, one might find that a particular means utilized by an alliance is in fact resulting in the attainment of multiple objectives.

BLURRING OF MEANS AND OBJECTIVES

In a simple alliance, the distinction between means and an objective attained by those means is usually evident. In most cases, an observer can see a direct, causal relationship between the means undertaken and the achievement of the objective.

Example 4 "Wild West"—The area is overrun with murderers and thieves. The alliance's objective is to attain "order and decency" by ending the reign of murderers and thieves. The means to this end is the mercenary (as well as his weapons and the force that he will utilize to run off the murderers and thieves).

As alliances become more complex, however, this distinction will tend to be less obvious and means might begin to resemble objectives.

Example 4 "Wild West"—The population of the community grows substantially over time. As a result, the mercenary's operations grow as well. The mercenary hires individuals to serve as deputy mercenaries, investigators, jailers, clerks, and so on. Soon, the mercenary has become the largest employer of the area and has a sizeable economic effect upon the community. The employees spend money in the local establishments and are generally thought to improve the prosperity of the community. The members take note of this fact and begin to believe that the mercenary should be maintained because of his positive economic effects upon the area. Additional funding is provided to support the hiring of more employees, although they are not needed to attain the objective of "order and decency."

In this example, the distinction between means and objectives has blurred. The mercenary is still serving as a means of attaining "order and decency." But the mercenary (and the positive economic effect associated with the mercenary) has become an objective as well. By retaining the mercenary, the alliance is pursuing two objectives: (i) Defense against Aggressors (that is, the murderers and thieves), and (ii) Generation of Prosperity (that is, create more wealth through stimulus spending).

As time passes, a means might be transformed fully into an objective.

Example 4 "Wild West"—As more time passes, order and decency are fully attained and there are no more murderers and thieves. It would appear that the objective underlying the alliance has been achieved and that the alliance should dissolve. Nonetheless, the alliance continues to fund the mercenary. The sole reason for the funding is the positive economic effect associated with the mercenary and his employees. As such, the means has now become an objective. That is, the fundamental purpose of the alliance is now to provide jobs and its objective has been changed from Defense against Aggressors into Generation of Prosperity.

The blurring of means and objectives is a confusing topic. Nevertheless, it is imperative that the issue be considered when analyzing complex, longstanding alliances.

MIXED-MOTIVE ALLIANCES

A mixed-motive alliance occurs when the members view and identify the objective(s) underlying the alliance differently. This situation can be caused by:

- *Means Achieving Multiple Objectives*—The members see the means as achieving different objectives. For instance, one group of members sees a means as attaining Objective A, another group sees the means as attaining Objective B, and a third group sees the means as attaining both Objectives A and B.

- *Blurring of Means and Objectives*—Some members see an endeavor as constituting a means to attaining an objective. Others view the same endeavor as an objective in and of itself.

What is the effect of a mixed-motive alliance? A mixed-motive alliance can function just as an ordinary alliance (where all of the members view and identify the objective the same way). However, mixed-motive alliances are often unsuccessful and unstable.

One reason for this tendency is the lack of coordination and unity of purpose. Because the members are "not on the same page," confusion and disorder can result when the alliance attempts to pool its resources into a combined effort. For instance, if a decision must be made, the decision-making process might become paralyzed by the different perspectives underlying the alliance. Some participants might advocate one approach which is consistent with their view of the objective. Other participants might push a contradictory approach which is nonetheless consistent with their view of the objective. Disharmony will result and the alliance will tend to fail.

Another cause of failure lies in contribution. If members view the objective underlying the alliance differently, they will tend to value the contribution supplied to the alliance much differently. As discussed in Chapter 6, the formation and existence of an alliance is directly related to the perceived benefit that it offers to its members. As such, if the members view the objective from substantially different perspectives, they will tend to place widely different values upon the contribution supplied to the alliance. The potential for these wide disparities can result in the inabilities to agree upon a suitable level of contribution in many situations. The result will be that the alliance will tend to not form or will subsequently fail.

Overall, a mixed-motive alliance is essentially a question of degree. If the differences over the objective underlying the alliance are not substantial or pervasive, the alliance will likely function and will attain some success (although a true alliance would tend to function much better). However, if the differences are sizeable and widespread, an alliance is not present. And anything that seems to resemble an alliance is probably best viewed as a semi-alliance or even an illusory alliance.

DEMOCRACY

What is a democracy? A democracy is nothing more than a name for a decision-making process used by a true alliance. Democracies can be divided into two broad categories: (i) pure democracies, and (ii) republics.

Pure Democracies

A pure democracy is a decision-making process by membership vote. All members of the alliance participate, or at least are eligible to participate, in a decision by casting a vote. The alliance's accord provides for the proportion of votes necessary for a proposal to constitute the decision of the alliance. Most often, this proportion is a simple majority. As was discussed in Chapter 7, other options include a plurality, a super majority, or unanimity.

Republics

A republic is a combination of membership voting and a delegated decision-making process. Republics are examples of decision-making processes that have multiple tiers and are interwoven. In its most simple form, a republic consists of (i) a membership vote to select an executive decision maker, and (ii) a single delegated executive decision maker to make all decisions. But infinite permutations are possible. Typically, most republics are characterized by a membership vote on selecting certain upper echelon executive and committee decision makers. The upper echelon executive and committee decision makers then make all of the decisions. In more complex republics, the upper echelon decision makers will delegate numerous decisions to executive and committee decision makers under their authority. These decision makers might then delegate a portion of decisions down to subordinate decision makers. Regardless of its structure, the common feature in a republic is that upper echelon delegated decision makers are selected by membership vote. In some republics, the members have further influence such as holding the sole authority to amend or modify the accord underlying the alliance or holding the authority to override the delegated decision makers through a referendum.

It is important to underscore that a democracy undertakes only those objectives desired by its members. Thus, a democracy can wholly ignore the interests of non-members. And a democracy can even constitute a tyranny to non-members.

As discussed in Chapter 7, the different types of decision-making processes have a variety of relative strengths and weaknesses. At times, an alliance might find that a democracy—either a pure democracy or a republic—is best suited to attain the objective. At other times, an alliance might conclude that a democracy is not suitable and that a permanent delegated decision maker (committee, executive, or both) is preferable.

SOVEREIGN

A sovereign is a delegated decision-making process and falls within the subcategory of executive decision makers. In this arrangement, the alliance vests all authority and power to attain the objective(s) in the sovereign. At the very least, the sovereign is authorized to implement the means (identified in the accord) and to collect contribution of resources from the members if necessary. In some alliances, the sovereign will also be authorized to select the means to achieve the alliance's objectives or to choose new objectives for the alliance to pursue. A sovereign is a permanent decision maker and is not subject to discharge.

In Chapter 7, it was observed that all delegated decision makers are granted a certain scope of authority. The delegated decision maker is allowed to make decisions falling within the parameters of the granted authority. If the alliance has a multiple-tiered or interwoven decision-making process, the decision of the delegated decision maker might not constitute the final decision. Instead, if a multiple-tiered process is in place, another decision maker (membership vote, committee, or executive) might have to review and endorse the decision in some fashion. Or, if an interwoven process is present, one or more other decision makers must be in agreement with the decision reached for it to become final.

The defining feature of a sovereign is that no multiple-tiers or interwoven processes are present. Instead, the authority granted to the sovereign is unfettered. No other decision-making process is involved in the making the decision. For any decision that must be made, it is made by the sovereign alone. The fact that the sovereign holds unrestricted discretion to make decisions within the scope of authority granted by the accord does not mean that a sovereign holds the authority to do anything. Instead, the sovereign's authority is constrained by the underlying accord.

Sovereigns go by many names including king, queen, monarch, chief, caesar, caliph, czar, emperor, empress, kaiser, khan, maharajah, mikado, mogul, pasha, potentate, prince, rajah, rex, shah, sultan, and so on. The name or title, however, is not controlling. The determining factors are whether (i) the alliance has a single executive decision maker, (ii) the accord grants (expressly or impliedly) the executive decision maker a scope of authority to make all decisions for the alliance, and (iii) the authority held by the executive decision maker is unfettered and is not otherwise part of a multiple-tier or interwoven decision-making process. For instance, although an executive decision maker might be called a "king," the executive is a not a sovereign if he is not authorized to make all decisions on his own. If this "king" must submit a decision to, or otherwise coordinate his decision making with, another process, the person is in reality an executive decision maker participating in either a multi-tiered or interwoven decision-making process.

Another feature of a sovereign is permanency. When the alliance is created, the accord provides that the sovereign will hold the position for life, or for as long as the alliance exists. Thus, if an executive decision maker is subject to periodic selection or recall by the members, the executive is not a sovereign. Instead, a republic is present.

Sovereigns are not tyrants. A sovereign's obligation is to serve as a decision maker for the alliance and otherwise fulfill the duties the sovereign has been charged with in the accord. In contrast, a tyranny is a structure resembling an alliance in many respects except that there are no members and no accord. Instead, the purpose of a tyranny is the furtherance of the interests of the tyrant. Tyrannies typically involve numerous individuals being compelled into contributing their resources towards a combined effort. These individuals have not agreed to this contribution. There is no accord. There is no objective that they mutually desire. Instead, the tyrant has one or more objectives that he desires and he uses force to coerce individuals under his power to achieve his objectives using their resources. Thus, although sovereigns and tyrannies might share similar features, they are very different. A tyrant seeks to further his own interests while a sovereign fulfills the obligations he is charged with by the accord.

As discussed in Chapter 7, all delegated decision makers are subject to three categories of limitations: (i) motivational, (ii) capability, and (iii) fidelity. Sovereigns are naturally quite prone to all of these limitations. As a result, many alliances often refuse to utilize sovereigns due to the presence of these limitations.

Sovereigns often constitute tyrannical alliances. In these situations, the sovereign is subject to persistent and often insidious limitations. For instance, the sovereign might ignore his duties due to motivational limitations, make imbecilic decisions caused by his capability limitations, and engage in horrendous corruption stemming from fidelity limitations. Nonetheless, the members might accept the sovereign because it provides a perceived net benefit and there are no other suitable alternatives.

OLIGARCHY

An oligarchy is a delegated decision maker and falls within the subcategory of committee decision makers. An oligarchy is nearly identical in all respects to a sovereign except for one primary difference. Instead of consisting of a single individual like a sovereign, an oligarchy consists of at least two individuals and can consist of numerous individuals. This group of individuals forms a committee that makes decisions for the alliance pursuant to a predetermined arrangement (for example, often a majority vote of the committee participants). All of the other aspects of a sovereign are the same for an oligarchy.

All oligarchies are committees. But observe that not all committees are oligarchies. If a committee does not hold unfettered discretion to make decisions or otherwise must work with some other decision-making process, the committee is part of a multi-tiered or interwoven decision-making process and cannot constitute an oligarchy.

Oligarchies are often viewed as the equivalent of tyrannies. This is not the case. An oligarchy is simply a delegated decision maker holding unfettered discretion to act with its scope of authority. Its obligation is to fulfill the duties it is charged with in the accord. Because an oligarchy is a delegated decision maker, it is subject to all three limitations associated with delegated decision makers. As a consequence, an oligarchy is prone to shirking its duties, making flawed decisions, and engaging in corruption. And, for the same reasons as a sovereign, it is possible for a tyrannical alliance to exist with an oligarchy. In this situation, the oligarchy exhibits many flaws. Nonetheless, the alliance members willingly accept the oligarchy as it provides a perceived net benefit over the available alternatives under consideration.

Oligarchies can constitute tyrannies to non-members. In such a situation, the alliance is composed of members who desire to exploit non-members in some fashion (that is, the objective is to exploit non-members). In this situation, the alliance delegates the exploitation to a committee. Because this committee holds sole authority to attain the objective, it is an oligarchy. And, because the alliance is exploiting other individuals, it constitutes a tyranny to those exploited individuals, but not to the members of the alliance.

Sometimes an ostensible sovereign is in reality an oligarchy. In this situation, the named sovereign appears to be all powerful and have all of the traits of a sovereign. In reality, however, the named sovereign holds no authority or power and is nothing more than a figurehead. Instead, the sovereign answers to the dictates of a small group of individuals constituting an oligarchy. These individuals select the sovereign and covertly instruct him regarding what he should and should not do.

ALLIANCES WITHIN THE DECISION-MAKING PROCESS

Certain decision-making processes are prone to the development of alliances within the process. For instance, if an alliance uses a membership vote to make decisions, this process will tend to have two or more voting-alliances within it. These voting-alliances are comprised of members supporting different proposals.

Example 5 "Help the needy"—The alliance selects the monthly means through a membership vote with a simple majority constituting the decision. Of the 100 members, 40 members support funding a soup kitchen. Another 40 support purchasing blankets and the remaining 20 members are undecided. The

40 members supporting the soup kitchen form a voting-alliance to push this idea on the 20 undecided. It is their goal to get 11 of the 20 undecided members to support the soup kitchen and therefore obtain a majority of the votes. These 40 members contribute money towards generating pamphlets explaining why the soup kitchen is the best proposal. The other 40 members supporting the blanket acquisition create a similar voting-alliance except that its goal is convincing 11 of the 20 undecided to vote for the blanket proposal. The blanket voting-alliance wins over 13 of the undecided members and its proposal constitutes the decision, receiving 53 of the 100 votes cast. Both voting-alliances terminate, with one having succeeded in attaining its objective and the other failing.

The accords underlying such voting alliances are usually spoken. The contributed resource is the vote itself (that is, the freedom of voting is fettered by a promise to vote in a certain manner). Depending upon the size of the membership and the number of supported proposals, it is possible for numerous voting-alliances to form within a membership-vote, decision-making process.

FACTIONS

If an alliance is long-term and regularly has membership votes on decisions, factions can form. Factions are long-standing voting alliances that form within the context of a membership vote decision-making process. Factions typically have a certain objective or set of objectives that they tend to advocate. Often, the relationships between competing factions are competitive or even quite contentious and ugly. If three or more factions are present within a process, it is possible for one faction to temporarily ally with another faction to compete against the other faction(s) in the voting process. This situation is an example of an alliance of alliances, which has been discussed earlier. These alliances are usually temporary and relate to a specific matter present in the decision-making process. Once the matter has been addressed, the alliance of factions usually terminates. However, sometimes allying factions can merge in a single permanent faction, if they conclude that it is advantageous to do so.

At times, one faction might strike a deal with another faction. The terms of this deal will be that each faction is to support a proposal favored by the other faction. It is tempting to consider this situation an alliance. But it is not an alliance because there is no mutually desired objective towards which the members are contributing resources. Instead, each faction desires a different proposal to constitute the decision of the alliance. If an alliance is not present in this circumstance, then what is? This situation is an example of an individually outsourced effort. For instance, Faction A agrees to support Faction B's proposal and Faction B agrees to return the favor and support Faction A's proposal. Faction A is individually attaining its objective through outsourcing a portion of the effort to Faction B. And Faction A is compensating Faction B by supporting its proposal. In effect, Faction A is buying Faction B's vote in the same manner as if money exchanged hands.

Voting-alliances and even factions are possible in a committee decision-making process. The same concepts discussed with membership vote are present in this situation. Namely, certain committee participants might temporarily ally with each other to convince other participants to support a certain proposal. Or certain participants might find that they have so much in common that it is useful to permanent ally together on most issues.

CHAPTER 13

Traits of Success

The purpose of an alliance is to attain one or more objectives. By their nature, these objectives either (i) cannot be achieved by individual effort or (ii) can be achieved more effectively or efficiently through a combined effort. Some alliances attain their chosen objectives while others do not. Some alliances achieve their objectives but not particularly well. Some alliances achieve nothing but instead slide into combined-effort entities such as illusory alliances and tyrannies.

This chapter generalizes regarding certain traits and characteristics of alliances that make attainment of objectives more and less likely. In making these generalities, it must be underscored that they do not constitute universal rules governing all alliances and that many exceptions exist. In fact, the traits and characteristics of successful alliances usually have one or more downsides. At times, these downsides might outweigh the benefits associated with the traits.

LIMITING MEMBERSHIP

In most situations, an alliance will want to control its membership. Why? Because the objectives pursued by the alliance typically cannot be enjoyed by an unlimited number of individuals. For instance, consider an alliance to construct a swimming pool. Obviously, there are only so many people who can use a swimming pool. If too many members are allowed to use a pool, there will be overcrowding and no one will be able to swim. Because the alliance effectively provides no benefit, most members will cease contributing resources to the alliance and it will fail. For this reason, many alliances must control their membership to insure that the objectives can be suitably enjoyed by the members.

The need to limit membership is not always advantageous. Some alliances will desire to have as many members as possible. Alliances pursuing law-compelled objectives typically want to be all-inclusive. This is because the specific objective (for example, no killing) is more likely to be attained if all individuals in a given area are part of the alliance and have contributed the resource (for example, the freedom to kill) towards attaining the objective. Generally speaking, if the objective is a tangible end (for example, a swimming pool), membership must be limited. Conversely, if the objective is intangible (for example, peaceful coexistence), membership should be as open as possible.

One drawback of limiting membership is miscalculation. Most alliances require a critical mass of members to contribute sufficient resources to attain the objective. Alliances bent on limiting the membership might tend to miscalculate and undershoot the necessary level of members. As a result, the alliance will fail. A related concept is the failure to recognize the benefits of additional members. Often, the downside associated with increased membership will be offset by an overall reduction in the amount of resources that each individual member must contribute. In this situation, the increased membership yields economies of scale that allow the overall contribution of each member to be less. If an alliance is too focused on preservation of access to the objective, however, it might fail to recognize the reduction of contribution brought by increasing membership.

Another drawback of limited membership is the provocation of outside revolutionary alliances. If a sufficient number of individuals are excluded from an alliance, they will tend to ally. The objective of this alliance will be Offense against Non-Members and the "Non-Members" will be the members of the original, exclusionary alliance. What would motivate the formation of such a revolutionary alliance? One reason might lie in the objective attained by the original alliance. If it is a tangible objective of value, the revolutionary alliance might strive to seize it. This result occurs because a successful alliance will tend to breed envy in non-members. Another reason is more akin to Defense against Aggressors. If the original alliance is perceived as exploiting or otherwise harming the members of the revolutionary alliance, the revolutionary alliance will strive to throw off that yoke of oppression.

To avoid provoking an outside revolutionary alliance, an alliance has several options. One is to conceal the benefits of the alliance from outsiders. Another is to pursue various means under the objective of Defense against Aggressors such as suppression of rebellion (for example, surveillance, prevention of organization, restraint of speech, and so on) or appeasement (for example, provide the outsiders with food and material comforts).

Another option is to allow the outsiders some manner of membership in the alliance. The membership can be:

- *Full Membership*—The outsiders are welcomed into the alliance and afforded the same rights and privileges of the original members.

- *Second-Class Membership*—The outsiders are afforded some of the rights and privileges of membership, but the original members are entitled to participate in additional alliance benefits not open to the second-class members.

- *The Promise of Membership*—The outsiders are offered membership in the future if certain conditions are satisfied.

- *Illusory Membership*—The outsiders are deceived into believing they are members (full or second class) in the alliance. In reality, the only members are the original members who are controlling the manipulation of the outsiders.

The presence of these options will tend to reduce the formation of an outside revolutionary alliance.

Another possibility is to aid the outsiders in forming their own, independent alliance. The premise underlying this option is that the outsiders will be less prone to attack the existing alliance if they have their own alliance to keep them satisfied. This option certainly has its dangers in that the new alliance will usually pose a viable threat to the existing alliance. As a result, this option will be undertaken only if the existing alliance is confident that a new alliance will not put the existing alliance in jeopardy.

On the whole, most alliances must limit membership in order to be successful. Such practices, however, have their drawbacks that must be carefully considered and evaluated when forming and structuring the limitations on membership.

A SUITABLE DECISION-MAKING PROCESS

If an alliance must use a decision-making process, it must select a process best suited for the specific situation presented. The benefits and disadvantages of each process are addressed in Chapter 7 but the following discussion will cover a few highlights.

It should be emphasized that successful alliances are never wedded to a particular process. There are manifold variations of decision-making processes with different benefits and different drawbacks. The successful alliances will select the processes most suited for the objectives at hand. For instance, if the objective requires quick action or expertise, an executive decision maker is usually best. If the objective requires deliberation, debate, and membership support for the final decision, a membership vote might be the best alternative. And, if the objective is somewhere in between, a committee might be the best alternative.

Another significant consideration is the use of more complex decision-making processes such as tiered processes and interwoven processes. These formats are useful to mix expertise, deliberation, and caution into the decision-making process. The drawbacks of these arrangements include slowness and bureaucratic indifference.

CAREFUL USAGE OF "MAJORITY-RULES"

If an alliance uses a voting process such as (i) a membership vote or (ii) a vote by a committee delegated decision maker, the most common vote total required is a simple majority or 51 percent of the votes cast. This concept is commonly known as "majority-rules."

Alliances that embrace majority-rules for any and all decisions tend to be unsuccessful. The reason is that the majority-rules concept is inherently unstable. The threshold of votes required for a proposal to become a decision is 51 percent of the votes cast. If a proposal passes with a simple majority, that means that 49 percent of the voters did not desire the proposal. These voters in the minority will tend to become resentful of the majority and the decision that it made. This spite will serve to erode the perceived value associated with the alliance and push the minority voters towards forming their own alliance.

Illustration—An alliance of 100 members is pursuing the objective of Defense against Aggressors and uses a majority vote decision-making process. The alliance members are being periodically attacked by raiders. One group of members proposes finding the raiders' camp site and attacking it. Another group of members proposes setting a trap and attempting to lure the raiders into it. A vote is held and the proposal to attack the raiders' camp passes by a vote of 54 to 46. The minority of 46 members disagrees sharply with the decision, and they refuse to go on the raid. Acrimony results and the alliance falls apart.

If the decision at hand pertains to whether the alliance should pursue an objective, majority-rules can result in severe destabilization of the alliance. The reason is that the alliance will be pursuing an objective desired by only 51 percent of the voters. Because this minority does not desire the objective, it will perceive no value from the objective. Further, if the minority finds the objective to be disagreeable or odious, the minority will perceive a negative value from the attainment of the objective. In addition, if pursuit of the new objective requires additional contribution from the members, the overall perceived value placed on the contribution by dissenting members will increase. The net effect will be to reduce the gap between the perceived values attributed to the alliance and the contribution supplied by the members. As this gap closes, the alliance will become more unstable.[1]

> *Illustration*—An alliance of 100 members is pursuing the objective of Defense against Aggressors and uses a majority vote decision-making process. One group desires to pursue a new objective, Aggression against Non-Members, and combine the members' resources towards raiding nearby villages. Another group opposes the objective. A vote is held and the proposal to undertake the new objective passes by a vote of 54 to 46. The minority of 46 members disagrees sharply with the decision. These members do not desire to raid the neighboring villages and in fact find the concept odious. Further, they recognize that participating in the raid will require them to risk injury or death (that is, a form of contribution), if the targeted villages fight back. Because of these changes, the gap between the perceived values attributed to the alliance's benefit and the contribution supplied closes completely for the minority members. As a result, they withdraw from the alliance altogether.

Successful alliances will take care in utilizing the majority-rules concept and limit its application only to situations where it is well-suited for the decision at hand. As a general rule of thumb, majority-rules is much better suited for decisions on means. The reason is that a dispute over the best approach to tackle an objective is less susceptible to discord and ill will. Although feathers might get ruffled over an argument regarding the best means, those feathers usually will smooth back down shortly. In contrast, a dispute over whether an alliance should pursue a certain objective is highly destabilizing because it usually has a sizeable effect upon the gap and the perceived values associated with the alliance. As a result, a successful alliance will tend to avoid using majority-rules on any issue relating to selection of objectives to pursue.

If a majority-rules process is employed, a successful alliance also tends to have voters that will not force a simple majority vote down the throats of the minority

---

[1] The mere fact that many members do not desire a particular objective does not necessarily destabilize an alliance. Recall Example 8—"Council of Elders" where the alliance is pursuing an open objective. As discussed in Chapter 10, the alliance members see value in having in place and ready for action a long-standing (or permanent) process for identifying commonly-desired objectives that are suitable for combined action. Having such an arrangement in place can offer advantages such as having the ability to take quick action when called for the circumstances. Implicit in this arrangement is an acknowledgment by all members that the alliance might undertake objectives from time to time that are not desired by all members. Because a member understands this fact, the perceived values attributed to the alliance by the member usually will not be offset substantially if the alliance pursues an objective the member does not desire.

voters. The voters in such an alliance will recognize the potentially destabilizing effect of this act. Further, if a proposal is controversial and can only pass by a simple majority, that fact suggests that the proposal might not be meritorious (that is, is it really a good idea if so many oppose it?). As a result, the alliance as a whole will tend to avoid divisive votes. If it appears that a proposal will pass only by a mere simple majority, voters in the majority will not vote for the proposal and will instead explore ways to build a greater consensus. They will confer with the minority and attempt to understand its viewpoints and concerns. If they find that the minority's points have validity, the majority will refashion the proposal and attempt to entice more in the minority to vote for the proposal.

This generalization does not mean that a successful alliance can never have a proposal pass by a simple majority. Several justifiable situations where a successful alliance might pass a proposal by a bare majority include:

- An urgent decision must be made and there is no time to form a consensus.

- There are inherent disagreements (that is, differences of opinion between reasonable minds) and no consensus is possible.

- The opposition is acting in bad faith in opposing a proposal.

CHECKS ON DELEGATED DECISION MAKERS

If delegated decision makers are under consideration, successful alliances will pay particular attention to the potential limitations associated with such decision makers. As discussed in Chapter 7, all delegated decision makers are subject to three limitations: (i) motivation, (ii) ability, and (iii) fidelity.

With regard to motivation, successful alliances will take care to see that the delegated decision maker is sufficiently stimulated to attain the objective. These enticements might include rewarding the decision maker with wealth, power, prestige, or a share in certain objectives pursued.

As for ability, successful alliances will attempt to insure that a delegated decision maker is actually capable of attaining the objective. As covered in Chapter 7, some alliances will merely assume that a desired objective can be attained. In these situations, no attention will be paid to whether even the most qualified delegated decision maker is actually capable of achieving the objective. This is the "magic wand" problem and occurs when an alliance essentially ascribes magic powers to a decision maker. It is as if the alliance believes that the decision maker holds a magic wand that, if properly waived, can attain the objective. This supposition is usually unwarranted and results in the alliance failing.

The third category of limitations that alliances should be concerned about is fidelity limitations. This topic is discussed in the following section.

SAFEGUARDS AGAINST FIDELITY LIMITATIONS

Recall that there are three sub-categories of fidelity limitations: (i) position protection, (ii) favoring the interest of a minority of alliance members or of an outsider to the alliance, and (iii) pure, unadulterated corruption. Almost any alliance with a delegated decision maker is subject to potential fidelity limitations. Exceptions to this generalization are very uncommon and are limited largely to situations where the actions of the decision maker are completely transparent and any failing of the decision maker will be immediately apparent.

Because of this inherent relationship, successful alliances institute safeguards against fidelity limitations. These measures might include:

- Codes of Conduct—Rules will be instituted prohibiting delegated decision makers from engaging in undesirable conduct. The rules will carry penalties or other punishments suited to deter misconduct.

- Audits—The alliance will have some type of internal investigatory procedure for reviewing the conduct of the decision maker.

- Interwoven Decision-Making Processes—This arrangement requires two more separate processes to approve a decision and tends to reduce the influence of corruption. In particular, an entity desiring to influence the decision maker will have to corrupt all (or most) participants in the interwoven process. In contrast, with one delegated decision maker, only one individual or committee must be influenced. Although interwoven processes are not a panacea, they generally are more difficult to corrupt. This concept is sometimes called a "Balance of Powers."

- Freedom to Critique—The members are allowed to speak freely and to point out any fidelity limitations exhibited in the decision makers. Such exposure will tend to decrease fidelity limitations.

- Disclosure Requirements—Rules requiring decision makers to reveal their sources of income and ties to interested parties or issues will tend to reduce fidelity limitations.

- Transparent Decision-Making Process—Decisions are made publicly where members can view the reasoning utilized.

A final mechanism for the reduction of fidelity limitations is to minimize the use of delegated decision makers. A membership vote is not prone to these limitations. As such, every time an alliance decides to use a delegated decision maker, it is risking incurring fidelity limitations. Because delegated decision makers can offer superior advantages to a membership vote, however, this risk is often worth it.

DECISION MAKER SELECTION AND REMOVAL PROCESSES

Useful mechanisms for both reining in and correcting the limitations of delegated decision makers are processes for the selection, and for the recall or removal, of decision makers. In these arrangements, no decision maker's position is completely secure. Instead, alliance structures allow for delegated decision makers to be removed from their positions. These removals can be conditioned upon specific acts or omissions committed by decision makers. Or the alliances might have periodic processes for the evaluation of their sitting decision makers. In many alliance structures, the members directly evaluate sitting decision makers and often replace them with new individuals based upon a membership vote process (for example, "elections"). Some alliances might provide for certain delegated decision makers to evaluate other decision makers and remove them if necessary.

These processes tend to reduce the limitations of delegated decision makers. One reason for this reduction is that the process removes incompetent or inadequate decision makers. Such removals naturally tend to improve the performance of the decision-making bodies as the poor performers are culled out.

More importantly perhaps, the removal processes provide important stimuli and incentives to decision makers. Any decision maker is naturally prone to exhibiting fidelity limitations. The removal processes check these natural impulses by subjecting the decision makers to both scrutiny and accountability. Without a removal process, a typical decision maker can flaunt fidelity limitations with little fear of losing his position. With the removal process, a typical decision maker will have to consider whether his fidelity limitations will be noticed and will serve as a catalyst for his removal from his position.

Why would members of an alliance be concerned with fidelity limitations? The answer is that a membership desires that the objective of the alliance be attained. If the decision maker is not focused on attaining the given objective, the membership will desire to remove the decision maker and install a new one that will work towards attaining the objective. In addition, if a decision maker is wasting alliance resources on special interests or personal corruption, the members will have to contribute more resources to attain the objective. This result is not desired by the members. The members will see a decision maker immune from the temptations of fidelity limitations as being able to attain the objective of the alliance at less cost.

Selection and removal processes are not a panacea. Compromised decision makers have a number of mechanisms to defeat removal. A primary method is to conceal the fidelity limitations from the membership. If the membership is not aware of the limitations, the members obviously cannot act upon them and remove tainted decision makers.

Another effective means of concealing fidelity limitations is indirect attainment. Recall that indirect attainment is achievement of an objective through a circuitous or roundabout method. At times, indirect attainment can constitute a bona-fide means of actually achieving an objective. At other times, indirect attainment is used as the smokescreen to disguise the true objective being pursued. In this latter situation, compromised decision makers will use indirect attainment to mask the illicit benefit to themselves or a special interest. Specifically, they will assert that a corrupt undertaking actually achieves an objective of the alliance in an indirect manner. In reality, the undertaking rewards a corrupt interest and either does not attain the objective, or attains the objective in a less effective manner.

As a final matter, it should be observed that removal processes have their drawbacks as well. For instance, the first category of fidelity limitations is position protection. Removal processes tend to reinforce this type of fidelity limitation. If a delegated decision maker is subject to removal, the decision maker will tend to take the safest, least controversial courses of action, even if they are not the best decisions. In contrast, decision makers not subject to recall will tend to feel more secure in their positions and will be willing to make the best decisions, even if they involve some risks. Further, the removal processes are not necessarily adept at making the best decisions. At times, a particular process might remove the superior candidate and replace him with an incompetent or corrupt individual.

EFFECTIVE RESOURCE CONTRIBUTION

An alliance is founded upon the pooling of contributed resources towards a mutually desired objective. If an alliance cannot obtain sufficient resources, it will fail.

In the most successful alliances, the members voluntarily contribute resources towards the alliance effort. This fact might seem strange to some. Why would a voluntary contribution ever occur? The most common reason is that the members value the objective sought by the alliance and fully believe that the alliance is the best mechanism for attaining the objective. Because these members have confidence in the alliance, they will willingly contribute resources to the alliance. In effect, a self-reinforcing cycle is created. The more resources an alliance has, the more successful it will be. The more successes that an alliance has, the more resource contribution it will generate. In short, effective resource contribution is often both a cause and an effect of a successful alliance.

In the same vein, the least successful alliances typically exhibit ineffective resource contribution. Often, resources must be compelled from the members by force or at least the threat of force. In most of these situations, resources are not voluntarily contributed because members question the value of the alliance. Another possible reason is free riders. The potential for free riders always exists with certain types of objectives, regardless of the effectiveness of an alliance. But the free rider scenario is less likely if an alliance is particularly valued by its members.

Another reason for an unwillingness to contribute resources is the fact that a true alliance might not be present. As a general rule, individuals in any combined-effort entity (other than a true alliance) do not readily contribute resources. For instance, a tyranny must forcibly extract contribution from the individuals that it subjugates. Similarly, a semi-alliance is in the grey zone where its true nature is not clear. The value of most semi-alliances is usually questioned by the members. As a result, members of semi-alliances are less willing to contribute resources to the entity. The exception to this generalization is an illusory alliance. By definition, an illusory alliance has duped subjugated individuals into believing that an alliance exists. As a result, these individuals usually are willing to contribute the requested resources.

EQUAL RESOURCE CONTRIBUTION

Alliances where the members each contribute the same amount tend to be more successful. Alliances with disproportionate levels of contribution can and do exist. Further, such alliances can be quite successful. However, alliances with different levels of contribution are likely to breed resentment and disharmony amongst the members. Recall that members are constantly weighing the perceived value of the contribution against the perceived value afforded by the alliance. As a part of this analysis, some members will scrutinize the benefits received by other members and balance that against their relative contributions. If certain members are receiving sizeable benefits from the alliance but are contributing a proportionately less amount of contribution, the members contributing more will tend to question the arrangement. Sometimes these questions will lead to nothing. But often they will lead to discord with members being more inclined to withhold contribution or to consider departing the alliance.

ESPRIT DE CORPS

Most successful alliances have esprit de corps. Recall that esprit de corps is a mood or atmosphere pervading through the members of an alliance. The concept is generally associated with high morale, a sense of belonging, and a comradeship amongst the members.

The presence of esprit de corps usually means that the members participate in the alliance with enthusiasm and willingly contribute resources to the alliance. In addition, if the value placed upon the esprit de corps is sizeable, members might also contribute resources valued more than the objective attained. These factors all tend to make an alliance successful.

ASSOCIATION GLORY

The presence of association glory can make an alliance successful. Recall that association glory is a pride-based emotion felt by members of an alliance. It is a feeling of honor or esteem stemming from a member's association with the alliance. It can take the forms of self-esteem flowing from being a member, public esteem by non-members towards members, and a combination of both types of esteem.

The desire of members to maintain or augment the association glory of an alliance will tend to make an alliance successful. In this regard, the alliance members are motivated not only towards attaining the objective at hand. The members also are motivated towards furthering the alliance's reputation or image so that they, as members of the alliance, might bask in its glory. A failure to attain an objective will cast a dark light on the alliance and harm the individual prestige of each member. As such, association glory can provide a powerful impetus towards the attainment of an objective and therefore can make an alliance successful. Significantly, the lack of association glory is not fatal to an alliance attaining an objective. Alliances without association glory can still be successful.

Association glory, however, has its negatives. As discussed in Chapter 12, association glory can push an alliance into imprudent undertakings. In this situation, the alliance pursues an unwise endeavor solely to maintain or enhance its association glory and is often severely harmed or destroyed as a result. Further, association glory can tend to dominate some alliances such that their original, unifying objectives are disregarded and all resources are expended upon furthering the glory of the alliances. Moreover, association glory can be exploited by corrupt decision makers to conceal their fidelity limitations or to delude an alliance into taking a course of action that is not truly desired by the members.

Overall, a successful alliance will strive to attain a proper balance between the positive and negative factors associated with association glory. Such an alliance will endeavor to uphold and maintain its pride and esteem in undertaking its objectives. At the same time, the alliance will also guard against being driven into taking certain actions in order to augment its association glory.

IDENTIFICATION OF
OBJECTIVES

A successful alliance tends to identify its underlying objective(s) and has a relatively firm concept of what the alliance is supposed to do and not do. Chapter 3 discussed this topic and set forward three classes of objectives:

Specific Objective	Indefinite Objective	Open Objective

These three classes vary according to the degree of specificity with which the objective is identified in the underlying accord. One extreme is specificity. A specific objective leaves no room for uncertainty as to what the alliance is and is not pursuing. The other extreme is openness. An open objective places no limits upon what the alliance might, or might not, undertake.[1] In between these two extremes in the middle ground is indefiniteness. An indefinite objective places some parameters upon what the alliance might and might not do. However, these parameters are fuzzy and allow room for interpretation.

How does the identification of the underlying objective tend to make an alliance more successful? Recall the concepts of objective creep, objective disguise, and indirect attainment. Although these phenomena have positive attributes, they also tend to have corrosive effects upon the functioning of alliances. As discussed in greater detail earlier, they allow for new objectives to slip into the alliance without much notice. The result often is that the perceived value of the alliance will tend to decrease as more objectives sneak into the alliance. As a consequence of this situation, members will tend to withhold contribution and termination of the alliance becomes likely. Further, these phenomena facilitate the occurrence of all three delegated decision maker limitations. As mentioned earlier, they greatly assist in the commission of various fidelity limitations by serving to mask the abusive behavior.

---

[1] Arguably, "open alliances" do not exist. Instead, what appears to be an open alliance is actually a single objective alliance that forms to pursue a particular objective and then terminates. Under this theory, no alliance exists most of the time. When an objective suited for an alliance effort is identified, the members then form an alliance to pursue it. The catalyst is usually a decision-making process. Specifically, the decision maker, such as the Council of Elders in Example 8, identifies an objective suited for an alliance effort and broadcasts this identification. The potential members then decide on a case-by-case basis whether to pursue the objective.

If an accord is specific, the chances of objective creep, objective disguise, and indirect attainment problems occurring are substantially reduced. The reason is that it is difficult for objectives to creep into an alliance if the underlying accord makes it evident what the objective is and is not. Specificity serves to shine a spotlight on a new proposal and to subject such a proposal to scrutiny. While specificity is not a panacea, it can go a long way towards reducing the problems associated with objective creep, objective disguise, and indirect attainment.

It has been observed that specificity has its drawbacks since it can prevent necessary change. In such situations, some degree of indefiniteness can be helpful by allowing the alliance to adapt to changing circumstances. However, if there is too much indefiniteness, the problems of objective creep, objective disguise, and indirect attainment are likely. As a result, the best situation is often for an alliance to strike a suitable balance between specificity and indefiniteness. Perhaps this could be best described as identifying the objective with substantial precision but at the same time leaving some "wiggle room" to allow for modest change.

ACCORD AMENDMENT PROCEDURES

As has been discussed at length in earlier chapters, change in an alliance often can be very important to the attainment of an objective. Further, change can be essential to the survival of an alliance. Recall that change can be effected by two mechanisms. A change effected through a provision in an accord is termed a contemplated change. In contrast, a fundamental change pertains to a radical alteration of an accord underlying an alliance in a manner not considered at the time the alliance was entered. In almost all circumstances, contemplated changes are much easier to achieve and also result in substantially less disagreement and acrimony, in comparison to fundamental changes.

Contemplated changes are the product of accords with amendment and modification procedures. Alliances with such procedures in the accord tend to be successful. Such alliances have the ability to change as called for by new situations in a fashion that is usually superior to that of alliances required by circumstance to change fundamentally. This is because a fundamental change requires much more energy, coordination, effort, and contribution to attain the desired result. In contrast, a contemplated change is usually attained by utilizing an agreed-upon decision-making process.

In addition, the very existence of procedures for amendments and modifications also tends to stabilize alliances and reduce violent revolutionary activity brought against alliances by their members. The reason is that such procedures offer both the hope and the mechanism for a perceived positive change. As discussed earlier, destabilization of alliances and inside revolutionary[1] fervor are usually the product of dissatisfaction with the undertakings of an alliance. When such dissatisfaction arises, discontent members will tend to either leave the alliance or attempt to foment an inside revolution through violent or other unsavory means. If the alliance has a mechanism for amendment or modification, however, the discontent members can strive to access that mechanism and change the alliance to their suiting. In such situations, the discontent members will weigh (i) departure from the alliance or revolutionary activity versus (ii) lobbying for an amendment or modification of the alliance to fix the perceived deficiencies in the alliance. In many situations, the discontent members will find that the second option (that is, sticking within the original alliance framework and lobbying for change) is preferable. Perhaps this is why members attempting to change an alliance through an agreed-upon mechanism often style their efforts as "revolutions."

RESTRICTIONS ON MEANS

A trait often associated with successful alliances is the placement of restrictions on the means available to an alliance. Recall that means are the tool used by an alliance to attain an objective. Some means are fully known when an alliance is first formed. This is usually the case in the simpler alliances. With more complex alliances and especially those with multiple objectives, the range of means available is potentially infinite, with each means being tailored to meet the particular objective of the alliance. In these types of alliances, the means are usually selected by some type of decision-making process.

It is likely that some alliances will be prone to selecting means that are undesirable. As noted earlier, decision-making processes are not perfect and often make mistakes or become thoroughly corrupted. For instance, an alliance's decision-making process could select means that:

- are wholly inadequate to meet the objective

- are not the best suited for the particular objective

- require too much contribution

- are prone to facilitating corruption or other fidelity limitations

---

[1] Recall that an inside revolution is an event that occurs inside an alliance. It is best summed up as a sudden and drastic change in the alliance's accord. In contrast, an outside revolution occurs when members form an alliance to take on another alliance, or tyranny, that exploits or otherwise directly harms them.

- constitute a pure ruse for corruption (for example, objective disguise/indirect attainment)

- result in harm or side effects that are undesirable

- utilize methods found odious to the members

If an alliance utilizes inappropriate means, the alliance will tend to fail at attaining its objective, or at least it will not attain the objective as effectively or efficiently as other available means. Such outcomes lead to the termination of alliances. Further, even if an alliance attains an objective, the controversy and displeasure caused by the use of disfavored means might cause such dissension that the alliance will dissolve. For these reasons, alliances with restrictions on the available means tend to be more successful. Such alliances are more likely to attain the chosen objective(s) and are less likely to incur negative fallout associated with loathsome or otherwise disagreeable means.

How do the restrictions on means work? In most circumstances, the restrictions will be structured in such a way as to afford the alliance substantial leeway in selecting from a multitude of means. For instance, the restrictions will prohibit only certain categories of means. All other means falling outside of the realm of prohibited means can be utilized.

> **Example 4 "Wild West"**—The accord prohibits the mercenary from using torture to attain order and decency. As such, all methods other than torture might be used.

> **Example 5 "Help the needy"**—To help the needy, the alliance purchases products such as food, clothing, and shelter. The accord prohibits the alliance from purchasing products from a certain business that are not favored by the members. Purchases from any other business are permissible.

Instead of prohibiting specific categories, another method is to focus upon an effect. This approach prohibits the usage of means that cause a certain result or consequence.

> **Example 5 "Help the needy"**—The accord prohibits the alliance from undertaking any endeavor that tends to demean or debase the needy. As such, so long as the chosen means do not result in humiliation to the needy, it is acceptable.

Often, these terms are rather indefinite and vague and a decision-making process might be necessary to ascertain their meaning.

Example 4 "Wild West"—The accord prohibits the mercenary from using any means that result in "cruelty." A five-member panel is appointed to determine what means are cruel and therefore prohibited.

Many restrictions are intended to protect only the interests of members. In these situations, alliances are free to pursue whatever means they choose, so long as the means do not harm the interests of members to the alliances.

Example 4 "Wild West"—The accord prohibits the mercenary from using deadly force, torture, and any other "cruel" means on members. The mercenary is free to use whatever means he chooses on non-members. Thus, if a non-member engages in robbery, the mercenary might shoot him down on the spot. If the same act of robbery is performed by a member, however, the mercenary is restricted to taking the member into custody.

Frequently, alliances will not form without an express accord containing firm restrictions on means. In these situations, the potential members will be very concerned with an alliance utilizing certain means. As a result, they will insist upon the restriction on means as a condition of entering the alliance.

RESTRICTIONS ON OBJECTIVES

Similar to restrictions on means, some alliances will find success in prohibiting the pursuit of certain objectives. These types of restrictions are necessary only in complex alliances pursuing multiple objectives with indefinite accords. (A single objective alliance is limited by its nature to pursuing the single objective.)

Typically, the members will conclude that an indefinitely described objective is a useful manner of identifying the objective underlying alliance. At the same time, the members will be concerned with the drawbacks of an indefinite objective (that is, the alliance's decision-making process interpreting the indefinite objective in an undesirable fashion). To prevent this result, the members will seek to constrain what the alliance might undertake with prohibitions on certain specific objectives that might fall within the indefinitely described objective.

Example 5 "Help the needy"—The objective underlying the alliance is indefinite—that is, help the needy. The members fear that the alliance's decision-making process might interpret this indefinite objective to pursue undesirable, specific objectives. As such, the accord prohibits the alliance from pursuing certain objectives (for example, art-appreciation classes). Under this framework, the decision-making process is free to select any specific objective, except for providing art-appreciation classes to the needy.

As noted earlier, indefinite (and even open objectives) afford certain benefits over specific objectives. However, these benefits are often outweighed by the dangers they bring including objective creep and a gradual slide into a semi-alliance, an illusory alliance, or an outright tyranny. Usage of restrictions on objectives can serve to reduce the likelihood of these dangers occurring. Further, as just discussed with regard to restrictions on means, many members might refuse to enter alliances unless restrictions are placed upon the objectives that might be pursued.

SUBSTANTIAL PROTECTIONS WHEN LIBERTY IS CONTRIBUTED

Liberty is often an important resource that must be contributed for an alliance to succeed. Liberty is particularly important to the attainment of most internal objectives. Law-Compelled Objectives are a good example. To achieve the objective of no stealing, members must agree both to forego taking the property of other members and to subject themselves to an enforcement mechanism (for example, police, investigations, trials, fines, prisons, and so on). Contribution of liberty, however, is important to external objectives as well. For instance, to attain the objective of Defense against Aggressors, members typically must subject themselves to the leadership of a decision maker. This decision maker will order the members to fight and will often have the authorization to punish or to execute a member if he disobeys an order.

Contribution of liberty is unlike the contribution of other resources. The reason is that it can make the members very vulnerable to abuse and can result in the alliance sliding into a tyranny. Recall the discussion of the tools of tyranny. These tools include:

- Suppressing information or knowledge tending to show that alternatives to the tyranny exist

- Issuing misinformation regarding the alleged limitations and failures of known alternatives to the tyranny

- Prohibiting any communications tending to expose the illusory nature of the benefits offered by the tyranny

- Forbidding any meetings or assemblies of exploited individuals whereby they might form a revolutionary alliance

- Preventing the illusory members from departing the illusory alliance or otherwise terminating their illusory membership

When members contribute liberty to an alliance, they are greatly facilitating these tools. They are making it much easier for a tyranny to arise and prevail over them.[1]

Successful alliances will recognize these dangers and institute safeguards to protect against a tyranny developing. These alliances will appreciate that the objective attained by the contribution of liberty is not worth it, if the alliance becomes prone to sliding into a tyranny. These types of safeguards are substantially similar to the restrictions on means and objectives discussed earlier. The focus will usually be more upon the means. The restrictions will target means that are prone to facilitating the development of a tyranny.

For the safeguards to be effective, the alliance typically must have an express, written accord detailing the relevant restrictions and protections. Restrictions that are not put in writing are often:

- Forgotten

- Subject to selective recollection

- Reinterpreted to suit the needs of a particular situation

- Ignored completely

- Denied as having never existed

Placing the restrictions in writing is not a panacea. However, it is much more difficult to forget, reinterpret, or ignore a written identification of the restrictions.

Interwoven decision makers are usually necessary to have effective safeguards in place. If there is a single decision maker, it is up to that decision maker to interpret and enforce the limitations. This arrangement can work but it is prone to failure. In effect, "the fox is guarding the henhouse." A more effective arrangement is to have a secondary decision maker that reviews and evaluates the actions of the primary decision maker. This secondary decision maker will hold the limited authority to prevent the primary decision maker from acting in the event the primary decision maker acts outside of the restrictions.

---

[1] The objectives of Leveling and Paternalism are internal objectives and therefore focus upon the conduct of individual members. In order to attain these objectives, alliances typically must employ means that are very intrusive upon the liberties of members. For the reasons just noted, pursuit of these objectives can ultimately yield to a tyranny. As such, successful alliances are hesitant to pursue the objective of Leveling and Paternalism.

RESPECT FOR THE ACCORD

The accord is the structure of the alliance. It contains all of the essential agreements and understandings underlying the alliance. The accord can contain provisions on all types of issues including:

- objective identification

- restrictions on objectives

- means identification

- limitations on the means

- member identification

- how members might join or depart the alliance

- contribution to be supplied

- consequences of not providing contribution

- procedures for modifying or amending the accord

- circumstances under which the alliance might terminate

- how tangible benefits of the alliance are to be distributed

The accord and its provisions are of no consequence unless the accord is followed by the members. If the accord is not adhered to, the alliance will likely perish for several reasons including a failure to attain the objective, usage of inadequate or odious means, higher than expected contribution, disproportionate contribution, and so on. The overriding reason for termination, however, will be either that (i) the members are not receiving the benefit they expected to obtain from the alliance, or (ii) the failure to follow the accord has created such uncertainty that the members conclude that the perceived value of the alliance is not as great as once thought.

In contrast, successful alliances have a strong respect for the accord and the members will always strive to abide by its provisions and requirements.[1] Even if members are not pleased with certain undertakings by the alliance, the members will nonetheless accept them if the accord authorizes the actions at issue. The most successful alliances consider the accord to be almost sacred and their members will always strive to see that the accord's provisions are strictly followed. This firm respect for the accord serves to both provide the benefit expected from the alliance, and

---

[1]Respect for the accord is generally not important in implied accords. Generally, respect is a significant factor in long-term, multi-objective alliances.

reinforce the perception in the minds of members that the benefit will continue in the future.[1]

FEW OBJECTIVES

The most common trait of successful alliances is the pursuit of a single objective or a very limited number of objectives. In general, a single objective alliance is the most effective form of alliance. The more objectives that an alliance strives to undertake, the more ineffective the alliance will become and a termination becomes more and more likely.

The reasons for this generalization should be evident. The overriding factor for judging the success of an alliance is the difference (that is, the "gap") between the perceived value of the alliance and the perceived value of the contribution supplied to the alliance. When this gap is large, it means that the alliance is attaining the objective and providing a net perceived value to the members. Further, a large gap means that the value of the alliance is manifest and the members will readily contribute resources to the effort and show respect for the accord. Overall, the bigger the gap, the better the alliance is doing. In effect, a large gap can be seen as a "bargain" for the members. The members are receiving a huge value on their respective contributions.

This gap is particularly large when an alliance undertakes in earnest the objective of Defense against Aggressors. In these situations, the lives of the alliance members and their families are in jeopardy. If the alliance is seen as the only means of defending against this threat, the gap between the perceived value of the alliance and the perceived value of the contribution supplied is usually immense. The reason is obvious. Most persons place the highest value on their lives and the lives of loved ones. The contribution required to attain this goal is miniscule in comparison.

As the danger posed by the aggressors declines, the gap will close as well. For instance, if members were originally under a real threat of annihilation from aggressors and undertake extensive measures to guard against the threat, the gap will be large. If the alliance succeeds in repelling and otherwise defeating the threat, the gap will decline over time. If the threat of the aggressors becomes a distant memory, the gap will close and the alliance might dissolve.

Alliances with numerous objectives are capable of maintaining a large gap and

---

[1] The degree of respect given to an accord correlates with the perceived value generated by the alliance. For instance, if the perceived benefit is low, the respect will tend to be low as well.

being successful. Nonetheless, the gap is difficult to achieve and maintain with multiple objectives. As more objectives are undertaken, the following situations are likely to occur:

- Contribution demands on the members will increase.

- Objectives will be pursued that are not desired by certain members, resulting in zero perceived value to these members.

- Objectives will be undertaken that are disliked by certain members, resulting in negative perceived value to these members.

- The decision-making process will become burdened with more responsibilities and its effectiveness at achieving objectives will decline as a result.

- The undertaking of new objectives often facilitates fidelity limitations, which then tend to reduce the perceived value of the alliance.

The combined result of these factors is that the addition of objectives tends to increase contribution and result in marginal (or even negative) gains in perceived value. The gap for each member narrows as a consequence and, if it completely closes, the member will quit the alliance and termination is likely.

WILLINGNESS TO FORM NEW ALLIANCES

Another trait of successful alliances is the readiness to form new alliances when appropriate. Often, members of an alliance will strive to have that alliance pursue all of their individually desired objectives. If all members desire these objectives and derive a net perceived value from their attainment, no problem is present. However, if less than all members support the pursuit of these additional objectives, trouble will arise. Debates and arguments over whether the new objectives should be pursued will tend to result in discord and disharmony and threaten the future of the alliance. Further, if the objectives are pushed through (for example, a decision-making process adopts them) without the agreement of all members, the respective gaps of net perceived values of the dissenting members will narrow and the alliance will destabilize and possibly terminate.

The solution to this problem is the formation of a new alliance pursuing the controversial objectives. In this situation, the original alliance will remain in effect and will pursue the original objectives. The new alliance will be comprised of only the members of the original alliance who desire the new objectives. These members can then contribute resources towards the new objective. Overall, the original alliance continues in existence and remains successful. At the same time, the new alliance attains the newly desired objectives for its members.

Example 7 "Buy the boat"—Three members—Bob, Joe, and Bill—are members of the alliance. Bob and Joe want to purchase a jet ski. Bill is not interested. As such, Bob and Joe form a separate alliance to acquire the jet ski. Bill is not a member of this new alliance and is not allowed to use the jet ski. But Bill remains a member of the original alliance to buy the boat and is fully entitled to utilize the boat.

The keys to this solution coming about are twofold. First, members must be cognizant of the essential purpose of an alliance and stick to that purpose. Recall that the purpose is to attain an objective desired by all members. If less than *all* members desire an objective, there should be recognition among all members that the objective is not suitable for pursuit by the alliance.

The second factor is a readiness of members to form new alliances. Instead of always focusing attention in a given alliance, members will consider the possibility of utilizing one or more new alliances to attain the objectives. This mindset serves to preserve the success of the original alliance and to foster the creation of additional alliances to attain objectives desired by only certain members. If this way of thinking is not prevalent, however, members will focus their activities on a single alliance, resulting in discord and destabilization of the alliance. Further, such members will be tempted to utilize objective creep and objective disguise to sneak the controversial objective into the alliance.

THE PARADOX OF SUCCESS

An alliance's successes can ultimately result in the collapse of the alliance. This paradoxical result does not occur over night. Instead, it takes place over extended periods of time.

The cause of this gradual collapse appears to be that the members gradually fail to recognize the value of the objective that the alliance attains for them. As a result, the perceived value of the alliance slowly declines until the alliance is at the point of collapsing.

The paradox is that the failure to appreciate the objective that has been attained occurs because the alliance has been so successful at attaining the objective. The members effectively take the attained objective for granted and fail to acknowledge the alliance's role in its attainment. Some common examples include:

- *Defense against Aggressors*—If an alliance attains peace for an extended period of time, its members will tend to slowly forget the terror they, or their forbearers, felt when they all faced a very real threat of death and destruction from aggressors.

- *Law-Compelled Objectives*—Law-compelled objectives tend to become ingrained in an alliance over time. As a result, there is a strong tendency to take the law-compelled objectives for granted and to not recognize the benefits such objectives provide.

- *Generation of Prosperity*—If an alliance successfully attains prosperity for an extended period of time, members will tend to forget the poverty in which they used to reside.

When the members take the attained objective for granted, the perceived value associated with the alliance declines as a result. Members will gradually be less inclined to contribute resources to the alliance. Further, if the objective is in fact taken for granted, members might fail to recognize that the alliance is responsible for attaining the objective. As such, if the alliance begins to not attain the objective, members might not realize the role played by the alliance and might actually be unable to take corrective action necessary to reorient the alliance towards attaining the objective once again.

PARTICIPATING MEMBERSHIP

A final trait of a successful alliance is a membership that actively participates in the operation of the alliance. When members participate, several positive results occur including:

- *Checks on Delegated Decision Makers*—If members are participating in an alliance, they will tend to notice limitations exhibited by delegated decision makers. Such observations will usually result in complaints which will then tend to reduce decision maker limitations.

- *Improved Performance*—When members participate, they tend to notice defects in the performance of the alliance. The members will then lobby for corrections and improvements.

- *Increased Contribution*—If members participate, they tend to contribute more resources towards the alliance. The reason is that the net benefit of the alliance is more apparent to them.

- *More Esprit de Corps*—For esprit de corps to develop, alliance members usually must work side by side in attaining an alliance objective. As such, active participation tends to engender esprit de corps.

CLOSING

There are no hard and fast rules for attaining a successful alliance. In some situations, a factor can be positive while the same factor can be negative under other circumstances.

Part IV

History and Alliances

CHAPTER 14

The Historical Theory

H istory is a very broad topic, and reasonable minds can easily disagree over the parameters of the concept of "history." The discussion within this Part of the book is cursory and no effort will be made to venture into complex definitions. Instead, "history" will mean simply the study and analysis of humans and their actions over time. To some, this discussion might seem more like anthropology, sociology, or even political science. Nonetheless, it will be referred to as "history."

Undoubtedly, alliances have played a substantial role in history. In some ways, history can be seen as the study of the growth, development, and demise of alliances. This Part will provide an overview of this theory by briefly touching upon various developments over the course of human history.

THE ROLE OF KNOWLEDGE

If something is not known by humans, it cannot be used, carried out, or otherwise done by humans. For instance, the wheel is ubiquitous in today's world and appears on everything from dump trucks to baby strollers. Yet there was a time when the wheel was not known to humans, and there were no carts, wagons, or anything employing a wheel. Things were moved by carrying, dragging, or sliding. At some point in time, a human somehow and somewhere stumbled across the idea of a wheel. At first, the use of the wheel was surely quite limited and simple such as a wheel barrow. Over time, however, other humans observed the wheel's inventor employing it to his benefit. These humans then attempted to replicate this use of the wheel.

As time passed, humans slowly discovered the different uses of the wheel and more complex innovations appeared (for example, two-wheeled carts, chariots, and four-wheeled wagons). These discoveries were noted by others and imitated. Slowly but surely, the concept of the wheel evolved into new and different forms. And, at the same time, these innovations spread to humans around the globe. Even today, novel uses of the wheel continue to appear.

This process of concept evolution is not unique to the wheel. No doubt agriculture, mathematics, physics, chemistry, engineering, accounting, business practices, and most areas of knowledge followed similar routes of development.

Alliances share similarities with these examples. It is not possible to identify the first alliance ever. But, at some time, humans had to have stumbled upon the concept of a very simple alliance. This alliance was notable because it offered advantages over individual human effort. Humans continued to use this type of an alliance until its usefulness ended. While this particular alliance was in effect, new alliances were conceived and developed. If these alliances were advantageous, they persisted. If they were not useful, they perished. Other humans took note of these alliances and attempted to replicate them. In copying the alliances of others, the participants adapted the alliances to their particular situations. As time passed, various types of alliances originated, evolved, and faded away. Further, new objectives and means were conceived or discovered and resulting new forms of alliances arose to address these new arrivals. This process has been ongoing for hundreds of thousands of years or more.[1] Today, the process of alliance creation, development, and death continues.

Just as in the case of the wheel, the key factor in the history of alliances is knowledge. A particular type of alliance cannot be expected to appear if it has never existed before or if it has never been conceived in a human mind. But once a particular type of alliance exists in the collective knowledge base of humanity or is conceived mentally in the mind of one person, the opportunity exists for that alliance to develop and expand across humanity. Over time, as more knowledge of alliances accumulates and, if it is effectively preserved through regular use, oral communications, or writings, this knowledge can serve as a foundation for further innovations. As more time passes, the wealth of information relating to various types and uses of alliances continues to grow. With this concept in mind, the history of alliances can be seen as the growth and expansion of simple ideas into more and more complex permutations.

---

[1] Arguably, the process of alliance development has been going on for much longer than a few hundred thousands of years. In fact, alliance formation might be natural to many mammals and other species. For instance, certain relationships between animals, especially herd animals and "pack" hunters, can be viewed as having alliance-like characteristics. This topic is not explored further in this book.

As the following chapters will touch upon, the most important development in the progression of alliances through history appears to be the concept of a multi-objective alliance. Recall that this is an alliance with two or more objectives. The underlying rationale for such an alliance lies in the difficulties associated with forming a separate alliance for each objective desired. Because of these difficulties, an alliance is formed to attain multiple objectives. The arrival of multi-objective alliances led to larger, more complex, and longer-lived alliances that have successfully attained numerous objectives over the course of history. Further, the idea of multi-objective alliances has resulted in the development of a variety of decision-making processes that are typically never necessary in small single, objective alliances. Finally, the concepts underlying multiple objective alliances have arguably given birth to and bolstered illusory alliances and allowed illusory alliances to exploit and tyrannize numerous individuals over the course of time. These topics will be explored in greater detail in the following chapters.

OVERVIEW OF THE REMAINING PARTS OF THE BOOK

Part IV marks a transition point in this book. Parts I, II, and III pertain to identifying and discussing the principles and concepts underlying alliance theory. Part IV and the following Parts V and VI focus upon applying these principles and concepts to historical events and trends.

Part IV Overview

Part IV is a general overview of historical developments. It offers theories and hypotheses regarding historical trends and events utilizing the principles and concepts set forward in Parts I, II, and III. No significant effort is made to substantiate or "prove" these theories as the breadth of the material tackled renders such an undertaking unattainable. Instead, these theories and hypotheses are offered in order to illustrate how alliance theory might be used to understand and analyze history and related topics.

Chapter 15 seeks to identify the earliest multi-objective alliances. These consist of (i) clans, (ii), tribes, (iii) villages, and (iv) city states, with clans being the earliest form of long-standing multi-objective alliances. The discussion suggests that each new form of alliance was born out of a desire to attain new objectives. For instance, tribes became necessary when clans were unable to adequately attain objectives like Defense against Aggressors and Offense against Non-Members. Villages probably developed to address the objectives associated with agricultural-based concerns such as Cooperatives, Uniting against Natural Obstacles, Mitigation of Catastrophe, Morality, and Law-Compelled Objectives. City states likely arose to pursue new objectives such as Generation of Prosperity and to improve upon the objectives pursued by villages by using better means and techniques such as high walls to attain Defense against Aggressors or the construction of large and impressive religious structures to attain Morality-Religious Concerns. This chapter indicates that older forms of multi-objective alliances do not necessarily disappear when a new alliance form appears. Rather, the older forms tend to continue on and can flourish or slowly fade away. Whether the older form continues in existence appears to rest upon whether it continues to offer a net perceived advantage to the alliance members. In addition, this chapter suggests that, as alliances grower larger and older, analysis of them becomes more and more difficult. This situation occurs because the magnitude and history of the alliance at issue can tend to overwhelm the cognitive faculties of the individuals engaging in the analysis.

Chapter 16 focuses upon kingdoms and empires. A kingdom is essentially a city state that conquers and subjugates a number of other city states. An empire is basically a kingdom that conquers and subjugates a number of other kingdoms. Kingdoms and empires tend to be alliances but membership in them is usually limited to a narrow group of persons. Most individuals residing within a kingdom or empire are usually not members. Most empires arise either by not imposing undue burdens upon the subjugated kingdoms and empires or by entering into alliance, semi-alliance, or illusory alliance relationships with the subjugated kingdoms and empires. Kingdoms and empires are not limited to governmental-type alliances. Religion provides a good example. Chapter 16 briefly explores the history of Christianity and suggests that it can be understood as an alliance that split into many different alliances but also evolved into what is effectively an empire.

Chapter 17 focuses upon ideas, mindsets, and worldviews. The general concept is that alliance development and evolution is directly associated with the prevailing views of a particular time. To illustrate this point, the European Middle Ages are first surveyed. The analysis suggests that the ideas, mindsets, and worldviews of the Middle Ages were of such a nature that alliance development and evolution remained largely static, although some developments did occur. The chapter then addresses the European modern age and its emphasis upon progress and the questioning of everything. The chapter indicates that this new set of ideas, mindsets, and worldviews resulted in a substantial change in the nature of alliances and the rate at which alliances evolved and changed over time.

Chapter 18 expands upon the points of Chapter 17 and explores modern developments in alliances. The chapter starts with the reformations of old alliances and new versions of old alliances. It then identifies brand new forms of alliances, accords, and decision-making processes. It also identifies the expansion of membership of most alliances and new means that alliances began using to attain certain objectives. The chapter closes by suggesting that an entirely new attitude towards governmental alliances developed in this era.

Chapter 19 is limited to Law-Compelled Objectives and their predominance in the modern age. The three subsets of this objective—Protection of the Person, Protection of Property, and Enforcement of Promises—are discussed in a fair amount of detail. The chapter also covers the subject of International Law. The chapter concludes by identifying composite objectives such as employment law or environmental law. It is suggested that these objectives are "composite" because they seek to attain a variety of different objectives and do not constitute pure Law-Compelled Objectives.

Chapter 20 concludes Part IV by surveying various modern objectives. Primary attention is given to Generation of Prosperity, Mitigation of Catastrophe and Social Insurance, Charity & Justice, Nationalism, Morality, Paternalism, and the Overlord Objective.

Part V Overview

Part V focuses upon the history of the United States of America. Alliance principles and concepts are used to analyze significant documents such as the Declaration of Independence, the Articles of Confederation, and the U.S. Constitution.

Chapter 21 theorizes that the Colonial Revolution against Great Britain constituted a termination of an alliance. In effect, the colonies concluded that Great Britain offered the colonies no net perceived advantage and that the colonies could attain desired objectives more effectively or efficiently on their own. As a result, the colonies revolted and the Declaration of Independence constituted the termination of the colonies' memberships in the Great Britain alliance. The Articles of Confederation was a first attempt to create an alliance among the colonies but it failed to attain many objectives and therefore the alliance was terminated. The United States of America replaced it.

Chapters 22 through 25 explore various provisions of the U.S. Constitution. The general theory is that the Constitution is an express, written accord underlying an alliance called the United States of America. The Constitution authorizes this alliance to pursue certain objectives and to use means to attain these objectives. The Constitution also imposes numerous restrictions upon the authority of this alliance to pursue certain objectives or to use certain means. The President, Congress, and the Courts constitute a complex tiered and interwoven delegated decision-making process. The states are effectively members of the alliance and the United States thus can be seen as an arch-alliance atop an alliance of alliances.

Chapter 26 touches upon the early history of the United States and the Civil War. The chapter identifies massive changes in the alliance nature brought about by the Civil War including the pursuit of the Overlord Objective and sizeable expansions in membership in the state alliances. The chapter also suggests that the Civil War resulted in the individual members of the states being made members of the United States.

Chapter 27 surveys the history of the United States from the 1870s up to 1980. The chapter identifies various trends and developments that occurred during this time period.

Part VI Overview

Part VI constitutes the conclusion of the book. Chapter 28 is entitled "Forecasts and Speculation" and offers various generalizations about the future of the United States. Many of these generalizations touch upon issues that might affect other parts of the world. Chapter 29 is oriented towards the individual reader and seeks to identify various questions and issues relating to alliances that might interest a typical reader.

CULTURAL CONCERNS

This historical overview will tend to focus on "Eurocentric" or "Western" or "Occidental" or "American" historical trends. This concentration should not be viewed as a suggestion that alliances arose only in European and American areas. Such a viewpoint is manifestly false. Instead, this focus on certain regions and cultures is the product of nothing more than the author's knowledge base and the fact that the history of the European area is fairly well documented and accessible. The concepts discussed in the following chapters should apply equally well to all other civilizations and cultures.

CHAPTER 15

Clans, Tribes, Villages, and City States

This chapter seeks to apply alliance theory to some of the earliest of human associations. The central hypothesis is that ancient clans, tribes, villages, and city states can be viewed as alliances (or, at times, some other form of combined-effort entity such as a semi-alliance, an illusory alliance, or a tyranny).

CLAN ALLIANCES

The prevailing anthropological view is that humans lived for tens of thousands of years or more in circumstances best described as "hunting and gathering" lifestyles. In this condition, most humans lived at a subsistence level. Almost all of their time was spent securing food. They slept in caves, primitive lean-tos, or the outdoors. They were constantly in fear of attacks by predatory wildlife or other humans.

At this point in human history, alliances did exist. However, they were rather limited. To attain objectives that interested an individual living in this time period, the individual had three options:

i) individual effort,

ii) small, short-term alliances (single objective alliances), or

iii) large, long-term alliances called "clans" (multiple objective alliances).

Individual Effort

For the most part, humans typically relied upon their own efforts to achieve most objectives that they desired. If a person was hungry, he located his food. If he was cold, he secured clothing. If he wanted a decent place to sleep, he scouted a location. If he was attacked, he fended for himself.

Small, Short-Lived Alliances

Although humans in this era achieved most objectives through individual effort, they undoubtedly formed alliances from time to time. These alliances typically were single-objective alliances with small memberships. The objectives were probably always external. Common examples of objectives pursued include:

Class of Objective	Example
Uniting against Natural Obstacles	• Hunting large animals • Moving heavy objects
Defense against Aggressors	• Uniting to fight off hostile humans
Offense against Non-Members	• Raiding other humans to take their possessions • Kidnapping other humans to use as slaves
Cooperative	• Sharing and maintaining rare and valuable things such as a fresh-water spring

These alliances typically terminated immediately after the objective was attained. If the alliance was successful, however, pervious members reconstituted similar alliances over and over as required by the members' needs. The accords underlying the alliances were usually implied and a formal decision-making process was rarely needed.

Large, Long-Term Clan Alliances

Most, but not all humans, were members of loose alliances best described as *clans*. The members of these clans did not number more than about 500 and were usually blood-related in some fashion. The clans rarely if ever were held together by express accords. Instead, almost all clans were united by implied accords.

A defining feature of these clans is that the clans pursued objectives that could be achieved more efficiently and/or effectively by large, combined efforts in comparison to individual efforts or efforts of small, short-lived alliances. The primary objectives were usually indefinite and external.

Examples of typical *external* objectives included:

Class of Objective	Example
Defense against Aggressors	• Uniting to defend against other groups of humans that sought to raid the members of the clan
Offense against Non-Members	• Creating large raiding parties to plunder sizeable groups of non-member humans

In addition, these clans had several new *internal* objectives such as:

Class of Objective	Example
Law-Compelled Objective	• Do not kill other clan members • Do not steal the possessions of clan members
Morality	• Common religious practices centralized in the clan
Customs	• "Common courtesy" rules such as keeping the noise level down at night, guest/host rules of conduct, and so on.

Clans pursued other objectives depending upon the facts and circumstances presented. For instance, in difficult times, some clans embraced the "open" objective where the clan might pursue any objective deemed to be in the interests of the members. When conditions improved, the openness of the objective usually declined in a corresponding fashion.

The typical clan was not a significant part of the daily lives of the individual members. Rather, these individuals spent most of their time on their own or engaging in short-lived, single-objective alliances. However, when an issue arose justifying the combined efforts of the clan members, they came together, combined their resources, and strove to attain the objective.

These clans rarely used formal decision-making processes. Instead, they operated largely based upon a nebulous process consisting of an informal consensus of clan members' opinions. For instance, the clan members met and conferred regarding an issue. Although a vote was not taken, an agreed course of action slowly emerged.

Some clans, from time to time, used a decision-making process consisting of a single chieftain (executive decision maker) or a council (a committee decision maker). Other clans used a dual process where an informal consensus made most big decisions but at times certain matters were delegated to executive or committee decision makers such as leading a defense against a band of raiders.

The decision-making processes of the clans were subject to limitations discussed earlier. Due to these limitations, clans often failed to achieve, or fully achieve, their objectives. Similarly, some clans showed signs of decision-maker corruption, and some clans can perhaps be more accurately described as semi-alliances instead of true alliances. However, because it was difficult to conceal corruption and hidden benefits in the relatively open clan system, such occurrences probably were not pervasive. Also, because of the loose nature of the clans, disgruntled members had more freedom either (i) to leave the clan or (ii) to form a revolutionary alliance inside the clan for the purpose of taking control of the clan from inept or corrupt delegated decision makers. These possibilities tended to reduce the negative effects of decision maker limitations.

Most clans exhibited esprit de corps in large measures. The blood-relation nature of clans promoted a sense of belonging and a comradeship amongst the members. In many ways, a clan was a large, extended family. In clans, esprit de corps was limited to an effect of the alliance, and clans did not attempt to attain esprit de corps as an objective. The esprit-de-corps effect typically boosted the performance of an alliance as members often willingly contributed excess resources (life and limb) towards attaining objectives like Defense against Aggressors.[1]

Non-Members in the Clan Setting

Most clans limited membership to only certain individuals. Typically, a clan recognized these individuals as members through membership rituals in which they were inducted into the clan. In the rituals, a new member was usually required to affirm in some respect an accord underlying the alliance.

---

[1] By "excess," it is meant that the perceived value of the resource contributed by the member exceeded the perceived value of the objective attained by the alliance for that member. This difference in perceived values, or excess value, constitutes the perceived value the member placed upon the esprit de corps associated with the alliance. Such contributions resulting in death or other catastrophic consequences are often termed "sacrifices" and the individuals making such contributions are usually thought of as heroes.

Non-members typically lived in proximity to clans. These non-members included hermits, pariahs, and recluses who did not fit into the clan or who desired a solitary life style. These individuals lived alone and achieved most objectives by individual effort. These individuals typically led difficult lives in comparison to clan members. At times, many of these non-members occasionally formed short-lived alliances with other humans to attain certain goals.

Other non-members living in the vicinity of a clan usually included women, children, and men who were sick, disabled, or otherwise infirm. The underlying rationale for the exclusion of these individuals from membership likely lay in the topic of contribution. During the era of clans, the contribution required of alliance members was almost always brute strength. Because the excluded members were viewed as lacking (in a relative sense) of this attribute, they were usually excluded from membership. If the clans, or their members, possessed slaves, these enslaved individuals were not members of the clan either.

The fact that an individual lacked membership in a clan was not necessarily a dire situation. Chapter 5 raised the topic of the "free rider." A free rider is an individual who is not a member of an alliance and does not contribute resources towards the alliance's efforts. Nonetheless, because of the nature of the objective attained by the alliance, this non-member benefits from the alliance. Applying this concept to clans, it is evident that many non-members—including women, children, infirm males, and even slaves—benefited at times from the objectives attained by the clans. For instance, although these individuals might not have been given much respect and led harder lives than the members of the clan, these non-members were likely protected from raids by outsiders and indirectly benefited from some of the internal objectives pursued by the clans. Further, the clans might have pursued some versions of the Charity & Justice objective where the focus was on the interests of the non-members such as the infirm or the elderly. And some of these objectives might have actually been a primitive form of the internal objective of Mitigation of Catastrophe (such as Social Insurance). In this regard, healthy male members likely all realized that they could, at some point in their lives, become injured, disabled, sick, old, or otherwise infirm. As such, it was in their long-term interest to support an internal objective that provided some support to individuals effectively expelled from membership due to their inability to contribute resources to the alliance.

Although females, children, infirm males, and slaves usually were not members of a clan, that does not mean they were not members of other alliances. These individuals undoubtedly formed their own, small-scale, single objective alliances from time to time. For instance, women excluded from the clan formed various alliances to attain certain objectives of interest to them. Similarly, infirm members combined their resources from time to time to their mutual benefit. And any slaves certainly allied among themselves when it was mutually advantageous. Thus, although the highest-profile alliance was the clan, there were numerous other alliances present as well.

TRIBAL ALLIANCES

The tribal way of life was substantially similar to the clan lifestyle. Individuals engaged largely in hunting and gathering activities. They relied upon individual effort to attain most objectives that they desired. From time to time, they entered small, short-lived, single-objective alliances to attain particular objectives. Furthermore, the status of non-members was substantially the same in the tribal way of life.

The main distinctions between a clan and a tribe are that the tribe is larger and more complex than a clan. A *tribe* is best described as an alliance of clans (or an "alliance of alliances" where the tribe is the arch-alliance). In this situation, the individual humans were members of a particular clan. Several of these clans came together and formed the tribe. The clans were the members of the tribe. A tribe composed of ten or more clans could have thousands of derivative members (that is, individuals that are members of the clans that constitute the tribe).

The typical tribe pursued objectives very similar to those pursued by clans. These included external objectives such as war-related defensive and offensive goals and internal objectives like law-compelled topics, morality, and customs. The real difference was the size of the endeavor. A tribe could collect and marshal substantially greater contribution and therefore could attain objectives much more effectively or efficiently, in comparison to a clan. This economies-of-scale feature of tribes was the primary rationale justifying a tribe's existence.

Tribal decision-making processes were most often committee delegated decision makers. Typically, each clan would send a delegate such as a chieftain to participate in the process. These chieftains would confer and reach a decision usually through an informal consensus. If required by the circumstances, a tribe's committee might select a tribal chieftain to serve as an executive delegated decision maker such as to lead the tribe into battle. Or, if the tribe was quite large, the committee might form a smaller committee of chieftains to address certain issues.

It is important to note that the small clan alliances largely remained viable alliances notwithstanding the existence of the tribes. Generally speaking, the clans addressed the issues of specific interest to clan members. The tribes, on the other hand, addressed those issues that (i) were of interest to all clans, and (ii) were particularly suited for tribal action.

Esprit de corps was usually present as an effect of a tribal alliance. In this regard, the members of the clan felt these sentiments with regard to both (i) the clan in which they were members and (ii) the tribe in which their clans were members. In most situations, the individual members felt greater esprit de corps towards their clan.

At times, association glory developed as an effect of a tribal alliance. In this situation, clans could increase their prestige and reputation through affiliating with a notable tribe. And, from time to time, certain tribes engaged in efforts to preserve or augment the association glory of a tribe.

As time passed, the clans tended to dissolve and the typical tribe began to resemble more an alliance of individual members rather than an alliance of alliances. This gradual transition occurred because the larger tribe tended to offer greater advantages over the smaller clans. As a result, clan members slowly began to identify themselves more as a part of the tribe. Notwithstanding this transition, the clans continued at least a nominal existence despite lacking a real substance. Often, combinations of esprit de corps and association glory held clans together long after all other functions of the clan had dissipated.

VILLAGES

One of the external objectives of all tribes was to defend their members from attacking raiders. If a tribe successfully achieved this objective, there was a very significant result—relative peace and stability. These conditions then lead to the development of villages.

Tranquil times allowed members to do things not possible in the harsher times of the past. For instance, the members were able to accumulate possessions, construct semi-permanent housing, and initiate agricultural endeavors. Conversely, when tribes failed to adequately defend against attacking raiders, such undertakings were largely impossible. The constant threat of attack rendered these undertakings of little value. If raids were a distinct possibility, the members needed to be able to flee at a moment's notice. Accumulation of property, living in homes, and farming were incompatible with this need.

Tribes that successfully defended against raiders gradually transitioned from mobile, loosely-organized alliances to village arrangements and corresponding new alliance structures. In this regard, the success of tribes seems to be an essential precondition for the development of villages.[1]

---

[1] Not all tribes transitioned to a village way of life. Even if a tribe attained great success in defending against invaders, it might have nonetheless preferred the mobile lifestyle of the tribe.

A *village* is characterized as an alliance supporting a community of members who situated themselves around a semi-permanent geographical location. A typical village had a nexus where a large group of members lived closely together. Other members lived farther from this nexus but maintained some degree of proximity. Typically, the members engaged in some type of agricultural activities. Often, members had claims to certain tracts of land upon which they constructed homes or farmed. Usually, the village was situated in a location that was suitable for an effective defense in the case of a raid by aggressors.

The village-alliance structure was substantially similar to those of clans and tribes. The decision-making processes varied but were characterized by informal consensuses, chieftains, committees of chieftains, or various combinations thereof.

As with clans and tribes, individuals in villages had various options to attain desired objectives:

- *Individual Effort*—Individuals achieved most desired objectives through individual actions.

- *Short-lived, single-objective alliances*—Individuals also formed small, short-lived alliances to achieve various objectives such as labor-intensive efforts of interest to only a few village members.

- *Villages*—Villages, like clans and tribes, were a form of long-term, multi-objective alliances.

Villages pursued many of the same basic, external objectives as tribes. However, villages typically attained these objectives with *improved means* such as:

Class of Objective	Improved Means
Defense against Aggressors	• Militia with some training and coordination • Defensive measure in place such as palisade walls or primitive towers • Diplomatic measures to prevent conflict • Entering alliances with other villages or tribes to fend off large forces of raiders
Offense against Non-Members	• Better organized raiding parties • More evenhanded distribution of booty • Entering alliances with other villages or tribes to raid non-members

Class of Objective	Improved Means
Offense against Non-Members	• More effective measures to retain slaves and prevent their escape

Aside from pursuing old objectives with better means, villages also sought to attain new objectives. In general, these new objectives could be pursued only because of the relative peace and stability associated with villages.

Examples of new *external* objectives include:

Class of Objective	New External Objectives
Cooperative	• Wells and canals for improved water supplies for agriculture • Mills for grinding grain
Mitigation of Catastrophe	• Aiding members suffering misfortune with food, clothes, shelter, etc.
Charity and Justice	• Helping non-members who are in need

New *internal* objectives include:

Class of Objective	New Internal Objectives
Law-Compelled Objectives	• Additional enforcement of property laws • More sophisticated property laws governing land such as where agricultural projects were undertaken

Class of Objective	New Internal Objectives
Morality— Religion	• More advanced religious rituals and practices
Morality— Bolstering	• Focus on physical health and mental toughness to insure the ability to contribute to the alliance

Esprit de Corps and Association Glory

Villages typically had less esprit de corps and association glory in comparison to clans and tribes. The blood-relations of clans and tribes tended to result in a heavy presence of both phenomena. A village alliance, in contrast, was more utilitarian and therefore less likely to have strong sentiments of esprit de corps or association glory.

If clan or tribe members formed a village, the association glory of the old clan or tribe tended to continue to some degree and to fuse into the village. Newcomers to the village could then join the village alliance and clothe themselves in the association glory of the former clan or tribe. Over time, such association glory tended to diminish.

Decision-Making Processes in Villages

Because of their more complex objectives, villages required more sophisticated decision-making processes including various forms of executives and committees. In comparison to clans or tribes, villages usually suffered from greater decision-maker limitations. This tendency was due in large part to the number and type of objectives that villages tended to pursue. For instance, villages pursued objectives that were usually more open and required greater delegated decision maker discretion. As such, the potential for ability limitations increased.

In addition, villages also suffered from greater fidelity limitations in their decision makers. This was because the objectives of villages typically required greater trust in the decision makers. And the nature of villages, with houses and buildings to conceal activities, allowed for many fidelity limitations to go undiscovered.

Village Membership

The composition of village membership often differed from that of clans and tribes. Although village membership continued to favor healthy males, membership ranks were usually opened to new classes of persons. Recall that the determinative factor of membership is the ability to contribute resources. In a village setting with objectives that did not focus solely upon brute strength capabilities, females and infirm or old males were able to contribute suitable resources. Further, while clans and tribes tended to limit membership to blood-relations, village membership was generally open to anyone who could supply needed resources towards the effort. As such, the rise of villages initiated a trend towards expanded alliance membership.

Villages were more inclined to have second-class members. Usually, this was a situation where a village-alliance would form a short-lived alliance with either (i) persons living near the village, or (ii) nearby clans or tribes. The objectives of these fleeting alliances were typically to fend off an attack by raiders, tackle a natural obstacle, or to undertake a similar one-time event. When the given objective was attained, the alliance typically dissolved. In these situations, the short-term new participants somewhat resembled members of the village. However, because they did not enjoy the full range of objectives pursued by the village, the individuals are best described as second-class members.

Transition to City States

The development of villages was marked by the end of nomadic lifestyles and in its place the arrival of semi-permanent residences. This change was made possible by tribes creating a relative peace so that the members could settle down in a particular place. This end to the nomadic wandering then allowed the accumulation of additional property, construction of housing, and agricultural endeavors. These accumulations resulted in additional resources to be combined towards the attainment of new objectives. In addition, a semi-permanent lifestyle allowed more time for contemplation and experiments regarding both new objectives to pursue and new means to utilize in attaining existing objectives.

The semi-permanency of the villages tended to create longer standing alliances with relatively stable accords and objectives. Although the accords (and decision-making processes) did evolve over time to meet changing circumstances, the rate and magnitude of the change declined in proportion to the stability brought on by the village lifestyle. This stability then led to the development of city states.

CITY STATES

A *city-state* alliance was similar to a village alliance in that it centered upon a permanent geographical area in or around which members lived. But the city state differed from the village in that the city state usually:

1) Was larger that a village;

2) Used more effective and/or efficient means to achieve objectives pursued by villages;

3) Pursued new and different objectives; and

4) Utilized much more formal decision-making processes.

The typical city state of the past resembled a modern, small city, except that it usually had a heavily fortified, defensive area to where members could flee in the event of raids. Members of city states engaged in advanced trade and commercial activities such skilled crafts, markets and bazaars, and imports and exports.

The key to success of any city state rested upon its ability to attain the related objectives of Defense against Aggressors and Offensive against Non-Members. City states typically attained these objectives through using new and better means, in comparison to villages.

For instance, some of the *improved means* included:

Objective	Improved Means
Defense against Aggressors	• Fulltime delegated decision-maker(s) such as warlords dedicated to defensive measures • Well-trained, armed, and standing militias • Stone walls, towers, and other fortifications • Stores of necessities in the event of siege • Proficient diplomats to resolve conflicts, sue for peace, and/or negotiate defensive alliances with other city states or tribes
Offense against Non-Members	• Experienced and competent decision makers to lead offensive efforts such as warlords • Well-trained and armed militias • Adequate supplies for extended campaigns • Proficient diplomats to negotiate offensive alliances with other city states or tribes

City states also used *improved means* to achieve other existing objectives (both external and internal) such as:

Objective	Improved Means
Uniting against Natural Obstacles (*external*)	• Improved pathways and roads • Harbor construction and maintenance for fishing and trade • Improved wells
Cooperatives (*external*)	• Common areas for commerce and public activities • Public baths
Mitigation of Catastrophe (*external*)	• Well-coordinated efforts to respond to natural disasters
Law-Compelled Objectives (*internal*)	• Standing decision-making process for enforcement of laws • Prisons and other punishments for violations • Extensive property rules addressing most disputes that commonly arose
Morality—Religion (*internal*)	• Religious buildings, statues, and other • implements to further the prevailing religion
Morality—Bolstering (*internal*)	• Emphasis upon development and maintenance of personal qualities believed to foster contribution such as health, strength, courage, selflessness, and so on

And city states also pursued *new* objectives including:

Class of Objective	Examples
Generation of Prosperity	• Promotion of crops or wares produced by members • Coinage
Law-Compelled Objectives	• Enforcement of promises • Remedies for broken promises
Conservation	• Basic efforts at conserving certain resources prone to overuse
Esprit de Corps & Association Glory	• Rousing speeches • Holidays to celebrate important events • Statues and monuments to commemorate great victories

The new objectives tended to strengthen the alliance. For instance, by promoting prosperity, fostering conditions favorable to commerce, developing functioning property laws, and initiating conservation, the result was that the members were more likely to have additional resources. These additional resources could then be used to contribute towards the attainment of new objectives. Or they could be used to craft better means of attaining existing objectives.

City State Decision-Making Processes

City states were notable for having much more formal and complex decision-making processes. The variations in the processes ran the gamut with one extreme being membership vote and the other being a single, executive decision maker. In between these extremes were tiered and interwoven decision-making processes using membership votes, committees, and executives. These processes were typically longstanding and not subject to much modification.

Most city states retained an executive decision maker in the form of a king or warlord. In many situations, a closer review of the circumstances might reveal that a committee decision maker such as an oligarchy was the true decision maker and the king was a mere figurehead that did as the oligarchy ordered.

City-State Membership

The location and composition of city-state membership entailed interesting new developments. For instance, the members were not necessarily situated physically within the city state. Typically, the city state was located in a relatively small area that was easily defended against attacks. Often, the location was atop a hill or an embankment of some sort and was surrounded by walls. Many members lived inside this defensive area. However, a significant portion of members lived just outside the walls where they constructed residences and commercial buildings. Further, a sizeable portion of members lived much farther away on agricultural estates. In a time of attack by raiders, these outside members would collect transportable possessions and flee to the defensive center of the city state and wait out the attack. When the raid ended, these members would then return to their outside residences and estates.

As noted earlier, villages saw the loosening of membership ranks to include new classes of persons aside from the traditional healthy male. City states continued this trend. Possible causes included the prosperity commonly associated with city states as well the development of sophisticated barter systems and coinage. As discussed in Chapter 5, money serves a very significant role in opening membership to a variety of persons. Instead of having to contribute a specific type of resource such as labor, a person could instead contribute a sum of money perceived to be equal in value to the necessary resource. Bartering and then coinage developments in city states allowed more and more classes of persons to enter the membership.

At the same time, a paradoxical result of this opening of the membership to new classes of individuals was the exclusion of the less prosperous from membership. In the past, the key resource necessary to most alliances was some form of physical labor such as brute strength or fighting skills. As a result, alliances tended to allow only healthy males to be members. With the development of coinage, the key resource shifted from labor to monetary prosperity. The main value of money from an alliance perspective was outsourcing. By collecting large sums of money from members, an alliance could then outsource the attainment of an objective to a third-party. For instance, if an old village alliance desired to have a paved road through the village, the village members had to contribute the labor resource themselves. That is, they had to personally collect the stones, transport them to the village, and then lay the road. Obviously, this would be quite a project and it would likely never be undertaken. In contrast, a city state could just collect money from its members and then hire a labor gang to do all the work. Thus, the result of the trend towards monetary contribution was that individuals without sufficient prosperity were not allowed to become members of many city state alliances.

In many situations, membership was originally limited to only land owners as these persons were the only prosperous individuals in the city state. As time passed, merchant classes developed that possessed sufficient monetary contribution to justify membership.[1] These two classes—the land owners and the merchants—then controlled the alliance. And the alliance undertook only those objectives that were in the interest of the membership classes. Naturally, only those classes participated in the decision-making process and contributed resources towards the effort.

The Masses and City States

With wealth limitations on membership becoming more common, a sizeable portion of the individuals living within or near the city state were not members of the city state. These newly excluded individuals usually consisted of laborers and servants. They joined the classes of individuals historically excluded from membership such as drifters, the destitute, the infirm, slaves, children, and women. This collection of non-members can be termed the *masses*.

The masses often enjoyed many of the benefits of the city-state alliance. This was because of the free-rider effect. For instance, when a city state was attacked, the masses were usually allowed to hide within the defensive walls of the city state. And, if a city state had public wells, the masses usually could use them. Further, if the city state was prosperous, the masses usually benefited from the prosperity in the form of higher wages, better food, and so on.

The city states treated the masses in many different ways. Some of the various manners include:

- *Ignoring*—The city state undertook only those objectives that were desired by the members. The masses were disregarded.

- *Exploiting*—The city state undertook objectives for the express purpose of taking advantage of the masses. For instance, Law-Compelled Objectives were structured to favor the members and to allow them to take property away

---

[1]City states with merchant classes were prosperous and could usually generate substantially more resources to attain objectives than city states without merchant classes. This material advantage often tipped the scales in conflicts between city states. For instance, these additional resources could be used to acquire better defensive and offensive weaponry. Further, they could be used to outsource military endeavors by hiring mercenaries to fight for the city state. It should be noted that the practice of outsourcing to mercenaries had its drawbacks as these individuals fought for a material reward only and lacked an esprit de corps towards the city state. This lack of an esprit de corps at times resulted in the mercenaries' lack of commitment to particular undertakings and resulting failures.

from the masses. These undertakings fell within the external objective of Offense against Non-Members.

• *Repressing/Appeasing*—The city state feared the masses creating a counter, revolutionary alliance that might revolt and upset the city state alliance. To guard against this occurrence, the city-state alliance maintained soldiers to put down any revolt and otherwise keep the masses in line. In addition, the city state undertook measures to keep the masses relatively content so that they would not feel the need to revolt. These endeavors fell within the external objective of Defense against Aggressors.

• *Furthering Charity & Justice*—The members of some city states might have felt compassion for the masses and undertook measures to aid them. These endeavors fell within the external objective of Charity & Justice.

• *Creating Illusory Alliances*—To stifle revolution and promote harmony, some city-states created illusory alliances whereby the masses perceived themselves as being bona-fide members of the city-state alliance. In reality, the only true members were the wealthy land owners and merchants. Again, such undertakings constituted the external objective of Defense against Aggressors. Many city states attempted to develop esprit de corps and association glory in order to further the semblance of an alliance.

• *Allowing Second-Class Members*—Similar to creating illusory alliances, some city states fostered second-class members. Typically, this was done in order to have sufficient manpower to fend off an attack by an aggressor. In this situation, the true members of the city state were the wealthy. These members enjoyed the benefits of the city-state alliance year round. And the non-member masses enjoyed some of these benefits as free-riders. But when an attack loomed on the horizon, the city state alliance in effect opened the membership to the masses. The masses then raised arms with the true members and defended the city state against the attack. When the attack was repulsed, however, the true members attempted to reinstate the prior system with membership being limited to the wealthy. But this was often difficult as the masses, having been allowed into membership, did not want to return to their non-member status. The result was usually an illusory alliance where the wealthy continued to be the true members and the masses were fooled into believing they were members. In other situations, there were two genuine alliances that allied together to form a single alliance. One alliance consisted of the wealthy class and pursued objectives desired by the members. The other alliance was of the masses. This second alliance generally did not pursue its own objectives. Instead, it existed to ally with the wealthy-class alliance from time to time on a few select objectives such as defense of the city state.

- *Holding Open the Promise of Membership*—With membership usually resting upon the ability to contribute necessary resources, the masses typically could enter the ranks of membership if they became wealthy. As such, many city-state alliances allowed individuals to move from the masses to membership. This served to increase the pool of resources contributed and to improve the alliance. In addition, the possibility of membership served to reduce revolutionary sentiments as the masses perceived that they—with hard work or luck—could join the wealthy and be admitted to the alliance as a full member. As such, a revolution was not necessary to improve one's situation.

- *Extracting resources*—Some city-state alliances sought to extract resources from the masses in the form of taxes. Usually, these taxes were some type of duty on goods sold or a user fee such as a toll for crossing a bridge. In this situation, the masses should not be viewed as true members contributing resources towards an alliance. Instead, two situations are possible. First, the city-state alliance was merely exploiting the masses and seeking to appropriate resources from them through a tax. Second, the masses constituted second-class members and the tariffs represented contributions of resources towards attainment of an objective desired by both the wealthy, member class and the masses. For instance, a bridge toll could be seen as benefiting the masses, if it was used to fund and maintain the bridge. In this situation, the wealthy were members of one alliance. And this alliance would then create an alliance with the masses for the purpose of pursing the objective of the bridge.

The size of the masses varied greatly with each city state. Some city states had very liberal terms for membership and their masses were therefore relatively small. Other city states strictly limited membership and therefore had large masses.

True Nature of City States

Over time, city states usually were in a state of flux. Earlier, it was noted that a combined-effort entity might fluctuate from a true alliance to a semi-alliance to an illusory alliance to an outright tyranny. City states exhibited these transformations frequently. Generally, city states resembled semi-alliances on most occasions. In this situation, characteristics of a true alliance were present but other factors raised questions as to whether an illusory alliance might actually exist.

The fluctuation in the nature of city states was generally tied to the perceived value of the objectives underlying the city state. As a general rule, when a compelling objective developed such as defense against a formidable aggressor, a city state would unite and usually transform itself into a true alliance. When the crisis subsided and the objectives pursued became of less immediate value, the city state might then slide into a semi-alliance or an illusory alliance. If another crisis arose, the city state might then slide back towards a true alliance until the crisis was averted.

Historical Examples of City States

Four historical examples of city states are Athens, Sparta, Carthage, and Rome. Athens and Sparta existed at the same time and often fought. Carthage and Rome also existed in the same time period and fought as well. All four of these combined-effort entities appear to have constituted true alliances. Of course, the four were subject to the fluctuations associated with combined-effort entities and therefore sometimes constituted semi-alliances, illusory alliances, or tyrannies.

- **Sparta and Athens**—Sparta was a city state located in the southern part of what is today known as Greece. Sparta was known for its military excellence, a morality-bolstering lifestyle that focused upon discipline and physical exercise, and a very strong emphasis on esprit de corps. Sparta utilized an interwoven decision-making process consisting of two kings, a committee decision maker, and occasional membership votes. Sparta's membership was hereditary and essentially was limited to the male offspring of members. Female Spartans were not allowed into membership, although they were accorded much more respect than females in Athens. Sparta's masses largely consisted of numerous slaves that performed most of the labor in the city state. Sparta expended substantial resources in controlling and repressing this slave population.

  Athens was a city state located in the area known today as Greece. It was known for having an open society where trade, commerce, arts, and creativity prospered. It employed a membership vote decision-making process. Athens' membership was conditioned upon owning a certain level of property. Generally, this property requirement was not difficult to meet and many individuals were able to become members of Athens. Numerous non-members lived in and around Athens. These non-members included women, slaves, and the poor, as well as various artisans, free laborers, traders, and merchants. These non-members typically benefited from Athens' attainment of various objectives.

  Athens fought with Sparta and other Greek city states in the Peloponnesian War, which lasted for about 30 years. Sparta ultimately prevailed and conquered Athens entirely. Sparta then magnanimously allowed Athens to maintain its independence and act as an autonomous city state. During this ensuing period, many aspects of Athens flourished. For example, it was during this period that Plato and Aristotle wrote their famous works that are still hailed today as masterpieces. Sparta dominated for some time after the end of the Peloponnesian War but ultimately collapsed when its huge slave population revolted. Athens, Sparta, and other Greek city states eventually came under the rule of the Macedonians.

- **Carthage and Rome**—Carthage was a city state located in modern Tunisia. It was known for its merchants and trading. Carthaginian ships traded around the Mediterranean and generated substantial prosperity for the city state. Carthage protected its trade routes with a large and powerful navy. The most famous Carthaginian was Hannibal who led Carthaginian forces against the Romans in the Second Punic War (218 to 202 BCE) and nearly defeated Rome. The precise nature of the Carthaginian decision-making process is unclear. Overall, it appears to have been an oligarchy whereby a committee consisting of aristocrats made most decisions. At times, there appear to have been other committee decision makers elected directly by the membership. The relationship between these decision makers and the oligarchy is unclear.

Rome was originally a city state located in modern Italy. It was known for an effective military, for instilling virtuous traits in its members, and for a strong sense of esprit de corps. Rome engaged in numerous public works projects, including the construction of complex systems of aqueducts and roads. Many Roman roads are still present today. Originally, Rome's decision-making process was a republic. This consisted of an intricate system of interwoven and tiered decision-making processes including votes by all members on certain matters, a committee decision maker called the Senate, and numerous executive decision makers such as consuls, magistrates, praetors, quaestors, and so on. The complexity of the process renders a thorough discussion not possible in this book. Interestingly, Rome also embraced the concept of a "dictator." In the event of an extreme emergency such as an invasion of Rome by a foreign army, the republic could appoint a dictator but for a period of no more than six months. The dictator was a single executive decision maker with the authority to make decisions upon any and all issues. The Roman Republic changed over time but remained a republic until Julius Caesar was made a seemingly permanent dictator. After Caesar was assassinated in 44 BCE, Rome's government was transformed into a sovereign whereby Augustus was the first of a long line of "Caesars" that ruled Rome as executive decision makers.

Carthage and Rome fought in three wars called the Punic Wars. In the First Punic War, Rome wrestled the island of Sicily away from Carthage. In the Second Punic War, Hannibal famously crossed the Alps with his elephants and then massacred several Roman armies and almost conquered Rome. Hannibal's invasion ended when Rome invaded Carthage and Hannibal was forced to retreat home to protect Carthage. The war ended with Carthage losing a major battle and entering truce whereby it ceded most of its power and autonomy to Rome. In the Third Punic War, Rome invaded Carthage, sacked the city of Carthage, and effectively destroyed the city and killed most of its inhabitants. Following this event, Carthage did not exist anymore and Romans occupied all of the former Carthaginian lands. Rome continued to prevail for many centuries afterwards.

GOVERNMENTAL ENTITIES

At this juncture, it is appropriate to identify the concept of a governmental entity. This is because historical study largely focuses upon the growth, development, and demise of governments. Further, the remainder of this Part will often concentrate on the rise of new governmental alliances and entities and will contrast these developments to non-governmental alliances and entities.

A *governmental entity* is a difficult concept to define with precision because it encompasses numerous different situations. To begin with, a governmental entity includes both true alliances and the three other types of combined-effort entities (semi-alliance, illusory alliance, and a tyranny). In addition, a governmental entity is long-term and pursues multi-objectives such as public-works projects, defensive undertakings, and Law-Compelled Objectives. The pursuit of other objectives is likely as well. Further, a governmental entity has a large degree of structure and formality, especially in its decision-making process. Governmental entities do not utilize nebulous decision-making processes. Finally, a governmental entity is what is traditionally considered to be a "government." This class of customary governments includes city and local governments, a national government, anything referred to as a "state," a noble with authority to rule over the masses, a kingdom, and an empire. Of the entities discussed in this chapter, the only true governmental entity is the city state. The clans and tribes, due to the nebulous decision-making process and informality, are not governmental entities. Villages can constitute governmental entities but most early villages were too informal to fall into this category.

CHAPTER 16

Kingdoms and Empires

Kingdoms and empires have played significant roles in human history. This Chapter seeks to identify the true natures of kingdoms and empires. Various historical examples are referenced.

KINGDOMS

Kingdoms arose around the same time as city states. A *kingdom* was a city state that was very successful at achieving the objective of Offense against Non-Members. As a result, the city state was able to subjugate neighboring city states and villages and to exploit them, resulting in a kingdom. In this situation, the surrounding city states and villages were not members of the kingdom alliance. Instead, the surrounding city states and villages were the targets of the kingdom, with the objective being to conquer these city states and villages and profit as a consequence.

A fundamental aspect of any kingdom was an outstanding, offensive military force. Historically, most kingdoms arose out of city-states that developed such forces. A city state used its superior force to subjugate neighboring city states and villages or to coerce them into submission. After conquering and subjugating several city states, the victorious city-state held the status of a kingdom. The subjugated villages and city states ("*subjugated entities*") were absorbed into the kingdom. The subjugated entities could include all forms of combined-effort entities (true alliance, semi-alliance, illusory alliance, or tyranny).

What was the relationship between the kingdom and the subjugated entities? In most situations, it essentially constituted a master-slave relationship. That is, the kingdom was the master and the subjugated entities were slaves exploited by the kingdom. This relationship was substantially similar to the manner in which an individual slave master might exploit an individual slave.

Within the framework of this master-slave relationship, a subjugated alliance typically retained its original alliance nature, with an accord, individual members, contribution, and objective. A subjugated alliance, however, was no longer an autonomous entity. Instead, it was subject to the dictates of the kingdom. Most kingdoms demanded tribute (such as precious metals, livestock, food, spices, oils, and so on), which were to be turned over by the subjugated alliance to the kingdom or serious military repercussions would follow. Often, but not always, the tribute included supplying military support (such as troops or ships) to the kingdom's offensive efforts. In supplying the tribute, the subjugated alliance was often attaining the objective of Defense against Aggressors. That is, through providing tribute, the subjugated alliance was in affect appeasing the kingdom and preventing military reprisals. And this tribute ultimately came from the individual members of the subjugated alliance as a form of contribution to effectively purchase peace and security from the kingdom.

Kingdoms represent an important refinement in the objective of Offense against Non-Members. Prior to the development of kingdoms, the typical alliance with a strong offensive military force engaged in what is best described as plundering. It would raid a neighboring village or city state and basically pillage, rape, destroy, and quickly depart with enslaved individuals and as much loot as could be transported. This process is obviously destructive and not particularly efficient. At some point, a wise executive decision maker must have realized that, instead of destroying a neighboring city state, it would make more sense to destroy only its military force and then compel it to pay a hefty tribute on an annual basis.[1] This concept then spread and more and more kingdoms arose over time.

VARIATIONS OF KINGDOMS

Kingdoms are somewhat confusing because of the complex relationships that can be present. At this point, it might be useful to reiterate a few points regarding the nature of kingdoms and related entities:

---

[1] The practice of seeking tribute instead of plundering probably initially arose out of a compromise. For instance, an offensive alliance might have assaulted a fairly well-defended village or city state and a stalemate resulted. The defending alliance then offered a tribute to avoid a protracted battle and possible devastation. The offensive alliance accepted the offer to avoid the casualties and costs associated with completing the assault and possible defeat. After receiving the tribute for several years, the offensive alliance likely concluded that a tribute-arrangement was preferable to plundering and attempting to carry off as much as possible at one time. That is, a steady stream of tribute was much better than a one-time plundering. After this conclusion was reached, more and more offensive alliances began structuring themselves as kingdoms and began seeking tribute instead of plunder.

- **Kingdom**—A kingdom is typically a true alliance with members. It always has a superior offensive military force that it employs to pursue the objective of Offensive against Non-Members. The members of this alliance contribute resources towards this objective. Usually the resources are life and limb as well as time. But sometimes the contribution might be money (or other fungible resources). Fungible resources allow the alliance to hire mercenaries to engage in the military efforts. The members have an expectation of receiving a material reward from conquering other villages or city states and having them render tribute onto to the alliance. The alliance might distribute this tribute to its members or might use it to offset or eliminate the contribution of monetary resources by members to the alliance. The decision-making process of a kingdom is most often a "king" and therefore the term "kingdom" is utilized to describe this entity. But the decision-making process can be other types of processes including an oligarchy, a democracy, or various permutations of these processes.

- **The Subjugated Entity**—This entity is typically a village or city-state alliance that has been conquered or otherwise subjugated by a kingdom alliance. To avoid death and destruction, this alliance has bought peace with the kingdom by agreeing to submit tribute to the kingdom, usually on an annual basis. As noted above, the subjugated alliance attains the objective of Defense against Aggressors by pooling contribution of individual members and using it to placate the aggressor kingdom. Importantly, the subjugated alliance usually remains an alliance to its individual members. However, it is not a member of the kingdom alliance. That is, there is no alliance of alliances. Instead, a tyranny essentially exists where the kingdom alliance constitutes a tyrant to the subjugated entity and profits from its hold on the subjugated alliances.

- **A Kingdom is Not Necessarily a Governmental Entity**—Earlier, the concept of a "governmental entity" was raised. Recall that governmental entities include things like city and local governments, a national government, anything referred to as a "state," a noble with authority to rule over the masses, a king, and so on. The concept of a kingdom, however, is not limited to governmental entities. Instead, any alliance or other combined-effort entity can constitute a kingdom and can subjugate other entities or individuals. Often, this subjugation might not be through military force. Instead, it might be through economic power or other indirect forms of coercion. For instance, many large, modern-day corporations appear to constitute kingdoms.

There are several exceptions to these generalizations:

- **Not All Kingdoms Are True Alliances**—With regard to individuals within a kingdom that might appear to constitute "members," the kingdom can be a semi-alliance, illusory alliance, or a tyranny. In this situation, the kingdom has effectively subjugated both (i) individuals residing in the kingdom's homeland, and (ii) the outside combined-effort entities that make up the kingdom. The subjugated individuals residing in the homeland typically fare well from the arrangement as they indirectly share in the spoils of the kingdom and its exploitation of subjugated entities. For instance, if the combined-effort entity is a tyranny, the tyrant will retain the tribute for his own purposes. However, the tyrant will usually share the spoils with the subjugated individuals in the homeland in order to placate a rebellion. Similarly, a kingdom that constitutes an illusory alliance to its ostensible members in the homeland will have to share the spoils with these ostensible members in order to preserve the illusion of an alliance. In each instance, the tyrant and the individuals controlling the illusory alliance will retain a large share of the spoils. As a result, the homeland individuals will typically receive a smaller share of kingdom spoils than they would receive in a true alliance.

- **Not All Subjugated Entities Are True Alliances**—The subjugated entities can also be semi-alliances, illusory alliances, and even tyrannies. For instance, a true alliance can subjugate a neighboring tyranny and receive tribute from it. Or a tyranny can subjugate another tyranny and receive tribute. Several other combinations are possible.

- **Some Subjugated Entities Do Become Members of a Conquering Alliance**— In the typical situation, a conquering alliance subjugates a combined-effort entity and compels it to pay tribute, resulting in a master-slave relationship. At times, though, the conquering alliance will open up its membership ranks and actually allow the subjugated alliance, or the individuals affiliated with a subjugated combined-effort entity, to join the conquering alliance. The conquering alliance will not do such a thing, unless it perceives that the benefit of allowing in new members outweighs the benefits of forcing the subjugated entity to pay tribute. For instance, if it appears that the persons within a subjugated entity will gladly join the conquering alliance, willingly contribute resources, and overall aid the conquering alliance in its attainment of objectives, the conquering alliance will tend to allow in new members. In contrast, if it appears that the subjugated entity, or individuals associated with it, will not willingly contribute resources and otherwise will be disruptive, the better alternative might be to close the doors of membership and maintain the subjugation.

- **Tyrannical Alliances**—At times, a kingdom's relationship with its subjugated entities might constitute a tyrannical alliance. In this circumstance, the subjugated entities might not have warm feelings towards the kingdom. However, they perceive that the kingdom offers a net benefit over other arrangements. For instance, although the kingdom might be abusive, its presence brings peace to the region and eliminates attacks by raiders. As a result, the tribute given to a kingdom will essentially constitute contribution towards an alliance effort (that is, the retention of the kingdom as a means of instituting peace and attaining the objective of Defense against Aggressors). As with all tyrannical alliances, the subjugated entities' willing acquiescence to the abuses of the tyrannical alliance constitutes a form of contribution towards an alliance effort.

- **Some Subjugated Entities Enter an Illusory Alliance with the Conquering Entity**—If a conquering entity is shrewd, it might dupe a subjugated entity into entering an illusory alliance. In this situation, the subjugated entity will perceive itself as being part of a true alliance. As a result, it will gladly contribute resources and be content with the situation. In reality, however, the conquering alliance will control the illusory alliance and manipulate it for the conquering alliance's benefit.

- **The Role of Outsourcing**—At times, combined-effort entities can enter into outsourcing arrangements with other combined-effort entities. These arrangements can be a little confusing and often resemble kingdoms. But scrutiny of the situation will reveal the true nature. For instance,

    Illustration—A city state fears an attack by another city state and therefore undertakes the objective of Defense against Aggressors. Rather than constructing large fortifications and building up a sizeable militia or standing army, however, this city state outsources the effort to a powerful kingdom. Specifically, it is agreed that the kingdom will defend the city state from attack. In return, the city state will compensate the kingdom with an annual payment of silver. In this situation, the city state is not part of the kingdom. Instead, the city state has outsourced its defense to a kingdom.

    Illustration—A tyranny fears an attack by another combined-effort entity (including a revolutionary alliance whose objective is destruction of the tyranny). The tyranny outsources the effort of defending against this threat to a kingdom, in exchange for compensation. In this situation, the tyranny is not part of a kingdom. Instead, an outsourcing arrangement is present.

It is difficult to define the parameters of kingdoms largely due to the question of membership. In this regard, it is often difficult to ascertain whether the subjugated entities, or their individual members, constitute:

- Subjugated vassals of the kingdom (essentially enslaved victims of a tyranny);

- Members of a kingdom alliance;

- Members of a tyrannical alliance utilizing the kingdom as a means to bring about order, stability, and peace;

- Deluded members of an illusory alliance; or

- Part of an outsourcing arrangement.

This difficult situation might be best solved by recognizing that kingdoms change over time. As a general rule, entities described as "kingdoms" that persist for long periods of time usually have evolved into true alliances (or at least semi-alliances) whereby the subjugated entities (or their members) are inducted into membership in the kingdom alliance. In contrast, kingdoms that do not evolve into a new form are usually short-lived. This tendency is explored in the next section.

DIFFICULTIES IN MAINTAINING A KINGDOM

Why would unchanging, static kingdoms tend to dissipate? The reason appears to be that maintaining a true kingdom (that is, a relatively small alliance that subjugates several other combined-effort entities into a tyrannical relationship) is usually very expensive and requires substantial contribution.

In many situations, members of the kingdom alliance perceive the value associated with subjugation and tribute as not being worth the contribution. In addition, the subjugated alliances (or other forms of subjugated combined-effort entities) typically do not like being subjugated. The reasons are obvious as the subjugated entities are paying tribute to avoid being destroyed by the kingdom alliance. As a result, the subjugated entities are usually looking for a way to escape the kingdom's dominance and expensive tribute. When the opportunity for freedom appears, the subjugated entities usually rebel. As a result of these factors, true kingdom alliances have difficulty surviving over time. Their ends are caused by a crumbling of support from the membership, rebellion by the subjugated entities, or a combination of these two factors.

To survive these difficulties, kingdoms expand their membership over time and allow the subjugated entities to become members of the alliance. In this arrangement, the tyrannical subjugation and extraction of tribute ends. In its place, contribution is more willingly supplied as the new members perceive a net benefit to the alliance. Because the alliance is perceived as being beneficial, the new members will not attempt to rebel. And this arrangement will benefit the original members as they will not have to expend contribution keeping the subjugated entities as members.

Sparta is a good example of a kingdom alliance that refused to expand its membership and ultimately collapsed. As discussed earlier, Sparta was a very successful city state that grew into a sizeable kingdom. It had an outstanding military force composed of members of the Spartan alliance. These members devoted most of their time towards military preparations and engagements. A substantial portion of this effort was expended upon enslaving thousands of individuals and holding other city states in a tyrannical alliance (or perhaps a tyranny). The means used by Sparta were very effective and the Spartan alliance became a prosperous and powerful kingdom. The slaves and subjugated entities, however, did not enjoy their situation and frequently sought freedom. Further, the heavy price paid by Spartan members (in terms of the complete dedication to warfare and the required austere lifestyle) became quite burdensome over time to many Spartans. As a consequence, the Spartan kingdom became unsustainable and ultimately collapsed.

Although Sparta did maintain a successful kingdom over the Peloponnesian peninsula in excess of 100 years, most kingdoms did not last very long in ancient Greece. Instead, Greek city states by and large successfully avoided becoming subjugated to a kingdom and maintained their autonomy. Why was this? The answer might lie in two features associated with the Greek city states.

First, the Greek city states were effective alliances. As a result, they were able to usually attain the objective of Defense against Aggressors time and time again and with great success. In particular, the Greek city states seem to have exhibited strong esprit de corps and association glory which often supercharged their battles against kingdoms.

Second, the Greek city states were adept at entering timely alliances with other city states against potential kingdoms. These alliances of alliances were usually successful and resulted in the defeat of formidable kingdoms (or empires) seeking to conquer the Greek city states. For instance, Persia invaded Greece with an overwhelming force around 480 B.C. A number of city states put aside their differences, allied against Persia, and defeated the threat. This result seemed unimaginable at the time but was made possible through an alliance. Overall, a review of the history of ancient Greece shows the continual birth, death, and rebirth of alliances between city states to defeat an aggressive kingdom.

In other parts of the world, however, kingdoms were more successful and lasted for hundreds of years or more. Particularly successful kingdoms were powerful enough to evolve into empires.

EMPIRES

An empire is a kingdom taken one step further. Recall that a kingdom is a successful city state capable of subjugating other city states into paying a tribute. In the same fashion, an *empire* is a successful kingdom that is capable of subjugating other kingdoms into paying tribute.

The same basic concepts governing kingdoms are applicable to empires. For instance:

- The objective of the empire alliance is to subjugate surrounding kingdoms and obtain tribute to benefit the members of the empire alliance.

- Empire alliances are often operated by a small group of individuals. As such, the typical empire alliance should be viewed as an alliance with a tiny membership that constitutes a tyranny to almost all individuals and lesser alliances within its domain.

- Some empires are true alliances with large memberships.

- Some subjugated kingdoms gradually become members of the empire alliance. The individual members of these subjugated kingdoms become derivative members of the empire alliance. Over time, these individual derivative members might become actual members of the empire alliance.

Overall, an empire is best viewed as an enormous kingdom that subjugates other kingdoms as well as some city states, villages, tribes, and clans.

DIFFICULTIES IN MAINTAINING AN EMPIRE

As just observed, kingdoms are typically difficult to maintain over time. Empires are subject to these same difficulties and also suffer from additional problems.

An empire always encompasses an enormous geographic area. As a result, effective administration of the empire by its decision-making process is very challenging if not impossible. As noted in Chapter 7, decision makers have three classes of limitations: (i) motivational, (ii) capability, and (iii) fidelity. The first two limitations are particularly prevalent in administration of an empire. A typical delegated decision maker lacks both sufficient motivation and capability to effectively oversee and govern a huge empire. The empire's delegated decision maker has so many subjugated kingdoms to watch over that he rarely can determine if the subjugated kingdoms have properly paid their tribute, if a rebellion is brewing, if the decision makers operating underneath his authority are engaging in corruption, stealing contribution, and so on.

Because of these limitations, empires are rare in the course of history. Although kingdoms might conquer large areas and therefore appear to constitute empires, it is usually the case that the kingdom cannot hold onto the areas for more than a brief period of time. The limitations of the decision-making process, combined with both the contribution required to maintain an empire and the propensity for the subjugated kingdoms to rebel, usually result in a quick dissolution of the apparent empire.

In light of these various difficulties, how do successful empires persist and even thrive? Generally speaking, successful empires employ one of two differing approaches: (i) the Non-Burden Approach, or (ii) the Alliance Approach.

THE NON-BURDEN APPROACH TO EMPIRE BUILDING

The Non-Burden Approach has two aspects. First, it allows the subjugated kingdom to operate largely as before its subjugation. The subjugated kingdom maintains essentially the same governing structure. Second, the empire imposes only a reasonable tribute upon the subjugated kingdom that can be met rather painlessly.

This approach can be very successful. Because the tribute is not onerous, the subjugated kingdom will usually pay it without balking. Further, the subjugated kingdom will tend to not rebel as the perceived costs associated with the rebellion (that is, war with the empire, death, destruction, and so on) typically outweigh the perceived benefit of the rebellion (that is, avoiding the tribute).

The Persian Empire (approximately 559–331 BCE) seems to have employed the Non-Burden Approach in crafting one of the world's first great empires. The Persian Empire was so successful that it swallowed up several other empires including the Babylonian, Median, Lydian, and Egyptian empires. At its height, the Persian Empire received tribute from more than twenty separate kingdoms (or lesser empires). This tribute included huge quantities of silver, livestock, food, weapons, ships, hides, and cloth. The founder of the empire was Cyrus the Great. Cyrus was noted for assembling the empire with surprisingly few major battles. Instead of fighting, Cyrus was able to convince most kingdoms to consent to subjugation through diplomatic endeavors. Of course, these diplomatic overtures were always backed by the threat of military devastation.

Once a kingdom entered the Persian Empire, the kingdom's institutions were largely kept in tact. For instance, if the kingdom had a king, he usually remained in power and the decision-making process underneath him stayed substantially the same. Further, most customs and religious practices were left alone as well. Finally, the tribute was never onerous or punitive and could be satisfied relatively easily. At times, the Empire required tribute in the form of troops to participate in a military effort. This donation of troops was often worthwhile. If the venture was successful, there was the opportunity for substantial plunder for the donating kingdom.

Overall, the Persian Empire was not unduly burdensome to the kingdoms within it. In exchange for the tribute, the kingdoms avoided military conflict and/or destruction and were allowed to function largely as before the subjugation. And the Empire provided a degree of stability in the region that had never existed before. These facts help to demonstrate why the Persian Empire was successful and long lasting.

The Persian Empire ultimately collapsed due to the same factors that made it successful. To briefly summarize its history, Cyrus founded the empire and was responsible for amassing most of the kingdoms within it. His successors expanded upon the empire further. One successor, Darius, attempted to expand the empire into Greece. Darius's invasion, however, hit a dead end at the battle of Marathon in 490 BCE, when a heavily outnumbered force of Athenians triumphed and drove the Persians out of Greece.

The Persians returned to invade Greece in 480 BCE under the leadership of Darius's son and newly crowned emperor, Xerxes. Xerxes assembled the largest military force ever seen at that time, consisting of hundreds of thousands of troops from most all of the Persian kingdoms. Despite the enormous odds, a collection of allied Greek city states (most notably Athens and Sparta) defeated the Persians in several battles, inflicted catastrophic losses upon them, and drove the Persians out of Greece for good.

Following the devastation in Greece, the Persian Empire began a slow but steady decline. The war with the Greeks demonstrated that the Persian Empire could not field a superior fighting force. The combination of troops from various kingdoms with different cultures and religions was not easy to control and properly utilize. Moreover, such fighting forces lacked an esprit de corps and/or association glory that often seems to make the difference in battle. As a result, the Empire stopped expanding and largely focused upon maintaining itself.

Notwithstanding its limitations, the Persian Empire remained viable and functioning for many more years. During this period, kingdoms steadily slipped away, the Persian military strength declined, and tribute waned. The Empire continued to persist, however, largely due to the traits that made it successful such as moderate tribute, stability, and so on. But the Empire was susceptible to a threat, and, when the threat materialized, the Persian Empire crumbled.

The threat was Alexander the Great. In a miraculously short period of time (336-323 BCE), Alexander not only conquered all of Greece and Egypt but the entire Persian Empire. Perhaps the most impressive aspect was that Alexander's army was relatively modest in size. Alexander's success appears to be due primarily to two factors, aside from Alexander's brilliant leadership and tactical skills.

First, Alexander's army was an extraordinarily effective alliance. Although the army was originally from Macedonia, it was independent of any state control and did not seek to further the interests of Macedonia. Instead, the members of the alliance were the soldiers themselves. The objective was to conquer kingdoms and obtain tribute and bounty for the soldier-members. The accord was implied and recognized Alexander and his officers as the delegated decision makers. (The alliance nature of the army manifested itself when Alexander reached India. There, the troops refused to go further and Alexander turned the army back west where he died shortly thereafter.) Aside from these factors, Alexander's army had a high degree of esprit de corps and/or association glory that fueled its endeavors. In fact, Alexander's near god-like status undoubtedly filled many members with association glory and drove them to maintain and further this glory as soldiers of the greatest army in history.

The second significant factor in Alexander's triumph lay in the inherently weak nature of the Persian Empire. Most of the kingdoms saw the Persian Empire as simply an entity to which they paid tribute in order to avoid military reprisals. When Alexander appeared, these kingdoms simply weighed the perceived values of paying tribute to Persia versus paying tribute to Alexander. As Alexander began racking up military victories, these kingdoms saw him as a preferable alternative to Persia and, by and large, willingly shifted their allegiance to Alexander. Alexander in turn followed the same practices of Persia such as a modest tribute, permitting the same customs and traditions, and so on.

When Alexander died, his empire immediately dissolved. Alexander left no successor and it appears that his army would accept no other executive decision maker to lead it. But instead of dissolving into complete chaos, Alexander's empire took shape as five mini-empires (or kingdoms), many of which persisted for hundreds of years. Had Alexander lived longer, however, it is unclear whether he would have been able to hold his empire together.

THE ALLIANCE APPROACH TO EMPIRE BUILDING

The second means of successful empire creation and maintenance is the Alliance Approach. This approach seeks to provide the subjugated with benefits resembling those of an alliance or to even allow the subjugated individuals to join the alliance as members.

An empire using the Alliance Approach dismantles the conquered alliance (or other combined-effort entity). In this void, the empire institutes a local decision-making process. This local process is an arm of the empire itself and reports up the decision-making chain to the higher elements of the empire's decision-making process. This local process will attempt to provide many benefits of the alliance to the residents of the conquered combined-effort entity. In some circumstances, it will also seek to allow these residents to join the empire as members. If this offer is taken, the new members will tend to willingly contribute resources to the empire alliance and not rebel against it. The overall point of the strategy is to persuade the residents of the conquered kingdom that the empire is better than the kingdom, or at least not much worse.

Does this approach result in the residents of the conquered combined-effort entity entering a true alliance? It depends upon the circumstances. Often, the resulting entity will be an illusory alliance. At other times, it will be a tyrannical alliance. But sometimes, a true alliance will result where the residents of the conquered combined-effort entity are truly incorporated into the empire alliance as bona-fide members.

The Roman Empire seems to have been particularly successful at using the Alliance approach. When the Romans conquered an area, they often quickly integrated Roman institutions into the conquered region. Usually, the Romans implemented a local official in the area that provided a fair degree of stability and drove off most raiders and plunderers. The Romans almost always laid sturdy roads in every area that they conquered. Other typical constructions included assembly halls, harbors, commons, market areas, aqueducts, fountains, public baths, and sewer lines. In addition, the Roman Empire had a very effective monetary system. Roman coins were used throughout the Empire and were always introduced into conquered regions. Roman law was well-developed and offered reasonable protection against offenses by neighbors and allowed for the protection of property. Although the Roman Empire was hesitant to grant official membership or "citizenship" to persons of conquered lands, the result of Roman institutions was a pseudo-membership for most inhabitants of the conquered lands.

In most situations, the effect of the Roman institutions was to at least placate the conquered regions, if not to make them actual members of the Empire. Although the Roman conquest of a region was often bloody and horrific, Roman occupation usually brought a relative peace. The typical conquered individual likely perceived the Empire as being not so bad, if not an actual improvement over the prior situation. It is important to note, however, that these Roman undertakings were not charitable. The Romans demanded and received large tributes from the conquered regions. And, as the regions were incorporated into the Empire, the Romans taxed the inhabitants and the Empire overall profited greatly.

The Roman Empire conquered so many areas that it would take an entire book to discuss each one. A brief consideration of a few examples might be useful. The region known today as Spain was largely ruled in 200 BCE by clans and tribal alliances of ethic people known as the "Celts." The Celtic tribes and clans in Spain were commonly known as the "Celtiberians." The Romans engaged in numerous bloody wars with the Celtiberians (and their allies, the Carthaginians). Slowly but surely, the Romans brought the Celtiberians into the Roman Empire with a combination of the stick and the carrot. This region came to be known as "Hispania" and was a very loyal and important part of the Roman Empire.

Another useful example is the Roman Empire's assault on another group of Celtic peoples known as the "Gauls," who resided in a region known today as France. This attack took place from 58–51 BCE and was led by the famous Julius Caesar. In an extraordinarily bloody war, Caesar killed hundreds of thousands, or even millions of Gauls, and essentially wiped out all vestiges of the prior Gallic alliances. But in their place, the Romans established numerous Roman institutions including governors, law, and public works. Within a short period of time, Gaul became a peaceful and productive part of the Empire.

The effects of the Roman Empire on Spain and France continue to this day. Many of their institutions and laws have their roots in old Roman institutions. The languages spoken in these lands—Spanish and French—are essentially heavily evolved versions of Latin.

ALLIANCES, KINGDOMS, AND EMPIRES OF RELIGION

As this book has made clear, alliances can take all shapes and forms. So far, the discussion of history has focused largely on alliances as such villages, city states, kingdoms, and empires. These types of alliances have been termed "governmental alliances" or "governmental entities." These governmental entities were usually long-term, multi-objective alliances. At times, these governmental entities were not true alliances. Instead, they were semi-alliances, illusory alliances, or tyrannies. Or they might have fluctuated from these various states from time to time. Typically, these governmental entities sought to attain a wide variety of objectives including Defense against Aggressors, Offense against Non-Members, Law-Compelled Objectives, Mitigation of Catastrophe, Uniting against Natural Obstacles, Cooperatives, and so on.

These governmental entities usually pursued the objective of Morality and its subset of Religious concerns, along with various other objectives. Governmental alliances, however, were not necessarily the only entities to pursue objectives like Religious concerns. At times, non-governmental entities sought to attain the objective of Religious concerns. These non-governmental religious entities sometimes became enormous and powerful, and resembled kingdoms or empires.

In most situations, the religious combined-effort entity began as a small alliance pursuing a religious-based objective. Members came together and pooled their resources towards attaining this objective. Often, the objective related to the construction of religious-oriented temples, shrines, or statues or to the maintenance of one or more priests to perform rituals, communicate with the applicable god(s), and provide any relevant religious instruction. The priests usually served as decision makers for the alliance as well.

Often, these small alliances grew in size and spread across wide geographical areas. As the alliances grew, they often lost their alliance-nature and were transformed into semi-alliances, illusory alliances, or perhaps tyrannies. At the same time, these growing combined-effort entities also resembled kingdoms and empires.

CHRISTIANITY

Christianity provides a useful example of the concept of an empire of religion. This religion undertook an alliance form shortly after the death of Jesus in approximately 33 CE. The original structure of the alliance was very loose. At the beginning, small communities of Christians developed in city states and villages around the eastern Mediterranean Ocean. The members learned of the tenets of Christianity through word-of-mouth and from important early Christian figures like Peter and Paul. Paul in particular wrote numerous letters to these alliances regarding Christian concepts. These letters were saved, reread, copied, distributed widely, and now make up much of the Christian Bible.

These early Christian communities were alliances. Typically, they were situated within a city state or a kingdom inside the boundaries of the Roman Empire. The accords underlying the alliances constituted basic agreements to combine resources towards attaining mutually desired Christian objectives. These objectives included learning about Christianity, spreading Christianity to others, reinforcing Christian principles in members, undertaking charitable endeavors, and creating a sustainable alliance structure. Of course, some individuals believing in Christianity saw no benefit from allying with other individuals to pursue Christian objectives and refused to join the Christian alliances. These individuals practiced the Christian religion on their own.

Christianity was an unusual alliance for its era in that its membership was essentially open to anyone. There were no class, heritage, or property qualifications. Women were eligible to join and in fact made up substantial portions of the membership of many Christian alliances. The sick, poor, aged, downtrodden, and infirm were encouraged to become members and were well-accepted in the alliances. This openness in the membership criteria was due in large part to the nature of the primary resource contributed. In order to become a member, individuals were usually required only to engage in a membership ritual such as baptism and make a solemn pledge to contribute the resource of liberty to the alliance. This contribution of liberty consisted of a commitment to adhere to the tenets of Christianity. Although not necessarily emphasized, other contributed resources included time, labor, effort, and money to be used in spreading and reinforcing Christianity. Christianity spread quickly throughout the Empire, with small alliances appearing in most villages and city states.

For a variety of reasons, the Roman Empire did not look favorably upon Christians and generally oppressed them sporadically for several hundred years. During this period, Christian alliances persevered and grew notwithstanding the oppression. Most Christian alliances pursued the objective of Defense against Aggressors in response to the Roman onslaught. Interestingly, this defense usually consisted of a commitment of Christian members to submit to the attacks, to not abandon the tenets of Christianity, to love and pray for the attackers, and to attempt to sway the attackers to the tenets of Christianity. As a result, many Christian members willingly submitted to torture and death at the hands of the Romans. This "defensive" tactic seems to have preserved Christianity and even inspired numerous others to join the alliance.

The efforts of the Christian alliances to sway opponents of Christianity to join Christian alliances were effective. In 313 CE, the Roman Emperor Constantine issued the Edict of Milan which ended the subjugation of Christians and provided for toleration. Over time, the toleration of Christians transitioned into acceptance, with the Roman Empire ultimately embracing Christianity by approximately 400 CE as the official religion of the Empire.

Soon thereafter, the accords underlying the Christian alliances became more express and specific. The decision-making processes grew more structured with the previously loosely organized and diffuse systems being more tightly controlled. Practices for collection of contribution (in particular money) evolved into rigid expectations.

By and large, small alliances were consolidated into large alliances during this time period. Early on, the structure of Christian alliances mostly consisted of alliances of alliances of alliances. At the bottom of the structure were the small community-oriented alliances with decision-making processes usually focusing around priests and committees of elders. These alliances allied together to form other alliances under single decision makers called "bishops." The bishops oversaw the alliances within particular regions, such as Jerusalem, Antioch, Alexandria, Constantinople, or Rome. These bishop-oriented alliances then usually allied from time to time on certain objectives. As Christianity became more accepted and widespread, the higher alliances became more and more significant. They began to exercise more control over the lower alliances. And members of the lower alliances started to see themselves more as members of the higher alliance.

This trend continued to the point where solid hierarchies and relationships between the various levels of alliances were established.

Ironically, during this period of consolidation, disintegration was also occurring. As the alliances became more structured, the underlying accords became more express and specific. As a result, heated dogmatic debates exploded from time to time over the particular beliefs and rituals underlying the alliances. Usually, these disputes were not resolved and sects splintered off, forming their own version of Christianity.[1]

Sects arising out of doctrinal differences began forming in the early years of Christianity and continue on to this day. This splintering effect reflects a fundamental characterization of alliances. As noted in Chapter 6, members will tend to compare the relative perceived value of their current alliance against the perceived value of alternative alliances, if any. In the case of earlier Christian doctrinal disagreements, members concluded on many occasions that the creation of alternative alliances embracing their viewpoints was preferable. As a result, these members created alternative sects, which flourished in many circumstances.

HERESY

At times, the splintering became quite disturbing to members of the dominant Christian alliance. Doctrines were developed to deter and punish members embracing conflicting dogmas and to suppress non-members in competing sects. The primary means was that of heresy. Individuals embracing beliefs or undertaking acts contrary to the accepted dogma were labeled "heretics" and were subject to discipline. The punishments ranged from reprimands to torture to death. Several different factors appear to have underlain applications of heresy:

- *Paternalism*—Early Christian doctrine recognized that it was easy for any member to stray from the fold and that the Church institution was present in part to draw these lost members back to the fold. In this situation, heresy served as a means of preventing and correcting an irrational tendency of members to embrace false doctrines.

- *Defense against Aggressors*—Many Christians saw sects as being harmful agents that might lure them or other innocent members into danger or damnation. Therefore, heresy was used as a means to guard against this perceived attack.

---

[1] For example, the Nicene Creed was agreed upon in 325 C.E. to clarify important doctrinal issues underlying the faith. Those members that disagreed with the Nicene Creed formed new Christian alliances.

- *Preservation of the Membership Base*—If members leave an alliance, the alliance loses the contributions of those members. Further, if a competing alliance is established nearby, it might serve to draw more members from the alliance and further reduce contribution. Because contribution is often vital to attaining the objectives of an alliance, heresy was used to check losses of members.

- *Association Glory*—The phenomenon of association glory was often present in Christian alliances. The identities, worldview, and self-esteem of many individuals were directly associated with their memberships in a particular Christian alliance. As such, if members began leaving the alliance or if non-members criticized the alliance, a sensitive nerve was often struck and the alliance would respond with heresy accusations. In this situation, heresy was used to preserve and defend the association glory of the alliance.

- *Fidelity Limitations*—At times, decision makers subject to fidelity limitations used dubious charges of heresy to further their own interests. Recall that the limitations include: (i) position protection, (ii) favoring the interest of a minority of alliance members or of an outsider to the alliance, and (iii) pure, unadulterated corruption. Heresy at times was associated with all of these limitations. For instance, a priest or a bishop might have feared losing his position and therefore accused a critic of heresy. Or a church decision maker might steal church funds but charge his accusers with heresy to fend off their accusations.

FIDELITY LIMITATIONS IN CHRISTIAN ALLIANCES

The last factor, fidelity limitations, is important to underscore. The Christian alliances had decision makers and these decision makers were subject to all of the fidelity limitations. Over the course of history, these limitations naturally manifested themselves time and time again. For instance, church leaders at times found the correct decisions to be too controversial or risky. To avoid endangering their positions, the decision makers would undertake a safer, but less appropriate, course of action. That is, the leaders' fears of comprising their positions as decision makers led them to not fully perform their obligations. Likewise, some leaders abused the authority of their positions to favor special interests over the interests of all members. Finally, some leaders engaged in outright corruption and stole funds, enforced rules to enrich themselves, and otherwise abused their positions of power to further their own interests.[1]

---

[1] The other two types of limitations—motivation and ability—were present as well. For instance, some church leaders grew weary or bored with their duties and therefore ignored them. Other leaders might have been highly motivated but simply were unable to attain the objectives set before them.

TRANSFORMATION OF CHRISTIAN ALLIANCES

Fidelity limitations were not the only operational difficulties faced by the Christian alliances. Many Christian alliances exhibited signs of second-class membership or were transformed over time into other combined-effort entities such semi-alliances, illusory alliances, and even tyrannies. The drivers of these transformations were the same basic factors discussed in earlier chapters.

Some of these transformed entities collapsed quickly while others lasted for extended periods of time. A quick collapse was usually the result of members recognizing that the entity was no longer an alliance. As a result, the members either (i) revolted and revived the alliance, or (ii) terminated their membership and formed a new alliance.

The non-alliance Christian entities that survived for extended periods of time did so typically by using the tools of tyranny discussed earlier. Some of these included:

- illusory benefits were used to obscure the entities' true natures;

- information relating to alternatives was stifled or distorted;

- dissent and criticism of the entities were suppressed; or

- members were deterred from terminating their memberships.

CHRISTIANITY'S RELATIONSHIP WITH GOVERNMENTAL ENTITIES

Over time, Christianity continued to spread and the various alliances and combined-effort entities associated with the religion grew. And these Christian entities slowly became interwoven in the structure of most other governmental entities such as villages, city states, kingdoms, and empires.

The relationships varied greatly but the governmental entities always paid at least a fair degree of homage to the predominant Christian entities. At many times, the governmental entities were under the effective direct control of the predominant Christian entities. At other times, the governmental entities were essentially allied with the predominant Christian entities. In almost all circumstances, the governmental entities drew legitimacy from their affiliation with a Christian entity. For instance, a particular decision maker of a governmental entity might maintain that he was chosen by the Christian God to be ruler of a land.

Often, the predominant Christian entities had a firm grip on the governmental entities. This grip was limited to religious issues—a specific but very broad sphere. The governmental entities usually tailored their actions so as to fall within the range of alternatives approved by the Christian entities. The governmental entities at times were required to seek the express approval of the applicable Christian entity prior to undertaking particular actions. Finally, these governmental entities usually submitted money and other valuables to the Christian entities on a periodic basis. Due to these typical characteristics, the Christian entities often resembled kingdoms or empires that had subjugated various governmental entities.

CHAPTER 17

Ideas, Mindsets, and Worldviews

The developments and transformations of alliances throughout the course of history appear to be directly associated with ideas, mindsets, and worldviews that prevail in a given time period. These concepts can have two important influences on alliances.

First, ideas, mindsets, and worldviews affect what is desirable. As discussed in Part I, the subjective desires of individuals change over time. The fluctuations in these desires affect the objectives that alliances pursue. If a sufficient number of persons desire a particular outcome and a combined effort can attain the outcome more effectively or efficiently than an individual effort, it is likely these persons will form an alliance to attain that objective. Similarly, if an objective pursued by an alliance is no longer desired, the alliance will tend to either terminate or find a new objective to pursue. Overall, ideas, mindsets, and worldviews control what is desired by the individuals that create, transform, and terminate alliances.

Second, ideas, mindsets, and worldviews affect what is believed to be attainable or "doable" by an alliance. As discussed in Part III, a particular course of conduct cannot be undertaken if no one knows how to do it. Instead, someone must accidentally stumble across the course of conduct and realize its value. Or someone must conceive the course of conduct in his head and then undertake it. Others will then witness the course of conduct being undertaken, recognize its value, and then replicate it in some fashion. After the course of conduct is undertaken by a sufficient number of persons, it will become prevalent in the realm of ideas, mindsets, and worldviews. If this process of discovery, experimentation, refinement, and circulation does not occur, the course of conduct is not known and it cannot be undertaken. A related concept is whether the course of conduct is considered to be a viable, workable alternative. Although a particular course of conduct might be known to many, the prevailing consensus can be that it is futile and worthless and, in addition, might entail negative consequences. As such, in looking back upon history, one must be mindful of the fact that the usages and structures of alliances could not occur unless they were both known and considered to be viable undertakings.

These two factors are interrelated and can slow or even prevent the development and transformations of alliances over time. The era of the European Middle Ages appears to be a good example of these phenomena.

THE EXAMPLE OF THE EUROPEAN MIDDLE AGES

The Middle Ages in Europe lasted from approximately 500 CE to 1500 CE. Their beginning is marked by the collapse of the Roman Empire and their end by the birth of modern nation states.

The thousand-year period prior to the European Middle Ages was marked by radical change and evolution in alliance structures in Europe. During this earlier era of 500 BCE to 500 CE, novel alliance structures developed in Europe and the Middle East with fundamentally new objectives being pursued and innovative means being utilized. City states rose to prominence. Several city states then transformed themselves into kingdoms. And a few kingdoms became empires. In particular, the Roman Empire arose and conquered much of Europe, importing new innovations in alliance structures to far-flung areas. The Law-Compelled Objectives embraced by the Roman Empire fostered the growth of numerous small, commercial-oriented alliances. In addition, other types of alliances arose and spread such as Christian alliances which evolved into massive entities resembling kingdoms or empires. Overall, the thousand-year period prior to the Middle Ages was an age of considerable innovation and development in alliance structures and forms.

In contrast, the European Middle Ages were marked by a much lesser degree of change in alliance structures, objectives, and means. Although alliances did evolve during this period, the rate of change and evolution was quite slow. Alliance institutions tended to become largely permanent and any transformation was gradual and subtle.

Why was alliance development and transformation largely stalled in the European Middle Ages? The answer might lie in the prevailing ideas, mindsets, and worldviews of the era. During the European Middle Ages, most individuals seemed to be relatively satisfied and content with the status of their alliance arrangements (and the relative lack thereof). Perhaps more importantly, most individuals seemed to have been unaware of any alternative to their predicament. The reason for these perceptions arguably lies in a concept known as the *Great Chain of Being*.[1]

THE GREAT CHAIN OF BEING

The Great Chain of Being was a worldview that seems to have pervaded Europe through most of the Middle Ages. It imposed a hierarchical structure upon the world and everything within it. This intrinsic hierarchy was organized from top to bottom as follows:

The Christian God
Angels
Humans
Animals
Plants
Earth material such as stones, metals, water, and so on.

Within each class existed sub-hierarchies. For instance, earth materials were ranked with gold being the supreme metal. Animals were graded with the lion being the king of all animals. Similarly, humans and their alliance structures were ranked within the sub-hierarchy such as:

Church
Emperor
King
Nobles
Peasants

These rankings then had further hierarchies within them. For instance, the Church was structured with the Pope at the top and then bishops, priests, monks, nuns, parishioners, and so on. Similarly, the relationships of the nobles were organized in various fashions with lords, barons, dukes, earls, counts, and so on. And even the peasants were organized in a family structure with elders holding the highest place and then husbands, wives, and children. Finally, even the children were ranked with predominance given to the eldest male.

Important relationships existed between the various components of these sub-hierarchies. For instance, peasants served a local noble and provided him with labor.

---

[1]The historical significance of the Great Chain of Being appears to have been first identified by the historian Arthur Lovejoy.

In return, the noble was obligated to the peasants such as looking out for their basic welfare. The nobles served the king and provided him with resources. In return, the king was to look out for the welfare of the kingdom and protect it from raiders. If there was an emperor, the kings were to support him with resources. In return, the emperor was to look out for the interests of the empire. At the top of this hierarchy was the Church headed by the Pope. The emperors and kings were to support the Pope, the kings and nobles were to support the regional bishops, and the nobles and peasants were to support the local Churches. In return, the Church institution would insure that all were in the good graces of the Christian God.

At most times, this hierarchy was largely unchallengeable. During the height of the Middle Ages, it was probably inconceivable for anyone to dispute the tenets of the Chain. Peasants knew their place in the hierarchy and stayed in that place, leading simple lives and obeying the nobles. Similarly, nobles understood that they were nobles and that their duty was to support the king. Children of a particular class learned of their class very early on and were taught to not stray from it. There was no concept of social mobility. The idea of a peasant rising in status to become a noble or a king was absurd. Peasants were and always would be peasants. Nobles were thought to be naturally different from peasants (that is, the nobles were superior). Kings were exceptional, with the royal bloodline having been set by God to lord over the nobles and peasants for eternity. This bloodline was to be preserved. The eldest, male offspring of the king was to always succeed the deceased king. And, if there was no male offspring, the next king (or sometimes queen) must be closely related to the deceased king by blood (for example, brothers, daughters, nephews, nieces, cousins, and so on). All of these classes—from peasants to kings—were subservient to the Church. In short, everyone had their natural place in the Great Chain of Being. Everyone was supposed to stay in that place and perform their respective duties.

Why would people stay in their place? Why would a peasant think it inconceivable to strive to become a noble? The answer is that the Great Chain of Being prevented such conceptions and ideas. The Great Chain of Being was pervasive. As noted earlier, the Chain not only concerned human relations, it governed the entire World and everything in it including animals, plants, and earth materials. The Chain was a natural state, a fundamental order that underlay all interactions with the world. It is comparable to contemporary prevailing views of physics, astronomy, and mathematics. Just as these worldviews are accepted without question in today's world, the Chain was accepted without question in the Middle Ages.

Because the Chain was a fundamental belief, it could not be ignored or tampered with or severe and catastrophic consequences were thought to result. The Chain was not only natural, it provided harmony and benefit to all in the World. By adhering to its tenets, the peasants, nobles, kings, emperors, and church officials could all lead proper and befitting existences. But if the Chain was disrupted or broken, all types of horrendous chaos and turmoil was thought to follow. As such, most individuals in the European Middle Ages perceived a strong value in the Great Chain of Being and would never conceive of breaking it.

THE STATIC WORLD

Because of the Great Chain of Being, alliance concepts were essentially locked in place and were not capable of significant growth and transformation. This static situation was primarily due to two factors discussed in the preceding sections.[1]

First, there were few new objectives to pursue because there was no significant desire for change. The Chain taught that the current state of affairs was natural and normal. As such, peasants by and large did not question their lots in life. It was natural for peasants to be poor. Nobles typically did not question the king's legitimacy. And no one questioned the Church. Because the state of affairs was natural and normal, individuals rarely could conceive of improving a particular situation. Persons accepted the status quo.

This acceptance of the status quo was reinforced by the lack of known alternatives. There was very little flow of information in the Middle Ages. If a new idea did develop somewhere, it was highly unlikely that others would learn about it. Books were extraordinarily rare and expensive and very few individuals could read. Travel was not common and most individuals resided in the same area for their entire lives. As a result of these factors, there were no new objectives to fuel new alliances. Subjective desires largely remained the same and so did the alliance structures.

Second, it was largely inconceivable to experiment with, or undertake, an alternative alliance structure. Even if individuals disliked the current state of affairs, they could not be changed. The reason was that the Chain demanded stability and permanence. Change and innovation were not desirable and were potentially dangerous. If anyone tampered with the Chain, chaos and catastrophe were likely to result. As such, the concepts of progress, innovation, and improvement largely did not exist. Inhabitants of the European Middle Ages largely accepted the state of the world in which they were born and rarely attempted to change it.

Although the alliance and other governmental concepts remained largely static during the Middle Ages, it is important to observe that there was some change and development. For instance, the rise of Charlemagne and the creation of the

---

[1]This is not to say that other factors did not contribute to the perseverance of the static nature of the Middle Ages. The Great Chain of Being, however, appears to be a very significant factor.

Holy Roman Empire constitute important alterations in alliance concepts and structures. Similarly, the development of chivalry is another useful example of change. The institution of chivalry appears to have been essentially an alliance among knights to pursue an internal objective consisting of engaging in exemplary conduct. This alliance tended to reduce rogue knights that pillaged the countryside and generally resulted in more peaceful times. Although these changes did occur from time to time, they were rare and much less frequent than at other times in history.

In addition, although the alliance and governmental-entity structures stayed largely static in the Middle Ages, there was frequent change within the structures. For instance, decision makers such as kings, nobles, and church leaders were often removed and new (but substantially similar) decision makers were installed in their place. Despite these changes, the alliance structures remained essentially the same for hundreds of years.

ALLIANCE OPERATIONS WITHIN THE GREAT CHAIN

Notwithstanding the dominance of the Chain, alliances did exist within its structure. The effect of the Chain was to slow down the growth, development, and modification of alliances and essentially lock many alliances in place for hundreds of years.

During the thousand-year period of the European Middle Ages, a wide variety of circumstances prevailed at different times. As such, it is difficult to generalize about the entire period. Nonetheless, the following generalizations will be identified, with the recognition that there were likely several exceptions to each one.

Peasants

At the bottom of the Chain were the peasants. Although they relied heavily upon individual effort to attain their desires, peasants formed a variety of alliances to attain certain objectives. These alliances were based upon implied accords, were typically very informal, and usually employed nebulous decision-making processes. The objectives pursued usually related to labor-intensive projects such as agriculture, construction, wells, extraction of natural resources, and so on. At times, peasants probably also pursued rudimentary Law-Compelled Objectives such as Protection of the Person and Protection of Property from other peasants. For instance, if one peasant attacked another peasant without justification, a mob of peasants probably formed to inflict a crude punishment upon the attacker such as a beating, destruction of his property, or death.

Nobles

The nobles relied heavily upon outsourced individual effort to attain many objectives. In this regard, a typical noble retained servants called "knights" to provide day-to-day assistance, to protect him from hostile forces, and to enforce the noble's control over the peasants. These arrangements usually constituted outsourcing because the nobles compensated the knights for the services rendered. Nobles also formed an assortment of alliances with other nobles which generally related to Law-Compelled Objectives such as land-property laws and mechanisms to keep the peasants in line. These alliances were based upon implied accords and usually had nebulous decision-making processes.[1]

Relationship between Nobles and Peasants

What was the nature of the interaction between peasants and nobles? The nobles are probably best viewed as having a tyrannical-alliance relationship with the peasants. For instance, in a given region, there would be an alliance of peasants with the decision maker being the local noble. There was an implied accord to obey the noble's dictates and to contribute to the noble certain resources such as agricultural products, labor, liberty, and so on. In return, the noble instituted a relative degree of peace and stability in the area and provided some form of Law-Compelled Objectives such as arbitration of disputes, some property rules, and so on. In addition, the noble could marshal forces to defend against non-member raiders such as thieves, robbers, and some attacking armies.

Why was the relationship typically one of a tyrannical alliance? The answer is that the peasants were subject to potential abuses from the local noble with little or no remedy. However, in return for suffering through these violations and ignominies, the peasants received the benefits of relative order and stability. Essentially, the peasants willingly tolerated the noble and the potential abuse because of the positive benefits the noble could achieve. The Great Chain, by effectively dictating the inherent natural aspect of the fashion, bolstered the perceived positive attributes of the noble.

At times, nobles constituted actual tyrants and exploited peasants in a purely tyrannical fashion. In these situations, there was no corresponding benefit to the

---

[1] In considering the "noble" class, it is important to emphasize that nobles did not live affluent, wealthy lifestyles in the Middle Ages. Nobles did live much better than the peasants. However, nobles generally had few luxuries, lived in uncomfortable strongholds or forts, ate poorly, and overall lived in dreary circumstances. The stereotypical life of a noble (that is, extraordinary wealth, luxury, decadence, and so on) came after the Middle Ages ended.

peasants or even a grudging toleration of the nobles. Instead, the nobles subjugated and exploited the peasants solely for the nobles' personal benefits. In these circumstances, however, the peasants were not without remedy. They could always ally and form a revolutionary alliance to topple a tyrannical noble.

Artisans

Aside from the peasants and nobles, the Middle Ages at times saw the presence of artisan classes. When this class was present, it fell in between the nobles and peasants. Artisans resided in urbanized places and produced skilled goods such as shoes, clothing, wares, baskets and barrels, iron products, and so on. Generally, the artisan class could exist only in times of long-term peace and stability. Because the Middle Ages often suffered from extensive wars, raids, and conflict, the artisan classes tended to be scarce.

Artisans usually formed alliances called "guilds." Express spoken, accords usually underlay guilds. Typically, guilds imposed price and quality standards on members and kept competitors away. Guilds adhered to variations of the Law-Compelled Objective of Enforcement of Promises.

Often, the artisans and other non-artisans such as merchants formed other alliances to govern towns and cities. These alliances usually had delegated decision makers such as mayor and councils to make and implement many decisions. These municipality alliances often pursued Law-Compelled Objectives generally protecting the interests of the artisans and defensive objectives to protect against raiders and attacking armies. Because municipalities were difficult to defend in the Middle Ages, they often failed and were not particularly populous in any event. Most persons instead resided in the countryside as peasants or nobles.

Kings

Kings had an unusual role in the Middle Ages. Like nobles, kings did not lead luxurious lives. Their so-called castles were inhospitable and kings rarely had much money to spend (if money even existed in a particular region). In addition, kings had very little authority and were sometimes essentially figureheads. This weakness resulted from the kings' heavy dependence upon the support of the nobles. Kings were rarely able to tax nobles and instead had to persuade nobles to contribute resources to various projects, which usually were military endeavors.

Kings held the potential to be immensely popular due to association glory. If a king obtained a particularly good result, both the nobles and the peasants could derive self-esteem from sharing in the glory of the achievement. This was particularly the case in the event of a significant military victory. The king, nobles, artisans, and peasants could all receive esteem from their affiliation with a triumphant military battle. At times, the perceptions of association glory might have stemmed from the existence of a true alliance between nobles and peasants such as to defend against a formidable invasion. At other times, the association glory might have been akin to an illusory benefit stemming from an illusory alliance or tyranny.

Kings were subject to all of the limitations associated with a delegated decision maker. Kings were often unmotivated and lazy. Some kings were incompetent or even suffered from mental defects. All kings exhibited fidelity limitations. With good kings, the fidelity limitations were manifested as some minor preferences for the king's family and friends, a pursuit of some luxuries, and acceptance of bribes but only where the course of action was reasonable. With bad kings, corruption was pervasive with the king showing no concern for the members of the kingdom and focusing all his efforts on the furtherance of his own prestige, power, and wealth.

Kings and Nobles

It is probably best to view a typical king as the decision maker in an alliance of nobles that usually pursued military objectives. In this arrangement, the nobles combined their resources from time to time to raise an army under the leadership of a king. This army could be employed to defend a region against an invasion. Or it could be used to subjugate a foreign region and capture its resources. Or the army could be used to neutralize or eliminate certain unfavorable nobles within the region. Overall, whatever the king did typically was of benefit to the nobles controlling the alliance. The king was usually one of these nobles so the activity was of benefit to his interests as well. If it was in their interest, towns and cities would join in these alliances from time to time. Usually, the towns and cities were interested in such alliances in order to obtain protection from attacking armies.

In many kingdoms, there were regional officers under the king with titles such as dukes, lords, earls, counts, barons, and so on. In some situations, these arrangements were effectively alliances of alliances. For instance, five alliances might each be headed by a separate noble called a "baron." These five alliances would then ally together to form a kingdom with a king at the head. The barons were responsible for most matters occurring within their specific alliance. The kingdom, which constituted an alliance of alliances, and its king would pursue only those objectives common to all five member alliances such as Defense against Aggressors, Law-Compelled Objectives, and so on.

In other situations, the titled nobles can be seen as decision makers within an interwoven decision-making process. These nobles held a sphere of decision-making authority for the particular region in which they governed. But these nobles reported to a king who held the ultimate authority to override any of their decisions.

The Church

In the Middle Ages, the Church generally stood on its own as a complex web of alliances of alliances. These concepts were discussed in an earlier chapter. At times, the Church allied with kings and nobles. At other times, the Church controlled the nobles and kings. And sometimes the Church was subjugated to kings. An interesting example is the Holy Roman Empire. The Holy Roman Empire was a vast collection of alliances across continental Europe that chose emperors through a complex decision-making process. These emperors had a long history of interactions with the Pope and the Catholic Church. Numerous disputes, controversies, and conflicts often broke out between the Pope, the Emperor, and the various members over this relationship.

Summary

The underlying point of this discussion is that the ideas, mindsets, and worldviews of the Middle Ages appear to have had a sizeable impact upon alliances. Although alliances undoubtedly existed during the Middle Ages, alliance development and growth was largely static due to the Great Chain of Being and a wide variety of other factors discussed in this chapter.

THE TYRANNICAL NATURE OF THE GREAT CHAIN

Was the Great Chain of Being representative of a true alliance? Or was it more akin to a semi-alliance, illusory alliance, or a tyranny? These are difficult questions to answer. The best answer is that, over the course of the history of the European Middle Ages, all of these combined-effort entities were manifested. For instance, a particular kingdom might have been a true alliance at its origin and then slowly decayed into an illusory alliance and then transformed itself into a semi-alliance. Or a local alliance headed by a noble might have been an illusory alliance for centuries but was then transformed into a semi-alliance and then a true alliance.

The Chain mandated submission to the dictates of the decision maker. Did this mean the decision makers could do anything they pleased? Was any action undertaken by a decision maker automatically sanctioned by the Chain? No, as noted earlier, the Chain imposed restrictions upon the actions of the decision makers. Middle Age decision makers were all taught the significance of the Chain and usually agreed to fulfill the duties that the Chain imposed upon them. As such, the typical decision makers did not intentionally shirk their obligations.

Moreover, even if a decision maker lacked motivation, suffered from incompetence, or was intentionally ignoring his obligations, the decision maker would find it difficult to wholly ignore his responsibilities. This was because the various individuals subject to a decision maker had certain expectations. Trouble would follow if these expectations were not suitably satisfied. The possible consequences included complaints, withholding contribution, unrest, riots, and rebellion.

Although the Chain dictated that rebellious actions by the lesser classes were wrong, the actions would be undertaken nonetheless if the pain and suffering caused by the decision maker's failures were of a sufficient magnitude. This principle was discussed in Chapter 6 where it was noted that members will adhere to an alliance structure only for as long as its perceived value is greater than that of alternatives. Decision makers were aware of the possible reactions of the lower classes and factored such possibilities into all of their actions. For instance, the Church was aware that kings might not adhere to its dictates. The king feared affronting the nobles and losing their support. The nobles worried about angering the peasants and causing unrest. Because of these concerns, the decision makers tended to fulfill the duties imposed upon them by the Chain.

In summary, this chapter has utilized the Great Chain of Being as a tool to demonstrate how ideas, mindsets, and worldviews can have a profound effect upon the development of alliances. The Chain largely locked alliance structures in place for hundreds of years. The Chain eventually deteriorated and passed away. When this occurred, the Middle Ages came to an end.[1]

THE EUROPEAN MODERN AGE AND THE ERA OF QUESTIONS

It is difficult to pinpoint when the Middle Ages ended and the Modern Age began. But it might be best to set the point of departure at the time when individuals began asking fundamental questions about the status quo and began seriously considering alternative arrangements. In common parlance, people began "thinking outside of the box."

Recall that the developments and transformations of alliances throughout the course of history are directly associated with ideas, mindsets, and worldviews that prevail in a given time period. The alliance structures of the Middle Ages were largely permanent because the prevailing worldview—the Great Chain of Being—stressed permanence. A corollary to this philosophical outlook was to never question existing institutions and beliefs.

Nothing lasts forever and the worldview of permanence obviously did not. Its demise was very gradual and without much fanfare. It is difficult to identify exactly

---

[1] Arguably, vestiges of the Great Chain remain in Europe today and shed light on its governments and social customs, especially in contrast to those of the United States.

when the erosion began and when it ended. Much of the uncertainty is due to the fact that the erosion began at different times, in different places, and in different ways. The defining feature of the erosion, however, was the questioning of institutions, ideas, and eventually everything. This questioning did not occur overnight. Instead, it gained speed slowly over time until it developed sufficient momentum to dethrone the old worldview of permanence.

Why did this questioning arise? The answer is difficult to ascertain with confidence and is beyond the scope of this book. But a few possible reasons include:

- *Exposure to New Societies*—Trade and travel exposed many Europeans to different languages, cultures, customs, and alliance structures. Such exposure is generally thought to breed cultural relativism which in turn would lead to the questioning of deeply-held beliefs. Columbus's voyage to North America undoubtedly opened many eyes.

- *The Printing Press*—The printing press appeared in Europe in approximately 1450 CE. Its arrival facilitated the recording and transmission of facts, ideas, thoughts, philosophies, and technologies across Europe. The printing press also allowed ancient texts of the Greeks and Romans to be reproduced relatively easily and disseminated widely. This spread of information likely sparked the imagination of countless individuals who began to look at their world in a new light.

- *Commercial Developments*—Commerce began expanding in the late Middle Ages which bread a new class of persons known as the merchant. These merchants did not fit into the old ways of thinking and challenged the conventional views of class structure. Further, merchants became wealthy and could use their wealth to influence existing alliance structures and to form novel alliances that suited their specific needs.

- *The Stability of the Late Middle Ages*—A primary means of maintaining the Great Chain of Being was the fear of the chaos and catastrophe that would result if it was broken. By 1500 CE or so, the reported misery following the collapse of the Roman Empire was a distant memory and some individuals were willing to experiment with new ideas. Furthermore, the relative peace and harmony of the late Middle Ages gave persons the time and luxury to contemplate their existences and the societies in which they lived.

MORE AND MORE QUESTIONS

The questioning of ideas, mindsets, and worldviews gradually grew like a snowball rolling down a hill, gaining more and more mass and momentum the farther that it rolled. The questions raised soon encompassed all areas including the large and small. A few Representative examples of the big questions asked and the resulting profound changes include:

- *Christian Dogma?—Martin Luther and the Protestant Reformation*—In the early 1500s, Martin Luther challenged the orthodoxy of the Catholic Church as being inaccurate and flawed. Luther proposed his own interpretation of Biblical scripture. Luther's criticisms led to widespread doubt of Church doctrine. These doubts in turn led to the Protestant Reformation, the creation of new church alliances such as the Lutheran Church and the Anabaptists, numerous wars of religion, and fundamental changes in the political landscape of Europe. At the end, the authority and influence of the Catholic Church had been markedly reduced.

- *The Church's Dominance of the State?—Henry VIII of England*—In the early 1500s, Henry desired a divorce from his wife because she was unable to bear him a male heir. When the Pope refused to grant the divorce, Henry questioned the Church's right to rule upon the issue of a divorce. Ultimately, Henry had England depart from the Catholic Church. Henry formed a new English Church at which he was the head. Henry also abolished the long-standing church structure, seized church lands, and closed all monasteries. Henry's actions resulted in decades of religious wars and disputes within England as well as the rise of numerous new Christian alliances within England including the Anglican Church, the Puritans, Presbyterians, and the Quakers. The end result was that England was no longer subservient to the Pope or any other religious authority. Instead, the king alone ruled England.

- *The King's Supremacy?—England's Beheading of Charles I*—After a bloody civil war and endless strife, the English nobles grew weary of the leadership of their king, Charles I. Having convicted Charles of failing to perform the obligations that a king owed to his people, the nobles publicly executed him by chopping off his head in 1649. This execution brought great instability and uncertainty to the land, with a variety of decision-making processes other than a king being utilized. These variations included (i) Parliament which was a committee decision maker, and (ii) a single, executive decision maker or "dictator" (Oliver Cromwell, the "Lord Protector" of England). Although Charles II, the son of Charles I, was later installed as King in 1660, few now believe that the King was selected by God. Instead, the King was installed by the people and was to serve the people. The fact that the people chose their King was further confirmed in 1689 when James II was deposed by his people and they then requested that William of Orange, a Dutch King, and his wife Mary of English descent move to London and become their king.

- *The Need for a King?—The Revolution of the American Colonies*—In 1776, the American Colonies declared themselves independent from Great Britain and its King. After winning the War of Independence, the American Colonies established a democratic republic consisting of decision makers that were mainly selected by all members of the alliance, including the most common of individuals. At the top of this alliance sat a delegated decision maker called a "President." Nearly any white male was eligible to hold this office. The overwhelming consensus view of Europe was that this radical new alliance structure was ridiculous and was doomed to imminent failure. Despite the pessimistic predictions, the alliance structure prevailed and became a model for numerous democratic republics.

These four actions all derived from the asking of basic questions about the status quo, combined with a willingness to act upon these questions and institute radical changes. These events set in motion chain reactions that continued for hundreds of years and probably are still being felt today. Martin Luther and Henry VIII most likely had no idea that their actions would result in numerous bloody wars or that the fabric of Europe would be irretrievably transformed. The English nobles who chopped off Charles I's head probably were unaware that they were calling into question the entire Great Chain of Being, including their own legitimacy as a special class, and that class warfare soon would be initiated against the nobles by the commoners. The American colonists were well aware that they were doing something unusual. However, it is unlikely that they realized that their revolution would lead to the French Revolution just a few years later, and numerous other revolutions throughout the world.

These four instances constitute only a few examples of situations where significant questions were asked and then answered with resulting profound consequences. Numerous other events contributed to the trend. During this era of questioning, all varieties of long-standing beliefs were examined and new answers were found. The new areas of inquiry were vast. A few examples include:

- *Art*—Two-dimensional images with unrealistic scenes were replaced with realist, three-dimensional images by artists such as Michelangelo and Da Vinci.

- *Philosophy*—The ancient teachings grounded in Christian theology and Aristotle were replaced by new philosophical worldviews grounded in reason or rationale inquiry. Notable examples are Des Cartes, Berkeley, Hume, Locke, Kant, and Leibniz.

- *Science*—The archaic science of Aristotle was replaced by revolutionary new methods and theories in astronomy, physics, mathematics, chemistry, and biology. Representative thinkers include Bacon, Copernicus, Newton, and Galileo.

- *Literature and Theatrics*—Religious-oriented productions were replaced by literature and plays on all topics, with Shakespeare being a prime example.

- *Music*—The old Church music (*a cappella*) was replaced with radical instrumental music by composers such as Bach and Handel and later by Mozart and Beethoven.

By and large, the asking of questions opened the door to the asking of more and more questions. The era of questioning eventually began putting everything under the microscope and demanding a justification for the existence of each institution, belief, relationship, and so on. As more questions were asked, more long-established, traditional institutions and ways of thinking deteriorated and collapsed. Into this vacuum emerged new ideas, mindsets, and worldviews. And these new arrivals resulted in new objectives, new means, and new alliance structures. These developments are explored in the next chapter.

CLOSING OBSERVATION

This Chapter has focused upon the European Middle Ages to demonstrate that ideas, mindsets, and worldviews of a particular era have a profound effect upon the growth, development, and termination of alliances. Any alliance, or the lack thereof, must be evaluated and reviewed in light of its historical time period. The views prevailing in that time period assert a powerful if not complete control over the alliances that exist. If a particular alliance structure is not present in a certain era, it is likely because (i) the objective to be pursued by the alliance was not considered desirable, or (ii) the objective was seen as being unrealistic and unattainable.

CHAPTER 18

Modern Developments

As discussed in the last chapter, the new era of questioning seems to have opened the door to substantial innovations in alliances. This experimentation and development of new alliance structures started out slowly but gained momentum as time passed. The examples are numerous and a comprehensive discussion of these developments will not be undertaken. But this Chapter will present a brief survey of particular developments.

REFORMATIONS OF OLD ALLIANCES

With the onslaught of questions and examinations, long-standing alliances and other combined-effort entities such as semi-alliances and illusory alliances attempted to correct their perceived deficiencies. These entities undertook a variety of corrective actions including pursuing new objectives, improving the means utilized to attain established objectives, attempting to reduce limitations associated with delegated decision makers, and sometimes utilizing the tools of tyranny to defeat alternative alliances. The common goal underlying these efforts was to increase the net perceived values associated with the existing entities, in comparison to the new, competing structures that were developing.

The Catholic Church provides an excellent example. Following the attacks of Martin Luther and Henry VIII and the numerous uprisings of new Christian sects, the Catholic Church undertook a variety of initiatives to improve the Church's standing in Europe. These actions are generally known as the "Counter Reformation." These efforts included substantial reductions of corruption in the decision-maker hierarchy, reviewing and largely affirming disputed issues of religious doctrine, and engaging in extensive, and at times brutal, reprisals upon non-Christians, Protestants, and dissenters within the Catholic Church.

Traditional governments also provide useful examples. The governments throughout Europe reacted with horror at the English's beheading of Charles I in 1649 and acted to prevent such uprisings and rebellions. By and large, these efforts were successful in the short run. Ultimately, however, they succeeded only at delaying inevitable revolutions. For instance, Louis XIV of France (1638-1715) proclaimed his doctrine of the divine right of kings to rule and cemented his control over France throughout his reign, instituting what appears to have been a tyranny.[1] But the Bourbon Monarchy's rule collapsed with the French Revolution and the beheadings of Louis XVI, Marie Antoinette, and thousands of French nobles in the 1790s. Other aging alliance structures in Europe suffered similar ends, although not as bloody.

NEW VERSIONS OF OLD ALLIANCES

As old traditional alliances became weak or collapsed, new versions of these long-standing alliances developed. The new Christian alliances formed during and after the Protestant Reformation, which were discussed earlier, are prime examples. Following the attacks on the Catholic Church by Luther and Henry VIII, numerous Christian alliances sprung to life. These new alliances were often very similar to the Catholic Church, especially the Anglican and the Lutheran churches. They were essentially new versions of the old Catholic alliance.

France serves as another good example of new versions springing out of old alliances. The bloodshed and turmoil of the French Revolution produced a confusing decision-making process probably best described as an oligarchy. This process was a failure and was quickly replaced by a single executive decision maker, Napoleon Bonaparte. Under Bonaparte, France was arguably a true alliance at least for a short period of time. Further, by conquering most of Europe, Bonaparte created a short-lived French Empire where he was the Emperor. When the remainder of Europe finally defeated Bonaparte for good at the battle of Waterloo and imprisoned him on the Island of St. Helena, France then went back to utilizing the old system of monarchs but continued to experiment with other forms of government from time to time.

England (and later Great Britain and the United Kingdom) is a useful example of efforts to remake an old institution from the inside. Following the beheading of Charles I and the subsequent rule by both Parliament and the Lord

---

[1] This probable tyranny was composed of the nobles and Louis XIV was its decision maker. The peasants were brutally taxed and received few if any benefits from the government. The nobles essentially paid no taxes and lived extravagantly.

Protector Cromwell, England restructured its government on multiple occasions. These efforts included Parliament's reinstalling the monarchy under Charles II, deposing James II and importing from Holland William of Orange to be king, confirming the legitimacy of Queen Anne as monarch, and finally importing George I from Hanover to be king. This reformed alliance structure is still present today in the United Kingdom. Although the sitting monarch technically possesses many powers dating back hundreds of years such as the authority to declare war, the monarch does not exercise these powers and Parliament effectively makes all decisions.

NEW ALLIANCES

In this new era, new types of alliances also arose. These alliances were the product of a variety of complex factors including the inquiring nature of the times, better education, improved channels to disseminate acquired learning, and greater prosperity. A few examples of new alliances include:

- *Modern political parties*—Alliances somewhat similar to political parties have existed for long periods of time. In general, these alliances were small-scale and usually existed to curry favor with a single executive decision maker such as a king, or with a committee decision maker such as a group of nobles that were integrated with a king into an interwoven and/or tiered decision-making process. In the new era, political parties such as the Tories, Whigs, Roundheads, and Jacobins appeared on the scene. These parties were formal, public, and had definite agendas or "objectives," including influencing the existing government to adopt the policies they desired as well as securing and preserving power. These parties fall within the concept of factions discussed earlier.

- *Business alliances*—Throughout the Middle Ages, industry and trade were rather limited. As discussed earlier, most commerce was controlled through long-standing alliances (or semi-alliances) known broadly as the "guild system." In this arrangement, merchants, manufacturers, and artisans were usually compelled to enter a guild in order to do business. The guild format tightly controlled the quality, quantity, and price of most goods that were crafted or sold in a particular region. In the new era, the guilds began to break down and were replaced by new, sophisticated forms of business alliances, such as joint ventures, partnerships, and corporations. The focus of these new alliances was to reap the benefits of combining the resources of each individual member to attain certain business objectives.

- *Labor Alliances*—As business reformed itself, so did the working class. Workers began allying together in order to negotiate better wages and working conditions. The typical accord was essentially an agreement to forego individual negotiations with an employer. Instead, the members delegated authority to negotiate on their behalf to a single representative who then negotiated with the employer. The result was that the representative could usually obtain better terms such as improved wages, working conditions, benefits, and so on by bargaining on behalf of all members.

- *Academic and scientific associations*—In the Middle Ages, education and learning was largely limited to the Church and monasteries. In the new era, all types of societies and associations developed that were devoted to the discovery and advancement of intellectual subjects including physics, chemistry, astronomy, mathematics, and biology. For instance, the famous Royal Society of Great Britain was originally a small group of scientific-minded individuals that met periodically to ponder novel and interesting subjects and to work together on these matters. Similarly, Paris became famous for its salons where various intellectual topics were debated. These entities all constituted new forms of alliances.

- *Insurance Alliances*—Insurance became more and more popular as the new era progressed. Individuals realized that, by pooling their resources together to guard against a catastrophe expected to be suffered by a small portion of the membership, all members could be safeguarded.

- *Non-Religious School Alliances*—In the Middle Ages, education was rare and was almost always taught through a Church institution. As the need for an education grew in the new era, parents began pooling their resources to form new school alliances devoted solely to the provision of education to their children.

NEW FORMS OF ACCORDS

The modern era saw substantial developments in the area of accords. In the past, most accords were implied. If the accords were express, they were made through spoken words and generally were a mix of implied components and express components. For instance, governmental alliances like the Roman Republic were based largely upon mixtures of implied and express (spoken only) components.

Express, written accords were very rare but they did exist in the past. For example, the many written documents associated with Catholic dogma (aside from the Bible) can be viewed as part of large, express, written accord. One of the most significant written accords was the Magna Carta. In 1215, various English nobles reduced to writing a detailed accord identifying various powers held by the King of England. This document also included numerous limitations on the power of the King. The nobles then forced the King to sign the document. The Magna Carta can be viewed as perhaps the first effort to reduce an accord underlying a governmental alliance completely to writing.

As literacy began increasing during the end of the Middle Ages, and then through the Renaissance and the Enlightenment, written accords became more prevalent. For instance, various commercial alliances were formed and written documents were created to memorialize the terms. Further, as governmental alliances began forming more treaties, they began reducing the agreements to writing. An excellent example of the trend towards reducing accords to writing is the Constitution of the United States of America. This written accord is discussed in greater detail later in this book.

The trend towards express, written accords arguably resulted in the formation of more alliances. Why? Recall that an alliance is formed only if the members perceive a net value in entering the alliance. If a written accord exists delineating key aspects of an alliance (for example, the objective, the decision-making process, the requisite contribution, and so on), the value associated with a proposed alliance is much more evident. As a result, potential members are much more likely to perceive substantial value in entering the alliance.

In addition, the trend towards express, written accords tended to make alliances more workable and effective. Why? If an alliance is founded upon oral promises and assurances, there is a high likelihood of disputes and controversies over the terms and provision of the accord. Memories are faulty and can fail. People can misinterpret spoken communications and might have radically different recollections of the material terms of a particular agreement. In addition, if an arrangement goes sour for one party, he can lie about what the agreement was in order to escape its obligations. The existence of an express, written accord does not eliminate these problems. But a written accord will substantially reduce their occurrences.

NEW DECISION-MAKING PROCESSES

The modern era saw the development of new forms of decision-making processes. The most notable development was the rise and ultimate dominance of membership voting as a decision-making process.

Democracy

As noted earlier, the membership-voting process was used thousands of years ago by ancient Greeks in the city-state of Athens. This process, termed a "democracy," was premised upon a majority vote of all members. Delegated decision makers were rare and usually were appointed only for short periods of time such as to lead an army to battle.

The Athenian democracy attained great successes and prosperity for the Athenians but ultimately it resulted in a horrible defeat. By majority vote, the

Athenian democracy led the alliance into devastating military engagements commonly known as the "Peloponnesian War." Athens ultimately was brought to its knees and was conquered.

History subsequently blamed Athens' democracy for the defeat. Various commentators attacked democracy as unworkable and instead favored delegated decision makers. Plato blamed the Athenian democracy for executing his teacher, Socrates, and famously argued that the only appropriate decision-making process was an enlightened "philosopher king." Although membership voting was subsequently intertwined into other processes such as the Roman Republic, democracy was essentially the pariah of decision-making processes for thousands of years.

The American Revolution reversed this trend by instituting an interwoven decision-making process relying heavily upon membership voting. The Americans called this process a "democracy" or a "democratic republic." When the United States was first formed, commentators in Europe saw it as an absurdity that was doomed to fail. To the surprise of all the critics, this new decision-making process was successful. Moreover, this new process sparked a trend that swept through Europe in the 1800s and much of the world in the 1900s. The trend is on-going with more and more areas of the world turning to democracy as a decision-making process.[1]

Bureaucrats

Another development in decision-making processes has been the rise of the professional bureaucrat. This person is typically an executive decision maker within a tiered decision-making process. As discussed in Chapter 6, alliances will stack executives on top of each other in a pyramid-hierarchy format where each executive reports to an executive above him until all reports channel up to one individual. The decision maker, however, does not have to be an executive. Committee decision makers can be woven into this format as well.

The bureaucrat has become quite popular in the past hundred years. This popularity has been driven by need. As governmental alliances (and other types of alliances) have undertaken more and more objectives, a complex decision-making

---

[1] The decision-making processes of modern "democracies" are never based solely upon membership voting. Instead, the system is always some form of interwoven decision-making process with executive and committee decision makers. However, the ultimate decisions are heavily influenced by the members through the voting process and their selection of delegated decision makers. In some democracies, the members have an even stronger influence by voting on referendums which can bind the decision-making processes to a large degree.

process employing numerous bureaucrats has become necessary to attain the objectives.

It should be remembered that bureaucrats are delegated decision makers and are subject to all of the corresponding limitations including (i) motivational, (ii) ability, and (iii) fidelity. As such, bureaucrats often fail to attain certain objectives and otherwise cause displeasure among the membership.

Programmed Decision Makers

Another development of the modern area has been the use of programmed decision makers. Recall that this is where decision-making authority has been delegated but in such a fashion that the decision maker has only nominal discretion or no discretion at all in reaching a decision. Instead, all decisions have been effectively predetermined by the alliance. The decision maker's role is essentially to look at the circumstances presented and determine which predetermined decision is to be implemented. Programmed decision makers are prominent in many alliances of the modern world.

The rise of programmed decision makers has been driven by several likely factors. One reason is the rise of literacy and convenient writing devices such as pens and paper, typewriters, modern word processing. With these new devices, it is relatively easy and convenient for an alliance to prepare specific programs for delegated decision makers to follow and effectively eliminate most discretion that they might have formerly held. In addition, with the rise of huge bureaucracies, the need for formal instructions has become more and more prevalent. Certain alliances have hundreds or perhaps thousands of delegated decision makers that must make decisions. Many of these alliances have found that they need to strictly control the actions of such decision makers with written, programmed decision-making processes. Although these programs attempt to reduce discretion, it is largely impossible to completely eliminate discretion held by decision makers.

Rational Chaos

Another interesting development has been the use of chaotic decision-making processes. This topic is covered in Chapter 19 and its discussion of free market Capitalism as a means of attaining the external objective of Generation of Prosperity.

EXPANSION OF MEMBERSHIP

The modern era has seen a radical expansion of membership in governmental alliances. For thousands of years, most long-standing, governmental alliances effectively limited membership to a relatively small percentage of the individuals residing in the local geographic region. In many situations, the true members of a governmental alliance were probably less than ten percent of the population of a particular region. In alliances with the most liberal membership rules, the true members were probably never more than one-half of the surrounding population. For instance, even in the case of the Athenian democracy, a substantial portion of the population was excluded from membership. This excluded group consisted of slaves, resident aliens, transients, and all women.

In the modern era, the membership ranks of governmental alliances opened slowly to include more and more categories of individuals. At the beginning of the modern era, membership in most governmental alliances was limited to wealthy, landowning individuals. Over time, governmental alliances began admitting more and more classes of persons. Examples of certain historically excluded groups that were admitted during the modern era include:

- Merchant and artisan classes—non-landowning individuals with money

- Males—regardless of land possession or wealth

- Racial and ethic minorities

- Women

- Immigrants

Why did the membership ranks of governmental alliances tend to open in the modern age? The answer probably lies in the following three factors.

1) Contribution

The first factor is the need for contribution. As discussed earlier, most alliances require a critical mass of members to attain an objective. Further, even if an objective is attainable, the admission of more members can reduce contribution levels for current members. As such, admissions of new members can be seen as attempts to develop additional contribution so as to either attain an objective or to attain an objective at a smaller cost.

One form of contribution often required by a governmental alliance is money. Approximately five-hundred years ago, the members of most governmental alliances were nobles and other landowners. As a merchant class expanded and began accumulating substantial wealth, these governmental alliances began courting wealthy merchants as members in order to receive their money as contribution to use in alliance efforts. As more merchants entered governmental alliances, the interests of the merchant class began to dominate the alliances while the interests of the nobles and landowners diminished.

Another form of contribution is manpower to fight wars. The past several hundred years have seen massive battles. These battles require large armies with tens of thousands of soldiers. Mercenaries are expensive and difficult to retain. In contrast, true members fighting to defend and protect their lives, families, property, and so on are both inexpensive and effective. Typically, such fighting members have esprit de corps and association glory that motivates them to fight with diligence and dedication. To draw large numbers of individuals into either volunteering to fight or fighting for paltry compensation, these individuals must be made members of the alliances. (Or at least illusory members tricked into believing they are in an alliance.) As such, it appears that the expansion of membership to include large portions of the population was motivated in part by a desire to attract inexpensive and effective fighting forces.

2) Conciliation

The second factor leading to increased membership is the need to placate potential rebels or trouble makers. Often, alliances observed sizeable and fearful revolutionary discontent brewing nearby. These pockets of dissent varied substantially over time. For instance, one common type of resistance was individuals subjugated and exploited by the ruling governmental alliance. Another common type consisted of persons with second-class membership within the ruling governmental alliance. These individuals received few benefits of membership and were not happy about it.

There was always a danger that these unhappy individuals would unite and overthrow the ruling governmental alliance. These possible revolutions often held the potential to be violent and bloody attacks. But some potential revolutions were likely to occur only within a membership-voting process (that is, discontent second-class members would successfully unite and choose delegated decision makers favoring their interests). The ruling governmental alliance typically would respond to such revolutionary threats under the external objective of Defense against Aggressors. The means employed included violent oppression, stifling of dissent, reduction of freedom of speech, and other tools of tyranny.

At times, however, some ruling alliances determined that the brewing rebellions either could not be defeated or that the costs of defeating the rebellions were simply too great. Instead of fighting the rebellions, the alliances made peace with them. The underlying rationale appears to have been the adage, "If you can't beat 'em, join 'em." By employing this approach, the ruling alliances often were able to structure the admission of new members (or the granting of additional benefits to discontent second-class members) on terms very favorable to the controlling alliance members.

These solutions rarely resulted in complete peace and happiness. The newly admitted members usually were second-class members with fewer privileges than old-line members. The existing second-class members receiving additional privileges often still did not hold the full range of benefits afforded to the first class members. Further, the old-line, first class members usually retained a large degree of influence over the decision-making process and used it to often (but not always) further their interests. Nonetheless, the solutions usually ended the likelihood of revolution. Although the newly admitted members remained discontent to some degree, the costs of rebellion were usually heavily outweighed by the benefits of the new or expanded membership. As such, although many individuals might have remained displeased, they were relatively satisfied with the new arrangements.

Were these governmental entities that admitted members solely for the purpose of conciliation true alliances? It is probably best to consider them as semi-alliances. They had many earmarks of true alliances and typically operated like alliances. Yet most of them possessed sufficient deviations such as second-class members that it was not clear that true alliances were in fact present.

3) Fairness and Rationality

The third factor contributing to the expansion of membership is a sense of fairness and overall rationality. As noted earlier, the modern age is the era of questioning. This questioning is often grounded in various reason-based concepts including common sense, a need to maintain consistency, and the avoidance of hypocrisy.

When individuals were excluded from an alliance, the excluded individuals (as well as some members) tended to inquire as to why the exclusions were taking place. Often, theories such as notions of inherent inferiorities based upon race, gender, or ethnicity were put forward to rationalize such exclusions. Although these theories were often accepted, they did not stand the test of time and the questioning of the modern age. When their flaws were exposed, the theories slowly crumbled and the excluded individuals were admitted into the alliance.

The American Civil Rights movement of the 1950s and 1960s provides a good example of this situation. A compelling argument can be made that World War II was the true catalyst for the success of the Civil Rights movement. During World War II, African Americans were drafted and forced to fight in the war. When the war ended, many African Americans likely asked why they were required to supply contribution such as life and limb to the war effort when they were largely excluded from true membership in the United States. These so-called members had very limited rights in most states. Extensive efforts were undertaken by many state governmental alliances to segregate them from White people. In sum, African Americans were second class citizens in most parts of the United States. Nonetheless, African Americans were required to supply full contribution to the various governmental alliances including taxes and the ultimate contribution of their lives in war efforts. This situation underscored a fundamental unfairness of the exclusion of African Americans from membership.

Moreover, all of the racial theories of inferiority began to collapse under the weight of empirical evidence. For instance, the war had shown that African Americans had no physical inadequacies. They could fight as well as Whites. Moreover, African Americans were competing with Whites in the Olympics, professional baseball, and other sports. In addition, African Americans had been generating impressive developments in science, literature, and music and cultured activities for some time. Overall, the accumulating evidence was making clear that theories of African American inferiority were groundless. This situation served to highlight the irrationality of the second class citizenship granted to African Americans.

Finally, World War II exposed a huge hypocrisy in the exclusion of African Americans from full membership. As the war progressed and ultimately ended, much was made of the racial bigotry of the Nazi regime and the extraordinary depravity of the Holocaust. It was not hard to see a similar (but not identical) parallel between the conduct of Nazi Germany to the Jews and the conduct of the United States towards African Americans.

In sum, these three factors seem to have worked together to break down the barriers to membership. Ultimately, African Americans were granted full membership in the United States with the right to enjoy all privileges. Nonetheless, some continue to criticize this solution as being inadequate and contend that African Americans are still second-class citizens.

NEW MEANS

The modern era has seen considerable development in the means used to attain various objectives. In fact, the development of many new objectives was likely made possible due to innovations in means. These innovations in means were in turn driven by new technologies and ideas. For instance, the printing press made it possible to codify Law-Compelled Objectives in numerous written documents that could then be distributed around to the members of a governmental alliance. Similarly, the advent of money allowed for the development of easy contribution collection and the use of non-member labor to attain objections.

The concept of indirect attainment has had a profound effect upon the development of novel and effective means. Recall that indirect attainment is achievement of an objective through a circuitous or roundabout method. For instance, an alliance will utilize a measure that has no direct causal relationship with the end desired to be attained. To underscore this point, it is useful to repeat the examples set forward in Chapter 12. The following is an excerpt:

All alliances use means to achieve their objectives. In most circumstances, alliances will employ means that *directly* accomplish the objectives.

> **Example 4 "Wild West"**—The mercenary uses direct means of force and imprisonment to attain the objective of order and decency. If a marauder appears in the community, the mercenary either runs him off using weapons or imprisons him.

> **Example 5 "Help the Needy"**—The direct means are the food and shelter provided to the needy. Provision of these items aids the needy to overcome their circumstances.

At times, though, alliances will use means that *indirectly* attain the objective.

> **Example 4 "Wild West"**—The mercenary dictates that all employers in the community must pay a minimum wage to laborers. The mercenary contends that higher wages will draw individuals into the workforce and away from a life of theft and murder. And, as a consequence, order and decency will be indirectly attained.

> **Example 5 "Help the Needy"**—The alliance provides job-skill training to the needy. It is thought that the training will allow the needy to find good employment and therefore raise themselves out of their circumstances. Although the training does not alleviate the plight of the needy, it is hoped that the training will indirectly result in improvement in their situation.

The modern era has seen an ever increasing use of the concept of indirect attainment to achieve a variety of objectives. Alliances constantly seek to employ measures that ultimately achieve objectives in a roundabout way.

As noted in Chapter 12, indirect attainment is not always used as a bona fide method of actually achieving an objective. In many situations, indirect attainment is used as a smokescreen to disguise the true objective being pursued. For instance, a compromised decision maker will adopt a measure for the purpose of profiting him or his cohorts. The decision maker, however, will conceal this purpose by asserting that the measure will indirectly attain an objective pursued by the alliance. Thus, the prevalence of indirect attainment in the modern era arguably provided more and more opportunities for fidelity limitations.

NEW ATTITUDES TOWARDS GOVERNMENTAL ENTITIES

One of the most significant developments in the modern era was the gradual change in attitudes towards governmental entities. This change was characterized by a slowly-developing recognition that the purpose of a governmental entity is to serve the interests of the individuals residing under its control and authority.

The Old Attitude

Prior to the modern era, few individuals consciously perceived governmental entities as being present to serve their interests. Instead, individuals took for granted that governmental entities such as kings and nobles were an inherent condition in the world and nothing could be done to change the situation. Further, when individuals actually took the time to contemplate governmental entities, their contemplation was more of a subconscious evaluation rather than a conspicuous, logic-driven analysis of the situation.

> *Illustration*—In the Middle Ages, a group of peasants are ruled by a regional noble. The arrangement is a tyrannical alliance, which is a form of a true alliance. The peasants submit to the authority of the noble and supply him with contribution in the form of crops and labor. In return, the noble pursues the objective of Defense against Aggressors and also provides some furtherance of Law-Compelled Objectives such as Protection of the Person and minimal Property Protections. At times, the noble also acts tyrannically and abuses the peasants.

> - **No Conscious Recognition of an Alliance**—Although a true alliance is present, neither the noble nor the peasants actually recognize that an alliance is in fact in place. Instead, both the peasants and the noble accept the arrangement as a fact of nature.

> - **Occasional Subconscious Recognition of the Alliance**—The region is attacked by raiders. The noble assembles his knights and fights off the attack. The peasants are grateful and acknowledge the value provided to them by the noble. Despite making this acknowledgment, neither the noble nor the peasants can see the big picture. That is, it is beyond their capacities to recognize that that a true alliance is in place including: (i) the presence of an implied agreement to submit to the authority of the noble and provide him with contribution, (ii) the fact that all peasants are members of this arrangement, and (iii) that the arrangement allows the peasant members to attain objectives that they could not obtain on their own (or not as effectively or efficiently).

---

[1]The use of the term "subconscious mind" is not intended to reference psychological concepts. Rather, it is simply a recognition that humans often make decisions without utilizing a formal, rigid, thought process. Decisions ranging from what clothes to wear to purchasing an expensive automobile to deciding what school to attend are often made without a deliberative analysis of the relevant facts. In other words, the decision is not consciously made in that the actor is not formally making a decision. Rather, the individual's

Although individuals living before the modern era were largely unable to recognize the formal nature of an alliance relationship, their subconscious minds[1] were aware of the arrangement to a large degree. Recall that members of an alliance constantly weigh the perceived value of an alliance against the perceived values of known alternatives. If this balance changed markedly, individuals took action.

Illustration—In the Middle Ages, the same tyrannical alliance noted in the earlier illustration is present. The noble dies, however, and is replaced by his son. The son decides to rule the region harshly and cruelly. He confiscates from the peasants as many crops and valuables as he can. He runs roughshod over the interests of the peasants and frequently abuses them. Further, the son ignores the Law-Compelled Objectives underlying the alliance and pursues the objective of Defense against Aggressors only when raiders threaten his property. The peasants slowly take note of the change in circumstances. They begin to fondly recall the old situation with the father. Although the father could be abusive at times, he generally provided numerous benefits to the peasants. The son, however, provides few or no benefits and generally oppresses the peasants. The peasants conclude that the situation is untenable. The peasants ally and join forces to fight the noble. A violent revolt ensues. Although the son ultimately puts the revolt down, he has learned of the powers possessed by united peasants. As a result, the son pledges to resume the practices of his father. Although the son acts cruelly at times in the future, he overall provides a net benefit to the peasants and the peasants are satisfied. A tyrannical alliance has been restored.

As this illustration makes clear, members have long implicitly recognized the alliance-nature of a governmental entity. In these situations, individuals subconsciously evaluated the net perceived benefit of the arrangement. If the perceived value was less than the perceived value of known alternatives, the members would tend to terminate their membership and form a new alliance. Despite the fact that individuals played out this fundamental concept time and time again, few if any individuals formally recognized the concept in the Middle Ages.

---

subconscious mind is effectively making the decision. This subconscious decision is based upon information that the actor has accumulated over time and processed into generalizations. For example, a young adult is deciding where to attend college. This person does not sit down and draw up a list of pros and cons for a particular college. Rather, this person bases his decision upon years of knowledge and information that he has accumulated about colleges while growing up. The individual's subconscious mind then processes this information into making a decision.

The New Attitude

The change in the Modern Era was the conscious recognition of the long-followed, but unappreciated, concept that:

1) The purpose of a governmental entity is to serve the interests of its members.

2) If a purported governmental entity is not serving the interests of its members, it is tyranny. The members should terminate their membership and form an alternative governmental alliance.

The primary driver of this recognition appears to be the political philosopher John Locke, who lived from 1632 until 1704. Locke argued that all governments have an underlying accord which he called a "social contract." This social contract consisted of an agreement whereby members submit to the rule of a monarch. This monarch's authority, however, is not unfettered. Instead, the monarch is obligated to respect certain natural rights held by all members including the rights to life, liberty, and property. If the monarch violates the restrictions imposed upon him, the members are free to terminate the social contract and revolt against the monarch.[1]

Locke's observations seem to have had a profound effect upon the attitudes of Europeans towards governments. The changes that took place certainly did not occur overnight. But it clearly appears that Locke's recognition of the alliance nature of the relationship between a monarch and his subjects substantially influenced the history of Europe. A primary influence of Locke was upon the American Colonies and their revolution in 1776. In fact, many commentators contend that the Declaration of Independence is essentially a mere restatement of Locke's principles.

NEW OBJECTIVES

The modern era has seen substantial development in the objectives pursued by governmental alliances. These objectives include both (i) new categories of objectives and (ii) permutations of existing objectives.

Prior to the modern era, most governmental alliances pursued a very limited range of objectives outlined earlier such as Defense against Aggressors, Uniting against Natural Obstacles, Law-Compelled Objectives, Morality/Religion, and so

---

[1] It should be underscored that Locke's views appear to have been largely of a moral nature. In his era, the concept of a revolution and attacking one's king was thought to be immoral and entirely unthinkable. Locke assailed this prevailing viewpoint and contended that an individual was entirely justified on moral grounds in attacking a monarch that failed to respect the inherent, natural rights of human beings.

on. With the explosion of alliances and expanded ways of thinking, alliances began pursuing a wide variety of new objectives.

Alliances began pursuing these new objectives, because the members saw the objectives as being (i) desirable, (ii) attainable, and (iii) well-suited for a combined effort in contrast to an individual effort. These objectives and the various means used to attain them did not arrive instantly. Instead, the developmental processes discussed earlier had to play out. Typically, persons stumbled upon the concepts underlying the objectives (or the means used to obtain the objectives). These persons put the ideas into action in their own alliances, or argued for alliances to embrace the ideas and use them in alliances. Alliances experimented and some new ideas were successful while others failed. Alliances, and members within alliances, watched what others were doing and often imitated their successes (and sometimes failures). As time passed, the more desirable objectives and the more successful means prevailed and became commonplace. At the same time, old objectives and means were often found stale, undesirable, ineffective, or better suited for individual effort and were discarded as a consequence.

Recall that, as a general rule, all members of an alliance desire the attainment of an objective pursued by their alliance. The modern era saw a sizeable rise in an exception to this general rule. This exception is that sometimes a minority of members will not desire one or more objectives pursued by their alliance. This exception typically arises in most long-term, complex, multi-objective alliances such as governmental alliances. Why does the exception occur in these types of alliances? It results from a variety of factors including the usage of indefinite or open objectives, the nature of the applicable decision-making process, and objective creep. In addition, the fact that an entity is pursuing one of more objectives not desired by its members might be a sign that a true alliance is not present. Instead, another combined-effort entity such as a semi-alliance or an illusory alliance might be present and pursuing these objectives.

The next two chapters will survey some of the more notable or prevalent objectives pursued in the modern age. Due to breadth and complexity of these objectives, an in-depth analysis will not be undertaken. Chapter 19 focuses on Law-Compelled Objectives and Chapter 20 addresses other modern objectives.

CHAPTER 19

The Ascendancy of Law-Compelled Objectives

G overnmental alliances have long pursued Law-Compelled Objectives. In the modern era, however, these pursuits have expanded substantially. Recall that Law-Compelled Objectives can be placed into three broad categories: (i) Protection of the Person, (ii) Protection of Property, and (iii) Enforcement of Promises. Modern developments in these three categories will be discussed separately in the following sections.

PROTECTION OF THE PERSON

This is the oldest of Law-Compelled Objectives. In the past, the objective principally focused upon protecting a member from suffering serious bodily injury or death at the hands of another member.[1] In the modern area, these protections have been expanded greatly.

Subject Matter

Substantial expansion has been in the subject matter of what is protected. Instead of just protecting against physical harm such as injury and death, the subject matter has been broadened to encompass areas such as:

---

[1] Recall that this objective does not focus upon preventing harm inflicted by non-members. That is a separate objective—Defense against Aggressors. A Law-Compelled Objective focuses only upon the conduct of *members* of the alliance. Its essence is that members will benefit in some fashion if all members agree to behave in a certain way.

Subject Matter	Common Name	Description
Reputation in a Community	Defamation	A person's reputation can be a very important asset in interactions with others, business dealings, and so on. The law should seek to protect one's reputation in a community from false and damaging remarks.
Personal and Confidential Information	Privacy	Everyone has secrets that they do not want revealed to the community for various reasons. The law should protect certain categories information against unjustifiable disclosures.
Vulgarities	Obscenity	A person viewing or hearing certain images and statements might suffer mental distress. The law should strive to keep such images or statements out of the public arena.
Exclusion and Differential Treatment	Discrimination	Groups often have an irrational tendency to treat a class of persons differently on the basis of one or more immutable traits. This treatment can cause the recipients to suffer economic and mental harm. The law should prohibit such irrational actions where they serve to substantially impair the ability of the recipients to live normal lives.

Means

The means employed to attain Law-Compelled Objectives have expanded greatly. Examples of commonly used means include:

- full-time police
- investigators
- prosecutors
- criminal courts

- prisons

- emergency report hotlines such as "911"

Preventative Measures

Law-compelled objectives also include prohibitions on conduct that is not injurious by itself, but instead holds the potential to cause injury to members. These laws are sometimes called "prophylactic." Examples include laws prohibiting:

- drunk driving

- firing guns in residential areas

- driving a car with bad brakes or bald tires

The rationale underlying prophylactic laws is to prohibit conduct:

1) that is likely to cause irreparable and grievous injury to others; and

2) in situations where the victims cannot adequately protect themselves (that is, a combined/alliance approach is therefore of value).

In recent years, the area of prophylactic laws has expanded substantially. These measures are often called "regulations." Examples of newly regulated areas include:

- *Food and Medicine*—Unsafe food and medicine are likely to cause serious illness and death. Moreover, it is difficult for individuals to adequately protect themselves against latent, non-obvious dangers associated with food or medicine. Specifically, at least one person (if not many) must become sick or die before other individuals are likely to know that the food or medicine is dangerous and should be avoided. A combined effort in the form of a Law-Compelled Objective setting minimum standards for food preparation and drug manufacture is therefore preferable to individual action.

- *Consumer Products*—Consumer products such as appliances, vehicles, toys, equipment are often regulated for latent, non-obvious defects that are likely to cause serious bodily injury or death. The rationale is same as with food and medicine regulations (that is, a Law-Compelled Objective setting minimum standards is preferable to individual action).

The Arena for Individual Action— The Courts System

Governmental alliances do not rely solely upon action by a governmental entity to attain a particular objective. Instead, governments often allow for individuals to protect themselves by maintaining an arena where individuals might undertake specific endeavors to protect their persons from harm or injury. This arena is the civil courts system. The government provides the judge, any jury, the underlying rules of conduct or the "law," and a mechanism for enforcing the outcome. Claimants in the court system might seek, for example:

- an order from the court directing another individual to cease undertaking a course of conduct likely to cause irreparable damage to the claimant

- a sum of money to compensate the claimant for an injury that has been inflicted upon the claimant by another person

- a sum of money intended to punish another individual for inflicting harm upon the claimant and to deter other individuals from causing similar injuries

The Standards of Conduct Imposed by the Civil Courts System

In the past, the standards of conduct imposed by the civil courts system were fairly lenient. Generally speaking, the courts would grant relief to a claimant only if the claimant could prove either:

1) *Intentional harm*—The defendant must have desired to cause bodily injury to the claimant (or been substantially certain that his action would cause bodily injury to the claimant).

2) *Negligent harm*—The defendant's conduct was unreasonable and caused the claimant's injury. In determining reasonableness, the court would determine what a typical, ordinary person would have done in a similar situation and then compared that benchmark to the conduct of the defendant. If the defendant acted below the benchmark, he was liable. If the conduct was equal to or above the benchmark, the defendant was not liable and the injury suffered by the claimant was seen as an unfortunate accident where no one was to blame.

In recent years, courts have largely adhered to this same basic format. Courts, however, appear to have substantially increased the standard of conduct (the "benchmark") for judging negligently inflicted harm. At the same time, the courts seem to have lowered expectations regarding the conduct expected of a typical claimant. These trends seem to have sizably increased the awards of compensatory damages to claimants in recent years.

Arguably, this higher standard of care of recent years is tied to a general rise in prosperity. As regions become more prosperous, precautions and safeguards for reducing injuries and death seem to be more affordable and realistic. As a result, the courts system tends to raise the benchmark for proper conduct. Similarly, if the costs of attaining the current benchmark standard of conduct appear too costly, the courts system will lower the standard to a less burdensome level. Ultimately, it seems that this raising and lowering of the benchmark is akin to raising and lowering the contribution required of members in order to attain an objective.

In recent years, the objective of Mitigation of Catastrophe has crept into the reasoning of the court's rulemaking. For instance, in setting the standard of care for manufacturers of consumer products that tend to cause personal injuries, courts often raise the benchmark of acceptable conduct under an "insurance" rationale. Specifically, the courts indicate that manufacturers can pass the costs of damage awards onto customers in the form of higher prices. As a result, when consumers purchase a product, a portion of the price is effectively a premium that provides insurance in the event that the product injures the customer. This viewpoint is controversial.

As final matter, it should be observed that the standards of conduct imposed by the civil courts system typically coexist with or complement government action seeking to attain the same objective. For example, a governmental entity might institute a specific safety regulation that a consumer product must satisfy. At the same time, the courts system might institute rules governing when an injured person by the product might recover compensatory damages from the manufacturer. Typically, these different means work towards attaining the same goal safety. But there usually are differences. The governmental regulation usually strives to prevent the harm from occurring. The civil rule, in contrast, strives to use compensation to remedy the harm caused by the product.

PROTECTION OF PROPERTY

Governmental alliances have offered some protections of property for many years. But the modern age has seen a sizeable expansion in these protections.

Land

The earliest laws generally protected interests in land. This began simply with establishing just who owned a particular track of land. This area has expanded into numerous other areas such as:

- leasing of land

- right to travel across another's land (an "easement")

- activities on land (noise and odor restrictions)

- protection of land from harm by others

- agricultural products grown on land

- usage of streams and rivers flowing adjacent to or through land

- resources found on the land's surface

- resources under the land's surface (oil, gas, and other minerals)

Personal Property

Aside from land, property laws have grown to include most tangible items of matter that are valued by individuals. Examples include:

- resources removed or severed from the land (gold, silver, iron, timber, stone, crops)

- implements and tools

- household items

- manufactured goods

- artistic works

Intangible Property

These laws also encompass intellectual property such as:

- writings, compositions, artwork, photographs, and music (copyright)

- images, slogans, and reputations (trademarks)

- inventions and innovative ideas and techniques (patents)

- confidential information and know-how (trade secrets)

Means to Protect Property

The primary means of protecting property is government action. Police and the criminal justice system usually fill these roles. If an individual trespasses on another's land, steals personal property, or makes too much noise at night, the police and courts will take action.

The modern era has seen increasing usage of the civil courts system to protect property. This arena allows property owners to defend and protect their interests through individual action. Examples of actions that the property owners might take include suits to:

- determine who owns property

- resolve a dispute over a lease to property

- keep someone from harming property

- determining if one has a right to use the property of another

- recover property that has been taken away wrongfully

- recover compensatory monetary relief for damage inflicted to property

Transfer of Property

Aside from defining and protecting property, another matter is effectuating the transfer of property. For example, an item of property is owned by one individual. This is usually described as the individual holding "title" in the property. If this individual desires to permanently transfer title in the property to another by sale or gift, rules governing this transfer are often useful. Historically, these rules were not needed until individuals began accumulating sizeable amounts of property.

Offense against Non-Members Disguised as Property Laws

As discussed in Chapter 8, there are usually two rationales underlying the protections of property. The first reason is a basic desire of members to protect the property that they currently possess. The second reason is recognition that persons will not create or secure property without a protection of that property. That is, the ability to enjoy the fruits of one's labor is a prerequisite to a person performing the labor in the first place.

In implementing property protections, alliances are guided by these interrelated concepts. For instance, the law did not recognize intangible property rights such as copyright, patents, and so on for a long time because individuals did not see a value in such recognition. At some point in time, however, the innovation and prosperity resulting from protecting intangible property was realized by members and the property laws were expanded to encompass such property.

In discussing property laws, it is important to observe that alliances protect only the interests of their members. As such, certain so-called "property" laws can be structured to harm non-members. For instance, an apparent "property" law might be employed to seize the property of non-members or prevent them from acquiring property. Or an ostensible "property" law might allow members to treat non-members unfairly in property transfers.

In these situations, it must be underscored that the alliance is not pursuing an internal, Law-Compelled Objective. Recall that a Law-Compelled Objective is premised upon obtaining a benefit for all members by compelling the members to all behave in a certain fashion. Property laws that target non-members are not consistent with this rationale. Instead, such laws actually constitute the external objective of Offense against Non-Members. Failure to acknowledge this point can result in substantial confusion in analyzing alliances. As such, when one considers a property-protection undertaking, one should first seek to determine whether it is (i) a Law-Compelled Objective, or (ii) a mechanism for engaging in Offense against Non-Members.

ENFORCEMENT OF PROMISES

The Law-Compelled Objective of Enforcement of Promises is relatively new in the history of alliances. It has existed in a rudimentary form for thousands of years but it has become formalized only in the past several hundred years. Moreover, it seems to not be present in much form in many parts of the world.

Overview

The gist of this objective is that all members benefit if they are held to the promises that they make. As noted in Chapter 8, individuals can protect themselves from broken promises in many situations. There are a number of other situations, however, where such protections are not readily available or effective. As a result, beneficial arrangements based upon exchanged promises will not come about and all members will suffer as a consequence. A Law-Compelled Objective seeking to enforce promises is the solution to this problem.

The specific rules governing enforcement of promises vary with the time period and the particular alliance. As always, the substance of the rules is driven by the needs and desires of the members. As a result, the rules will change over time to adapt to new needs and situations. Typically, the rules of enforcement of promises fall into three categories: (i) identifying enforceable promises; (ii) evaluating the subject of the promise for policy reasons; and (iii) the remedy or cure for a broken promise.

1) *Identifying Enforceable Promises*—The first category constitutes rules for determining when an enforceable promise exists. These rules focus on a variety of issues including:

- whether a promise was in fact made

- what the substance of the promise was

- whether the promise was extracted through some form of deception, duress, or coercion

- whether the party making the promise should be excused from it.

In sophisticated alliances, complex default rules have been developed. Default rules are essentially "gap fillers." In most negotiations, it is rare that two parties entering promises reach specific agreements on every single issue. Often, the parties will fail to agree upon a very important issue and a "gap" will result. Some alliances have complex rules that fill in these gaps. Usually, the parties are free to contract around these rules. If they fail to agree upon an important issue, however, the gap-filler rule comes into play.

> *Illustration*—A store sells a lawnmower to a customer. The customer uses the lawnmower and concludes that it does not cut the grass well. When the sale was made, the store made no promises regarding how the mower would cut the grass. What happens? Many governmental alliances have a gap-filler rule that any product sold must be of average quality or "merchantable." This means that the product is compared to similar products available on the market and the analysis must show that the product is at least average. As such, if the mower does an average job of cutting the grass, the customer has no legal claim. It should be emphasized that this gap-filler rule applies only if there is no agreement on the mower's performance. For instance, the store and the customer negotiate over the mower before the sale takes place. The store promises that the mower will cut grass to a certain objective standard. If the mower does not perform to this standard, the customer has a claim against the store.

The gap-filler rules often exist with regard to implied contracts. This topic was discussed in Chapter 4 regarding implied accords. Just as alliances are often formed on the basis of unspoken agreements, parties sometimes enter into enforceable contracts based upon implied conduct. Often, Law-Compelled Objectives recognize the implied contracts and provide background rules governing them.

> *Illustration*—An individual enters a restaurant, sits down, orders an entrée from the menu, and eats it. He is then presented with a bill for $15 and refuses to pay it, arguing that he never agreed to pay for the food and that the restaurant gave the meal to him. The gap-filler rule is that these circumstances give rise to an implied promise by the individual to pay for the food.

> *Illustration*—An individual walks past a restaurant and a waiter is standing outside with a tray of bite-sized foods with toothpicks in them. The waiter offers the tray to the individual and he takes one of the items and eats it. The waiter then demands $5 for the food. The gap-filler rule in this case would be that the waiter gave the food to the individual and that there is no obligation to pay.

2) *"Policy" Concerns*—The second category of rules governing promises pertains to "policy" concerns. The term "policy" is not a very descriptive term but

it is the best one available. These policy concerns pertain to the subject matter of the promise and control whether the Law-Compelled Objective should enforce it. The policy concerns incorporate two objectives identified earlier: (i) Paternalism, and (ii) the Law-Compelled Objective of Protection of the Person or Property. Morality Objectives might play some role here as well.

The Paternalistic concern focuses upon whether the party entering the promise is doing something not in his interests. Recall that the Paternalistic rationale is based upon an assumption that the members have agreed that the alliance should prevent them from doing things that are not in their interests but that human nature and its accompanying frailties might induce them into doing. Examples of promises that might be voided under a Paternalistic rationale include:

- agreements to work as a prostitute

- promises to pay debts with extraordinarily high interest rates

- obligations entered into by youths or mentally incompetent persons

- commercial transactions considered grossly unfair and one-sided

- gambling debts

The other concern pertains to the Law-Compelled Objective of Protection of the Person or Property. The concept here is that the subject-matter of a particular promise is likely to result in harm to a member of the alliance that is not party to the agreement. This harm can be a personal injury or harm to a member's property. To protect others from the likely effects of the promise, the alliance refuses to enforce the promise and might prohibit it (under a prophylactic rationale):

- contracts to murder another person

- sales of explosives or other highly dangerous items

- agreements to form trusts or monopolies that unduly restrain trade ("antitrust laws")

3) *Remedy for a broken promise*—The third category of rules pertains to the remedy for a broken promise. Should the promise breaker be required to perform the promise in full? Should the promise breaker instead be required to pay a monetary sum compensating the other individual for the harm suffered as a result of the broken promise? Should the promise breaker be punished? Different alliances follow different rules.

A Catalyst to the Formation of Smaller Alliances

The pursuit of the objective of enforcement of promises by governmental alliances has had the remarkable effect sparking the creation of numerous other alliances within the framework of the governmental alliance. As discussed in Chapter 12, an alliance must have an underlying accord and it must be adhered to for the alliance to function properly. If the accord is not followed, the alliance will fail and collapse. Or the alliance might not even form if potential members fear the accord being ignored. The promise-enforcement mechanism serves as a powerful tool for holding small alliances together and forcing adherence to the accord. Further, in the case of disputes over the accord, the promise-enforcement mechanism serves as a readily available means for resolution of controversy.

The prevalence of promise-enforcement mechanisms in certain regions has resulted in a flourishing of alliances that operate within the alliance. A few examples include:

- *Partnerships*—A partnership is an alliance consisting of two or more members to pursue an objective that either (i) they cannot achieve on their own or (ii) is more suited to a combined effort. These objectives almost always relate to some type of profit-making activity such as factories, stores, banks, mines, professional firms, and so on. The promise-enforcement mechanism greatly enhances the operation and functioning of these partnerships. Many governmental alliances have developed elaborate rules to aid and streamline the operation of partnerships. In addition, default rules are often instituted for situations where the partners might not agree upon an important topic. For instance, one default rule might be to identify a decision-making process that governs the partnership if there is no express provision in the accord. Another example is a default rule governing implied partnerships (that is, the accord is never expressed or fully expressed).

- *Corporations*—A corporation is substantially similar to a partnership and the rules governing disputes and the background rules are similar. Instead of partners, however, the alliance members of a corporation are shareholders. Another difference is that most decisions relating to the operation of a corporation are made by delegated decision makers such as the board of directors and officers and not the shareholders. In recent years, many governmental alliances have imposed significant rules on corporations intended to protect the shareholders from fidelity limitations exhibited by the delegated decision makers. Another difference between partnership law and corporate law is that a corporation allows its owners (that is, the shareholders) to be insulated from most liability of the corporation in the case of a legal issue. (Partners are generally liable for all legal problems suffered by the partnership; shareholders typically will lose only their investment or shares in the corporation in the event of a legal issue.) This concept was an important development in the history of Law-Compelled Objectives. The underlying rationale is that there is a benefit to limiting the liability of shareholders. This benefit is the willingness of shareholders to contribute money and other forms of a capital to the creation of corporations. Without the limitation of liability, few individuals will be willing to contribute due to a fear of liability. Corporations therefore will not form, valuable commercial endeavors will not be pursued, and members of the alliance as a whole will suffer as a consequence.

- *Labor Unions*—The rise of labor unions has been aided by the existence of a promise-enforcement mechanism. A labor union is an alliance where the workers are members. Most unions make decisions through a combination of membership vote and delegated decision making. The promise-enforcement mechanism plays two, distinct roles in enforcing labor-union agreements:

  - *Negotiations between a union and an employer*—Many governmental alliances have developed elaborate rules in recent years to govern these negotiations and any controversies that might arise. Other objectives have been imported into this area as well. For instance, the Generation of Prosperity Objective has been used to compel parties to negotiate and reach agreements under certain circumstances. The rationale is that the prosperity of all members in the overarching alliance will suffer if an agreement is not reached between the union and the employer. Further, the other Law-Compelled Objectives of Protection of the Person and Protection of Property have been imported to support specific rules governing violence and destruction of property that tend to arise in labor disputes. Similar rules prohibit employers from retaliating against employees for associating with unions.

  - *The Decision-Making Process*—Numerous rules have been imposed on the decision-making processes governing unions. These include membership votes and as well as delegated decision makers. Union decision makers are often perceived as being particularly susceptible to various fidelity limitations. As such, special rules have been devised to deter the occurrences of fidelity limitations and to remedy the consequences when fidelity limitations do arise.

- *General Associations*—The availability of a promise-enforcement mechanism has spurred the development of countless different types of alliances. The explosion of all types of alliances in recent years is a testament to the effect of the promise-enforcement mechanism. These entities exist only because of the ability of the members to enforce the underlying accords with a promise-enforcement mechanism. Examples include:

- *Mutual Insurance Companies*—To pursue the objective of Mitigation against Catastrophe, individuals create a non-profit alliance to acquire insurance. If the alliance has lower than expected losses, the excess contribution is typically refunded to the members in the form of dividends.

- *Charitable Associations*—Numerous alliances have sprung up to pursue the objective of Charity & Justice. Members contribute sizeable sums of money to these entities largely because they trust that the charitable alliance will be operated within the confines of the legal structure and the delegated decision makers will not engage in fraud.

- *Neighborhood Associations*—Many neighborhoods have alliances that pursue Law-Compelled Objectives relating to residences in the neighborhoods such as noise reduction, appearance standards, home-building practices, and so on. These entities are founded upon a promise-enforcement mechanism.

The Effect upon Outsourcing

As discussed in Chapter 12, the promise-enforcement mechanism has greatly enhanced the ability of persons to attain objectives through individually outsourced efforts. The reason has been discussed earlier. People are not likely to enter outsourcing arrangements unless there is some means for enforcing the promises made, seeing that the service is performed as expected, insuring that payment is made, and so on.

The prevalence of a promise-enforcement mechanism in the modern world has resulted in the eruption of outsourcing arrangements. Consider, for instance, food preparation. In the past, individuals largely had to attain this objective through their own individual efforts. They had to obtain the food, wash it, cook it, and so on. Today, a person can readily outsource this entire effort to others such as restaurants, fast food, frozen dinners, prepared-meal delivery, and so on.

Another useful example is home maintenance and repair. In the past, individuals usually did their own cleaning and laundry and repaired most problems that arose at the house. Nowadays, a person can readily outsource every single one of these tasks to house keepers, dry cleaners, repair persons, and so on.

Essentially, any task can now be easily outsourced. The only requirement is money. This development has been made possible by the prevalence of promise-enforcement mechanisms.

The Monetary System

The vast monetary system of the modern world is essentially a product of a complex network of promise enforcement mechanisms. Bonds, certificates of deposit, loans, credit extensions, IOUs are all made realistic, viable options in today's world due to the presence of promise-enforcement mechanisms. If no such mechanisms existed, these financial creations would largely not exist. In fact, currency is essentially a huge promise made by the governmental alliance issuing the currency to stand behind it. In the past, many governmental alliances would exchange a set amount of gold or silver if presented with currency issued by that governmental alliance. With the extensive size of the modern economies, this option is no longer viable and has been replaced by a governmental promise to stand behind the currency.

INTERNATIONAL LAW

The past several hundred years has seen the substantial development of international law. This topic holds the potential for confusion but it is quite simple. Briefly, international law is nothing more than a Law-Compelled Objective pursued by an arch-alliance of governmental alliances.

Alliance Elements of International Law

The member alliances are nation states with various types of decision-making process including membership votes, executive decision makers, committee decision makers, interwoven processes, and so on. Members do not have to be alliances. Members might be other combined-effort entities such as semi-alliances, illusory alliances, and tyrannies.

These members (true alliances or other combined-effort entities) form an alliance to pursue one or more Law-Compelled Objectives. These can fall within any or all of the three preceding categories: (i) personal protection, (ii) property protection, and (iii) enforcement of promises.

Examples of international law include:

- *War-Conduct Rules*—To pursue the objective of Personal Protection, the members agree on certain standards to govern warfare when it breaks out. For instance, the members agree to not kill or torture prisoners and to not attack civilians. Or they agree that all soldiers must wear uniforms and that certain weapons cannot be used.

- *Identifying Property Borders*—To pursue the objective of Property Protection, the members agree to certain rules defining the geographic borders of land possessed by various members.

- *International Commerce*—To pursue the objective of Enforcement of Promises, the members agree to rules governing international trade and commerce between their respective members.

Implied and Express Accords in International Law

International law provides an excellent example of implied accords. A substantial portion of international law is based upon customs, traditions, and understandings that have developed over time, instead of express, written documents. For instance, the old codes of warfare usually were never reduced to writing. Consider the ancient rule that a side does not kill captured prisoners of another side. This rule was probably never placed in writing in the past. Further, it is likely that it was rarely even acknowledged in spoken words. Nonetheless, combating sides usually followed this rule and did not kill prisoners. The underlying reason is that, if all sides adhere to this rule, all sides will benefit if their soldiers are captured. Moreover, if a side failed to comply with the rule and killed prisoners, that side was usually perceived as no longer being in the implied-accord alliance. As a consequence, the side could expect to have its soldiers killed if they were taken prisoner. Finally, if raiders from far away attacked an alliance following this rule, the alliance typically would not follow the rule and would kill the raiders if captured. Why? The reason is that the raiders are not perceived as being members of the alliance. As such, the raiders might be killed without consequence.

Most international law is based upon rather amorphous concepts. These ideas are useful and can provide benefit to all members of a particular alliance. However, the typical vagueness of international law often results in confusion and disagreements.

In recent years, accords underlying international law have been reduced to writing with greater frequency. These express accords are usually called "treaties." For example, many nation states have participated in the various Geneva Conventions where specific rules governing war and treatment of prisoners and civilians have been identified and reduced to writing. The Twentieth Century saw the enactment of numerous other treaties on a variety of international topics.

United Nations

The best example of an express accord in international law is the charter underlying the United Nations. Although people have different views of the successes and failures of the United Nations, it is clear that the United Nations has striven to attain a variety of Law-Compelled Objectives. (It should be noted that the United Nations also pursues objectives other than international law. These include Charity & Justice, Mitigation of Catastrophe, and the Overlord objective.)

The Difficulty of Enforcing Promises in International Law

A serious limitation on international law is the difficulty of enforcing the accord and its requirements. Many members appear to enter international-law alliances with little intention of actually performing whatever they have promised to do. Typically, there is no mechanism to force compliance with the promise other than a draconian measure such as warfare. Furthermore, due to the separation of nations and their respective autonomies, it is usually difficult to determine whether a member is in compliance or not. The result of this situation is that international law often falls short with regard to what is attainable in other Law-Compelled Objective situations.

A Long History

As final matter, it should be observed that international law is not new. It has been around for thousands of years. For instance, the ancient Greek city states had various implied accords governing their warfare including not killing prisoners, not attacking towns, allowing the dead to be removed from the battlefield, and so on. Overall, wherever there has been some form of governmental alliance (or other combined-effort entity), it was likely that an implied accord regarding an international law objective was present. The real change in recent years appears to be the prevalence of written accords in the area of international law.

"LAW" OBJECTIVES THAT ARE COMPOSITE OBJECTIVES

In the modern world, governmental alliances often target topics from a number of different angles. This situation will usually obscure the precise nature of the objectives that the governmental alliance is attempting to pursue. In effect, because the governmental alliance is pursuing multiple objectives, it is sometimes useful to describe the area or topic as a *composite objective*.

Composite objectives are particularly prevalent in the area of law. A particular field of law might seek to attain a wide variety of objectives other than pure Law-Compelled Objectives. Consider the following two examples.

Employment Law

Employment law is a broad topic and is prevalent in most well-developed countries. As the following chart demonstrates, employment law typically seeks to further a number of different objectives.

Objectives	Explanation
Enforcement of Promises	Enforce the deal struck between the employer and employee including the payment of all agreed-upon compensation and benefits.
Protection of Property	Protect the employer's property such intellectual property from misappropriation by the employee.
Protection of the Person	Protect the employee and/or applicant for employment from injury to his person. Injuries include (i) physical harm caused by unsafe workplaces, or (ii) economic or emotional harm caused by irrational prejudice or discrimination.
Paternalism	Impose substantive parameters upon the employment relationship perceived to benefit the employee. The underlying rationale is that the employee will be unable to look out for his own interests on these subject matters.
Generation of Prosperity	Structure any employment rules to minimize negative effects upon the generation of prosperity within the alliance.
Mitigation of Personal Catastrophe	Compel all employers to hire and reasonably accommodate applicants with disabilities or other limitations, even if the employers must assume additional costs to do so.
Leveling	Force the transfer of resources from the employer to the employee to attain perceived states of equity.

Environmental Law

Environmental law is another field where numerous, different objectives are pursued.

Objectives	Explanation
Protection of Property	Prevent land owned by alliance members from being damaged by pollutants.
Protection of the Person	Prevent alliance members from being poisoned or injured by environmental toxins.
Conservation	Restrict access to or use of a natural resource that is limited in quantity and threatened with exhaustion if overused.
Charity & Justice	Preserve animals or certain environments not out of a self-interested benefit to members but because it is perceived to be the "right thing" to do.
Generation of Prosperity	Structure any environmental rules to minimize negative effects upon the generation of prosperity within the alliance.

These are but a few examples of the various objectives pursued in a particular legal field. In the complexity of the modern world, one will typically find that few legal endeavors seek to pursue a single, discreet objective.

CHAPTER 20

Other Modern Objectives

The modern era has seen substantial innovations and developments in objectives pursued by governmental alliances. The last chapter focused upon new Law-Compelled Objectives. This chapter focuses upon modern developments in other categories of objectives.

GENERATION OF PROSPERITY

The objective of Generation of Prosperity is relatively unique to the modern era. In the past, governmental alliances and other combined-effort entities might have pursued objectives that tended to increase the prosperity of a region. These undertakings, however, were not particularly extensive or significant.

The Predominance of the Objective in the Modern Era

In the modern era, governmental alliances and other combined-effort entities pursue the objective of Generation of Prosperity with fervor. This development was probably a product of two factors: (i) increasing desires for material wealth, and (ii) the revolutions in the sciences and philosophy.

For most of the Middle Ages, an interpretation of Christianity prevailed that advocated pursuit of a spiritual life and avoidance of material wealth and accumulations. Many embraced this viewpoint. Because the actions of alliances are driven by the desires of the membership, the lack of desire for material wealth meant that governmental alliances did not strive to increase prosperity while this viewpoint prevailed. With the rise of the Enlightenment and Renaissance around 1500 CE, the Christian emphasis on avoidance of material wealth declined. As a result, governmental alliances began pursuing the objective of generation of prosperity with greater fervor.

The second possible factor lay in the scientific and philosophical revolutions. The scientific revolution was premised upon a belief that humans could manipulate and alter the natural world through meticulous study and ingenuity. The philosophical revolution was a mindset that demanded inquiry and analysis into all topics and matters. These two, new forces focused attention upon the ability of humans to generate prosperity through methodical approaches. Ultimately, these musings and theories became actual undertakings. Governmental alliances came to believe that they could produce, through combined efforts utilizing the newly conceived methods, greater material wealth for their members.

Over the course of the modern world, the objective of Generation of Prosperity has been pursued with a wide variety of means and approaches. The unifying concept of all variations is the goal of increasing the material wealth of the members of the alliance. A few examples are discussed in the following subsections.

Mercantilism/Colonialism

The Mercantilism/Colonialism approach was used by European governmental alliances when they held numerous colonies. The focus was upon enriching the members of the homeland alliance. The primary concern was to maximize the homeland's possession of valuable metals such as gold and silver. As a result, mercantilism heavily regulated trade with an intention of maximizing the wealth flowing into the homeland region and minimizing the outflow of wealth.

> *Illustration*—Great Britain required the American colonists to trade only with licensed British merchants and not with traders from other countries such as Holland or France. The colonists' primary export was natural resources like wood and cotton. These resources were taken back to Britain where they were resold to other countries or manufactured into new products that were then sold to other countries.

With mercantilism, the delegated decision maker was the government. The underlying rationale was that mercantilism internalized trade within the alliance and prevented wealth from seeping outside of the alliance. As a result, it was believed that the prosperity of all members of the homeland alliance was enhanced. The colonists, of course, did not like the policy as it restricted their freedom to sell to merchants from other countries. Mercantilism was largely eroded by the development of free-market principles.

Free Market/Capitalism

Adam Smith identified the Free-Market theory in 1776. It is essentially a rejection of mercantilism. The underlying principle is that the best means of generating prosperity is a free, unregulated market where buyers and sellers are permitted to trade with whomever they please and without any governmental regulation or interference. Instead of focusing upon possession of precious metals like gold or silver, Smith argued that material prosperity is best attained by maximizing the supply of products and services at the lowest price. This situation can be attained only by a free market guided by the "invisible hand" of free competition.

In mercantilism, the decision maker is the government. Who is the decision maker with the free market? The decision maker is Rational Chaos or the "invisible hand" of the marketplace. Recall that a rational-chaos decision-making process is any method for making decisions where a seemingly chaotic concept or process is utilized which ultimately results in a sensible and sound decision, or what is at least to be perceived as a sensible and sound decision. In the free market approach, the chaos of the market is thought to lead to the highest level of material prosperity.

Communism / Socialism

Communist and Socialist theories are complex and have many facets. A primary objective of these theories is often leveling as in undertaking the objective of Offense against Non-Members (that is, proletariat members form an alliance to seize the material wealth and power of the non-member bourgeoisie). Notwithstanding these complexities, most Communist and Socialist theories also pursue an objective of Generation of Prosperity.

The means of attaining this objective are centralized planning and control of all property, capital, and economic assets. The premise is that an enlightened and competent group of delegated decision makers (such as a committee or perhaps a single executive decision maker) can generate prosperity by allocating resources in an optimal manner. It is thought that this centralized planning and management is superior to the free market.

Free Market/Central Planning Hybrid

In recent years, governmental alliances have mixed certain central planning concepts of Communism/Socialism with Free Market concepts to produce a hybrid approach. The typical approach recognizes that the free market has many advantages. As a result, it largely predominates as the primary mechanism for generation of prosperity. At the same time, the governmental alliance intervenes heavily into the free market with various central planning projects and endeavors. These efforts typically consist of the governmental alliance operating certain businesses and services while leaving many other endeavors to the free market. A different approach allows the free market to predominate and government stays out of operating business and services.

At the same, the government planners regulate the freedom of the market by imposing various minimum standards on the operations of businesses.

Free Market/Monetary Policy Hybrid

This approach is similar to the Free Market/Central Planning Hybrid approach. In this arrangement, the Free Market predominates. At the same time, the government attempts to influence activity within the free market by (i) controlling the money supply (that is, the "supply" of money that can be borrowed) and (ii) engaging in targeted spending thought to provide a stimulus to economic activity. Essentially, this approach operates within the free market since the premise is that an effective monetary policy increases the number of transactions occurring in the free market. A newer aspect of this approach is tax policy. With this approach, the government attempts to foster material prosperity through certain reductions in contribution by members to the alliance. It is thought that these reductions can spur activity within the free market yielding greater prosperity to all members.

As the last two examples indicate, the divisions between the theories seem to have largely broken down. Arguably, some governmental alliances in today's world can be seen pursuing combinations of mercantilism, free market, and communism/socialism at the same time.

Influence of the Objective in Other Areas

The objective of Generation of Prosperity often spills into other objectives and can make analysis cloudy. Typically, Generation of Prosperity slips into another objective in two manners: (i) an objective will *conflict* with the Generation of Prosperity, and (ii) an objective will *further* the Generation of Prosperity. Often, great weight will be attached to the effect that a particular objective will have upon Generation of Prosperity.

Law-Compelled Objectives constitute a prime example of the influence of the Generation of Prosperity objective. When an alliance considers the pursuit of various Law-Compelled Objectives, the effect that a particular undertaking will have upon the Generation of Prosperity is almost always explored. In many situations, a Law-Compelled Objective will not be pursued because it will be viewed as having too large of a negative effect upon the Generation of Prosperity. Other objectives that tend to conflict with Generation of Prosperity include Conservation, Paternalism, Leveling, and Charity & Justice.

Generation of Prosperity also conflicts with means used to attain various other objectives. Often, a particularly useful means to attaining an objective will be rejected due to its negative effects upon Generation of Prosperity.

Not Universally Accepted

As a final matter, it should be observed that the objective of Generation of Prosperity is not necessarily desired by all individuals living in today's world. In recent years, some individuals have asserted that the objective is not desirable, that prosperity does not further the well-being of members, that prosperity results in harm to members through pollution, decadent lifestyles, and so on. Proponents of this view typically argue the goal of government should be either "sustainable" growth or "steady state growth" in prosperity. A very small minority in this area contends that there should be declines in prosperity and that all will benefit as a result.

MITIGATION OF CATASTROPHE
AND SOCIAL INSURANCE

Mitigation of Catastrophe is another objective that has risen to predominance in recent years. As discussed in Chapter 9, mitigation of the consequences of a catastrophe is an external objective that is particularly well-suited to a combined effort. There are two types of catastrophes. A *group catastrophe* pertains to natural disasters like earthquakes, floods, or epidemics and tends to strike across wide swaths of individuals. A *personal catastrophe* is a disaster that typically afflicts only one individual at a time. Examples of personal catastrophes include a house burning down, a disabling injury or illness, or financial bad luck.

Alliance efforts geared towards mitigating a group catastrophe have been around for thousands of years. In contrast, the concept of using an alliance effort towards mitigating a personal catastrophe is a relatively new idea. It is true that certain small alliances in the past undertook limited measures to mitigate personal catastrophes. These measures were typically in the form of a "community-chest" concept. Alliance members would deposit necessities in a chest or something similar. A member in need could then retrieve items from the chest when misfortune struck. Members would continue to replenish the chest as needed. Any member who utilized the chest was expected to resume making contributions when he got back on his feet.

In the modern age, these types of undertakings have become substantially more formal, structured, and expansive. Many governmental alliances undertake programs encompassing hundreds of millions of members. These programs are sometimes called "Social Insurance." The gist of these Social-Insurance programs is to reduce or eliminate the consequences of personal catastrophes suffered by members. A few examples will be discussed in the following paragraphs.

Destitution Insurance

The underlying concept is that anyone can fall into poverty and destitution. This predicament can result from a person's simple bad luck, calculated risk taking, negligence, or even stupidity. If all members pool their resources, however, the consequences of poverty can be reduced or eliminated. Typically, the means of attaining this objective in the modern world is to accumulate monetary contributions from members and then disburse a sum to members in need. In recent years, some governmental alliances have imposed various conditions on these programs to deter exploitation of the system, reduce dependency, and to otherwise wean participants off of the programs.

Old-Age Insurance

There is a presumption underlying these programs that old age inevitably causes financial hardship and need. These consequences can be reduced if all members pool their resources and then distribute a set amount annually to each person over a certain age.

Disability Insurance

Anyone can suffer a debilitating injury or illness that renders him unable to care for himself or earn a living. The economic consequences of such a disability can be offset by all members pooling their resources and then distributing need-based sums to those beset by disabilities. In recent years, some governmental alliances have expanded disability endeavors to include what appear to be Law-Compelled Objectives. These laws obligate members to accommodate the limitations of disabled persons in the workplace and to reduce structural barriers limiting the movement of disabled persons in public. In actuality, these undertakings appear to be a form of mitigation of the consequences of a personal catastrophe.

Bankruptcy

Bankruptcy laws are probably best seen as a mitigation of personal catastrophe. In effect, all members of the alliance agree that a member's debts might be discharged if that member suffers certain types of financial losses. If the debts are discharged, the individual might start over without the burden of the prior debts.

This system constitutes a mitigation effort because it obtains the same result as if the alliance paid off the debts of the individual with pooled contributions. The only difference is that the burden of contribution is instead placed upon the creditors who are owed money by the debtor. These creditors lose their claims upon the debtor. And presumably the creditors pass these costs onto all other members in the form of higher lending rates and prices. (A rationale for burdening creditors is that they can protect themselves with individual efforts such as being careful in making loans, background checks, collateral, security interests, and so on).

Health Insurance

The typical rationale here is that a governmental alliance pooling contributions can reduce the cost of health care. Other objectives creep into these programs, including Leveling, Paternalism, and Charity & Justice.

Redistribution of Wealth and its Relationship to Social Insurance

At times, a mitigation-of-personal-catastrophe endeavor can be confused with a redistribution-of-wealth effort. *Redistribution of wealth* is a form of Leveling whereby material wealth is taken from certain individuals and given to others. The individuals losing the wealth can be members if the alliance seeks to limit the wealth of all members as a form of an internal objective. Or the individuals can be the targets of an Offense against Nonmembers external objective whereby an alliance is formed to seize the wealth of the targets and provide it to the members of the alliance.

Mitigation-of-personal-catastrophe endeavors should not be equated with a redistribution program. The purpose of a Mitigation effort is not to seize wealth of certain individuals and provide it to other individuals. Instead, the purpose is to mitigate the consequences of a personal catastrophe through pooling combined resources.

The determinative factor here is the purpose of the program. If the purpose is to pool contribution to provide benefits to certain members if they suffer from personal catastrophes, it is a Mitigation program. If the purpose is to seize material assets of one group and transfer them to another, the program is pursuing some type of Leveling objective. It might be very difficult to ascertain the true purpose of a particular program. For instance, an undertaking might be styled as a destitution-insurance program but in practice it really acts as a Leveling program targeting non-members. This confusion can result in objective disguise and can allow other objectives to sneak into alliances.

Paternalism and Social Insurance

Often, a Paternalistic objective will sneak into mitigation programs. For example, if participation in the program is mandatory for all members (that is, no one can opt out of contribution even if they are willing to assume and suffer the risk of the consequences occurring), the governmental alliance is acting in a Paternalistic fashion. It is substituting its judgment for that of the members and compelling them to participate in the program, regardless of their desires and opinions.

Defense against Aggressors

Another objective that tends to sneak into mitigation programs is the external objective of Defense against Aggressors. This objective manifests itself as appeasement efforts undertaken to quell revolutionary fervor. In the case of a Mitigation program, the true aim is not to insure members of the alliance against personal catastrophes. Instead, it is to placate non-members that might form a revolutionary alliance and attack the sponsoring alliance. This objective is discussed in greater detail subsequently.

Limitation of the Benefit to Members Only

An important aspect of a Social Insurance endeavor is that eligibility to receive insurance benefits is always limited to members of the alliance. These members have contributed resources towards the objective (if they are able to do so) and therefore are to participate in the benefit should they have the need. If a program provides similar benefits to non-members, it is not a Social Insurance program. Instead, it is a Charity & Justice undertaking towards non-members. This topic is discussed in the next section.

The Potential for Abuse

Most of these programs are subject to abuse by members. This abuse occurs when individuals seek benefits when they do not meet the applicable criteria. In effect, they are seeking benefits to bolster their incomes. This misconduct threatens the viability of the program. As a result, most alliances develop complex decision-making processes to identify and deter such abuse.

Comparison of Social Insurance Endeavors to Individual Effort

Social-Insurance programs are often controversial. Critical members typically contend that an alliance effort is not warranted or justified. These critics argue that individual effort is usually, or even always, superior to an alliance effort. The following table identifies some common arguments made against Social-Insurance programs.

Objective	Individual Means
Destitution and Poverty	Savings account/"Nest Egg" Reducing expenses "Living beneath one's means"

Objective	Individual Means
Destitution and Poverty	Avoiding risky activities No gambling No speculation Prudent investments Outsourcing for business-interruption insurance, credit-protection insurance, etc.
Old Age	Savings account/"Nest Egg" Reducing expenses "Living beneath one's means" Planning ahead Securing living conditions in advance Obtaining long-term health insurance through mutual association or outsourcing to private health insurer Living with children
Disability	Obtaining disability insurance through mutual association or outsourcing to private health insurer Saving money or "self insurance" Avoiding risky conduct and lifestyles prone to causing a disability
Bankruptcy	Avoiding risky investments Limiting debt/incurring no debt Avoidance of speculation/gambling
Health	Self insuring by paying for health care individually (that is, in the same manner other expenses are paid) Obtaining health insurance through a mutual association or outsourcing to private health insurer Joining discounting associations that negotiate with health care providers to give discounts to members Purchasing catastrophic health insurance with a high deductible (that is, self insure up to the deductible and then have the insurer pay the remaining amount) Practicing a healthy life style

Members supporting the Social-Insurance programs usually respond that such individual efforts are not sufficient and that a combined effort is superior. In the end, it is always up to the governmental alliance's decision-making process to determine whether the alliance should undertake the program.

CHARITY & JUSTICE

Governmental alliances have pursued the objective of Charity & Justice with increasing frequency in the modern era. Recall that the objective of Charity & Justice pertains to aiding *non*-members in some fashion (and can include recipients other than humans such as animals or nature). The Charity & Justice objective is pursued when the members of an alliance desire to aid non-members because it is the "right thing to do." The members expect no reward or return from the endeavor, other than the satisfaction that they have contributed towards "doing the right thing."

Historical Absence of the Charity & Justice Objective in Government Action

Over the course of history, governmental alliances have rarely pursued the external objective of Charity & Justice. In general, any type of assistance provided by a governmental alliance has been to its members and has always had earmarks of a Mitigation of Catastrophe endeavor. When governmental alliances have provided assistance to non-members, the action was not motivated exclusively towards "doing the right thing." Instead, such assistance programs have been motivated by a variety of ulterior motives.

Example of Aid	Explanation of True Motive
Roman Empire	Free bread was often distributed to the masses in order quell uprisings.
The American Revolution	France provided aid to the American revolutionaries in order to undermine the British Empire.
Natives living in Colonial Empires	The homeland provided assistance to the natives living in the colonies to appease them and stifle uprisings.
World War II	The United States provided aid to the Soviet Union to allow it to fight Nazi Germany, which was an enemy of the United States.

Example of Aid	Explanation of True Motive
Cold War	The United States aided many third-world countries to keep them from turning to Communism. The Soviet Union propped up Eastern Block and other Soviet satellite countries to keeping them from turning to Capitalism.
Middle East	The United States and various European countries aided Middle Eastern countries in return for a stable supply of oil and natural gas.

For the most part, the Charity & Justice objective has been pursued only by non-governmental alliances such as religious and charitable organizations. Governmental alliances have largely limited their endeavors to situations where they could expect to receive or obtain something of value in return.

The Trend towards Government Alliances Pursuing Charity & Justice

In the modern age, a slight trend has developed towards governmental alliances pursuing the objective of Charity & Justice. Although it is very difficult to ascertain the true motives of a governmental alliance, it appears that many endeavors have been undertaken solely to provide assistance and without any ulterior motive. These efforts have typically related to mass famine, disease prevention or inoculation, and natural disasters. The motivation for these undertakings seems to be only the subjective desire of the members of the governmental alliance to aid people in far away lands.

The Penetration of Charity & Justice into Social-Insurance Programs

In recent years, certain Social Insurance programs seem to be morphing into Charity & Justice endeavors. Recall that the purpose of a Social-Insurance program is to insure *members* against the consequences of personal catastrophes. In recent decades, governmental alliances have been allowing more and more *non-members* to participate in these programs. Typically, these non-members are residing within the geographic boundaries of the governmental alliance either temporarily or without official permission. Because these non-members are not contributing resources to the Social-Insurance program and otherwise are not a part of the governmental alliance, their receipt of benefits can be characterized only as a Charity & Justice undertaking. The non-members are receiving these Social Insurance benefits solely because the alliance desires to aid them in the event of personal catastrophe.

Recent developments indicate that the inclusion of non-members in Social-Insurance programs might be jeopardizing the viability of the programs. As discussed earlier, if an alliance provides a tangible benefit, there is only so much to go around. As a result, alliances must limit membership and receipt of the tangible benefits of the alliance. In the case of Social Insurance, the non-members are not contributing resources to the program but are receiving the tangible benefits of the program. As more non-members are included, the system will eventually become unsustainable. The reason is that the members are, in theory at least, contributing resources sufficient only to cover the members' personal catastrophes, and not those of the non-members. When the number of participants receiving benefits increases but no more contribution is added, the program will run a deficit and will fail. Many governments are making up the deficits by supplementing the programs' budgets with additional resources. As these supplementations grow larger, they are being questioned. It is unclear whether the members of governmental alliances will continue to allow this situation to persist.

Controversy

A governmental alliance's pursuit of Charity & Justice is not universally accepted. Members will often ask why a governmental alliance is pursuing such an objective. These critics will assert that individuals interested in pursuing Charity & Justice can form separate alliances to undertake these endeavors. For instance, a private charitable alliance can collect contribution from its members and use it to aid victims of natural disasters in other countries.

ASSISTANCE PROGRAMS AS MEANS OF STIFLING INTERNAL DISSENT

Social-Insurance programs can constitute viable objectives within the alliance framework. Members of an alliance will often recognize that pooling their resources to guard against personal catastrophes offers many advantages over individual effort. However, when certain governmental alliances pursue Social-Insurance objectives, it is often unclear if this rationale is actually motivating the undertaking. At times, it appears that the decision-making process selecting a Social-Insurance program might be doing it for a different reason. This reason is to stifle internal dissent with an eye towards preventing an uprising by the recipients of the Social Insurance.

As noted earlier, one external objective pursued by many alliances is Defense against Aggressors. The means used to attain this objective are usually militaristic such armies, walls, navies, and so on. Alternative means, however, include diplomacy and appeasement. Appeasement is essentially deterrence of aggression through "buying off" the aggressor. Social-Insurance programs at times might constitute a form of appeasement. Alliances will use Social-Insurance programs to stifle dissent and in effect "buy off" potential revolutionaries or trouble makers.

Historically, this situation seems to have arisen in Europe in the late 1800s in the context of the battles between competing Generation-of-Prosperity endeavors. For instance, most European governmental alliances utilized free-market Capitalism to generate prosperity. This approach provided great benefits to all individuals able to participate within its framework. These individuals included bankers, factory owners, merchants, and so on. But they also included ordinary individuals that could better themselves such as artisans, skilled labor, or entrepreneurs (the "bourgeoisie").

The group of persons benefiting from a capitalistic framework excluded large numbers of individuals (the "proletariat"). Typically, these individuals were stuck in a cycle of poverty, debt, illness, ignorance, and disability. As a result of these conditions, these individuals were not able to better themselves within the capitalist framework. Although some could "pull themselves up by their bootstraps" and become rich industrialists, few actually did. The proletariat had essentially nothing to look forward to except daily labor, toil, suffering, and an early death.

The result was that the proletariat was not fond of the capitalistic system. It offered the proletariat few perceived advantages, if any. On the other hand, various versions of Communism and Socialism appeared attractive to many in the proletariat. One particularly attractive objective was Leveling. Typically, this objective included the expropriation of all material wealth possessed by the bourgeoisie and the redistribution of it among the proletariat. Other perceived advantages included increasing the material prosperity of all members and fair allocation of all wealth. This would be achieved by superior planning and allocation of resources. The Communist slogan was, "From each according to his ability, to each according to his need."

Because Communism and Socialism offered many perceived advantages, there was a real threat that the proletariat would form a successful revolutionary alliance and topple the existing government alliances in Europe. Undoubtedly, the bourgeoisie, nobles, and other powerful figures feared this possibility and likely undertook measures to combat it. One of these measures might have been the Social Insurance programs that were first instituted in Europe in the late 1800s. Although these could have been adopted under a true Social-Insurance rationale, it is likely that their enactment was motivated at least substantially by a desire to appease the proletariat and weaken the appeal of Communism and Socialism.

This appeasement rationale might have underlain the enactment of a variety of Social-Insurance programs over the past hundred years. In particular, the rise of the Soviet Union and its pursuit of global domination throughout the Twentieth Century might have contributed to this phenomenon. From a review of the history of the century, it is evident that there was an on-going debate regarding the relative values of Communism versus Capitalism.[1] Many governmental alliances pursuing capitalist theories might have been concerned about poverty and suffering within their membership. The existence of these circumstances might have been perceived as signs that the capitalist system was failing and that Communism was a better alternative. As such, some governmental alliances might have been motivated at least in part to pursue Social-Insurance programs in order to shore up the perception of Capitalism as a superior alternative to Communism.

Overall, undertakings to stifle dissent will always be difficult to ascertain. An alliance that pursues them will rarely, if ever, actually admit that they are attempting to stifle dissent by undertaking a particular endeavor. Instead, the alliance will attempt to disguise the endeavor as pursuing a different type of objective.

NATIONALISM

Nationalism is an elusive concept that has arisen in the last several hundred years. Essentially, nationalism is probably best described as esprit de corps, association glory, or a combination of both.

Concept Review

Recall that *esprit de corps* is a mood or atmosphere pervading through the members of an alliance. The concept is generally associated with high morale, a sense of belonging, and a comradeship among the members. In addition, the presence of esprit de corps often results in enthusiastic contribution of resources to the alliance. In contrast, *association glory* is a pride-based emotion felt by members of the alliance. It is a feeling of honor or esteem stemming from a member's association with the alliance. It can take the forms of self-esteem flowing from being a member, public esteem by non-members towards members, and a combination of both types of esteem.

---

[1] A classic example is the "Kitchen Debate" between Nixon and Khrushchev in which the merits of each system were explored.

In the context of governmental alliances, nationalism seems to develop as a product of a successful response to a severe challenge or crisis. Typically, a governmental alliance is faced with some type of impending disaster. The members unite behind the governmental alliance and the crisis is averted. By working together to avert the disaster, the members of the governmental alliance usually develop esprit de corps. Further, when the crisis is averted, the members typically feel proud of the accomplishment and association glory results. These combined sentiments of esprit de corps and association glory will continue on long after the crisis has been averted.

The Relevance of Warfare

In almost all circumstances, the crisis faced is warfare. In many situations, an outside aggressor attacks the governmental alliance and the alliance members unite and successfully defeat the onslaught. As a result, the alliance members feel both comradeship and pride-based glory from the victory. In other situations, the governmental alliance successfully conquers another governmental alliance or alien peoples and the members feel the same sentiments.

The Basis of "Nationalism"

Successful military adventures along with perceived cultural superiorities such as language, literature, music, art, science, food, and so on typically combine to form "nationalism." These factors are all combined within the "nation state."

Most nation states are based upon a common culture, history, or language thought to represent a "nation." Because of this common national background, members of a governmental alliance usually feel both comradeship with fellow members (esprit de corps) and pride in the nation (association glory). A member of a nation state typically feels a bond with everyone else in his nation state.

The Boost Effect

Recall that the presence of either esprit de corps or association glory will tend to result in the boost effect. The boost effect results a sizeable increase in the contribution that members are willing to make towards an alliance effort. The motivating factor for this increase is not the objective being pursued, but rather the alliance members' love for the alliance as reflected in esprit de corps, association glory, or both. In effect, the love of one's nation will drive members to contribute additional resources. This love of a nation state is some times called "patriotism."

The boost effect can result in one governmental alliance triumphing over another. A governmental alliance with strong nationalism is very powerful and difficult to defeat. In contrast, a governmental alliance with no nationalism is rather weak and often will quickly collapse when faced with a military attack.

Illustration—At the beginning of World War II, French nationalism was low and Nazi Germany quickly conquered France.

Illustration—When Nazi Germany routinely bombed British cities, Winston Churchill famously reminded the British of their proud heritage and motivated them to withstand the attack. Hitler eventually gave up attempting to conquer Great Britain.

Illustration—When Nazi Germany was conquering the Soviet Union, the Soviet troops made their last stand in Stalingrad. Josef Stalin urged the soldiers to fight for "Mother Russia." The Soviet troops won the battle and ultimately conquered much of Germany.

The Glue Effect

Nationalism can serve to bind seemingly diverse and different types of individuals into one alliance. It is as if nationalism is an adhesive that holds persons of diverse backgrounds together.

Illustration—Great Britain historically has exhibited a very rigid class structure. Examples of the various classes included the nobles, the merchants and bankers, the artisans and craftsmen, the laborers, and the destitute poor. Despite these glaring differences, Great Britain has demonstrated an impressive degree of unity and coherence in its history. This trait is probably due to its strong Nationalism. Historical events that stoked this Nationalism include England's shocking victory over the Spanish Armada and its defeat of Napoleon Bonaparte.

Nationalism as an Objective

Nationalism always begins as an effect of a great success by a governmental alliance. As time passes, nationalism can become an objective. Alliances will undertake efforts to preserve and augment nationalism. Examples of some endeavors include:

- Monuments

- Parades

- Holidays

Usually, governmental alliances pursue nationalistic objectives as a result of sincerely held nationalistic beliefs. The alliance members and the decision makers of the alliance love their nation state and undertake various endeavors to further these sentiments.

In some circumstances, however, nationalism is exploited for other ends. For instance, an alliance's decision-making process might be corrupt. The decision makers' participating in the corruption will pursue nationalistic objectives to cover up their corruption. This concept is the source of the expression, "Patriotism is the last refuge of the scoundrel."

MORALITY AND PATERNALISM

The objectives of Morality and Paternalism have shown both considerable growth and sizeable retraction in the modern area. As a part of this development, Morality and Paternalism have become intertwined to a large degree. As a result, it is often difficult to determine which objective is in fact being pursued by a particular alliance.

Concept Review

Morality is an internal objective. The focus is upon the conduct of the members. There is an expectation that the common conduct will result in a desirable situation for all members. Recall that Moral objectives can be divided into two broad sub-categories: (i) Religious concerns, and (ii) Bolstering concerns. In the case of *Religious* concerns, the matter typically relates to the appeasement or gratification of a religious deity. Specific rules of conduct are identified that are thought to please, or not offend, a deity. If these rules are adhered to by all members of an alliance, it is believed that the members will benefit in their relations with the deity. In contrast, the concept of *Bolstering* pertains to conduct thought to provide strength and vigor to a long-term, multi-objective alliance. If alliance members behave in a certain manner often described as virtuous (for example, good health, exercise, education, and so on), such conduct is thought to strengthen the ability of the members to contribute resources to the alliance.

Paternalism is a very different concept. The objective differs from all other internal objectives, because the benefit of the objective is not derived from common conduct by all members. Instead, Paternalism focuses on each individual and his following of a prescribed course of conduct for his own personal benefit. In this regard, if a member follows the prescribed conduct, there is no resulting benefit to alliance members. Instead, the benefit is to the member only. The rationale underlying paternalism is to guard against known, human frailties that (i) tend to have a severe and adverse effect upon a person, and (ii) cannot be adequately avoided by the typical person.

Religious Institutions

In the past, governmental alliances have often endorsed, supported, and at times fostered religious institutions.[1] These religious institutions usually have sought to further, often at the same time, several different objectives including: (i) Religious concerns, (ii) Bolstering concerns, and (iii) Paternalistic concerns. In the modern era, governmental alliances have tended to reduce or eliminate their support of religious institutions and the objectives typically pursued by such institutions.

Christianity provides a good example of governmental alliances' past support of religious institutions and current lack of support.

Objective	Old Concept	Current Concept
Religious Concerns	A worry over the "Sodom-and-Gomorrah" effect used to prevail. Members felt that the Christian God would punish an entire community if members behaved in decadent, immoral manners.	Few if any believe that there will be divine retribution imposed upon an entire community for the sins of others. Those that believe in divine retribution largely think that it will be inflicted upon only the individual sinners and not upon a community as a whole.
Bolstering Concerns	Most adhered to a belief that religious faith and rituals were necessary for a healthy, effective community and governmental alliance.	The old concept persists today in some regards. But most governmental alliances do not pursue the objective, largely due to disagreements over the correct tenets and practices.
Paternalistic Concerns	A concern that decent individuals would succumb to temptation without governmental alliances preventing their misconduct.	The concern that individuals will succumb to temptation remains intact. But the decision to succumb to such temptations is seen as a matter of individual choice.

---

[1] The term "religious institution" is meant to encompass only a means undertaken by governmental alliances and not an objective. As the analysis should demonstrate, a "religious institution" supported by a governmental alliance does not necessarily pursue only religious objectives. It can pursue numerous other objectives as well.

Why did governmental alliances largely stop pursuing religious objectives? There appear to be primarily three factors causing this decline.

First, certain objectives are no longer desired in today's world. In the past five-hundred years, Christian doctrine has gone through a number of transformations. Many of the old beliefs are no longer embraced by most Christians. As a result, many governmental alliances have ceased undertaking endeavors to attain these discarded objectives.

Illustration—Consider a natural disaster devastating a community. Five-hundred years ago, there would be a strong tendency to blame this disaster upon the moral failings of the community such as a failure to follow applicable religious tenets. Today, such disasters are seen as ordinary, natural phenomena fully explainable by science.

Illustration—The past one-hundred years has seen a substantial rise in atheism, agnosticism, and non-associational spirituality. These developments have resulted in many individuals having no interest in governmental-alliance support of religious institutions.

Second, the multitude of differing and conflicting beliefs has effectively prevented governmental alliances from supporting traditional religious institutions. If the members of a governmental alliance adhere to many variations of Christianity with different tenets and practices, there is no common ground. If there is no common ground, the governmental alliance cannot act. A precondition for an effective alliance effort is all (or most) members being in agreement on the objective pursued. If a governmental alliance embraces a particular sect, it will be acting contrary to the viewpoints all of the other sects. The members of these ignored sects will receive no benefit, and they will tend to terminate their membership as a result. In addition, they likely will become angered and will tend to form revolutionary alliances. Conflict and prolonged acrimony will result and violent war usually follows.

Illustration—Consider the so-called "Thirty Years War" (1618-1648 CE). This war was a series of battles fought across Europe with mass carnage and destruction. The subject matter largely consisted of conflicts between Catholics and Lutherans over religious doctrine (as well as a few other topics).

Illustration—Consider the recent hostilities between Protestants and Catholics in Northern Ireland.

Illustration—Consider the United States and its constitutional prohibition against the establishment of a religion. This prohibition seems to be a recognition that no agreement can be reached among the members regarding the appropriate religious tenets. Because there is no consensus, the governmental alliance is barred from endorsing any religious institution.

The results of these constant conflicts vary. But the long-term outcome seems to be that religion is recognized today as a point of controversy upon which members of most governmental alliances cannot agree. As such, there is no perceived net benefit to having a governmental alliance pursue religious endeavors. Instead, if individuals desire a combined effort regarding a religious objective, the solution is for the individuals to form smaller, non-governmental alliances such as churches that pursue the viewpoints held by them.

The third reason seems to be a recent, implicit recognition that governmental alliances are not capable of successfully attaining religious objectives. This concept ties into the big-picture idea that an alliance will pursue an objective only if the members believe that existing means can in fact attain the objective.

Illustration—In the past, Christianity largely focused upon ritual. Governmental alliances could attain some positive results in this area. For instance, governmental alliances could compel members (and non-members) to engage in the requisite rituals such as attending church services, observing certain practices, and so on. As time passed, Christianity began focusing more and more on developing a certain state of mind in all persons, with less emphasis on rituals. This goal, however, was largely unattainable by governmental alliances. A state of mind cannot be forced upon individuals, like a ritual. Because governmental alliances could not attain this objective, governmental alliances gradually stopped attempting to pursue the objective. At the same time, it was recognized that individual churches were more adept at attaining this state-of-mind transformation. As a result, governmental support of religious institutions declined.

Overall, it is difficult to pinpoint the causes of a decline of governmental support of religious institutions. However, these three factors do appear to have combined to decrease the pursuit of traditional Christian religious objectives by governmental alliances.

Obscenity

Obscenity is a famously hard-to-define concept. Obscenity regulations usually take the form of banning most forms of public nudity, swearing, profane language, and other vulgarities. Various objectives underlie obscenity regulations. The two most common are Morality and Paternalism.

Historically, Morality-Religious concerns served as a primary influence on obscenity endeavors. Tenets of Christianity, as well as most other religions, forbid conduct considered obscene. As discussed in the foregoing section, most governmental alliances have stopped pursuing religious-based objectives. This reduction has translated into a corresponding reduction in obscenity regulations.

The Morality-Bolstering concerns also motivated many obscenity initiatives. In the past, it was likely thought that a governmental alliance could not succeed if its members were engaging in lewd acts and decadent lifestyles. Prohibiting obscene matters was perceived as enhancing the character of the members and, as a result, the effectiveness of the governmental alliance. In recent years, this causal relationship has been challenged. The prevailing view of today seems to be that decadent lifestyles do not harm the overall contribution to the alliance by members. As a result, this justification for obscenity has faded and obscenity regulations have declined.

The Paternalism rationale has had a sizeable effect upon the pursuit of obscenity measures. In the past, decadent lifestyles were seen as a trap for the unwary. A typical individual was thought to be prone to pursuing obscene items against his will and otherwise acting against his best interests. As a result, obscenity undertakings by governmental alliances were viewed as valuable safeguards against this irrational tendency of most persons. In recent years, a decadent lifestyle has been viewed in a different light. For the most part, such a lifestyle is viewed as choice made freely by individuals and not as an irrational action compelled by irresistible urges. As a result, this rationale for obscenity prohibitions has declined.[1]

In the modern world, what are the prevailing objectives underlying most existing obscenity laws? The answer is that underlying justifications for most obscenity laws appear to have little to do with: (i) Morality-Religion, (ii) Bolstering, or (iii) Paternalism. Instead, the rationale appears to be a variation of the Law-Compelled Objective of Protection of the Person. Most obscenity laws focus upon shielding certain persons from being unwillingly exposed to obscene images or materials. In this regard, obscenity can be viewed as something akin to a physical injury. If an unwilling person views or witnesses obscene material, he in effect becomes "injured." As a result, most current undertakings focus upon prohibiting the public display of obscene materials where unwilling persons might come into contact with them. That is, the obscenity can exist but only as long as it is concealed from public view.

---

[1]With the rise of Internet pornography, interest in Paternalistic concerns appears to be making a comeback. In this regard, some contend that Internet pornography is highly addictive and can result in mental disorders.

Another possible rationale underlying many current obscenity efforts is Charity & Justice. The focus here is to protect unwilling participants in obscene activities, regardless of whether they are members of the governmental alliance. These participants are usually children. Most governmental alliances prohibit obscene acts involving children. These undertakings are done both to protect the children against predators and to guard against the perceived effects of exploitation of such children. With regard to the latter, it is commonly believed that exposure to child-obscenity spurs a viewer into attacking and preying upon children.

In closing, it must be observed that Paternalism still holds some sway in the regulation of children and obscene matters. This rationale is essentially that children cannot willingly agree to participate in obscene actions as they are not capable of adequately fending for themselves. Similarly, children may not be allowed to view obscene images. Once the children become adults, the rationale vanishes as adults are considered capable of selecting appropriate lifestyles without governmental oversight.

Overall, obscenity undertakings are motivated by a wide variety of objectives.[1] At this time, however, the primary objective appears to be Protection of the Person, with small roles played by Charity & Justice and Paternalism.

Alcohol, Tobacco, Narcotics, and Other Harmful Conduct

Like Obscenity, the regulation of alcohol, tobacco, narcotics, and other harmful conduct was regulated in the past under Morality-Religious concerns. As religion has moved out of government actions, so has this rationale.

Current prohibitions in these areas seem to be based upon three objectives. The first is Morality-Bolstering concerns. The concept here is that the alliance will not function properly if its members are utilizing substantial amounts of alcohol, tobacco, and harmful narcotics. As such, by regulating or banning the use of such items, it is thought that the governmental alliance as a whole will be better off.

The second is Paternalism. The concept is the same as other Paternalistic endeavors. A typical person is thought to be irrationally prone to using alcohol,

---

[1] In some cases, the objective of Charity & Justice appears to be present. This objective is present if non-members are being exploited and harmed by the obscenity and the alliance members undertake an endeavor designed to protect these non-members.

tobacco, and narcotics against his interests. As such, the government should step in and prevent him from using these items.

The third reason pertains to Mitigation of Catastrophe and Social-Insurance programs. It is thought that alcohol, tobacco, and drug use increases claims made on various types of Social Insurance including disability, destitution, and health. As such, some governmental alliances pursue alcohol and drug endeavors to reduce the burdens placed upon the Social-Insurance system.

Regulation of alcohol, tobacco, and drugs is often controversial. Critics of the regulations attack on several fronts. Some contend that the objective (that is, having persons free of the influence of drugs, tobacco, narcotics) is not necessarily desirable and should not be pursued by a governmental alliance. Another argument is that the means (that is, prohibiting the use of the items) will never work and people will continue to use alcohol, tobacco, and narcotics regardless of the regulations. This argument is usually paired up with the sizeable costs of most prevention programs including the time and money spent on the programs and the number of individuals imprisoned under the regulations. Finally, some argue that the Social-Insurance programs should not cover the consequences of using alcohol, tobacco, and narcotics. Instead, the user should bear the costs of the use of these items completely.

Other Topics—Old Issues on the Decline

In today's world, many prior objectives in the realm of Morality and Paternalism have faded away. As discussed earlier, the Religious concerns subset of Morality has little influence on most governmental alliances. There are exceptions of course. Middle Eastern governments and other Muslim-based governments pursue this objective. However, outside of these regions, Morality—Religious concerns have little influence.

Other objectives tied to Morality—Bolstering concerns and Paternalism are on the decline. These appear to be withering because either the objective is no longer desired or governmental alliances are not viewed as effective means of attaining the objective. Some examples of old-style objectives that are either on the decline or non-existent include regulations banning:

Gambling
Prostitution
Sexual Practices
Homosexuality
Inter-racial relationships
Suicide

Religion (that is, novel or peculiar religions)
Obscenity

Other Topics—New Issues on the Rise

In contrast to these objectives on the decline, governmental alliances are pursuing variations of old-style objectives. Although Religious concerns play little role in this area, it seems that Morality concerns and Paternalism have teamed up to fuel the pursuit of many measures. At times, this duo is joined by the Social-Insurance rational discussed briefly in the preceding section. The result is that many undertakings are justified by three separate rationales:

1) *Morality / Bolstering*—The endeavor will improve the members and make them more able to contribute to the governmental alliance.

2) *Paternalism*—The endeavor will safeguard against irrational tendencies of members to undertake acts not in their interests.

3) *Social Insurance*—The endeavor will reduce costs tied to bad lifestyles and therefore maintain the viability of Social-Insurance programs.

Examples of means used to further these modern objectives include:

- Compulsory education for children

- Healthy lifestyle education

- Tobacco regulation

- Seatbelt, helmet, and other safety mandates

- Alcohol regulation

- Narcotics bans

- Public education campaigns in general

The last item has been prominent in recent decades. Many governmental alliances have undertaken a wide variety of public education programs on various topics such as health, environment, diversity, and so on. The underlying premise of these endeavors usually lies in one or more of the three objectives identified above.

OVERLORD OBJECTIVE

Recall that an overlord objective is applicable only where there is an alliance of alliances. It is an internal objective that focuses upon the conduct of the member alliances. The arch-alliance is the "overlord." The overlord alliance watches over the member alliances and imposes a prescribed course of conduct upon them. Just as an alliance of individuals will pursue internal objectives that strive to impose a prescribed course of conduct on the individual members, an overlord alliance seeks to compel the alliances' members to follow a certain course of conduct. This prescribed course of conduct relates to the manner in which the member alliances act towards their individual members (that is, the "derivative members" of the overlord alliance). Typically, the overlord objective seeks to protect the interests of the individual members of the alliances. Almost always, this protection is to protect the individuals from abuses by the member alliance.

In recent years, more and more governmental alliances appear to be entering larger alliances that pursue overlord objectives. The purpose of this overlord objective is always to prevent the member alliances from abusing their individual members. In these situations, the overlord alliance is usually authorized to review the conduct of member governmental alliances and to issue verbal reprimands regarding any abuse of members. In many circumstances, the overlord alliance is permitted to use military force against a member governmental alliance in order to protect its individual members from abuse.

Further, many governmental alliances appear to be pursuing the Overlord objective with regard to private alliances. For instance, a corporation is usually an alliance. The shareholders are the members and the management and board are committee and executive decision makers. Much corporate law is arguably based upon the Overlord objective as the law strives to protect the interests of the shareholders and prevent abuse by the decision makers.

Closing

These chapters in Part IV have explored the concept of using a theory of alliances to understand history and to trace historical developments. Part V will use this same approach to study the development of the United States of America.

PART V

---•---

The United States
of America

CHAPTER 21

The Revolution

Part IV offered a theory that history can be analyzed and understood through the concepts and principles identified in Parts I, II, and III. Part V continues the exploration of this theory by focusing upon the history of the United States of America.

In the same vein as Part IV, the topic of the United States of America is extraordinarily broad and properly constitutes the subject of at least an entire book. As such, this Part should be viewed as only a brief discussion of alliance-related issues pertaining to the United States of America.

THE DECLARATION OF INDEPENDENCE

The Declaration of Independence[1] is a notice of termination of a relationship with Great Britain. Prior to July 4, 1776, the thirteen Colonies were in a combined-effort-entity arrangement with Great Britain. Each Colony was ruled by a governor appointed by the British government. The governors supplied the inhabitants of the Colonies with certain services and collected various taxes from the Colonies.

Reasonable minds can disagree as to whether the arrangement between Great Britain and the Colonies was a true alliance, tyrannical alliance, semi-alliance, illusory alliance, or blatant tyranny. Some will argue that the benefit provided to the Colonies by Great Britain greatly outweighed any meager contribution required of the Colonies and that a true alliance undoubtedly existed. Others will argue that the Colonies were effectively enslaved by Great Britain and its mercantilist economic objective and that the relationship can be viewed only as a tyranny.

---

[1] A copy of the Declaration of Independence is included in Appendix A.

Regardless of how the relationship is viewed from today's perspective, the structure of the Declaration is premised upon the existence of a purported alliance relationship between the Colonies and Great Britain. The Declaration itself effectively constitutes a determination by the Colonies that they perceived no net value from the perceived alliance relationship (and that it was in fact a tyranny or was transforming itself into a tyranny). This point is made clear by the text of the Declaration.

For instance, a discussion of the lack of perceived value of Great Britain takes up most of the text of the Declaration. Early on, the Declaration recognizes that governments are not perfect and often inflict "Evils" upon "Mankind." The Declaration goes on to observe that these "Evils are sufferable" and must be accepted. The gist here appears to be that of a tyrannical alliance (that is, the benefits of a government outweigh the costs or "Evils" imposed by the government).

The Declaration identifies an exception to the generalization that government evils must be tolerated. Specifically, if a "long Train of Abuses and Usurpations" occur and it becomes evident that the "Government" seeks to impose "Despotism" upon its members, the members have the "Right" and "Duty ... to throw off such Government, and to provide new Guards for their future Security." This exception is based upon the concept that the benefits of an alliance must outweigh the costs. If the costs (or the price of "Despotism") are greater than the benefits, the alliance must be "throw[n] off."

Having made these observations, the Declaration then charges Great Britain's executive decision maker, King George III, as "having in direct Object the Establishment of an absolute Tyranny over these States." The Declaration then recites the multiple abuses inflicted upon the Colonies by King George. The accusations against King George encompass numerous different topics and are offered to "prove" that the relationship with Great Britain both not only lacks advantages but it also causes net harm to the Colonies.

Having made its proof, the Declaration concludes by proclaiming that the thirteen Colonies are "Free and Independent States" with the "full Power to levy War, conclude Peace, contract Alliances, establish Commerce, and to do all other Acts and Things which Independent States might of right do." With this proclamation, the Colonies terminate their relationship with Great Britain and King George. In so doing, the Colonies elect to stand upon their own as thirteen independent alliances.

What happened in 1776? The Colonies declared that an alternative to the British Government existed. That alternative was the *individual* effort of each Colony. Members to an alliance weigh the perceived values associated with the alliance against individual effort. In 1776, each Colony weighed the perceived advantages and disadvantages of (i) participating in the British Government versus (ii) standing upon their own and pursuing objectives as individual Colonies. The Colonies determined that their own individual efforts offered more advantages. As a result, the Colonies "threw off" the British Government.

THE REVOLUTIONARY WAR AND A NEW ALLIANCE

The British Government rejected the Colonies' notice of termination contained in the Declaration of Independence. The decision-making process of the British Government (including the executive King George) concluded that keeping the Colonies within the British Empire was a worthwhile objective. As a consequence, the British Government sent substantial military forces to America to coerce the Colonies into rejoining the British Empire. A lengthy war resulted.

Overview

The Colonies' war against the British can be viewed as an alliance effort. To begin with, the Colonial alliance was an alliance of alliances. The members of the Colonial alliance were the thirteen Colonies. The thirteen Colonies each constituted separate alliances with individual members residing within in each Colony. The individual members of each Colony constituted derivative members of the Colonial alliance (that is, the arch-alliance").

Accord and Decision-Making Processes

The accord underlying the Colonial alliance was a combination of express and implied agreements. The express agreement was the Articles of Confederation that was drafted in 1777. (The Articles of Confederation are discussed in greater detail in the next section.) Although not all Colonies officially adopted the Articles of Confederation until 1781, it appears to have formed the foundation of the accord underlying the Colonial alliance. Other spoken and implied agreements supplemented the Articles of Confederation to form the complete accord underlying the alliance effort.

The alliance possessed a variety of decision-making processes. The primary process was the meetings of the Continental Congresses. Each Colony selected Representatives to attend these Congresses. The Congresses then made various decisions relating to the alliance effort. In addition, the Congresses usually selected other delegated decision makers such as military leaders and ambassadors. For instance, the Congresses selected George Washington to serve as the executive decision maker heading up the military effort and Benjamin Franklin, John Adams, and John Jay to form a committee decision maker to negotiate a peace with Britain.

Objective

The primary objective underlying the alliance was Defense against Aggressors. The British were the aggressors and the Colonies desired to be free of the British aggression. The Colonies saw that uniting together against Britain was superior to fighting the war effort individually. The alliance also sought to pursue other objectives as reflected in the Articles of Confederation, which are discussed in greater detail subsequently.

Resources

The resources contributed varied but included men to fight in the war effort, raw materials, weapons and provisions, and money. Resources were also raised by obtaining loans from European creditors.

Result

The Colonial alliance did not function to perfection. Numerous disputes and heated differences of opinion took place. Colonies often teetered upon surrendering and rejoining the British Empire. Contribution of resources (for example, militia men, money, gunpowder, supplies, and so on) was often not available or was withheld. Nonetheless, the alliance ultimately held together and succeeded in defeating the British military. After this victory, the delegated committee of Franklin, Adams, and Jay negotiated a compromise with Britain in 1783. The compromise recognized the independence of each Colony. The Colonies obtained their goal—independence from Britain.

Alliance with France

It should be observed that the Colonial alliance (that is, an alliance of alliances) formed yet another alliance to further the war effort. This alliance was with the French Government and the result was effectively an alliance of alliances of alliances. The arch-alliance at the top was the alliance between France and the Colonial alliance. The Colonial alliance was an alliance of member Colonies. And each Colony was an alliance of individual members.

Why did this alliance result? At the time, France and Britain were enemies and France concluded that weakening the British Empire was a worthwhile aim (that is, pursuing the objective of Offense against Non-Members). By joining forces with the Colonies and fighting Britain, France furthered this goal of weakening Britain.

What were the essential alliance elements of this Colonial-Franco relationship? The underlying objective was to run the British out of North America. The Colonial alliance desired this end to be free of British control. France desired this result to weaken Britain. But both desired that Britain leave North America. There were two members—France and the Colonial alliance. The accord was express and was entered into in 1778 as a product of diplomatic negotiations. The accord was an agreement to combine forces and wage war against Britain in and around North America. The resources the Colonial alliance supplied were largely soldiers. France supplied additional soldiers, naval power, money, weapons, provisions, and training.

THE ALLIANCE NATURE OF THE ARTICLES OF CONFEDERATION

As noted in the preceding section, the Articles of Confederation represented the core agreement underlying the Colonial alliance. It was express and was reduced to writing.[1]

The fundamental alliance nature of the Articles of Confederation is made clear by its introductory provision which states in part:

> The said States hereby severally enter into a firm league of friendship with each other, for their common defense, the security of their liberties, and their mutual and general welfare, binding themselves to assist each other, against all force offered to, or attacks made upon them, or any of them, on account of religion, sovereignty, trade, or any other pretense whatever. [Article III]

While this language is lacking in specifics, it reveals a clear intent to combine resources through "binding" the Colonies together to work on issues of common interest. These topics of common interest include defense, security of liberties, attacks, and the "mutual and general welfare." The underlying rationale is that the Colonies perceive a net advantage to combining their efforts in order to tackle certain issues, in contrast to the individual efforts of each colony.

What were the objectives of the Articles of Confederation? Their primary objective was to defeat Britain and obtain independence. Obviously, this goal could be obtained more effectively if the Colonies all fought together. The alliance, however, also pursued various other non-military objectives which are identified in the document itself. These objectives largely consisted of Law-Compelled Objectives relating to interactions between the Colonies on land disputes, trade, diplomacy with foreign states, and so on. These objectives all share a common thread in that the Colonies perceived an advantage to tackling them with an alliance effort, in contrast to an individual effort.

---

[1] A copy is included in Appendix B.

When the Revolutionary War concluded and independence was confirmed, the Colonies were now independent "states" free from Great Britain. These new states attempted to operate within the framework of the Articles of Confederation. However, the states quickly found the arrangement to be of little value. The primary flaw appears to have been the decision-making process. It seems that little or nothing could be achieved by the Colonial alliance under the Articles of Confederation.

As noted in Part I, members of an alliance typically are on the lookout for alternative alliance structures that provide a perceived net advantage over an existing alliance. Having noted the problems with the Articles of Confederation and recognizing the possibility of a more preferable alliance, the Colonies or "states" convened to discuss the subject. All states sent Representatives to a convention to participate in forming a new alliance. In September 1787, the convention produced a proposed accord for a new alliance. This new accord was in writing (that is, an express accord) and was referred to as the "Constitution of the United States of America."

By 1788, the states accepted the Constitution, and agreed to be bound by it. This accord has remained in effect for more than 200 years and is discussed extensively in the next chapters.

CHAPTER 22

The Constitutional Structure

Before discussing the structure of the Constitution, it will be useful to briefly summarize the alliance and its key components. In discussing this alliance, it will usually be referred to as the "federal government."

ALLIANCE CHARACTERISTICS OF THE FEDERAL GOVERNMENT

Members

When the Constitution was first adopted in 1788, the members of the federal government were the thirteen states. Each of the thirteen states constituted independent alliances with their own individual members. Since 1788, additional states have been admitted as members of the federal government so that the total membership is presently fifty.

The states have individual members. These individuals were originally derivative members of the federal government (that is, the arch-alliance). As time passed, the individual members tended to resemble actual members of the federal government, while continuing to be members of the state governments. This transition was probably due to constitutional changes brought about after the end of the Civil War.

Accord

The Constitution[1] is an express, written accord underlying an alliance of alliances. It is not a long document but it contains many complex and significant provisions. For instance, the Constitution has provisions pertaining to:

---

[1] A copy of the Constitution is included in Appendix C.

- A tiered and interwoven decision-making process
- Objectives* that might be pursued by the alliance
- Means* that might be employed to obtain the objectives
- Means* and objectives* that the alliance might *not* pursue or utilize
- Collection of contribution from the members
- Procedures for admitting new members
- Procedures for amending the accord

  * The Constitution does not refer to these concepts as "objectives" and "means." Instead, it lumps these concepts together and identifies them as "powers."

Some of these provisions will be discussed in greater detail subsequently.

Despite its breadth, many provisions of the Constitution are not particularly precise. This situation has resulted in some confusion and conflict. Some of these issues will be explored later.

Objectives

The federal government is a multiple objective alliance and therefore pursues a variety of objectives. All of the objectives pursued by the federal government are identified in the Constitution. Most of the objectives are fairly specific and a few are indefinite. One or two are arguably open. The indefinite objectives (as well as the arguably open objectives) have caused confusion and discord over the history of the federal government.

The Constitution sets forward "powers" that the federal government holds. These listed powers constitute either objectives or means that can be used to attain objectives. At times, a power might constitute both an objective and a means.

A review of every objective in the Constitution will tend to demonstrate that it is consistent with the principles discussed in Part I. Specifically, each objective is an end desired by all of the states and is one that an individual state either (i) can attain only by combining efforts with other states, or (ii) can attain more effectively or efficiently by combining efforts with other states.

Contribution

The Constitution does not specify the contribution required from the member states. It does, however, authorize the federal government to require certain types of contribution from the states. The federal government, however, does not hold unfettered authority to demand contribution. The Constitution does place certain restrictions on how that contribution might be obtained from states.

Because the Constitution does not specifically identify the contribution to be supplied, it is probably best to view the true contribution as being liberty. Prior to joining the federal government, each state was free to act as it saw fit. By joining, each state voluntarily relinquished a substantial degree of freedom by agreeing to be ruled by the federal government in certain limited areas. In effect, each state agreed to abide by dictates of the decision-making process of the federal government (that is, provided that the action dictated was authorized by the Constitution). By relinquishing this freedom of action, each state contributed liberty to the alliance effort. And by foregoing this liberty, it was believed that all states would benefit as a consequence.

OVERVIEW OF THE DECISION-MAKING PROCESS

The Constitution's decision-making process is consistent with alliance principles. The following discussion will outline the various components of this process and show how these parts work together to make decisions.

A Formal Process

In their simplest form, decision-making processes can be characterized as being either formal or nebulous. A formal process is one that has structure and is recognized by the members as constituting a decision-making process. Formal processes are common in alliances with express accords. In contrast, a nebulous process is common to alliances with implied accords. With a nebulous process, a decision is typically reached as a product of unspoken group dynamics (for example, a consensus appears to have been reached but without a vote).

The Constitution's process is undoubtedly formal. A number of rules and procedures must be adhered to and followed for a decision to be reached. If this arrangement is not complied with, no decision is made.

The Role of Membership Vote

Formal decision-making processes can constitute either (i) a membership vote, or (ii) some type of a delegated decision maker (that is, executive, committee, or nonstandard). In a membership-vote situation, the decision is made if a sufficient portion (for example, plurality, majority, supermajority, unanimity) of the members vote in favor of a proposal. In a delegated decision-maker situation, the delegate makes the decision for the alliance.

The role of membership vote in the Constitutional scheme is complex. To begin with, because the Constitution underlies an alliance of alliances, the "members" must be identified in order to properly analyze the issue. For purposes of analyzing this topic, the members of the federal government are the states. The individual members of each state are derivative members of the federal government.

In the Constitutional scheme, the state members and the derivative members play the following roles with regard to membership vote:

- *State Members*—The state members engage in a membership vote only on limited topics:

    - **Amendments**—A proposal to amend the Constitution might be submitted to a membership vote by all states.

    - **President**—A membership vote of all states is employed to select the President. This process is called the Electoral College. Each state has a certain number of electors to send to the Electoral College to decide who shall be the President.

    (It should be observed that the votes of Senators and Representatives do not constitute a membership vote. These individuals are delegated decision makers that are sent by the states to participate in making decisions upon their behalves. Each state alliance selects its Senators and Representatives through its own state-based decision-making process.)

- *Derivative Members*—The individual members of the states do not participate in the decision-making process of the federal government. There is no membership vote for these derivative members of the federal government. Instead, these individuals participate in various membership-vote processes as established by their state alliances. For instance, these individuals participate in a state-based membership vote to select electors to the vote in the Electoral College.

Overall, membership vote does not play a large role in the decision-making process of the federal government. Instead, delegated decision makers make most decisions.

The Delegated Decision Makers

The Constitution identifies three key delegated decision makers:

Congress	President	Supreme Court

As the following discussions will demonstrate, this framework produces a decision-making scheme that is both multi-tiered and interwoven.

The Multi-Tiered Process

In a multi-tiered process, a decision moves vertically through two or more levels of decision makers. Within the three delegated decision makers, there are various tiers of decision-making authority. For instance:

- **Congress**—Congress utilizes a committee structure to make decisions. Most proposals are first presented to a committee for evaluation. If the committee rejects a proposal, it will typically end at that point. If the committee accepts a proposal, it will then be forwarded to Congress for a final decision.

- **President**—The President is a single executive decision maker. Nonetheless, the typical President delegates most decisions to numerous sub-executives operating under his authority. The President might overrule the decisions of these sub-executives and make a decision that he feels is appropriate. If the President does not overrule a decision of a sub-executive, it will become the decision of the President.

- **Supreme Court**—The Supreme Court sits atop a hierarchy of courts, including courts of appeal, trial courts, and other lesser courts. In most situations, each of these courts is authorized to make a decision. This decision usually might be appealed upwards through the tier with the appeal stopping when it reaches the Supreme Court. If no appeal is made, the decision of the lesser court is final.

The Interwoven Process

The Constitutional decision-making process is interwoven in that most decisions involve the interplay of all three decision makers. For instance, as will be discussed in greater detail subsequently, Congress typically is the first to make a decision such as passing a piece of legislation. But this decision is in no way final. The President might reject the Congressional decision with his veto. The Supreme Court might also void the decision by declaring it unconstitutional. Overall, because one of these three decision makers rarely can make a decision without the direct or indirect approval of at least one of the other two decision makers, the process is best described as being interwoven.

The following sections will discuss each major delegated decision maker separately.

THE CONGRESS

Article I of the Constitution pertains to the legislature or "Congress." This discussion will focus on the decision-making processes of Congress.

A Committee Decision Maker

In its simplest conception, Congress is a committee decision maker. This committee is composed of two members—the House of Representatives (the "House") and the Senate. For Congress to make a decision, both of these members must support it. If one component fails to support a proposal, it will not constitute a decision of Congress. Effectively, the vote required is unanimity.

Two Committee Decision Makers within a Larger Committee Decision Maker

Aside from combining to form a committee decision maker called Congress, the House and the Senate can be each viewed as separate committee decision makers. In this regard, the House is one committee and its members are the Representatives sent to it by the states. Similarly, the other committee is the Senate and its members are the Senators chosen by the states.

As just observed, the committee called Congress requires unanimity for a proposal to become a decision. In contrast, the Senate and House usually require only a simple majority of votes (that is, more than 50%) for a proposal to become a decision. Thus, if a typical proposal receives more than 50% of the votes in both the House and the Senate, it becomes the decision of those respective entities. Because the House and the Senate consist of two committee decision makers to Congress, the decisions of the House and Senate will then become the decision of Congress.

Selection of the Representatives and the Senators

As touched upon above, the decision-making processes of the individual states largely determine which individuals will be sent to participate in the House and the Senate. Representatives are selected by a membership vote of the citizens of the state. Each state is afforded discretion in deciding how to select its Representatives.[4]

Originally, individual citizens of states did not select Senators. Instead, the decision-making process of each state government chose the two Senators. In 1913, the Constitution was amended to allow for the individual citizens of the states to select Senators in the same manner Representatives were selected (that is, through membership vote).

---

[1] In recent years, the federal government has regulated this area but states still hold sizeable discretion in controlling how Representatives are selected. For instance, a common controversy in today's world is the structuring of congressional districts and the practice of gerrymandering. These practices are the products of the state decision-making processes.

The number of Representatives that a state might select is directly tied to the state's population.[1] The states with more individual members have more Representatives and thus a larger voice in the decision making of the House. As for Senators, each state might select two Senators regardless of the population of the state. Each state is on equal footing in the Senate. Why is this? It appears that the authors of the Constitution concluded that the structure of the Senate would tend to offset undue power in the House that populous states might possess.

Procedural Rules

The Constitution provides several mandatory rules relating to voting (for example, quorum, notification of votes, recording votes, when Congress must meet, removal of members from Congress, and so on). At the time the Constitution was founded, these issues were seen as being of sufficient importance that they must be spelled out in the Constitution.

In addition, the Constitution authorizes both the House and Senate to establish procedural rules governing their operations and day-to-day activities. Both the House and Senate have since created intricate rules governing voting procedures and related matters.

The Usage of Lesser Committees within the House and Senate

Both the House and Senate have used the rule-making authorization to create numerous specialized committees to investigate and make recommendations relating to proposals under consideration. Often, these committees determine whether a proposal will be presented to the House or Senate for a vote. Sometimes, even sub-committees are created within a larger committee.

The committee structure creates a tiered process, because the committees often control whether a decision moves forward to the House or Senate. The committees, however, hold no authority to transform a proposal into the decision of the House or Senate. Thus, the decision can move only up the tier, with the House or Senate possessing the final decision-making authority.

The Power to Legislate and its Limits

All legislative powers are vested in Congress. "Legislate" means to make law. The

---

[1]Originally, the population used for determining Representatives included non-members such as slaves. However, the number of slaves in a state was recognized as constituting only three-fifths of their number for purposes of determining the population of the state.

other two delegated decision makers (that is, the President and the Supreme Court) are not authorized to legislate. The powers of these two decision makers will be discussed subsequently.

What powers to legislate does Congress have? This topic relates directly to the subject of permissible objectives and means, a complex topic which will be addressed in greater detail in later chapters.

THE PRESIDENT

Article II pertains to positions termed the "President" and "Vice President." These positions constitute executive delegated decision makers.

Selection

Effectively, the President is selected by a membership vote of the states. The Constitution sets forward complex rules for this selection. Generally speaking, the members of each state select "electors" in a manner determined by the state. These electors are charged with making one decision. That decision is to choose between the various Presidential candidates and to cast one vote for a single candidate.[1] The votes of electors from all states are then tabulated. A candidate must have a simple majority to become President. If no candidate has a majority, the Constitution provides for additional procedures whereby the House selects the President.

Overview of Presidential Duties

The President is a single delegated decision maker. The President's duties can be divided into two areas:

1) Participation in the decision-making process, and

2) Presidential duties and obligations.

These two areas will be discussed separately in the following section.

Participation in the Legislative Decision-Making Process

The President participates in the legislative decision-making process in the form of

---

[1] The electors also select a Vice President. Originally, the Vice President was the candidate coming in second place in the Presidential election. In 1804, the procedures were modified by amendment to create the "Presidential ticket" whereby a Presidential candidate and Vice Presidential candidate were effectively paired together.

the veto. As noted in the discussion of Congress, the Constitution employs an interwoven decision-making process for decisions on legislation. This process requires in part that two committee decision makers—the House and the Senate—both agree upon a proposal for it to become a decision of Congress. In most situations, this decision pertains to a piece of legislation.

The Constitution provides that the President might overrule or "veto" the decision of Congress. Thus, Congress does not have unfettered discretion to legislate, as the President is capable of stopping any legislation in his complete discretion. The President, however, holds no authority to create legislation, a power vested in only Congress. Although the President might propose legislation to Congress, such a proposal is of no consequence if Congress refuses to vote upon it or fails to vote in favor of it.

The Presidential veto is not all powerful. Congress might trump a Presidential veto if a two-thirds supermajority (that is, greater than 66.33%) of both the House and Senate vote in favor of a proposal.

Presidential Duties and Obligations

What are the duties and obligations of the President? Is the President vested with some type of unfettered authority to do as he sees fit? No, the President's duties and obligations are limited to two areas: (i) matters expressly provided for in the Constitution, and (ii) execution of the laws of the United States.[1] Each of these will be discussed separately in the following sections.

Specific Constitutional Obligations

Article II of the Constitution identifies certain specific duties of the President. These include the following:

- Serving as commander and chief of the military forces

- Granting pardons

- Entering treaties, subject to a two-thirds supermajority vote by the Senate to approve the treaty (that is, an interwoven decision-making process)

---

[1] The Constitution grants the Vice President no authority whatsoever except to cast a tie-breaking vote in the Senate and replace the President if he leaves office in the midst of his current term. Essentially, the Vice President appears to constitute a predetermined replacement for the President to avoid the difficulties of selecting a new President on the spur of the moment.

- Appointing ambassadors, judges, and all officers of the United States (but again requiring a majority vote by the Senate for approval)

- Receiving ambassadors and ministers from foreign states

These enumerated authorities can be summarized into the following functions:

- *Military*—The President holds complete and unfettered authority to direct the military. Observe that the Constitution, however, appears to not authorize the President to raise revenue to pay for military efforts. Instead, only Congress is authorized to raise revenue to fund military endeavors. In addition, the Constitution limits the authority to "declare war" to Congress. As such, although the President is clearly authorized to command the military, the Constitution seems to require Congress to give the President a specific authorization in order to initiate "war."[1] Further, certain provisions of the Constitution as well as amendments impose other limitations on the authority of the President as well as the government in general.

- *Foreign Policy*—The Constitution grants the President near complete authority to represent the United States in interactions and dealings with foreign states. This authority includes the direct dealings of the President as well as the interactions of U.S. ambassadors appointed and supervised by the President. The only limitation is that the President might not bind the United States to any treaty without the approval of two thirds of the Senate.

- *Appointing and supervising sub-executive decision makers*—The Constitution provides for numerous executives to exist below, and subject to, the President. This is a tiered decision-making arrangement because decisions are often made at a lower tier and then might flow upwards. At times, the President will make a decision. At other times, the President will authorize a sub-executive to make a decision on his behalf but retain the right to overrule the decision. And, many times, the President will have a sub-executive investigate a proposal and then make a recommendation to the President. If the President sees merit in the recommendation, it becomes the decision of the President. These sub-executives often have more executives below them that are directed to review proposals and/or make decisions in the same manner. This process can be seen as the passing of the "buck" where the responsibility moves through various tiers of the President's sub-executives. However, ultimate responsibility for a decision lies with the President. The immediate sub-executives below the President are commonly referred to as "Cabinet" officers (for example, Secretaries of State, Defense, Treasury, and so on). The executives beneath

---

[1] The questions of the circumstances under which the President might direct the military and whether Congress must first declare war are unresolved at this time.

these immediate sub-executives have similar titles (for example, Deputy Secretary reports to the Secretary of State, Secretary of the Army reports to the Secretary of Defense, and so on). As the U.S. government has grown, this tiered decision-making process of the President has grown quite large and very complex. Today, thousands of sub-executives exist beneath the President. These sub-executives make a multitude of decisions, subject to the President's ultimate authority to overrule or modify them.

- *Pardoning*—The power to pardon can be seen as a check on the criminal justice system. The President is granted the authority to pardon any violation of U.S. law (except for cases of impeachment). Thus, the President might trump any decision made by the criminal justice system in his complete discretion.

Execution of the Laws of the United States

As just observed, the Constitution places several specific duties upon the President. The Constitution places one other duty on the President. It is that the President "shall take Care that the Laws be faithfully executed."

This provision relates to the role of the President as an *executive* in that the President *executes* the laws. The President is obligated to perform all acts called for by whatever is properly made into law by Congress (and not vetoed by the President).

For instance, Congress early on passed laws related to the raising of revenues through taxes and also passed certain criminal laws. The President was obligated to enforce these laws (or have sub-executives under this authority enforce them).

Law	Enforcement
Collections of Taxes	The Secretary of the Treasury originally executed this law by collecting taxes from the taxed persons or entities. Today, many of these tasks have been delegated downward to a committee decision maker under the Secretary of the Treasury. This decision maker is the Internal Revenue Service.
Criminal Laws	The Attorney General executes these laws, or delegates their execution to a regional U.S. Attorney to handle under the Attorney General's supervision.

A Programmed Decision Maker?

In Chapter 7, there was a discussion of a programmed decision maker. Recall that this type of decision maker essentially holds no discretion in making decisions. Instead all decisions have been predetermined. The programmed decision maker essentially puts these dictates into action.

In executing the laws, is the President a programmed decision maker? The answer is not crystal clear. The best view, however, is that the President is not a programmed decision maker.

To begin with, the Constitutional duties of the President do not specify the actions that the President is to take. As such, the President holds substantial discretion in fulfilling these obligations and cannot be viewed as a programmed decision maker.

Similarly, the laws that the President is required to execute rarely if ever constrain the discretion of the President such that he is effectively programmed in making decisions. Instead, most laws are crafted in a manner that requires the President, and those under the President's supervision, to use substantial discretion in determining how to go about enforcing the laws. For instance, in executing a law, the President typically must make numerous decisions including the hows, whats, whens, and wheres to execute laws. Overall, although the President is somewhat "programmed" in that he is obligated to enforce the specific provisions of the laws, the President typically makes many additional decisions in executing the laws.

Removal from Office

As final matter on the President, the Constitution provides that the President might be removed from office by a complex decision-making process termed "impeachment." This is yet another example of a decision-making process within the Constitution.

THE JUDICIARY

Article III pertains to the judiciary or the "Supreme Court." The Supreme Court is a committee decision maker charged with exercising "judicial power." The committee members are called "Justices."

Selection of the Justices

The Constitution provides that the President is to appoint the Justices, subject to the Senate approving the selection by a majority vote. Unlike Congress and the President, the Constitution does not state when the justices are to vacate their offices. As such, justices remain in office until they resign, die, or are removed for misconduct.

The Number of Justices

The Constitution does not indicate how many justices are to be appointed to the committee comprising the Supreme Court. Over the history of the United States, Congress has set, through legislation, the number of justices on various occasions. The number has ranged from five to ten justices. Since 1869, the number of justices has been fixed at nine.[1]

The Multi-Tiered Process

The Constitution provides for Congress to establish through legislation additional courts to serve under the Supreme Court. The Constitution terms these entities "inferior courts." This arrangement constitutes a tiered decision-making process. In almost all cases, an inferior court (that is, the district or "trial" court) makes a decision. This decision might then be appealed to an intermediate inferior court (that is, the appellate court), which might reverse the decision. The decision of the appellate court might then be appealed to the Supreme Court, which may then reverse that decision. Thus, decisions flow upward through these tiers. The decisions are not final until the Supreme Court has issued its decision (or has declined to hear the appeal).

The Making of a Decision

How does the Supreme Court make a decision? Being a committee, the justices meet and cast their votes for a particular outcome. The Constitution does not provide what number of votes is necessary to constitute a decision of the Supreme Court. Convention has dictated that a simple majority is sufficient.

When the Supreme Court makes a decision, one or more of the Justices will prepare a written opinion explaining the reasoning for the decision. Typically, this opinion will contain a conceptual framework for the analysis of the decision.

The inferior courts within the tiered decision-making process carefully review the Supreme Court opinions. When the inferior courts are presented with matters to adjudicate, they will attempt to locate a conceptual framework endorsed by the Supreme Court in one or more written opinions. If an inferior court can find such a framework, it will use it to analyze the issue at hand and to reach a ruling.

---

[1] In the 1930s, there was a movement to increase the number of justices from nine to fifteen.

Because the Supreme Court opinions control the actions of the inferior courts, the opinions are termed "precedent." Once precedent is set, it is extraordinarily uncommon for the Supreme Court to later disregard or "overrule" it. Instead, the precedent continues in perpetuity.[1] This concept is sometimes called "stare decisis."

The Subject Matter of the Decisions

What does the Supreme Court (and its inferior courts) make decisions regarding? This topic is complex but perhaps can best be divided into two areas:

1) Law cases, and

2) Constitutional cases.

Each of these will be discussed separately.

The Law Cases

The law cases take up the bulk of the Supreme Court's decision making. In almost all circumstances, the cases before the Supreme Court begin in inferior courts. For instance, an inferior court will try a case and reach a decision. If a party to the case does not like the decision, he might appeal it upwards through the tiered decision-making process. The case might ultimately be appealed to the Supreme Court.

As a general rule, all cases in the federal courts are premised upon laws passed by Congress. If a party desires to assert a claim premised upon a law passed by a state, that party typically must file the claim with the relevant state court. This fact reflects the alliance of alliances nature of the federal government. That is, state laws are for state courts; federal laws are for federal courts. There are, however, some exceptions to this generalization where state-law claims might be brought in federal court, and federal-law claims might be brought in state court.

The subject matter of the law cases can be subdivided into criminal and civil cases. These topics will be discussed separately.

---

[1] Precedent of the Supreme Court might be changed or nullified by other mechanisms. If the Court issues an opinion on the meaning of a provision of the Constitution, the Constitution might subsequently be amended to alter the effect of the Court's ruling. Similarly, if a law passed by Congress is ambiguous and the Supreme Court gives a particular meaning to it, Congress might subsequently pass a new law changing the meaning given to it by the Supreme Court. These examples serve to underscore the interwoven nature of the Constitutional decision-making process.

Criminal Cases—In a typical criminal case, a sub-executive under the President brings criminal charges against another person or entity. This sub-executive is usually termed a "U.S. Attorney" and operates under the authority and supervision of the U.S. Attorney General, who reports to the President. The criminal charge is premised upon a law passed by Congress forbidding a type of conduct or action (for example, tax evasion, mail fraud, money laundering, drug trafficking, and so on).

The inferior courts serve as decision makers of these cases. The courts and Congress have developed intricate rules of procedure for the making of these decisions. At times, the courts enlist the assistance of a committee decision maker called a "jury." A jury will usually be asked to make determinations of fact necessary to resolve a case. The inferior court will ultimately make a final decision on the case, usually with the assistance of a jury. If a party does not like a decision of the inferior court, it might appeal the decision upwards through the tiered process of courts to the Supreme Court.

The Constitution imposes strict limits upon what the federal courts might do to individuals accused of crimes and individuals convicted of crimes. These are contained in certain amendments to the Constitution (for example, the "Bill of Rights") and are discussed later.

Civil Cases—The typical law case relates to a claim by one individual for some type of relief against another individual. The relief sought is usually a monetary sum intended to compensate the individual for some type of harm or injury. Other types of relief include a court order forbidding an individual from engaging in a course of action causing harm to the complaining party.

The inferior courts serve as decision makers in resolving these disputes. Juries are often enlisted to aid these courts in making decisions. The final decision of an inferior court might be appealed upwards to the Supreme Court.

The Constitution also imposes certain limits upon what the federal courts might do in adjudicating civil cases. Generally, these limits are not as stringent as those imposed upon the adjudication of criminal cases.

Constitutional Cases

The Constitutional cases pertain to the Supreme Court's role in determining what the Constitution allows and what the Constitution prohibits. Generally speaking, the Supreme Court is authorized to decide what the Constitution means. As a result, the Supreme Court can nullify actions of both Congress and the President if such actions are contrary to the meaning ascribed to the Constitution by the Court. As such, the Supreme Court can be seen as being a part of the interwoven decision-making process relating to the passage of legislation.

How does this work? Typically, an individual will file suit, contending that either Congress or the President has acted contrary to the Constitution. The Supreme Court will consider the contentions and make a decision. Importantly, the Supreme Court is not authorized to nullify an action of Congress or the President because the Court does not favor it or feels that it is an unwise action. That is, the Supreme Court is to avoid making "policy" judgments, such as assessing whether a particular decision of Congress or the President was wise, prudent, or otherwise justifiable. Instead, the Court is to defer to the discretion of (i) Congress in making legislation, and (ii) the President in carrying out his duties. Essentially, the Supreme Court is to simply determine whether the action of the Congress or President was authorized by the Constitution.

The Supreme Court's decision is final and binding upon both Congress and the President. Thus, through its power of nullification, the Supreme Court can be seen as a check upon the authority of Congress and the President. Ultimately, the Supreme Court might be viewed as the enforcer of the accord (that is, the Constitution) underlying the United States alliance.

Interestingly, the Constitution does not clearly grant the Supreme Court the authority to interpret the Constitution and nullify actions of Congress and the President. How did this power come about? In the early stages of the United States, the Supreme Court proclaimed that it held this authority based upon certain language and concepts in the Constitution. Although this proclamation was controversial, it was ultimately accepted and has endured.

Fitting the Three Decision Makers Together

How do the three delegated decision makers fit together? It is complicated. But to boil things down to the essentials, the starting place is Congress. It decides what the laws are, subject to a President's veto and the possibility that the Supreme Court might later nullify the law as unconstitutional. The President and his many sub-executives execute and otherwise enforce the laws. Typically, these efforts relate to prosecuting civil and criminal activities, and pursuing on various projects authorized by Congress such as the military, post offices, and so on. The Supreme Court and its inferior courts resolve criminal and civil cases that arise. Occasionally, the courts interpret the Constitution and might nullify an action of Congress or the President.

Overall, the three delegated decision makers work in separate ways towards the same goal. That goal is the attainment of the objectives identified in the Constitution. What are these objectives? Constitutional objectives, along with the topic of means, are the subjects of the next discussion.

CHAPTER 23

Constitutional Powers

Recall that an objective is an end result that is desired by all alliance members. The members form the alliance to attain this objective and willingly contribute resources towards a combined effort at achieving this objective. The alliance members choose to use an alliance, because they perceive either that (i) they cannot attain the objective using individual effort, or (ii) an alliance effort is more efficient or effective at attaining the objective in comparison to an individual effort.

As discussed in Chapter 4, "means" constitute the manner in which individually possessed resources are to be combined and utilized to attain an objective. Means can be a way, method, technique, or procedure for achieving an objective. Means is a very broad term and can encompass a variety of matters. Perhaps the best way to look at means is as a tool that the alliance is using to achieve the objective. In essence, that tool is either the combination of the resources of the members, or another tool acquired through such combined resources. There are no set or predetermined categories of means. Anything can be the means so long as it achieves the objective.

As observed in Chapter 12, objectives and means are at times clear and distinct. But at other times, it is difficult to determine whether a particular endeavor is an objective, a means to attain an objective, or both. A classic example in the Constitution is taxation. At first consideration, taxation would appear to be only a means. Specifically, the government obtains contribution of resources through collection of taxes. These resources are then used to fund the attainment of other objectives such as Defense against Aggressors. If the circumstances are perused, however, one might find that a certain tax is actually an objective. How? It might be the case that the members desire leveling (that is, restrictions on the material possessions of fellow members). As such, taxation is pursued not to obtain revenue but to level the material wealth of members.

The Constitution does not utilize the concepts of objectives and means. Instead, the Constitution lumps these ideas together and refers to them as "powers." For instance, Section 8 of Article begins, "The Congress shall have the Power To lay and collect Taxes, Duties, Imports and Excises ...." As noted above, the power to tax seems to be a means to an end. But is it also an objective? The Constitution is not clear on this point. This confusion will be elaborated upon in the following sections.

THE SOURCES OF CONSTITUTIONAL POWERS

The overall structure of the Constitution indicates that it does not grant Congress the unfettered authority to undertake whatever objective is selected by its decision-making process. Instead, the federal government is an alliance of limited authority and might pursue an objective only if it is authorized by the terms of the Constitution.

To utilize concepts from Part I, recall that the Constitution is an accord. An accord is an express or implied agreement between the members to contribute resources towards attaining one or more mutually desired objectives. Fundamental parts of an accord are the objective to be attained and some conception of the means to be employed to attain the objective. The accord might describe the objective and means with varying degrees of clarity:

Specifically	Indefinitely	Openly

As noted in the introduction, the Constitution does not differentiate between objectives and means. Instead, it lumps these concepts together and terms them "powers." The powers identified by the Constitution are typically specific. Some of these powers, however, are indefinite and afford the relevant decision maker leeway in determining whether a particular action falls within the scope of the indefinitely defined power. One or two powers are arguably open.

The federal government's powers might be categorized into four areas. The following sections will discuss each category in greater detail:

Category	Substance	Objective or Means?	Nature
The Enumerated Powers	Powers held by the federal government are listed out in the text of the Constitution	Both	Some are specific and some are indefinite
The Necessary & Proper Clause	Authorizes Congress to make all laws necessary and proper to execute the Enumerated Powers	Means	Open?
The General Welfare Clause	Authorizes Congress to provide for the general welfare of the United States	Objective	Open?
The Commerce Clause	Authorizes Congress to regulate inter-state commerce	Both	Indefinite

This table summarizes the authority of the federal government to take action. If a particular action cannot be grounded in one of these four categories, the federal government is not authorized to undertake the action.

THE ENUMERATED POWERS

Most of the Constitution's powers are listed out in the article pertaining to Congress' legislation authority. The specific provision is Section 8 of Article I. The powers listed in this section are commonly known as the "Enumerated Powers."

To briefly summarize the Enumerated Powers, they include the authorizations allowing the federal government to do the following:

- Set and collect taxes

- Borrow money and pay debts

- Provide for the common defense

- Provide for the general welfare*

- Regulate commerce internationally and between the states*

- Set immigration rules (that is, rules regarding membership in the alliance)

- Formulate bankruptcy rules

- Coin money

- Fix standards for weights and measures

- Prevent counterfeiting

- Establish post offices and postal roads

- Create patents, copyrights, and other protections of intellectual property

- Establish courts subject to the authority of the Supreme Court

- Combat piracy on the high seas

- Declare war

- Create a standing army and navy

- Formulate rules for the army and navy

- Call up state militias

- Arm and regulate militias (subject to control by state government)

- Suppress insurrections

- Govern the geographic area where the government is situated (that is, the District of Columbia)

- Make laws necessary and proper for carrying into execution the foregoing powers*

    *These three powers form the basis of the three other categories of powers, which will be discussed in greater detail in the following sections.

Are the Enumerated Powers Objectives or Means?

As noted earlier, some of these powers constitute objectives. Others constitute means. And some appear to constitute both objectives and means. For instance, consider the following table:

Power	Objective or Means?	Explanation
Provide for the common defense	Objective	Defense against Aggressors is an end goal.
Borrow money and pay debts	Means	Borrowing money and paying debts constitute a mechanism for funding the attainment of objectives such as providing for the common defense.*
Coin money	Both	Coined money can be viewed as an end in itself. Alternatively, it can be viewed as a means towards: (i) the efficient raising of tax revenues to attain objectives requiring monetary funding, or (ii) attaining the objective of Generation of Prosperity (that is, the presence of coined money facilitates transactions and increases prosperity as a consequence).

*In today's world, the borrowing of money by the federal government might also be used to indirectly influence the economy. As such, it arguably constitutes a means towards attaining the objective of Generation of Prosperity.

This table should make evident that analysis of objectives and means in the Constitution is a complex and difficult topic. In many situations, there is no clear answer and reasonable minds can easily disagree regarding whether a power identified in the Constitution is an objective, a means, or both.

The source of this uncertainty ultimately lies in the fact that the federal government is a long-term, multi-objective alliance with certain objectives and means (that is, "powers") that are not specifically identified. As discussed in the preceding chapters, the more complex that an alliance becomes, the more difficult analysis of its circumstances becomes.

Practical Analysis of the Enumerated Powers

How do the Enumerated Powers work? The Constitution does not specify a procedure or format that must be applied in analyzing the Enumerated Powers. Nonetheless, a general framework has emerged over time. This framework is probably best viewed as an implied element of the federal accord (that is, the Constitution).

The framework typically works as follows. Laws originate in the Congress. If Congress is considering legislating on a topic, Congress will consult the Enumerated Powers to determine if the Constitution authorizes Congress to legislate upon the matter in question. If the authorization is located, Congress will then proceed to pass a law that arises out of that Constitutional authority. Laws are always in writing. Usually, the text of the legislation will reference the specific power or powers in the Constitution that authorize the law.

If Congress passes a law, the President might then veto the law or sign it, making it a law of the federal government. If the President vetoes the law, the underlying rationale might be that the President feels it is unwise policy. At times, however, the President might veto the law on the basis of Constitutional interpretation. In these situations, the President has essentially concluded that the Constitution does not authorize the law in question.

If Congress passes a law and the President signs it, the Supreme Court might ultimately be asked to review whether it is authorized by the Constitution. This question is sometimes framed as whether the law is "constitutional." As noted above, a party typically will file a lawsuit in a trial court (that is, a lesser court under the Supreme Court). The party will assert that the law is not constitutional or is "unconstitutional." Usually, a sub-executive operating under the authority the President will appear in the lawsuit and contend that the law is constitutional. After a trial, the trial court will issue a determination as to whether the law is constitutional. The trial court's ruling might then be appealed up through the tiered process to the Supreme Court. The Supreme Court will review the law, the Constitution, prior opinions or "precedent," and any other matters of relevance. The Supreme Court will then issue an opinion regarding the laws constitutionality. If the Supreme Court finds that the law is constitutional, the law remains in full force and effect. If the Supreme Court finds that it is unconstitutional, the law is void and null.

Analysis of Congressional powers can be quite straightforward at times. For instance, many of the Enumerated Powers are rather specific with only a small degree of indefiniteness.

- *Borrowing Money*—Congress is quite clearly authorized to borrow money. It seems that no controversy can arise over this topic.

- *Establishing Post Offices*—Again, this power is pretty straightforward. There is little or no ambiguity here.

- *Establishing Patents, Copyrights, and other protections of Intellectual Property*— This power is not so clear. It is evident that Congress is authorized to make patent laws and similar statutes, that the laws must be directed towards promoting "the progress of science and useful arts," and that the patent laws must be for a limited time. But the details of what Congress is allowed to do are not evident. As such, the parameters of this power are somewhat indefinite. As a result, Congress must engage in decision making to determine what those specific parameters are. Congress's decision can then be vetoed by the President (for any reason including the President's opinion that Constitutional authority is lacking) or nullified by the Supreme Court (only on the grounds that Constitutional authority is lacking).

- *Punishing Piracy on the High Seas*—Again, this power is not so clear. Congress is undoubtedly authorized to "punish" piracy on the high seas. But this concept is not precise. What exactly can Congress do in combating piracy? Substantial decision making is required on this topic.

Overall, these examples illustrate some relatively straight-forward decision making that must be undertaken by Congress, the President, and the Supreme Court. The focus of the decision making is whether Congress, and therefore the United States government, is authorized to undertake a particular action. In some cases, the answer is obvious (for example, the power to coin money). In other cases, the answer is not as clear (for example, patent law).

The next sections will focus upon the harder cases: (i) the Necessary and Proper Power, (ii) the General Welfare Power, and (iv) the Commerce Power. Each power is contained within the Enumerated Powers. Due to their indefinite nature (or even open nature), however, these three powers are quite broad and merit separate recognition and discussion.

THE NECESSARY AND PROPER POWER

The "Necessary and Proper" power comes last in the list of enumerated powers of Section 8 of Article I. The entire clause reads as follows:

> To make all laws which shall be necessary and proper for carrying into execution the foregoing powers, and all other powers vested by this constitution in the government of the united states, or in any department or officer thereof.

What does this power constitute? Is it an objective, a means, or both? A review of the text indicates that the power is intended to enable the federal government to take actions required to carry out the Enumerated Powers. As such it appears to be only a means. There is nothing indicating that it expands upon the areas in which the federal government is authorized to act.

The parameters of this power, however, are not clear. As a result, this clause caused considerable confusion in the early years of the United States. All agreed that the language was intended to clarify that Congress could pass laws required to carry out the various enumerated powers. For instance, one of the Enumerated Powers is, "To coin money." The language, however, does not provide insight into how Congress might go about exercising this power. But the necessary and proper clause makes clear that Congress, for instance, might pass a law authorizing the construction of a mint to manufacture the coins.[1]

The relationships between the necessary and proper clause and other Enumerated Powers are not so clear cut as this example of a mint. For instance, can Congress legislate the construction of a system of federal banks? A bank is not identified anywhere in the Enumerated Powers. But is a federal banking system "necessary and proper" to perform other Enumerated Powers? Is a banking system a convenient and effective means of raising and collecting taxes, paying for governmental expenditures, supporting the military, borrowing money, regulating commerce, etc.?

Controversy simmered over this issue for many years. One side contended that the necessary and proper clause authorized endeavors only if they were absolutely essential or indispensable towards performing an Enumerated Power. As such, this side argued, a federal bank was unconstitutional.

---

[1] Observe that Congress would not actually construct the mint. Instead, the construction of the mint would be arranged and supervised by the President or one of his sub-executives. In this regard, the President would be "executing" the law passed by Congress.

The other side argued that the necessary and proper clause did not require essentiality or indispensability. Instead, the clause required only a reasonable and plausible relationship towards performance of an Enumerated Power. Thus, this side contended, a federal bank was constitutionally permissible because it greatly aided in the execution of the Enumerated Powers.

The issue eventually made its way to the Supreme Court where the second, more expansive view was adopted. The Supreme Court determined that the necessary and proper clause did not require indispensability. Instead, the necessary and proper clause contained substantial flexibility. It afforded Congress considerable discretion in passing legislation that could aid in the performance of the Enumerated Powers. The Court identified this standard as:

> Let the end be legitimate, let it be within the scope of the constitution, and all means which are appropriate, which are plainly adapted to that end, which are not prohibited, but consist with the letter and spirit of the constitution, are constitutional. [*McCulloch v. Maryland*]

How does this standard work? The "end" (that is, the objective) is first scrutinized to determine if it falls within the "scope of the constitution." If the objective is authorized, then any means "plainly adapted" to achieving the objective are permissible. This standard is quite broad and essentially requires only that there be a reasonable relationship between the means and the objective. The Court will not scrutinize the reasoning and effectiveness of Congress's selection of a particular means. Instead, the Court will find that a chosen means is constitutional so long as it is plausibly tied to the performance of a constitutionally permitted objective.

The effect of the Supreme Court's ruling was to substantially extend the parameters of permissible means that might be employed in exercising the Enumerated Powers. Arguably, any types of means might be used, unless if they are specifically prohibited. (The prohibitions on means are discussed subsequently.)

To use concepts from Part I, the Supreme Court's interpretation of the Necessary and Proper clause indicates the analytical focus is largely upon the objective pursued, rather than the means. Essentially, the Necessary and Proper power grants the federal government the freedom to use any means it deems appropriate to attain a constitutionally identifiable objective.

THE GENERAL WELFARE POWER

Recall that an open objective is one that more or less has no constraints. For instance, Example 8 "Council of Elders" pertained to a tribal council that was impliedly authorized to undertake any action in the benefit of the tribal members including organizing a defense against raiders, moving the tribe, and so on.

In the Constitution, one of the Enumerated Powers pertains to the general welfare of the United States. The clause reads in part:

> The Congress shall have power to lay and collect taxes, duties, imposts and excises, to pay the debts and provide for the common defense and *general welfare* of the United States ..." [Article I, Section 8]

The question naturally arises as to whether the "general welfare" language is an open objective? Does it authorize Congress to legislate upon any matter that is perceived as providing for the general welfare of the United States? Observe that if the Necessary and Proper power is incorporated, the language arguably authorizes Congress to utilize any means plausibly related to the general welfare of the United States. That is an extraordinarily broad and indefinite objective. Its breadth is so sizeable that the objective is probably best described as being open. Under such a viewpoint, Congress is essentially authorized to undertake anything so long as it is thought to provide for the general welfare.

Is this the correct interpretation of the Constitution? If the power of the federal government is essentially open, why does the Constitution bother to list out the Enumerated Powers? The express identification of Enumerated Powers suggests that the federal government is an alliance of limited authority or power.

Arguably, the General Welfare clause is not a grant of power but instead constitutes a limit on Constitutional powers. That is, the language effectively mandates that no action might be taken by the federal government unless it provides for the general welfare of the United States. Such a limitation would be consistent with the concepts identified in Part I. Namely, members form an alliance for the purpose of attaining an objective desired by all members. The General Welfare clause encapsulates this concept by requiring that any power exercised by the federal government be for the general welfare of all states. Effectively, this reading of the General Welfare clause prohibits the federal government from taking an action designed or intended to be of benefit to a particular state, or a small group of states.

The puzzle surrounding the General Welfare clause remains unresolved to this day. The Supreme Court has on occasion considered what the general welfare language means. But it has skirted the question and left it unanswered. A primary reason has been the convenience of the Commerce Power.

THE COMMERCE POWER

The last of the four categories of power is the Commerce Power. In the present day, the Commerce Power is the most formidable of all Constitutional powers and underlies most actions undertaken by Congress.

Similar to the Necessary and Proper Power and the General Welfare Power, the Commerce Power is contained with the list of Enumerated Powers. The language provides that the federal government is authorized:

> To regulate commerce with foreign nations, and among the several states, and with the Indian tribes. [Article I, Section 8]

A portion of this power pertains to regulation of commerce among the several states. This concept is usually termed "interstate commerce." Simplifying the language, the Constitution provides that Congress holds the authority *to regulate interstate commerce.*

But what does this mean? What is regulation of interstate commerce? Presumably, it means that the federal government is authorized to impose terms and conditions upon commercial transactions that cross over state lines.

If the necessary and proper language is considered, however, does the language mean that the federal government holds the authority to undertake any action plausibly related to regulating interstate commerce? For instance, can the federal government undertake an action so long as its subject-matter involves commercial transactions that actually cross state lines? What if the transactions might only potentially cross state lines?

The Supreme Court has answered these questions affirmatively. The history of the Supreme Court's analysis is complex, lengthy, and evolving to this day. The following discussion will briefly survey the topic.

For approximately 100 years, Congress rarely enacted legislation under the Commerce Power.[1] Because such legislation was uncommon, the Supreme Court

---

[1] The Supreme Court nevertheless considered the commerce language in thorny cases addressing the authority of state governments to regulate interstate commerce, which is a different but related concept. In these cases, the Supreme Court was considering whether the Constitution forbids the states from regulating interstate commerce. Often, the Court found that a state was not authorized to regulate certain commercial transactions because they constituted interstate commerce, an area left to the federal government.

did not have the opportunity to consider the issue of what exactly the Commerce Power authorized Congress to do.

In the late 1880s, the federal government began regulating the conduct of business, with an aim towards decreasing anticompetitive business conduct, improving working conditions of employees, increasing the safety of products, and pursuing Morality-related objectives. Questions were raised as to whether the federal government was in fact authorized by the Commerce Power to legislate in such a fashion. Opponents contended that regulation of interstate commerce was a very limited field. Interstate commerce, these opponents argued, did not encompass business activity that occurred entirely within one state (that is, where all transactions occurred within a state's boundaries and nothing crossed state lines). In response, supporters of the regulation maintained that interstate commerce was quite broad. These supporters asserted that interstate commerce included any activity that was related to, or had an effect upon, interstate commerce.

The arguments raged for decades until the 1930s when the Supreme Court resolved the matter. In several decisions, the Supreme Court made clear that the Commerce Power granted the federal government broad and flexible powers to act upon any matter that has a reasonable relationship to interstate commerce.

This standard continues to this day. In every case presented to the Court for consideration from the 1930s until the 1990s, the Supreme Court always adhered to this broad standard of Commerce Power. In a typical case, the Supreme Court analyzed the legislation to determine whether it had a plausible relationship to interstate commerce. The Supreme Court always found such a relationship and concluded that the Commerce Power authorized the legislation.

A few examples are illustrative. In considering these examples, it should be kept in mind that the issue is whether the federal government holds the power to pass the legislation at issue.

- *Can the federal government criminalize kidnapping?*—Yes, but only if it relates to interstate commerce. As most people are aware, the Federal Bureau of Investigation holds authority to intervene into a kidnapping case only if the victim is transported across state lines. Why is this? Congress imposed this limitation to comply with the Commerce Power, because transporting a victim across state lines relates to interstate commerce. The text of the federal kidnapping statute makes this point evident:

  > Whoever unlawfully seizes, confines, inveigles, decoys, kidnaps, abducts, or carries away and holds for ransom or reward or otherwise any person, except in the case of a minor by the parent thereof, when ... the person is willfully **transported in interstate or foreign commerce**, regardless of

whether the person was alive when transported across a State boundary if the person was alive when the transportation began ... shall be punished by imprisonment for any term of years or for life and, if the death of any person results, shall be punished by death or life imprisonment. [18 USC §1201(a) (emphasis supplied)]

- *Can the federal government set minimum standards for wages?* Yes. Work performed by employees has an effect upon interstate commerce. This is true even if employees do not cross state lines in their work. As such, federal regulation of employees' wages is permissible.

- *Can the federal government regulate the garden products grown by a person for individual use and consumption at his home?* Yes. By growing one's own food and consuming it, the person is not purchasing food on the market. Because one is not purchasing food on the market, the demand for food declines. As a result, the conduct has an effect upon interstate commerce. As such, Congress is authorized to regulate one's home-grown crops, even if the person will never sell them in commerce to others.

- *Can the federal government impose standards upon hotels and restaurants regarding how they behave towards potential patrons?* Yes. Hotels might be regulated because patrons are often travelers coming from out of state and traveling to other states. Restaurants might be regulated because a sizeable portion of the food they prepare and sell comes from out of state.

Aside from utilizing this analytical standard since the 1930s, the Supreme Court has consistently found that Congress was authorized to undertake every action presented to the Court for review. That is, the Court has always concluded that every questioned action by Congress was within its Commerce Power.

The only exception to this generalization has been in the 1990s. During this decade, the Court found on a few occasions that certain laws did not have rational relationships to interstate commerce and therefore were not authorized. For instance,

- *Can Congress criminalize the carrying of handguns near schools?* No. The carrying of a handgun near a school does not have an effect upon interstate commerce. The Commerce Power does not authorize the federal government to criminalize the conduct.

What is the significance of the Commerce Power? It is undoubtedly the most potent of all Congressional powers. So long as a proposed action can be related to interstate commerce, it is within the authority of Congress. Most Congressional actions taken in the past 100 years have been under the Commerce Power. And these actions have not been of little consequence. The scope of the undertakings of the United States has expanded tremendously in the last 100 years and this expansion was made possible through the Commerce Power.

SUMMARY

Consistent with the concepts set forward in Part I, the Constitution is an accord underlying a complex, multi-objective alliance called the federal government. The federal government holds sizeable authority to pursue numerous objectives. However, the objectives that the federal government might undertake are not boundless. Instead, for each and every objective that the federal government seeks to undertake, it must be matched up with a specific provision in the text of the Constitution authorizing the pursuit of such an objective.

Because the Constitution merges objectives and means into one concept termed "powers," analysis of this subject can be cloudy. Nonetheless, the two generalizations might be made.

First, the objectives that the federal government might pursue are limited. In the chapter, it was observed that there are four categories of powers: (i) the Enumerated Powers, (ii) the Necessary and Proper Power, (iii) the General Welfare Power, and (iv) the Commerce Power. Of these four categories, the second category (that is, the Necessary and Proper Power) is only a means. The third category (that is, the General Welfare Power) has never been officially recognized as being a power. As a practical matter, the only real powers in the Constitution authorizing the pursuit of objectives are the Enumerated Powers and the Commerce Power. These clauses in the Constitution form the basis of all objectives pursued by the federal government. Further, these objectives are, in principle, consistent with alliance principles. Namely, the objectives pertain to desires of the states that can be obtained either (i) only through a combined effort of the states, or (ii) more efficiently or effectively through a combined effort of the states.

Second, the Constitution authorizes the federal government to utilize any means to attain constitutionally permissible objectives. In terms of authority, the federal government's discretion is largely unbounded. As such, while the objectives that the federal government might pursue are limited, the means are not.

In closing, this chapter has summarized the powers held by the federal government. An action might be taken only if the Constitution authorizes it. But the fact that the Constitution authorizes an action does not necessarily mean that it might in fact be taken. The Constitution also imposes a number of restrictions upon actions that it authorizes. These restrictions are discussed in the next chapter.

Chapter 24

Restrictions on Constitutional Powers

The discussion of the previous chapter pertained to the powers of the federal government. The issue discussed was whether the Constitution authorized or empowered the federal government to undertake a particular action.

In contrast, the subject matter of this chapter pertains to the restrictions imposed by the Constitution upon these powers. Chapter 4 outlined the concept of restrictions. In many circumstances, accords contain restrictions that limit the ability of alliances to take action in one or more areas. The most common reason for such restrictions is that alliance members do not fully trust the decision-making process of the alliance. Often, members will perceive the process as being prone to making mistakes or susceptible to corruption. To attempt to reduce these possibilities, the accord might contain specific restrictions on the objectives, means, or both.

The Constitution has a number of provisions restricting the powers of the federal government. As noted in the last chapter, for the federal government to take an action, the Constitution must authorize it. To use the parlance of the Constitution, the federal government must have the "power" to take the action in question. Once a power has been identified, it must be ascertained whether the Constitution imposes a restriction upon the exercise of that power. Considering the power and the restriction together, it can be said that the federal government holds a broad authority to take a particular action but such an action may not be taken in certain circumstances.

Recall this example from Chapter 4:

Example 4 "Wild West"—The objective is order and decency. The means are to hire a mercenary to achieve this objective. Since the mercenary will be dealing with many violent individuals, the members recognize that the mercenary often will have to use violent methods to achieve this objective. But the members are concerned with what the mercenary might do. As a result, the accord includes specific restrictions on the mercenary's activities (that is, the means) including:

1) The mercenary may kill only in self-defense. If the mercenary believes that a person should be executed, he must bring that person before a committee of alliance members and have them decide the issue.

2) The mercenary may never use torture as a means of bringing order and decency.

The Constitution is not clear regarding whether its restrictions are upon objectives, means, or both. As noted earlier, the Constitution does not differentiate between objective and means and instead lumps both concepts together under the term "powers." The Constitutional restrictions follow this conceptual framework by not specifically referencing objectives or powers.[1] Instead, some of the most important restrictions focus upon effects of actions.

In reviewing the Constitutional restrictions, it should become apparent that the restrictions serve important purposes. At the time the Constitution was created, it was feared that the federal government might transform itself into an oppressive tyranny. As such, many of the restrictions appear to be focused upon constraining the power of the federal government. Other restrictions seem directed at protecting the interests of the derivative members (that is, the members of the state governments) from certain perceived abuses. For instance, the first ten amendments (that is, the "Bill of Rights") largely target the treatment of individuals and restrict the federal government from taking certain actions with regard to these individuals.

Where are the Constitutional restrictions on powers? They can be found in three sources:

Text accompanying the Enumerated Powers	Others Articles of the Constitution	Amendments to the Constitution

---

[1] Some restrictions appear to be specifically directed at means. For instance, one of these restrictions is contained in the Fourth Amendment which provides, "The right of the people to be secure in their persons, houses, papers, and effects, against unreasonable searches and seizures, shall not be violated, and no Warrants shall issue, but upon probable cause, supported by Oath or affirmation, and particularly describing the place to be searched, and the persons or things to be seized." This provision seems to have little to do with objectives. Instead, it serves to constrain only means by forbidding the federal government from ever engaging in unreasonable searches of persons or their property except under very narrow circumstances.

Each of these items will be discussed separately in the following sections.

RESTRICTIONS WITHIN THE ENUMERATED POWERS

Some of the Enumerated Powers are coupled with a restriction. For instance, the power to tax is enumerated as follows:

> The Congress shall have power to lay and collect taxes, duties, imposts and excises, to pay the debts and provide for the common defense and general welfare of the United States; *but all duties, imposts and excises shall be uniform throughout the United States.* [Article I, Section 8]

This language indicates that the federal government holds the power to tax but is restricted from imposing taxes that are not "uniform throughout the United States." Recall from Chapter 4 that many accords impose significant restrictions upon the collection of contribution from members. The restriction on taxation is consistent with this concept and seems to be concerned with insuring that all members contribute to the alliance proportionately (that is, to insure that contribution is equal and that certain members are not compelled to contribute more than others). This restriction was later eliminated by the Sixteenth Amendment which, among other things, allowed taxation that was disproportionate across the states.

Another useful example pertains to the power to create and maintain a military. An Enumerated Power specifically authorizes the creation of an army but then imposes a significant restriction upon it.

> To raise and support armies, *but no appropriation of money to that use shall be for a longer term than two years.* [Article I, Section 8]

This provision clearly allows the federal government to build and fund an army. However, it also prohibits the long-term funding of an army (that is, the army might be funded for a maximum of two years).

The concern here is with checking the power of the army. Recall that the army is under the control of the President. With this restriction, the President's control of the army is not unlimited. At least every two years, the army will run out of funding, and the President will have to seek additional monies from Congress through the interwoven decision-making process discussed earlier. The net result is that, although the President holds sizeable power to control the army, the power is not absolute. Instead, Congress can restrain this power by not authorizing additional funding or by imposing restrictions upon how the funding might be used.[1]

RESTRICTIONS WITHIN OTHER PARTS OF THE CONSTITUTION

Section 8 grants the federal government the various Enumerated Powers. Section 9 immediately follows Section 8 and restricts these powers in certain instances. These restrictions upon the federal government include:

- *Slavery*—The government was forbidden from restricting the importation of slaves until at least 1808. It seems apparent that slave-holding states demanded this firm limitation upon the power to regulate slavery as a condition of entering the alliance.

- *Habeas Corpus*—Habeas corpus is an old British legal doctrine that allows a court to inquire into why a person has been imprisoned or otherwise detained by a governmental entity. If no legitimate basis is identified by the governmental entity, the court will free the person. The Constitution prohibits the federal government from suspending the availability of habeas corpus. However, an exception to this limitation provides, "unless when in cases of rebellion or invasion the public safety might require it." Overall, habeas corpus serves as an important check upon the power of the federal government to detain persons without justification.

- *Ex Post Facto Laws*—The federal government may not pass legislation criminalizing conduct that has already occurred. Criminal laws may look forward only (that is, apply to future conduct occurring after the legislation has become effective). The net result is that, although the federal government holds the power to pass many criminal laws, no such law may be ex post facto.

- *Taxation*—The federal government may not tax unless it is in proportion to the population of a state. This restriction appears to be redundant. There is a very similar provision in the Enumerated Powers of Section 8 as noted above.

---

[1]The source of the Iran-Contra controversy is associated with this concept. In the early 1980s, Congress passed legislation that barred the President from using funds to support Nicaraguan rebels called the "Contras." The Contras were attacking the communist government of Nicaragua. The President or his sub-executives attempted to skirt this restriction by selling weapons to the government of Iran and then having the proceeds from this sale channeled to the Contras. This indirect funding of the Contras was considered to be an unlawful effort to evade a legal restriction.

- *Commerce between the States*—The federal government is limited in how it might impose taxes and duties on commerce. A significant restriction bars the federal government from targeting certain states for preferential treatment. It seems that the purpose of this restriction is to insure that all regulations are imposed equally upon all states. Further, this restriction can be seen as a check on corruption. In particular, if a group of states effectively control the decision-making process, they might not twist the federal government to favor their specific interests.

- *Funding*—Monies held by Treasury may not be withdrawn, unless the federal government has passed a law making specific appropriations for such monies. Further, the federal government must keep careful records of all funds and expenditures and publish them periodically. This restriction appears to be a check upon corruption and mismanagement.

- *Nobility*—The government may not grant any titles of nobility. No government officer may accept a title of nobility from any other government. This restriction appears to be a limitation on objectives. The federal government may never pursue the objective of instituting an aristocracy.

Other parts of the Constitution have limits intermixed with certain provisions. For instance, Article III pertains to the Supreme Court and includes the following:

- *Jury Trials*—All criminal trials must be by jury. This restriction seems to pertain to means only. While the federal government is authorized to pass criminal legislation furthering Law-Compelled Objectives and to convict individuals for committing crimes, jury trials must always be utilized in these undertakings.

- *Treason*—Treason is specifically defined and rules of proving treason are mandated. Presumably, treason was seen as a potential abusive undertaking. As such, the Constitution subjects treason prosecutions to strict limitations.

RESTRICTIONS WITHIN THE AMENDMENTS

The Amendments to the Constitution contain numerous restrictions on federal government action. The limitations in these amendments generally pertain to protection of the interests of the derivative members of the federal government (that is, the citizens of the states).

The first ten amendments contain various restrictions on the power of the federal government. These restrictions largely protect individual persons and are commonly referred to as "rights." As a result, the first ten amendments are called the "Bill of Rights."

The Bill of Rights was adopted contemporaneously with the Constitution. History indicates that many states feared the Constitution and believed that it granted far too much authority to the federal government. As such, enactment of the Bill of Rights was coupled with the ratification of the Constitution in order to assuage their concerns.

A short summary of the restrictions within the Bill of Rights includes provisions prohibiting the federal government from:

- Establishing a religion

- Prohibiting the exercise of a religion

- Abridging the freedom of speech or press

- Preventing peaceably assemblies

- Preventing the petitioning of the government for a redress of grievances

- Infringing upon the keeping and bearing of arms

- Quartering soldiers in individuals' houses

- Engaging in unreasonable searches and seizures of individuals and their property

- Trying a person for a crime without first securing an indictment from a grand jury

- Trying a person twice for the same alleged crime (that is, "double jeopardy")

- Compelling a person accused of a crime to testify against himself

- Depriving a person of life, liberty, or property without due process of law

- Taking private property for public use without just compensation

- Denying an accused a speedy and public trial

- Preventing an accused from confronting the witnesses testifying against him

- Denying an accused the assistance of counsel

- Failing to try civil cases (where more than $20 is in dispute) without a jury

- Utilizing law other than the rules of British common law

- Imposing excessive bail on an accused

- Inflicting excessive fines or cruel and unusual punishment on persons

These limitations all seem premised upon a certain mistrust of the federal government and its decision-making processes with regard to the treatment of individual persons. There appears to be an underlying presumption that an unchecked federal government will be prone to mistreating persons. Because of these concerns, the Bill of Rights imposes various restrictions upon the federal government and its actions.

Some of the concerns can be grouped into categories:

Category	Description
Religious Freedom	Persons may freely exercise their chosen religion.
Secular Objectives	The federal government may not pass legislation "respecting an establishment of religion."
Communication Freedom	Persons may speak freely, publish newspapers and books without restrictions, assemble peaceably (that is, no riots or mobs allowed), communicate with the federal government for regarding complaints, and so on.
Personal Autonomy	Soldiers may not be quartered in persons' houses. Persons may not be searched without a compelling reason. Their houses may not be searched without a search warrant.
Protection of the Accused	A person accused of a crime must be: (i) indicted prior to a trial, (ii) tried by a jury, (iii) not tried twice for the same crime, (iv) not required to testify against himself, (v) not denied due process, (vi) given a speedy trial, (vii) allowed to confront any witnesses testifying against him, (viii) allowed an attorney, (ix) granted a reasonable bail prior to conviction, and (x) not subjected to cruel and unusual punishments.

The Bill of Rights can also be viewed as means to prevent utilization of the "tools of tyranny." Recall from Chapter 11 that tyrannies use many mechanisms to preserve their power including:

- Manufacturing illusory benefits to deceive the victims into believing they are in a true alliance

- Suppressing information or knowledge tending to show that alternatives to the tyranny exist

- Issuing misinformation regarding the alleged limitations and failures of known alternatives to the tyranny

- Prohibiting any communications tending to expose the illusory nature of the benefits offered by the tyranny

- Forbidding any meetings or assemblies of exploited individuals whereby they might form a revolutionary alliance

- Preventing the illusory members from departing the illusory alliance or otherwise terminating their illusory membership

Not all of the amendments in the Bill of Rights focus upon restrictions. For instance, the Ninth Amendment is different and provides:

> The enumeration in the Constitution, of certain rights, shall not be construed to deny or disparage others retained by the people. [Amendment IX]

This language is not intended to place clear restrictions upon the power of federal government, in contrast to the previous eight amendments. Instead, the Ninth Amendment clarifies that the rights identified in the Constitution and in the first eight amendments are not an exhaustive list of all rights. As such, the possibility exists that other rights (or limitations on federal government action) exist, although they are not explicitly provided for in the Constitution. This possibility has been the source of many controversies regarding what unidentified rights might exist.

The Tenth Amendment is similar to the Ninth Amendment in that it does not restrict any specific federal government action. Instead, the Tenth Amendment provides:

> The powers not delegated to the United States by the Constitution, nor prohibited by it to the States, are reserved to the States respectively, or to the people. [Amendment X]

As noted in the discussion of Constitutional powers, the fact that the Constitution enumerates certain powers strongly implies that the federal government is limited to only those specific powers. The Tenth Amendment confirms the limited powers of the federal government. In this regard, unless the Constitution grants a specific power to the federal government, it is without authority and has no power to act.

SUMMARY

The Constitution is an accord. Often alliances are not formed because an accord cannot be reached. It appears evident that the restrictions on the powers of the federal government were crucial to the formation and acceptance of the Constitution. Many potential members undoubtedly had reservations about creating a federal government with sizeable powers. There were fears that this government would grow out of control and become abusive.

Why? Delegated decision makers control almost every action of the federal government. And delegated decision makers are subject to many imperfections and weaknesses (that is, motivational limitations, ability limitations, and fidelity limitations) as surveyed in Chapter 7. In light of these flaws with delegated decision makers, potential members were concerned that the power granted to the decision makers would be used carelessly and negligently or for corrupt ends. These concerns, however, were addressed by placing express and specific restrictions on the power of the federal government. These precautions, it was hoped, would check carelessness and abuse. With these safeguards in place, members were willing to join the alliance and form the United States of America.

In effect, the Constitutional restrictions carve out exceptions to the powers bestowed upon the federal government by the Constitution. Consider the example of criminal laws:

Power	Offsetting Restriction
Power to Make Criminal Law— Congress's decision-making process passes a law criminalizing certain behavior. The President signs the law and it becomes effective.	*Restrictions on Criminal Law*—The Supreme Court might subsequently declare the law void if the law is found to be prohibited by a Constitution limit.
Investigation of a Crime—An individual is accused of violating the law. The Attorney General and his subexecutives, acting under the ultimate authority of the President, investigate the allegation and bring charges against the individual.	*Restrictions on Investigations*—The investigation must not involve unreasonable searches and the accused's due process rights must be protected. Further, an indictment must be secured prior to formally charging the accused and the accused usually must be given the option of bail.

Trial of the Accused—A federal court, under the ultimate authority of the Supreme Court, is authorized to try the accused and adjudge him guilty or not guilty of the crime.

Restrictions on the Trial—Numerous limitations are imposed upon the trial of the accused including a speedy trial, trial by jury, a privilege to not testify against oneself, the ability to confront a witness, having an attorney present, and so on. Further, the accused must be given the opportunity to appeal a conviction to a higher court.

Punishment of the Accused—A federal court is empowered to punish the accused with a fine, imprisonment, or death. The degree of punishment depends upon the ranges set in the law and the circumstances presented.

Restrictions on Punishment—The punishment of the accused must not be cruel or unusual.

As a final note, it should be observed that the Constitution is not the only source of a restriction on a governmental action. In making laws, the federal government is always free to impose its own restrictions upon a particular law that it creates. The source of such a restriction is not a Constitution restriction. Instead, the source is the federal government itself and the power held by its decision-making process.

Illustration—Congress passes a law mandating the construction of a post office. The law specifies that the post office must be constructed of brick. The President and his sub-executives, in executing this law, are constrained to using brick in the construction of the post office. This restriction is not based in the Constitution. Instead, it arises out of the law making powers held by Congress.

CHAPTER 25

Other Notable Provisions

The discussion of the previous chapter demonstrated that the Constitution and the Bill of Rights are by and large composed of (i) provisions describing the various delegated decision makers, and (ii) grants of powers and authorities to the federal government coupled with numerous restrictions on those powers. But there are other important provisions in the Constitution.

AMENDMENTS

As discussed in Chapter 4, many express accords contain formal and detailed procedures for amending the accord.[1] Such amendment procedures are typically present only in long-term, complex, multi-objective alliances. In contrast, a single-objective alliance usually has a simple accord and there is rarely a perceived need to amend it in the future.

Amendments to the accord are required only when the accord (i) does not authorize the alliance to perform a particular action, or (ii) prohibits the alliance from taking a particular action. Because the alliance is powerless to take the action in question, the accord must be amended to allow it.

Amendments to the accord can pertain to any subject and typically include changes pertaining to:

• Objectives that might be pursued

---

[1]Amendment procedures are not present in implied accords, since an implied accord has no formalities and instead is based upon the facts and circumstances underlying an alliance. Because an implied accord has a high degree of fluidity, it is subject to being effectively amended at any time through the conduct of the members and the actions of that the alliance undertakes.

- Means that might be utilized

- Refinement or modification of the decision-making process

- Rules relating to membership

- Contribution rules

- Administrative rules

The Constitution's Amendment Procedure

Article V of the Constitution pertains to amendments. The clause identifies a two-step, decision-making process by which the Constitution might be amended.

Step One: An amendment is proposed.

Step Two: The proposed amendment is accepted and made a part of the Constitution.

The first step of proposing an amendment can be accomplished in two manners. Congress might make the proposal if supported by super-majority votes (that is, two-thirds or 66.33% of the votes in both the House and the Senate). The other method is by the states through what is called a "Constitution Convention." In this situation, a super majority of two thirds (66%) of the states is required in order to propose an amendment to the Constitution.

The second step is accepting the proposed amendment and making it part of the Constitution. This acceptance is performed through two different kinds of votes of the states. One way is for the legislatures of the states to vote on a proposed amendment. A super majority of three quarters (75%) of the states is required. The other method is up to Congress to specify but essentially requires each state to hold a convention on the proposed amendment. Again, a super majority of three quarters (75%) of the state conventions is required. If a proposed amendment is passed with the requisite super majority, it is effective and becomes a part of the Constitution.

Rationales Underlying the Constitution's Amendment Procedures

The amendment procedure of the Constitution can be seen as a mechanism to serve several purposes. One end is to correct any conceptual mistakes within the Constitution. For instance, after the election of 1800, a consensus quickly developed that the decision-making process for selecting the Vice President was deficient and the Twelfth Amendment was quickly passed to remedy the procedure. This change resulted in the "Presidential Ticket" of voting for a President and Vice President together instead of separately.

Another end is to adapt the Constitution to changing desired objectives. As discussed in Chapter 2, objectives change over time due to new circumstances, altered subjective desires, and so on. The federal government is of limited, enumerated powers and cannot undertake new objectives not authorized by the Constitution. As such, if desired objectives change, the Constitution will not authorize the pursuit of these newly desired objectives.[1]

The amendment procedure, however, allows the Constitution to be modified to address new objectives. For instance, the Constitution was amended in 1919 by the Eighteenth Amendment to prohibit the sale and consumption of alcohol and to authorize the federal government to enforce this ban. By 1933, there had been a change in attitudes and the Twenty-First Amendment was passed which annulled the Eighteenth Amendment.

Further, the amendment procedure might be used to address any other aspect of the alliance that is perceived as being in need of modification. For example, women were granted a firm right to vote in all elections by the Nineteenth Amendment which was passed in 1920. Similarly, in 1971, the right to vote was given to all adults over the age of eighteen.

The Internalization of Revolutions?

The Constitution's amendment procedure can be viewed as a substitute mechanism for a revolution. As discussed in Chapter 12, a revolution is an alliance whose objective is to defeat another combined-effort entity, which is usually a tyranny. Revolutions are most commonly conceived as violent undertakings resulting in death and destruction. This carnage results because the opposing sides usually must employ violent mechanisms to achieve their desires. Argument, debate, and the voice reason rarely can play any role in a revolution.

The Constitution's amendment procedure arguably allows for all of the radical change associated with revolution, minus the violence and carnage. Under the amendment procedure, everything in the Constitution is up for modification, deletion, or addition (subject to two exceptions). The only thing required to effect

---

[1]If an objective within the Constitution is indefinite, however, a new desire might fit within the existing objective and might be pursued as a consequence. For instance, when the Constitution was created, airplanes and jets did not exist. When airplanes and jets became commonplace in warfare in the Twentieth Century, Congress created a separate entity, under the authority of the President, called the "Air Force." There was no need to amend the Constitution to allow for the creation of the Air Force as it was seen to fall within the provisions of the Constitution relating to the creation and maintenance of an Army and Navy.

such radical change is a super-majority voting power. This super-majority vote might be roughly equated to the physical force required by a revolution to overthrow an existing combined-effort entity. Moreover, because change is effected through a vote, there is a sizeable role for argument, debate, and the voice of reason prior to the vote taking place. Instead of using violence, proponents of change might state their case for change grounded in logic and common sense. If their case is persuasive, the change is likely to be adopted through the membership vote. On the whole, if a radical and fundamental change of the Constitution is effected through the amendment procedure, it can be viewed as a non-violent revolution.[1]

Prohibited Amendments

The Constitution places only two substantive limitations on the amendment procedure. First, as noted earlier, the Constitution banned any measure to stop the importation of slaves until 1808. The amendment procedure forbids any modification of this ban by amendment to the Constitution. This forbiddance terminated by its own terms in 1808, effectively resulting in an authorization to ban slave imports after 1808.

Second, the amendment procedure prohibits any deprivation of each state's equal voting proportion in the Senate. Presumably, this measure demonstrates the perceived significance of the Senate in the decision-making process. Other than these two provisions, the Constitution apparently might be amended in any other fashion imaginable.

OBLIGATIONS HELD BY THE STATES

As noted in the foregoing chapters, the Constitution focuses almost exclusively upon the federal government. It contains various provisions on the federal government's decision-making processes, its powers, and restrictions on power. The members (that is, the states) receive very little attention in the document. The Constitution, however, does impose certain obligations upon the states.

These duties include:

- *Honor the Acts and Judgments of Other States*—This duty is a complex concept but essentially requires one state to respect and adhere to a final court ruling rendered by another state.

---

[1] The existence of an amendment procedure, of course, does not always reduce violence and carnage. The American Civil War is a classic example of this fact.

Illustration—A Vermont court issues a final judgment on a lawsuit in favor of a defendant. The plaintiff then refiles the same lawsuit in Maine. The Maine court is obligated to dismiss the suit and recognize the judgment rendered by the Vermont court.

- *Treat Citizens of All the States the Same*—This duty essentially requires each state to afford citizens of other states the same "privileges and immunities" granted to citizens of that state. The Supreme Court has allowed a few exceptions to this general rule. For instance, the states might impose time-based residency requirements and reasonable restrictions on out-of-state visitors seeking to benefit from certain services offered by a state. The rationale for these exceptions is undoubtedly to allow states to deter against the "free-rider" effect discussed in Part I.

- *Extradition*—The Constitution requires one state to turnover fugitives wanted by another state.

- *Return Escaped Slaves*—States must return any slaves that might escape into their borders.

These obligations all constitute objectives that can be obtained either (i) only through a combined effort of the states, or (ii) more efficiently or effectively through a combined effort of the states. Essentially, they are all Law-Compelled Objectives constituting a promise by all states to behave in a certain manner that is perceived as being mutually advantageous to all states.[1]

SUPREMACY OF THE FEDERAL GOVERNMENT

Recall that the federal government is an alliance of alliances. The states are the members of the federal government alliance but also all constitute separate and independent alliances. The state alliances pursue various objectives in their own respective realms. At times, a particular state's actions might overlap or conflict with the action taken by the federal government.

What happens if there is a conflict between state law and federal law? The Constitution has a provision for this situation. It states that the Constitution and all laws made under it constitute the "supreme law of the land." This language makes clear that the federal government prevails over any state in such a conflict.

---

[1] The only exception is the return-of-slave provision. This would have been of benefit only to the slave-holding states. As such, it is a special interest objective that the slave-holding states apparently negotiated to place within the Constitution for their exclusive benefit.

Does the Supremacy Clause then make the federal government all powerful? No, the Supremacy Clause does not increase the powers and authorities of the federal government. The federal government has limited powers and those powers are supreme when exercised. The federal government controls a restricted realm of authority and its control of that realm is all powerful.

As a practical matter, the federal government typically allows states to legislate in most areas where the federal government holds an Enumerated Power. Occasionally, the federal government will prohibit states from legislating in any fashion in a particular area. For instance, the federal government has preempted the field of patent law and prohibits states from regulating the field in any fashion.

PATERNALISTIC OBJECTIVE

The Constitution contains one apparent Paternalistic objective pertaining to the states. Recall that Paternalism is an internal objective that strives to guard against some defect in the members. Paternalism is founded upon a notion that members desire a certain course of conduct but that an anticipated shortcoming will tend to prevent the members from attaining this course of conduct. As a consequence, the paternalistic objective requires the alliance to undertake measures to combat or prevent this shortcoming from occurring.

The apparent paternalistic objective of the Constitution provides:

The United States shall guarantee to every state in this union a republican form of government, and shall protect each of them against invasion; and on application of the legislature, or of the executive (when the legislature cannot be convened) against domestic violence. [Article IV, Section 4]

The precise meaning of this clause is a bit unclear. Although some might argue that it pertains only to invasions by a foreign force or large-scale, violent uprisings, the language appears to be much broader. In fact, the clause seems to require the federal government to monitor the states to insure that their respective governments are in fact behaving as "republics."

What is a "republican form of government"? Definitions of this concept vary to some degree but the common characteristic is a decision-making process by delegated decision makers who are ultimately selected by membership vote. The United States government is a "republic" in that the members do not participate directly in any decision making. Instead, the members select most decision makers by membership vote. These decision makers then make most necessary decisions but also select other decision makers to make certain decisions. Ultimately, however, the entire decision-making process is answerable to the members.

Overall, it seems that the clause obligates the federal government to insure that states continue to use delegated decision-making processes that are ultimately answerable to the members of each state. The parameters of this obligation, however, are entirely unclear.[1]

In any event, the clause represents a fairly clear paternalistic objective within the Constitution. If a state for instance transforms into a tyranny, presumably the federal government is obligated to intervene and restore a republic in the state. On the other hand, if a state's decision-making process is making poor decisions, the federal government probably has no duty to act.

MEMBERSHIP

The Constitution certainly did not address every possible issue. One perplexing issue in the text of the original Constitution is membership. Specifically, who were the original members to the alliance? Were the members the states, the individual persons living in each state, or both? There are no easy answers to these questions.

Evidence that the Members are the States

The name of the alliance ("The United States of America") implies that the members were the states themselves. Otherwise the alliance would have been called something like, "The United *People* of America." Further, the Constitution was drafted by delegated representatives from each state and each state accepted or "ratified" the Constitution, rather than the individual persons of each state. In addition, the Constitution's rules governing the admission of new members pertain only to the admission of new states. Briefly, the Constitution provides that Congress might admit new states, no proposed new state that borders an existing state might be admitted without that border state's approval, and existing states might not split themselves into two or more states. There is no provision about admitting individual persons as members.[2]

---

[1] When the Civil War ended, the federal government took control of the confederate states and imposed rule over them, until each state was slowly readmitted to the United States. The federal government's authority arguably was exercised under this clause.

[2] The fact that the Constitution imposes constraints on admitting new members corresponds to the concept that membership in an alliance is not always open to all comers. Instead, an alliance will admit a new member only if there is a perceived value associated with the admission.

Evidence that the Members are the Individual Persons

On the other hand, the Constitution's Preamble refers to "the people" as the establishers of the Constitution. Moreover, the Constitution uses the term "citizen" to refer to certain individual persons, although it does not elucidate what this term in fact means. Further, the Bill of Rights largely focuses upon protecting individual persons from the powers of the federal government, instead of shielding states from federal abuse.

Resolution of the Conflict

Although reasonable minds might disagree, the most suitable answer is to consider the original members to be only the states. Under this framework, the federal government was an alliance of alliances. The individual persons were members of their respective state alliances and were derivative members of the federal government.

Individual persons were referenced in the Constitution because they were the ultimate parties in interest in the entire arrangement. The objective common to all state alliances was to secure a larger alliance with other states to pursue objectives where a combined effort was advantageous. In securing this larger alliance, each state was ultimately seeking to attain an objective desired by, and of benefit to, its individual members. In effect, the states were separate, collective bargaining units that negotiated on behalf of their members. As a result, the states bound themselves (that is, the states) to the Constitution in order to secure an arrangement that ultimately benefited the individual members of each state.

The framers of the Constitution underscored in the Preamble that the fundamental object of the Constitution was to benefit the individual members of each state. Specifically, the Preamble recited that it is the "people" that are establishing the Constitution. At the same time, the reality of the matter was that only the states were accepting the obligations of the Constitution.

As for the individual rights contained within the Constitution and the Bill of Rights, the states recognized that the new federal government would have extensive dealings and interactions with the members of each state. As a result, the states took care to insert numerous provisions into the Constitution to protect the individual members. Overall, when the Constitution was first enacted, the individual persons were members (that is, citizens) of their respective alliances (that is, the states) which were in turn members of the larger alliance (that is, the United States).

As will be discussed subsequently, the nature of membership in the federal government has undergone sizeable changes since the Constitution was first put into place. In today's world, the members of the federal government appear to be both the states *and* the individual citizens of the states.

Who are the Members of the States

A related and intriguing question is who were the members of the states? That is, were all of the individuals living within each state an actual member of that state?

The answer is that many of these individuals were not members. For instance, slaves residing in the south undoubtedly were not members of the state alliance. And women were probably not members as they were not allowed to vote. Further, many states restricted voting eligibility to land owners or other propertied classes. As such, when the United States was formed, the membership of most states was not inclusive and was instead limited to only certain classes of individuals. As the United States grew and evolved, the doors of membership were opened to more and more classes of persons.

CHAPTER 26

The Early Days and the Civil War

In its early days, the federal government underlying the United States was of extremely limited power. Most individuals saw individual effort and outsourcing as the primary means of attaining desired objectives. If an individual conceived of a governmental alliance pursuing a particular objective, it was almost always a local government or state government. Simply put, most individuals did not expect much from the federal government.

In the 1860s, the United States was ripped apart by the Civil War. After the war ended, several amendments were passed which radically altered the nature of the federal government and its relationship with the state governments. This concept will be explored in this chapter.

SIX MECHANISMS FOR THE ATTAINMENT OF OBJECTIVES

After the Constitution was ratified and the United States came into effect, most individuals residing in the United States had various methods available to achieve objectives that they desired. These can be categorized into six areas.[1]

1) Individual Direct Effort

Individual direct effort achieved most objectives at this time. By direct effort, the individuals attained the objectives through their own personal labors and endeavors. For instance, most individuals (or families) produced much of their own food,

---

[1] Not all of these mechanisms were available to all individuals living in the United States. For instance, many individuals were excluded from membership in some of the alliances discussed.

constructed their own houses, made many of their tools and implements, sewed probably all of their clothes, prepared all of their food, usually defended themselves against attackers, and so on.

2) Individual Outsourced Efforts

Outsourced efforts were used at times. Typically, outsourced efforts consisted of tasks that were highly specialized, difficult to perform, and/or time consuming to do individually. Examples of outsourcing included blacksmithing, shoe making, furniture, education, medicine, and law.

A person outsourced efforts to such industries when he would rather pay for these individuals to attain the objectives, opposed to attempting to do the work himself. Generally speaking, city dwellers outsourced many more endeavors than country folk.

3) Small Alliances

Individuals often entered a variety of single objective alliances based upon implied or short-lived and vague express accords. These alliances usually related to small endeavors such as barn raising, agricultural activities, and other labor-intensive efforts. Occasionally, individuals formed business partnerships to combine their resources towards a business end.

In addition, nearly everyone was a member of various religious alliances such as churches. Churches typically sought to attain objectives relating to Morality (religious instruction) and Charity & Justice. Some education was provided through church-based alliances as well.

Further, most everyone participated in extensive alliances that pursued the internal objective of Customs. As discussed in Chapter 8, customs are always based upon implied accords and few members, if any, actually recognize that the customs they adhere to form the basis of an alliance. In the early United States, the customs essentially were informal rules regarding interactions between neighbors. Specific objectives typically included matters such as loaning things to neighbors, not being a nuisance to neighbors, holding open doors, and so on. If individuals failed to exhibit the conduct required for by the custom (that is, provide the requisite contribution), other alliance members effectively ostracized these non-contributing individuals from the benefits of the alliance.

4) Local Governmental Alliances

Most individuals were members of some sort of local government alliance. Typically, these were cities, counties, or both. These local governments sought to obtain objectives such as defense against aggressors (for example, constables or sheriffs), public works (for example, meeting halls, commons areas, and street construction and maintenance), and mitigation of catastrophe (for example, volunteer fire efforts).

Membership in these local government alliances was not open to all. Women, children, and slaves were excluded. Usually, the poor and drifters were excluded as well. Often, membership was essentially limited to those individuals who supplied contribution (that is, paid taxes on land and property).

Many local governmental entities were not true alliances. At times, a single individual (or a small group of allied individuals) could rule a town. This individual or small group could turn the decision-making process governing the town into a tyranny whose sole purpose was to serve the interests of the governing individual or group. Such tyrannies were rarely recognized and were therefore illusory alliances (where the ruse of an alliance was furthered). At other times, the decision-making process of a town might be only partially compromised so that it instead constituted a semi-alliance.

5) State Alliances

Consistent with the nature of objectives, the state alliances pursued objectives that either: (i) could not be achieved by a local government or (ii) a state government could achieve more efficiently or effectively. Some of these endeavors overlapped with actions taken by local governments. Conflicts were usually resolved with the entity best suited to tackle the objective taking responsibility for it.

All states pursued Law-Compelled Objectives including protection of the person, property laws, and enforcement of promises. States established and administered a court system to adjudicate the various criminal and civil disputes. This court system was usually tiered where there was at least a trial court and one appellate court. The states typically instituted law enforcement to keep the peace and prosecute accused criminals. The states usually created and administered prison or jails.

States sometimes pursued the objective of Generation of Prosperity. For instance, some states instituted measures favorable to a local industry in an effort to make all citizens profitable.

6) Federal Government Alliance

Originally, the federal government was an entity of extremely limited power. In the early days of the United States, it really did not undertake many actions. Derivative members of the federal government rarely looked at it to attain many objectives. Instead, these derivative members relied upon the five other mechanisms noted above.

As a practical matter, the objectives pursued by the federal government were restricted largely to:

- *Defense against Aggressors / Offense against Non-Members*—These were attained with various means including the army, navy, militia, and diplomacy.

- *Law-Compelled Objectives and "Law" Composite Objectives*—Examples included uniform regulation of interstate commerce, patent and copyright laws, bankruptcy laws, weights and measures standards, coinage and counterfeit laws, criminal laws relating only to purely federal issues such as the postal system, and the court system.

- *Cooperative*—The primary instance here was the federal postal system.

- *Paternalistic*—The only example was the obligation to guarantee a republican government to every state.

Summary

Overall, in the early days of the United States, individuals obtained their desired objectives through a mix of these various individual efforts and alliance-based efforts. In general, individuals looked to the various governments only to attain specific, limited areas of objectives. Most objectives desired by individuals were satisfied through their own efforts or through small, non-governmental alliances.

This arrangement largely continued in place from 1788 until the outbreak of the American Civil War. The Civil War took place between 1861 and 1865 and substantially altered the nature of the federal government and its relationship to individuals and the states.

THE CAUSES OF THE CIVIL WAR

Why did the Civil War occur? Historians have debated this topic for many decades. But the answer seems quite simple. The seceding Southern states saw a viable alternative alliance to the United States. That alternative was an alliance composed of only Southern slaveholding states.

Why were Southern states contemplating an alternative alliance? The answer appears to be that, by 1861, the Northern and Southern states were no longer in agreement regarding objectives for the United States to pursue. As the nation aged, the overall perceived value attributed to the alliance by the Southern states slowly declined. This decline cumulated in the conclusion by Southern states that an alternative alliance composed of only Southern states was preferable to the United States.

Decline in the Threat Posed by Europe

A primary reason for the decline in the perceived value of the United States lay in the diminishing threat posed by Europe and in particular Great Britain. At the time the United States was created in 1776, a single overriding objective united the various states into an alliance. That objective was Defense against Aggressors (that is, defeat the British military and win independence). After the Revolutionary War was won, apprehension over Great Britain and other European powers continued to prevail. This fear, coupled with a perceived benefit in a federal alliance pursuing other objectives, motivated the formation of the United States.[1]

By 1861, however, the fear of Great Britain and Europe had diminished substantially for many reasons. A very likely reason lies in the Napoleonic wars. For more than a decade, Napoleon waged war across the European continent and devastated existing governmental structures (that is, various forms of combined-effort entities including true alliances, semi-alliances, illusory alliances, and tyrannies). These wars left most European governments either destroyed or in a very weakened stated. At the conclusion of Napoleon's reign in 1815, sizeable instability persisted in Europe which culminated in the numerous European revolutions of 1848. These revolutions served to disrupt the power structures of European combined-effort entities. As a consequence of this disruption, the various European power structures focused their attentions largely upon activities on the European continent.

Another likely reason for this decline in the perceived European threat pertains to the changing relationship with Great Britain. Throughout the early 1800s, Great Britain's textile industry became heavily dependent upon importing Southern cotton. Further, Great Britain engaged in various other forms of trade with the United States. As a result, Great Britain faced strong economic incentives to avoid warfare with the United States.

Overall, the fear of warfare with Europe prevailed in the United States in the early 1800s. The member states saw the United States as the best means of deterring and defending against this threat. In effect, the concern with European warfare constituted strong glue that bound the states together. By 1861, this dominant fear had largely dissipated. As a result, the states attributed little value to the United States and were receptive to alternative arrangements.

Slavery

Rancorous and at times violent debates raged over slavery and whether it should be

---

[1]The concern regarding Great Britain was validated when the United States and Great Britain went to war again in 1812.

abolished. The South was committed to the institution of slavery. The North was divided with a substantial portion of the North being adamantly opposed to slavery and demanding its abolishment. By the 1850s, the debates regarding the slavery reached a boiling point and served to highlight the profound differences in desires possessed by the various states.

Overall Lack of Commonly Desired Objectives

Aside from the issue of slavery, the relationship between the Northern and Southern states became more and more acrimonious throughout the early 1800s. The North and South rarely saw eye to eye on any matter.

A particular contentious area was the objective of Generation of Prosperity. The North embraced restrictive import tariffs in order to shield the United States' fledging industries from foreign competition. The South, in contrast, pushed for lower tariffs in order to increase the United States export of agricultural products. The source of this conflict lay in the fact that the two regions had very different economies. The Southern economy was agricultural and exported large quantities of cotton and other raw materials. The Northern economy was becoming ever increasingly industrialized and needed protection from foreign competition.

Collapse of the Alliance and the Rise of the Confederacy

In 1861, the "mental scales" in the minds of the Southern States that weighed the relative value of the United States tipped in favor of secession. The Southern states concluded that an alternative alliance of only Southern states was preferable and offered a net perceived value over the United States. This alliance as conceived would pursue only objectives that the Southern states desired. It was called the Confederate States of America. The Confederacy was founded upon an express, written accord, had a complex decision-making process, and was similar in structure to the United States.

THE CIVIL WAR

As a consequence of the South's secession, a long and bloody civil war broke out between the North or the "Union" and the South or the "Confederacy." In this conflict, the two opposing alliances were each united behind attaining the interrelated objectives of Defense against Aggressors and Offense against Non-Members.[1]

---

[1] Of course, not all of the states perceived a value in participating in the Civil War. Several states remained neutral and attempted to not fight in the war. In the case of Maryland, this was difficult as a very significant battle occurred in the state.

The North's primary objective was to compel the Southern states back into the United States. The South's primary objective was to defeat the North and attain independence. These objectives were not uniformly or consistently held among the members, or at least the respective derivative members of the Union and the Confederacy. Support for the war seesawed throughout the North. In the South, various regions withdrew from the war effort including the western part of Virginia, which joined the United States in the midst of the war as the state of West Virginia.

The dissensions in both the Union and the Confederacy were the product of individuals disputing the value of the objectives underlying the various alliances. The Northern dissenters contended that that any value associated with having the Southern states in the Union was outweighed by value of the contributed resources (that is, the price of war). Similarly, the Southern dissenters believed either: (i) that the United States was preferable to the Confederacy or (ii) that, while the Confederacy might be a preferable alliance, the price of war required to establish the Confederacy was not worth the perceived value associated with the Confederacy.

Despite the dissensions, the Northern and Southern alliances held together and the war raged from 1861 to 1865. In 1865, the North compelled the unconditional surrender of the South and won the war. The Southern states were occupied by Northern troops and slowly readmitted into the United States in a period termed "Reconstruction." By 1877, Reconstruction had concluded and all the states had been readmitted to the United States.

CHANGES WROUGHT BY THE CIVIL WAR

The Civil War marked substantial changes in the structure of the United States and the federal government. The changes largely were the product of three amendments to the Constitution that were enacted between 1865 and 1870.

The following discussion will address these three amendments in detail. This discussion will demonstrate that the amendments had the following effects upon the federal government and the United States:

- Regulation of the internal operation of the states through the Overlord objective

- Clarification of membership rules governing the federal government alliance

- Imposition of membership rules upon the state alliances

- Growing conception of the federal government alliance as the primary mechanism for attainment of objectives, in contrast to prior views favoring state or local alliances.

AMENDMENT NO. 13—THE PROHIBITION OF SLAVERY

In 1865, slavery was prohibited throughout the United States by the Thirteenth Amendment. Prior to this time, slavery had been an issue subject to regulation by the states only. For instance, the Northern states enacted laws banning slavery since the beginning of the United States. In contrast, the Southern states not only permitted slavery, they enacted laws governing the ownership and sale of slaves and undertook measures to prevent slaves from escaping or rebelling against their enslavement.

The Thirteenth Amendment changed the landscape significantly. No longer was slavery an issue of state control. The Thirteenth Amendment made it a federal issue. The amendment fully forbade slavery from existing in the United States *and* expressly authorized Congress to enact legislation to enforce the ban on slavery.

Motivation for the Amendment?

What was the underlying motivation of this objective? At the time the Thirteenth Amendment was passed, the Southern states had just been conquered and were under occupation by the Northern military. As such, it cannot be said that the Southern states desired the passage of this amendment. Instead, the ban on slavery was an objective sought, by and large, only by the Northern states.

Why did the North desire the Amendment then? What objective was being pursued? The North appeared to be pursuing three classes of objectives. Not all Northerners subscribed to these viewpoints. Some might have adhered to one or two instead of all three.

1) Charity & Justice—The first objective desired by the North was Charity & Justice. The Northern states were concerned with the wellbeing of non-members (that is, the slaves). As such, the Northern states enacted the Thirteenth Amendment to better the situation of the slaves and free them from bondage. Because the Northern states could expect no real benefit from this action and were instead acting to satisfy their subjective concerns for the predicament of others, this objective is best described as being Charity & Justice.

2) Morality—The second objective is Morality including both subsets of (i) religious concerns and (ii) bolstering concerns. Each of these concepts will be discussed separately.

The *religious* concern is similar to the Charity & Justice objective in that the Northern states were concerned with the wellbeing of others. But the religious concern is not identical to Charity & Justice, because the Northern states were looking out for their own wellbeing in pursuing the religious component of the

Morality objective. That is, their motivation was not to help others but to further their own direct welfare.

What is the basis of this belief? Many in the Northern states believed that the institution of slavery was prohibited by religious tenets and that a grave sin was being committed by the United States in allowing slavery to exist within its boundaries. As a consequence of this sinful conduct, these individuals saw the United States as suffering direct negative consequences ultimately imposed by a religious deity or a religious-based structure of the Universe. In effect, the religious deity or cosmic force was punishing the United States as a whole (including the Northern states) for the sin of slavery. To eliminate this state of sin and to avoid its repercussions, the Northern states concluded that slavery had to be abolished.

The *bolstering* concern was a viewpoint that slavery was impairing the virtues of the United States. As a consequence of this corrupting influence, it was felt that the alliance could not function properly. For instance, those states tainted with slavery might grow slothful and therefore would not be able to properly contribute resources. To improve the functioning and efficiency of the alliance, the North concluded that slavery must be eliminated.

3) Offense against Non-Members—In some ways, the ban on slavery can be seen as fulfilling the objective of Offense against Nonmembers. In this regard, slavery was a valuable resource of the Southern states largely because it provided substantial cheap labor. The South exploited this labor for numerous agricultural efforts and in particular cotton. Slaves even played sizeable roles in supporting the Southern armies.[1]

The North had just fought a long and bloody war with the South and probably feared the possibility of another war breaking out. By banning slavery, the North markedly reduced the power of the Southern states and effectively eliminated the possibility of another war. Moreover, many in the North had very negative feelings towards the South at the conclusion of the horrendous and costly war. As such, some might have been motivated by a desire for vengeance against the South. This retribution was attained in part by freeing the slaves.

The Significance of the Thirteenth Amendment

Structurally, the Thirteenth Amendment is significant because of its focus. As discussed earlier, the Constitution largely pertained to the powers of the federal

---

[1]Although the slaves did not fight, they appear to have accompanied the Southern troops and were employed in numerous war-related activities such as building fortifications and camp labor.

government, the restrictions on those powers, and the overall decision-making process. The original Constitution did impose a few obligations on the states (for example, honor the judgments of other states, treat citizens of other states the same, extradite accused criminals wanted by other states, limits on state regulation of interstate trade) but these were extremely limited in scope. The original Constitutional structure of the United States essentially allowed the states to do as they pleased and with little to no federal oversight.

The Thirteenth Amendment substantially changed this situation by shifting attention to the states and activities going on within the states. Specifically, the Thirteenth Amendment authorized the federal government to intervene into an area that was previously exclusively state territory. After 1865, if anyone was enslaved in a particular state, that was now a federal issue. The federal government was authorized to intrude into that state and take whatever measures it deemed appropriate to end the enslavement. This was a radical departure from the constitutional structure existing before the Civil War.

The Shortcomings of the Thirteenth Amendment

It is also interesting to note the limitations of the Thirteenth Amendment. By its express terms, it banned only the institution of slavery and authorized the federal government to utilize means to enforce the ban. But it authorized the federal government to do nothing else.

If individuals were enslaved, the federal government was authorized to intervene and act. But if freed slaves (or anyone else for that matter) were subjected to any other forms of oppressive conduct not rising to the level of slavery, the federal government had no authority to act. It was up to the states to address such matters as they saw fit.

Illustration—In a state, an individual imprisoned ten persons on his property and forced them to do labor. These ten persons were enslaved. After the Thirteenth Amendment, the federal government was empowered to take action and force the individual to free the enslaved persons.

Illustration—In another state, freed slaves were often robbed, beaten, and murdered. The state government did little to stop these crimes from occurring and rarely sought to punish the criminals. In addition, the state did not allow the freed slaves to vote in any elections, own land, or have a fair trial if accused of a crime. These were considered to be purely state matters. The federal government was not authorized to intervene into these areas under the Thirteenth Amendment as they did not rise to the level of slavery.

Overall, the Thirteenth Amendment banned only slavery. Because freed slaves were often subjected to numerous abuses not rising to the level of slavery, the Thirteenth Amendment had many significant gaps. To fill in some of these gaps, the Northern states passed the Fourteenth Amendment.

AMENDMENT NO. 14—THE RADICAL CHANGE

The Fourteenth Amendment was passed in 1868 and marks a fundamental alteration in the structure of the United States. The Thirteenth Amendment, with its authorization to the federal government to regulate a sizeable area of state conduct, was a only small harbinger of the radical change soon to be brought by the Fourteenth Amendment.

Recall the earlier discussion of the subject of membership in the original Constitution. From reviewing the text of the Constitution, it is not entirely clear who were the original members of the alliance comprising the United States. For instance, were the members the states, individual persons living in the states, or both? Although not conclusive, the best viewpoint is to consider the states to be the only members of the United States, with the Bill of Rights being safeguards the states placed in the Constitution to protect their individual members from abuse by the federal government.

When the Civil War ended and the slaves were freed by the Thirteenth Amendment, the status of the freed slaves was up in the air. Clearly, the slaves had to be freed and could not be enslaved again. But what did this freedom mean? Were the freed slaves now "members" of the state they lived in (that is, citizens of the state in which they were originally enslaved)? Or were the freed slaves more like aliens only residing within the state? Could the freed slaves be subjected to abuse and torment, so long as the mistreatment did not rise to the level of slavery?

The Fourteenth Amendment was passed to answer these questions. It is a complex amendment. Section 1 is the crucial part and it addresses two key areas: (i) membership, and (ii) the Overlord objective.

AMENDMENT NO. 14—MEMBERSHIP

The Fourteenth Amendment left no doubts about the topic of membership. The amendment provides in part:

> All persons born or naturalized in the United States, and subject to the jurisdiction thereof, are citizens of the United States and of the State wherein they reside.

This provision makes clear that anyone born in the United States is a "citizen" of both (i) the United States, and (ii) the state where they are living (that is, residing). As such, if a person was physically born in the United States, he is a citizen of the United States. Further, he is a citizen of any state where he resides.

How does this provision resolve uncertainty regarding the membership status of freed slaves? Because almost all freed slaves living in the United States in 1868 had been born in the United States, they fell within the provision and automatically were deemed citizens of both the United States and the state where they resided.[1]

The membership provision of the Fourteenth Amendment is significant for two reasons. First, without the amendment, individual membership in a state was a concern of that state and that state alone. It was up to the states to determine who their members were. The Fourteenth Amendment took this authority away and transferred it to the federal government. The federal government now held the authority to determine who was a citizen of a particular state.

Second, the Fourteenth Amendment clarified the confusion over whether individuals were citizens of the federal government by specifically providing that all individuals born in the United States were "citizens of the United States." This clarification served to chip away at the concept of the federal government constituting an alliance of alliances. It indicated the individuals were now members of two separate alliances: (i) a state government alliance, and (ii) the federal government alliance (that is, the United States). Further, this clarification of membership arguably initiated a trend towards emphasis upon the federal government as the primary alliance to attain objectives desired by individuals, in contrast to the states' role.[2] This trend would grow and grow and continues to this day.

AMENDMENT NO. 14—OVERLORD OBJECTIVE

Recall that an Overlord objective is applicable only where there is an alliance of alliances. The Overlord objective is an internal objective that focuses upon the

---

[1] The importation of slaves into the United States ceased around 1808. Although there were certainly some freed slaves still alive in 1868 who had not been born in the United States, these individuals were the rare exception.

[2] As noted earlier, individuals viewed local governments and state governments as the alliances best suited to address most of their desired objectives (that is, objectives that were appropriate for a combined effort). After the Civil War, the federal government began to be viewed as the more suitable alliance to pursue these objectives.

conduct of the member alliances. The arch-alliance is the "overlord." The overlord alliance watches over the member alliances and imposes a prescribed course of conduct upon them. Just as an alliance of individuals will pursue internal objectives that strive to impose a prescribed course of conduct on the individual members, an overlord alliance seeks to compel the alliance members to follow a certain course of conduct. This prescribed course of conduct relates to the manner in which the member alliances act towards their individual members. Typically, the Overlord objective seeks to protect the interests of the individual members of the alliances. Almost always, this protection is to protect the individuals from abuse by the member alliance.

The Fourteenth Amendment pursues a sizeable Overlord objective. The amendment provides in relevant part:

> No State shall make or enforce any law which shall abridge the privileges or immunities of citizens of the United States; nor shall any State deprive any person of life, liberty, or property, without due process of law; nor deny to any person within its jurisdiction the equal protection of the laws.

This provision is a radical and fundamental alteration of the relationship between the states and the federal government. Prior to its enactment, states had the near unfettered ability to act as their respective decision-making processes deemed appropriate. The Constitution imposed only a few, very limited restrictions upon state actions. The Fourteenth Amendment, however, changed the landscape by placing significant restrictions on every action that a state might take. These restrictions upon state action were remarkable and revolutionary.

What are the restrictions? There are three restrictions on state action. In undertaking any action, a state:

1) May not abridge the **privileges and immunities** of any citizen of the United States;

2) May not deprive any person of life, liberty, or property without **due process of law**; and

3) May not deny any person the **equal protection** of the laws.

How do these restrictions operate? Essentially, any action of a state must be examined to determine whether it violates any of these three restrictions. A state retains sizeable power and authority to act as it sees fit. However, if a state takes an action that violates one of the restrictions, the action is unconstitutional and therefore not permitted. These three restrictions each have different meanings.

AMENDMENT NO. 14—PRIVILEGES AND IMMUNITIES

Recall that the original text of the Constitution (that is, Article IV, Section 2) requires all states to treat citizens from other states the same, subject to certain exceptions. The privileges and immunities restriction presumably restates the obligations of all states to adhere to this obligation. In addition, the language suggests an obligation of a state to allow all citizens to participate in an evenhanded fashion in the endeavors undertaken by a state. For instance, if a state establishes "privileges and immunities," all citizens of that state must be allowed to utilize or otherwise access those "privileges and immunities."

This privilege and immunities provision appears entirely consistent with alliance principles. The fundamental reason for the formation of any alliance is that its members commonly desire an objective and believe that the alliance is the preferred means of attaining that objective. When this objective is attained, all members obviously desired to enjoy in the benefits of the objective. If they are not allowed to reap this reward, they will withdraw from the alliance and it will likely collapse due to lack of contribution. The privilege and immunities clause serves to prevent this result by mandating that all alliance members be allowed to enjoy the benefits of the objectives attained by each state government. The federal government is the overlord that enforces this obligation. As a result, the state alliances should operate properly and avoid collapse.

As a practical matter, however, the privilege and immunities clause has no real role in today's world. The Supreme Court has not attempted to interpret this provision in any meaningful way to date.

AMENDMENT NO. 14—DUE PROCESS

The obligation of due process has been one of the most significant restrictions on the powers and authorities of states. It subjects almost every action of states to "due process" analysis by the federal government. Specifically, before any state acts to deprive anyone of "life, liberty, or property," the state must insure that due process obligations have been satisfied.

What does "due process" mean? There is no easy answer to this question and it has been the subject of hotly contested debates that continue to this day. The subject is extraordinarily complicated to say the least.

Briefly, analysis of the due process restrictions can be subdivided into three areas: (i) procedural rights, (ii) the Bill of Rights protections, and (iii) unspecified rights.

Procedural Rights

In its most basic sense, due process means that individuals are afforded some type of opportunity to explain or defend themselves prior to being deprived of life, liberty, or property. If a state unilaterally deprives a person of life, liberty, or property without first giving them the chance to at least argue against the deprivation in some type of procedural format, the individual's due process rights have been violated.

Bill of Rights

As discussed earlier, the first ten amendments to the Constitution are the Bill of Rights and they originally imposed limitations upon the actions of *only the federal government.*

> *Illustration*—The First Amendment protects freedom of the press. In 1845, a state government shuts down a newspaper business. There was no federal issue. The First Amendment did not protect the newspaper business's freedom of the press from action by a state government.[1]

> *Illustration*—In 1845, the federal government shuts down a newspaper business. This action was unconstitutional. The First Amendment protects the newspaper business from action by the *federal government.*

Following the enactment of the Fourteenth Amendment, most of the Bill of Right protections were applied to actions by the states. How did this result occur? The answer is interpretation of the "due process" language by the Supreme Court. In a variety of cases, the Supreme Court concluded that the Fourteenth Amendment's guarantee of due process incorporates *most* of the Bill of Rights protections.

> *Illustration*—In 1875, a state government shuts down a newspaper business. There is now a federal issue, because the state government's action denies the newspaper business's due process rights. In this regard, a portion of the newspaper business's due process rights is the First Amendment's protection of freedom of the press.

Most of the restrictions in the Bill of Rights are generally applicable to the state governments through the due process clause of the Fourteenth Amendment. In other words, the due process clause can be paraphrased as stating:

---

[1] Most state governments, however, had instituted rights in state constitutions that guaranteed state citizens the right of freedom of the press.

If a state government denies a person the protections afforded by the Bill of Rights, that action is a violation of the due process guaranteed by the Fourteenth Amendment.

Not all protections in the Bill of Rights, however, are applicable to the states. The Supreme Court addresses each right in a case-by-case situation to determine whether it constitutes a due-process right against the states. Examples of restrictions in the Bill of Rights that have been imposed on the states through the Fourteenth Amendment include:

- Freedom of speech

- Freedom of religion

- Right to a jury trial in a criminal case

- Privilege against self incrimination

- Ban of imposing cruel and unusual punishments on convicts

- Right to an attorney

To review, the Fourteenth Amendment requires all states to provide any person with due process of law before depriving them of life, liberty, or property. The Supreme Court has considered what "due process" means and found that it includes many of the protections included in the Bill of Rights.

Unspecified Rights

At various times over its history, the Supreme Court has found that a particular action of a state violated "due process." These decisions are significant because the Supreme Court did not base the decision upon (i) a denial of procedural process, or (ii) locate a right within the Bill of Rights and graft it onto the due process obligations of states.

Instead, the Court reviewed various parts of the Constitution, the history of the United States, and policy concerns. After doing this, the Supreme Court concluded that certain unspecified rights were in the Constitution, although they were not clearly specified within its text. And the Court found that it would be a violation of due process for a state to act contrary to these unspecified rights.

For instance, the Supreme Court found in 1905 that the Constitution protected a "liberty to contract" and that was part of the due process restrictions on states. As such, no state could pass legislation that interfered with the freedom to contract.

Illustration—A state passed a law mandating that laborers may not work more than 60 hours per week. This law was found to violate business owners' due process rights. In this regard, the Supreme Court determined that businesses and laborers have a fundamental due process right to negotiate over how many hours are to be worked and that no state might interfere with that right by mandating a maximum amount of hours to be worked in a week.

This right to contract was subsequently discarded by the Supreme Court in the 1930s as a misreading of the Constitution. As a result, legislation regulating business-labor relationships increased markedly as well as other types of legislation regulating business activities.[1]

In more recent years, the Supreme Court has used a similar reasoning process to conclude that the Constitution recognizes a "right to privacy." This right to privacy is probably better described as a right to personal autonomy. This right to personal autonomy essentially affords one the ability to make important decisions about one's life without governmental interference or regulation.[2]

Illustration—A state government forbids the usage of contraceptions. This action is found to violate due process because all citizens have a right to decide if they want to use contraceptions.

Illustration—A state government forbids abortions. This action is found to violate due process because all citizens have a right to decide if they want to have abortions.

---

[1] Arguably, the ultimate cause of these interpretations of the due process clause lies in the Generation of Prosperity objective. In 1905, free-market concepts were seen as the best mechanism of generating prosperity. As such, the Supreme Court appears to have interpreted the due process clause in a manner thought to further economic prosperity. In the 1930s, the country was in the midst of the Great Depression. Free-market concepts were out of vogue and socialist/controlled economy theories were in style. As a result, the Supreme Court seems to have found that the 1905 interpretation of due process actually did not further prosperity and should be overruled.

[2] The creation of the right to privacy/autonomy by the Supreme Court appears to track prevailing viewpoints in the same manner as the liberty to contract right followed earlier prevailing viewpoints. Specifically, the laws that were negated by the right to privacy/autonomy were essentially means to attain Morality-based objectives. The decisions of the Supreme Court appear to be reflective of a determination that Morality was no longer a suitable objective to be pursued by governments. These decisions were made in the 1960s and 1970s and appear to correspond to the prevailing sentiments to the effect that Morality was not an objective properly suited to government action.

The Court's interpretation of the due process clause to determine unspecified rights has been very controversial and has lead to many heated disputes. The critics charge that the Court's finding of unspecified rights grants the Court far too much power to trump decision-making processes of the states (and Congress). Instead, the critics argue, such unspecified rights should be specifically adopted into the Constitution by the process of amending the Constitution. The supporters of unspecified rights recognized that the Court should not have unfettered power to find any right and contend that the Court has not been creating wholly new rights. Instead, the supporters assert, the Court has only reinterpreted existing rights in light of new circumstances and that such a practice is authorized by the Constitution.

AMENDMENT NO. 14—EQUAL PROTECTION OF THE LAWS

Like the due-process obligations, the equal protection of the laws provision has been very difficult to interpret and has given rise to many controversies. By its text, the clause mandates that a state must provide all persons "with equal protections of the laws."

What does that mean? The language suggests an obligation of a state to allow all citizens to participate in an evenhanded fashion in the endeavors undertaken by a state. That is, no state might limit an undertaking to a group or segment of citizens. This reasoning indicates that (i) the benefits of state action must be distributed equally among all citizens, and (ii) the contribution necessary to fuel the state action (and attain the objective) must be borne equally by all citizens. These concepts correspond to alliance principles discussed in Part I.

The Supreme Court has struggled with the meaning of the equal protection clause. Briefly, the Supreme Court has concluded that "equal protection of the laws" means that a state government might not treat one group differently from other groups, *without a rational and legitimate reason for doing so.*

The Supreme Court's interpretation and application of the equal protection clause has varied widely over the years. Many of the cases have related to state laws segregating the races. In 1896, the Supreme Court interpreted the clause as mandating equality in distribution of the benefits of state action. That is, if a state acted, it could segregate and separate by race the benefits of the action, provided that all citizens ultimately received an equal benefit. This interpretation was termed the "separate but equal" doctrine. In 1954, the Supreme Court discarded this doctrine as a misinterpretation of the equal protection clause. In its place, the Court adopted a new approach of balancing the relevant interests to determine whether the equal protection obligation has been met.

Nowadays, in performing equal-protection analysis, the court typically weighs the objective pursued by the state against the detriment inflicted upon the targeted group. The Court also usually considers whether other means exist that could attain the objective with less or no harm to the targeted group. The gist is that the Court is to analyze the reasoning process of the state and determine if it appears sound and legitimate.

The degree of analysis that the Court engages in depends upon the group targeted by the law. In general, most all laws pass equal-protection analysis so long as there is some plausible basis for distinguishing between two groups. Laws typically fail equal-protection analysis only when a group of persons with an immutable trait is singled out for special treatment by the law in question. Groups with these immutable traits include groups based upon race and national origin. Groupings based upon gender and other traits sometimes fall within this area as well.

Illustration—A state imposes higher income tax rates on individuals with higher rates of income. The individuals paying higher taxes complain, asserting that the tax laws are not being applied equally. The law will pass equal protection analysis so long as there is a plausible basis for it. It should be underscored that this analysis is very limited. The Court will not delve into the issue in any significant detail.

Illustration—A state provides subsidies to a certain business but not others. The businesses not getting the subsidies complain, asserting that they are not being allowed to participate in the benefits of the state action. The law will pass equal protection analysis so long as there is a plausible basis for it.

Illustration—A state passes a law providing preferential treatment to individuals within a certain racial category. This type of a law is treated with great suspicion and the courts are to strictly scrutinize the law. As a general rule, such laws will survive equal protection analysis only if (i) the purpose of the law is extremely compelling, and (ii) there are no other means available to attain the objective.

The rationale underlying the Supreme Court's equal protection decisions seem to correspond with alliance principles. As noted above, the equal protection clause appears to mandate that (i) the benefits of state action be distributed equally among all citizens, and (ii) the contribution necessary to fuel the state action (and attain the objective) be borne equally by all citizens. The Supreme Court arguably has taken a relaxed interpretation of these two points. Instead of applying the two points to any and all actions taken by a state, the Supreme Court instead applies them only actions relating to suspect classes noted above (for example, race, gender, and so on). The underlying rationale appears to be that decision-making processes of the state governments can be trusted, in almost all situations, to (i) distribute the benefits of state action equally among all citizens, and (ii) compel contribution equally from all citizens. The only situations where the states are not to be trusted are laws relating to certain classes of members. Laws touching upon these classes will therefore be scrutinized closely.

By its text, the equal-protection clause applies only to the states, and not the federal government. As such, can the federal government deny individuals the equal protection of the laws since there is no specific provision limiting federal action? The Supreme Court has concluded that the federal government is subject to equal-protection restrictions, although there is no specific provision applicable to the federal government in the Constitution. As a result, both actions by the states and the federal government are subject to the same equal-protection analysis.

AMENDMENT NO. 14—UNDERLYING RATIONALE

Having summarized the Fourteenth Amendment, it is appropriate to reiterate its nature. With the passage of the Fourteenth Amendment, the states still held substantial authority to do as they felt appropriate in governing their respective territories and citizens. In fact a state was free to enact any legislation and undertake any action so long as the endeavor did not violate the restrictions of the Fourteenth Amendment (and a few other limitations of the Constitution discussed earlier). Thus, the Fourteenth Amendment essentially served as a screening process on state action to insure that a particular endeavor did not contravene a basic fundamental right of a state citizen. Under this framework, for instance, a state could undertake an action that might appear unfair or unreasonable, but it would be constitutionally permissible so long as it did not violate (i) the privileges and immunities clause, (ii) the due process requirement, and (iii) the equal protection restriction.

In interpreting the Fourteenth Amendment's restrictions, the Supreme Court has taken care to afford the states substantial discretion in undertaking endeavors. The Supreme Court has never interpreted the Fourteenth Amendment as imposing common-sense or prudence analysis on state action. States remain free to make good, mediocre, and bad decisions. The only requirement is that the states' endeavors do not trample a fundamental right of their citizens guaranteed by the Fourteenth Amendment. Thus, the states can be viewed as actors holding substantial power, subject to the narrow and limited review of an overlord (that is, the federal government).

An interesting aspect of the Fourteenth Amendment is its uniformity in application. The purpose behind the Fourteenth Amendment was obvious. It was to protect newly freed slaves from abuse by states. The Fourteenth Amendment could have been fashioned to specifically reference newly freed slaves and limit it application to this class of citizens. But the amendment is not race or class specific. And it is not tied to particular actions or endeavors by states. Instead, the amendment is open and uniform. It applies to all citizens of the United States and all actions by state governments.

This uniformity is consistent with the rationale underlying alliances. Specifically, members of an alliance choose to follow an objective only if the objective is desired by all members. In the case of the Fourteenth Amendment, the amendment itself was presumably viewed as an objective that would benefit all citizens of the United States by (i) providing some degree of Overlord protection against abuse by a state, and (ii) furthering a Charity & Justice objective of insuring that other citizens (for example, newly freed slaves) were afforded basic protections against abuse.

AMENDMENT NO. 15—VOTING RIGHTS

The Thirteenth Amendment restricted states from allowing slavery to exist within their borders. The Fourteenth Amendment limited states from undertaking endeavors that violated certain basic fundamental rights. Although these measures did much to protect newly freed slaves from abuse, an important element was missing—voting.

Notwithstanding the Thirteenth and Fourteenth Amendment, the states were still free to fashion their own voting and election rules. And this was problematic because newly freed slaves were often excluded from the voting process. Why? The states still held substantial power to govern their territory and citizens. The federal government limited this power by prohibiting slavery in any state. And the federal government limited this power by requiring all states to not violate the rights in the Fourteenth Amendment. But the states still held the power to control the election process and voting.

Presumably, voting and elections were subject to the Fourteenth Amendment. And any state action that prevented newly freed slaves from voting would violate at least the equal protection clause. However, to insure participation in the voting process, the Fifteenth Amendment was passed in 1870. The amendment provides in part:

> The right of citizens of the United States to vote shall not be denied or abridged by the United States or by any State on account of race, color, or previous condition of servitude.

The amendment also authorized Congress to enact legislation to enforce this restriction.

With the passage of the Fifteenth Amendment, states were subject to another limitation on their authority. States still retained substantial power, even in formulating voting and election rules. The only real limitation of the Fifteenth Amendment was race. The states remained free to deny voting privileges on other bases such as gender or age.[1]

RESULTS OF THE CIVIL WAR AMENDMENTS

The primary reasons for the passage of the Thirteenth, Fourteenth, and Fifteenth Amendments were (i) to abolish slavery and (ii) to offer membership in the United States alliance to newly freed slaves. The amendments were entirely successful with regard to abolishing slavery. After the passage of the Thirteenth Amendment, slavery was wiped from the face of the United States and has never returned. This almost overnight change is noteworthy in light of the fact that slavery had been entrenched in the Southern states for centuries.

The amendments, however, attained mixed results at offering membership to newly freed slaves. On the positive side, the Civil War amendments granted citizenship to a newly-freed slave in both the United States alliance and in the state alliance where he resided. This membership, however, was largely in name only. It is important to not exaggerate the point and contend that the newly freed slaves received no benefits whatsoever. The applicable governmental alliances did provide the new newly freed slaves with certain alliance benefits. These benefits, though, were limited. The newly freed slaves undeniably were not afforded the full range of alliance benefits.

After the passage of the Civil War amendments, the best way to describe the status held by the newly freed slaves is that they constituted second-class members. They were technically citizens of the governmental alliances and did enjoy some of the benefits of citizenship. Nonetheless, they were denied a sizeable number of the benefits provided to first-class citizens.

This second-class status undeniably continued until at least the 1950s. In that decade as well as the 1960s, the United States alliance and many state alliances instituted new changes and measures designed to insure that the ancestors of the newly freed slaves were afforded all benefits of membership. This topic and others will be discussed in greater detail in the next chapter.

---

[1] In 1920, the Nineteenth Amendment was passed allowing women to vote. The language of the amendment was identical to the Fifteenth Amendment. The only difference was that "sex" was substituted in the place of "race, color, or previous condition of servitude."

CHAPTER 27

1870s to the 1980s

This chapter will quickly move through a roughly one-hundred year period of time in United States history. This review will be cursory and will omit many important events and topics. The point is to generalize regarding alliance trends and developments in this period of time.

1870s TO 1900

This period of time was marked by the substantial economic and geographic expansion of the United States. Several alliance trends occurred during this time.

Prevalence of Individualism

During this time period, individual effort was seen as the primary mechanism for attaining most objectives. Although the federal government had grown sizably during the Civil War, it stopped growing, or even retracted, at the conclusion of the fighting. Following the war, most Americans seemed empowered to create their own future through individual action or through non-governmental alliance efforts. Small businesses and individual farms flourished. Because of the optimistic view of human nature and the belief that individuals could fend for themselves, pursuit of the Paternalistic objective declined in this era.

Westward Expansion

During this time, the actions of federal government and local governments largely focused upon facilitating expansion into the new western frontier. A portion of these undertakings include the pursuit of the objective of Offense against Non-Members. In this case, the non-members were the Native Americans and the objective was to remove them from certain lands. In some cases, American settlers tried to live in peace with the Native Americans but were raided and attacked by them. In these situations, the governmental alliances pursued the objective of Defense against Aggressors. The Native Americans were viewed as the aggressors. Ultimately, the Native Americans lost these conflicts and were conquered. Subsequently, individual Native Americans were admitted to the United States as members or "citizens." Interestingly, most Native Americans are also members of their ancestors' tribes, which constitute alliances as well. The United States recognizes many of these tribes as independent entities existing within the geographic confines of the United States.

Law-Compelled Objectives

The objective of Enforcement of Promises became very important in this era. With the rise of numerous commercial activities, the need for reliable and effective rules governing commerce became paramount.

Generation of Prosperity

During this era, the free-market approach was viewed as the best means of attaining economic prosperity. As a consequence, there was very little governmental regulation of the market. The virtues of capitalism, industry, and manufacturing were extolled. Although socialist concepts were gaining strength in Europe at this time, they had marginal effects upon the United States. In fact, free-market concepts were so grounded in the prevailing views that the Supreme Court interpreted the due-process clause of the Fourteenth Amendment as guaranteeing a freedom to contract without governmental interference. (This decision was later overruled in the 1930s.)

Labor Unions

During this period, workers began to see the value of organizing. Labor unions became popular in this era.

Mitigation of Catastrophe

Governmental alliances continued to pursue this objective in terms of guarding against group catastrophes (for example, floods). Governments, however, did not pursue the objective in terms of guarding against personal catastrophes (for example, poverty, disability, and so on). Individual effort was seen as the best means of guarding against such calamities. Alternatively, individuals were able to enter non-governmental alliances to attain this goal. These non-governmental alliances were the various mutual insurance companies that flourished during this era.

Charity & Justice

Governmental alliances did not pursue this objective. It was left to individuals to pursue on their own or through non-governmental alliances. As a result, charitable alliances did become popular during this era.

Morality

Governmental alliances were heavily influenced by both aspects of this objective. The first aspect is the Religious component of Morality. Many undertakings of governmental alliances were sought to further, at least indirectly, Religious concerns. The second aspect is the Bolstering component. Governmental alliances frequently undertook endeavors for the purpose of fashioning healthier citizens. The banning of alcohol in many regions of the country is a classic example of an undertaking designed to further both Religious and Bolstering concerns.

1900 TO THE 1930s

During this era, the objectives from the previous era carried over but were modified and refined to meeting changing desires and perceptions.

Governmental Regulation and Intervention

Although individualism and free-market concepts continued to dominate from 1900 to the 1930s, governmental alliances embraced exceptions to these bedrock principles. In this regard, individual effort continued to be seen as usually constituting the best mechanism for attaining most desires. Further, the free market was still held to be a superior means of increasing material prosperity. Nonetheless, governmental alliances began regulating certain aspects of business activity. This trend was often called the "Progressive Movement" and included goals such as regulating food preparation, restricting child labor, restricting monopolies and anti-competitive behavior, legislation favoring struggling farmers, and protection for the indebted. These goals are probably best seen as composite objectives constituting combinations of objectives such as Cooperative, Charity & Justice, Morality, Paternalism, Leveling, Mitigation of Catastrophe, and Law-Compelled Objectives. Underlying all of these endeavors was a perception that governmental action offered more net advantages than both individual action (including individually outsourced action) and non-governmental alliance action.

Generation of Prosperity

As just noted, free-market concepts prevailed in this era. A particularly notably exception, however, was the Federal Reserve Act of 1913. This legislation was passed in response to several financial crises thought to have been caused by the private banking system. The result of the legislation was a system of federal banks that could insure an adequate supply of money through loans to commercial banks. This system was perceived as fostering greater prosperity and forestalling panics that occasionally arose when the cash in a particular region was low. This banking system is still in place today. The loaning practice of the Federal Reserve

Bank heavily influences the prevailing interest rates in the United States and is thought to have a sizeable effect upon the economies of both the United States and the World.

Leveling Concepts

During this era, some began to view the capitalists as "robber barons" that were appropriating most of the material wealth of the country. As a consequence, many advocated the objective of Leveling, which required some type of limit on the wealth that one could possess. Others advocated pursuing the objective of Offense against Non-Members. These proponents saw the new corporate titans as non-members that needed to be stripped of their material wealth. Although these leveling concepts were often popular, they appear to never have been directly enacted into legislation. Instead, they influenced other types of objectives.

Decision-Making Process Reform

In 1913, the Seventeenth Amendment was passed which mandated the direct election of U.S. Senators. This reversed the prior practice whereby state legislatures selected the Senators. This change was thought to put more decision-making power in the individual members of the states (that is, derivative members of the United States) and to take such power from small, powerful alliances that tended to control state legislatures.

Morality Efforts

In 1919, the Eighteenth Amendment was enacted which banned the manufacture, sale, and transportation of intoxicating liquors in the United States. This law was thought to further both the Religious and Bolstering aspects of the Morality objective.

Expanded Membership

In 1920, the Nineteenth Amendment was passed which guaranteed the right of all women to vote in elections. This entitlement applied to all federal, state, and local elections. Due to its application to state and local elections, it has elements of the Overlord objective.

Rise of Executive and Committee Decision Makers

Governmental alliance began employing these types of delegated decision-making processes during this time period. In most situations, the processes were used in fulfilling administrative tasks associated with governmental alliances. These arrangements came to be called "bureaucracies."

Conservation

Under the leadership of President Theodore Roosevelt, the federal government began pursuing the objective of Conservation by seeking to protect natural lands from development and exploitation. This largely new objective was spurred by recognition that westward expansion and development jeopardized the environment.

World War I

This war lasted from 1914 through 1918. The United States refused to join the war until 1917. Initially, Americans saw the war as a European affair and that America had no interest in contributing resources towards it. This perception changed in 1917 when the German Navy began targeting U.S. ships that were trading with Great Britain. In addition, evidence surfaced that Germany had some intentions of allying with Mexico to invade the United States. These events changed the perception of the war in the eyes of most Americans. Americans saw the Germans as aggressors and joining the war as being necessary to attain the objective of Defense against Aggressors.

1930s TO THE 1980s

This period saw a radical altering of the United States and its governmental alliances. A significant cause was the Great Depression which began in 1929 and probably ended (according to the prevailing viewpoint) when the United States emerged from World War II in 1945. Other causes included World War II, the Cold War, and the substantial prosperity that followed World War II which made numerous governmental undertakings appear viable and affordable.

Generation of Prosperity

The Great Depression was viewed as proof that the free market and capitalism were not the best means of generating prosperity. In the 1930s, a new theory of prosperity generation became popular. This theory held that governmental intervention into the economy with targeted spending and other measures was the best mechanism for attaining prosperity. Although this theory left the free market and capitalism in place to some degree, it substantially reduced their influence and pervasiveness. The result was a mixture of capitalism and centralized governmental control of the economy. During this era, socialist and communist theories were often popular as well but were not particularly influential.[1]

---

[1] Many governmental undertakings in this era have been labeled "socialist" or "communist." Such labels have adequate foundations and are reasonable. Such governmental endeavors, however, could be considered outside of the spheres of Socialism and Communism and as instead constituting limited situations where action by a governmental alliance was

Expansion of Federal Government Power

As noted in an earlier chapter, the U.S. Constitution was viewed as authorizing the federal government to pursue only a limited number of objectives specifically identified in the text of the Constitution. In the 1930s, the Supreme Court held that the Commerce Clause authorized the federal government to undertake any action that had a reasonable relationship to interstate commerce. This finding of Commerce Power radically increased the power and authority of the federal government. The substantial increase in the size of the federal government during this period appears to be directly tied to this new interpretation of the Commerce Clause.

Decline of Individual and Non-Governmental Alliance Efforts

In this era, individual effort lost much of its luster and was not viewed as being very effective at attaining many desires. The same viewpoint also developed with regard to action by non-governmental alliances. As a result, many came to view governmental action as the preferred mechanism for attaining desired goals. Thus, when individuals wanted a particular objective, they typically demanded that it be attained by a governmental alliance.

Decline of Local Government Effort

Similar to the decline in emphasis upon individual effort, there was a decline in the roles played by local governmental alliances in obtaining many objectives. Instead, the federal government was increasingly looked upon as the proper mechanism for pursuing most desired objectives.

Mitigation of Catastrophe / Social Insurance

Governmental alliances began to embrace these objectives as legitimate undertakings. In the 1930s, the federal government enacted Social Insurance programs such as Social Security. In the 1960s, a number of other Social Insurance programs arose such as Welfare, Medicare, Medicaid, and Food Stamps. Similar programs were enacted by state governmental alliances. The underlying rationale of these programs was that governmental alliances could effectively insure individuals against

---

seen as offering net advantages over actions by individuals or private alliances. For instance, a Social Insurance program could be viewed as socialist or it could be viewed as a limited exception to a presumption that individual effort was always preferable in guarding against personal catastrophes. In addition, a Social Insurance program could also be viewed as an appeasement undertaking furthering the objective of Defense against Aggressors. Under this perspective, the "aggressors" were the socialists and communists and the Social Insurance program was employed to placate these groups and prevent a revolution.

financial calamities. As discussed earlier, Charity & Justice rationales and Defense against Aggressors (that is, appeasement) tend to underlie Social Insurance programs. These concerns probably motivated the enactment of some of these programs. As such, the Social-Insurance undertakings of this era are probably best viewed as composite objectives.

Charity & Justice

This objective developed substantially during this era. In the past, governmental alliances rarely or never pursued this objective, and every governmental undertaking was intended to directly benefit the citizens of the governmental alliance. After World War II ended in 1945, the federal government began various international undertakings where the primary objective was to aid non-members living in other countries. Like Social Insurance, the international Charity & Justice undertakings are probably best viewed as constituting composite objectives. For instance, aside from reducing pain and suffering in foreign countries, international aid programs were thought to reduce the likelihood of destabilizing revolutions occurring in other countries. Such revolutions were perceived as tending to harm the economic and security interests of the United States. As a result, these programs can be seen as pursuing the objectives of both Defense against Aggressors and Charity & Justice.

Paternalism

From the 1870s to 1930 or so, most members were confident that individuals were able to look out for their best interests. During the 1930s to the 1980s, this confidence eroded substantially and governmental alliances began pursuing various Paternalistic endeavors. The basic assumption underlying these actions was that individuals could not adequately look out for themselves. Safety endeavors are a good example. Governmental alliances enacted numerous safety-based laws which effectively prevented individuals from undertaking certain acts, even if the individuals clearly desired to take such acts. Examples include seatbelt and helmet laws, public health campaigns (for example, anti-smoking), and the banning or regulation of various leisure activities that entailed serious risks of injury or death. Other examples include workplace regulations that set certain mandatory floor requirements for the employer-employee relationship that could not be negotiated around (for example, set payday rules, overtime, child labor, and job safety).

Law-Compelled Objectives

This era saw an explosion in Law-Compelled Objectives. The changes are so numerous and profound that this discussion will be cursory.

Protection of the Person—A major development was in the area of Protection of the Person. Following World War II (that is, 1945), legal theories offering protections to the person from injury expanded substantially. These changes included new civil lawsuit claims such as strict liability for defectively manufactured or designed products, failure to adequately warn of dangers, unsafe premises, and discrimination in employment on the basis of legally protected categories (for example, race, gender, age, national origin, and so on). The changes also included new types of injuries such as mental anguish. The cause of these changes appears to be the substantial prosperity of the United States following World War II. In this regard, it was thought that the United States could easily afford to pay for the costs caused by the expanded liabilities (for example, the contribution of resources was worth the resulting enhanced safety). These changes all pertained to civil lawsuit claims. At the same time, however, criminal laws were refined considerably to meet changing circumstances.

Protection of Property—In contrast to the expansion of Protection of the Person, the pursuit of Protection of Property declined substantially in this era. Prior to the 1930s, the prevailing view of property rights held that ownership was essentially absolute. Once a person "owned" something, that property was his and could not be taken away or interfered with in any fashion. As the new era progressed, this view declined and numerous exceptions arose. These exceptions essentially consisted of allowing governmental alliances substantially more flexibility to regulate the usages of property and to seize properties under a greater number of circumstances. These diminutions in property protections were often thought to be necessary to obtain other objectives such as Law-Compelled Objectives, Conservation, Charity & Justice, and Mitigation of Catastrophe / Social Insurance.

Enforcement of Promises—Commerce continued to expand in this time period. As a result, new and more complex rules were required to facilitate commercial transactions. Many of these endeavors were composite objectives. For instance, the Enforcement of Promise objective was often intertwined with the Generation of Prosperity objective such that the law would seek to enforce promises in a manner that increased prosperity. Another fusion was Enforcement of Promises and Paternalism where the law would strive to assist individuals not sophisticated in business to fend for themselves in commercial transactions (for example, debts, usury, deceptive schemes). At times, Morality and Enforcement of Promises were blended such as to deter individuals from entering transactions inconsistent with Religious or Bolstering concerns.

Predominance of Executive and Committee Decision Makers

Bureaucracies within governmental alliances continued to grow throughout the 1930s through the 1980s. More and more tasks were assigned to bureaucracies and their power became immense. At the same time, the limitations associated with delegated decision makers grew as well. The 1930s also saw a substantial decline in the respect for membership voting as a decision-making process. In Europe, fascist theories of government were prevailing in Germany, Italy, and Spain. [1] By and large, these theories focused upon the need for one executive leader (for example, Hitler, Mussolini, Franco) to make all necessary decisions. Fascist theories did become popular among many in the United States during the 1930s, although they were not put into action.

Morality

This era saw a sizeable decline in the pursuit of Religious concerns but an increase in the pursuit of Bolstering concerns. The decline of Religious concerns was exemplified by the repeal of the Eighteenth Amendment's ban on alcohol. Further, this time period saw an ever-increasing secularization of governmental actions. This change was often driven by the Supreme Court's interpretation of the First Amendment's "establishment" clause. This clause restricts the federal government (and all other governmental alliances through the Fourteenth Amendment) from making laws "respecting an establishment of religion." The Supreme Court tended to interpret this clause as prohibiting any governmental alliance from undertaking almost any actions with religious connotations. The rise of Bolstering objectives was exemplified by governmental alliances pursuing matters such as widespread mandatory public education, educational loans, health initiatives, and other programs intended to make more productive, effective citizens. The Cold War with the Soviet Union appears to have spurred on numerous Bolstering endeavors in order to prove that the United States was superior to the communists. A very important Bolstering concern in this era was the prohibition of narcotics. Although this endeavor has some composite objective aspects (that is, regulation of narcotic use is consistent with a Paternalistic objective), the primary motivation underlying the ban on narcotics appears to be a Bolstering concern. In this regard, it was thought that the United States could not succeed as a nation if its citizens were under the influence of debilitating narcotics.

---

[1] In arguing for adoption of fascism, most fascists used an analogy based upon sticks. Mussolini, for example, frequently pointed out that anyone can snap a single stick with his hands but that, if many sticks are bound together, no one can break them. This analogy arguably is based upon alliance concepts because it relies upon the advantage of individuals combining their resources towards a common goal. (Incidentally, the term "fascist" is derived from the Latin word "fascis," which refers to a bundle of sticks.)

Indirect Attainment

Indirect attainment is a means used to attain an objective. The effort is "indirect" because the objective is achieved through a circuitous or roundabout method. From the 1930s through the 1980s, the use of indirect attainment became more and more common. If a governmental action could be shown to further indirectly a well-accepted objective, that action was likely to be supported by the membership. For instance, many argued in favor of public-works projects not because they were needed but because the money spent on the projects would stimulate the economy and further the objective of Generation of Prosperity. This trend towards use of indirect attainment likely led to corruption as the theory could be used to mask the fact that a government project was actually intended to benefit someone other than the members. The prevalence of the indirect attainment concept was probably tied to the development of Commerce Power because of its focus upon the effects of an action upon interstate commerce.

World War II

This was a very important event in the era. The war began in 1939 but the United States refused to enter the war, believing that it was a European affair. After Pearl Harbor was attacked in 1941, however, the United States saw an interest in fighting and declared war on both Japan and Germany. In joining the war effort, the United States entered into alliance with Great Britain and the Soviet Union. What resulted was a remarkable mobilization of resources through vast, interlocking alliances. The conduct of the United States and its membership was particularly telling. The American citizens saw the seriousness of the war and felt that their lives and futures were in serious jeopardy. In a brief period of time, the United States military went from a state of disrepair to one of massive size, strength, and capability and the war was ultimately won. This result appears to have been attained through the very effective nature of the various alliances making up the United States.

Civil Rights

The 1950s and 1960s saw substantial changes in the area of civil rights. In 1954, the Supreme Court issued its famous opinion of *Brown v. Board of Education of Topeka*. In this opinion, the Court interpreted the Equal Protection Clause of the Fourteenth Amendment as prohibiting differential treatment on the basis of race by governmental alliances. This decision radically altered the nature of governmental services and ended racial segregation, a practice dating back to shortly after the slaves were freed by the Thirteenth Amendment. In 1964, the Civil Rights Act was passed which drastically changed how private individuals and businesses were permitted to act towards minorities.

These measures can be seen as focusing upon two different but related concerns. The interpretation of the Equal Protection clause was an alliance membership issue. Prior to *Brown v. Board of Education of Topeka*, African American citizens were often provided with governmental benefits on terms that were different from those offered to White citizens. The legal subterfuge was that African American citizens were given benefits that were *equal* to those provided to White citizens, but such benefits were provided through a *separate* mechanism (that is, "separate but equal"). For instance, if a state government erected a public university that only White students could attend, this arrangement was acceptable so long as a seemingly equal African American university was constructed nearby. Similarly, a state was allowed to maintain White-only public facilities such as drinking fountains and restrooms so long as separate and equal facilities were made available for African Americans nearby.

The *Brown* decision held that the Equal Protection clause did not permit the provision of governmental benefits that were separate but equal. Instead, governmental benefits had to be provided to all citizens and without regard to a citizen's race. In the end, *Brown* can be seen as proclaiming simply that African American citizens are full members of the various governmental alliances within the United States and must be afforded all benefits generated by those alliances.[1]

The civil rights acts of the 1960s largely focused not upon governmental benefits but upon what is best considered to be the objective of Protection of the Person.[2] Prior the civil rights acts, individuals could discriminate against other individuals on the basis of race in all regards. For instance, restaurants could ban African American patrons, department stores were allowed to admit only Whites, and hotels were permitted to exclude African Americans. Furthermore, employers were free to refuse to hire African Americans. This conduct was quite detrimental to African Americans. African Americans were substantially restricted in their ability to lead normal lives, because they were excluded from most jobs and customary businesses and activities.

---

[1] It should be noted that *Brown* had such an effect because of the Overlord objective contained with the Fourteenth Amendment. Prior to the Fourteenth Amendment, the U.S. Constitution focused almost exclusively on the federal government and not on the states. The states were largely free to do as they pleased. The *Brown* decision was not just a reinterpretation of the term "equal." It was also a decision by the Supreme Court to embrace and enforce the Overlord objective contained with the Fourteenth Amendment and, as a result, subject the actions of states and local governmental alliances to scrutiny. In particular, the courts would scrutinize the membership benefits offered by states and local governmental alliances and insure that they were not differentiated on the basis of race.

[2] The civil rights acts of the 1960s also focused on membership issues as well. For instance, the Voting Rights Act strove to insure that all members were allowed to vote on equal terms. Most of the new developments in the 1960s, however, focused on private conduct.

Furthermore, the exclusion inflicted mental harm (that is, insult, degradation, feelings of inferiority, and so on) upon many African Americans as well.

As noted earlier, these harms are akin to the interests protected by the objective of Protection of the Person. In effect, the civil rights laws view the consequences of racial discrimination as being intolerable injuries inflicted upon African Americans. By prohibiting racial discrimination, the laws were intended to shield African Americans from such injuries.

Two factors should be emphasized regarding the civil rights laws. First, their scope was limited to banning racial discrimination only in areas that have a substantial impact upon the lives of the victims of discrimination. The laws did not ban discrimination wherever it might occur. For instance, the laws forbid employers and businesses providing services to the public from discriminating on the basis of race. Private citizens, however, are free to discriminate on the basis of race in other matters such as their friendships or private clubs. The underlying concept is that such exclusions, while unsavory, are not sufficiently detrimental to justify laws forbidding such practices. This conclusion is particularly evident if the contribution required to obtain the objective is considered (that is, forbidding racial discrimination in friendships, clubs, and so on). Specifically, to attain this broad objective, all citizens must yield the freedom to associate with whom they please and to submit all personal relationships to governmental regulation.

Second, although the civil rights laws were concerned primarily with discrimination against African Americans, the provisions of the laws are race-neutral.[1] The laws prohibit discrimination against any person on the basis of race. The reason for this appears to be the alliance-based nature of the United States government and the need to make benefits available to all members of the government. Thus, instead of seeking to protect only African Americans, the law is universal in its application and protects any and all races from discrimination.

The Cold War

The Cold War lasted from the late 1940s through the 1980s. The objective pursued by the United States in this undertaking was Defense against Aggressors. The Soviet Union and communist actors were the aggressors and were seen as being bent on conquering the United States and dominating the world. The United States' pursuit of the Defense against Aggressors objective varied in degree from the late 1940s up

---

[1] The civil rights laws did not focus exclusively upon race. For instance, the Civil Rights Act of 1964 prohibited discrimination on the basis race, color, religion, sex, and national origin.

through 1980 (that is, the end period for this chapter's discussion). During most of this period, the United States committed massive amounts of resources towards this objective. These resources included billions of dollars spent on anti-communist efforts around the world. The resources also included the casualties sustained in the Korean and Vietnam Wars. In the late 1970s, the anti-communist efforts of the United States substantially declined due to the failures in the Vietnam War. Many United States citizens considered the contribution required to fight communism (that is, casualties, billions of dollars) as being too expensive relative to the benefit of curbing communism's growth. This perception was furthered by a decline in the value attributed to a world free of communism. Many began to believe that communism was not particularly bad or was actually a positive thing.

The United Nations

The United Nations was created in 1945 to pursue various objectives including Law-Compelled Objectives, Charity & Justice, Mitigation of Catastrophe, and the Overlord objective. From 1945 through 1980, the United Nations attained these objectives with mixed success. For instance, the United Nations led a fairly successful effort in the Korean War, and undertook various projects to reduce poverty and disease around the world. During the same time period, the United Nations had many struggles and failures.

SUMMARY

This chapter has sped through United States history to demonstrate how alliance concepts can be used to analyze certain events and trends. If one were to explore certain epochs of United States history in depth, one should find that alliance concepts can explain trends and events occurring within those time periods.

As this chapter and the preceding chapters demonstrate, the growth and achievements of the United States are quite remarkable in the course of human history and in comparison to its contemporary peers such as the governmental alliances of Central and Southern America. Undoubtedly, numerous factors contributed to relative successes of the United States including, but not limited to, the rich natural resources present in the land and the oceans that protected it from many aggressors. Nonetheless, it appears indisputable that the alliance structures of the United States, the smaller governmental alliances within the United States, and the prevalence of non-governmental alliances within the United States contributed significantly to these accomplishments.

PART VI

---·---

Future Developments
and
Individual Concerns

CHAPTER 28

Forecasts and Speculation

This chapter will attempt to forecast future developments in governmental alliances. The focus will be primarily upon developments within the United States, but many discussions can be applied elsewhere in the world. The analysis will not be comprehensive but instead will highlight only certain topics.

MEMBERSHIP IN GOVERNMENTAL ALLIANCES

A pressing issue facing the United States as well as all successful governmental alliances is whether to allow new members into the alliance. This issue is commonly referred to as "immigration."

A Concern Specific to Successful Governmental Alliances

Along with the United States, certain governmental alliances have been remarkably successful at establishing conditions desirable to peoples living around the world. The United States, Canada, Australia, and most European governmental alliances are prime examples. These alliances have successfully attained numerous objectives including Defense against Aggressors, Law-Compelled Objectives, Generation of Prosperity, Mitigation of Catastrophe, and so on.

These successes stand in stark contrast to the dire living conditions in many other areas around the world. In these parts, governmental alliances are either non-existent or ineffective. Most entities purporting to be governmental alliances are illusory alliances. Outright tyrannies are commonplace.

Individuals living in these calamitous regions see the successful alliances as very desirable places to live. Further, these individuals aspire to become members of the alliances. As a result, millions of individuals around the world are trying to join the successful alliances as members.

445

As general rule, most successful governmental alliances are hesitant to allow additional individuals to immigrate to their countries and join the membership. Many governmental alliances enact elaborate measures to prevent individuals from entering the geographic boundaries of the alliance. Why? The prevailing reasons appear to be concerns with the objectives of (i) Generation of Prosperity, (ii) Social Insurance, (iii) Defense against Aggressors, (iv) Association Glory / Esprit de Corps (or "nationalism"), and (v) Charity & Justice. The following analyses are specific to each concern.

Generation of Prosperity

Immigration is often seen as decreasing the prosperity of a region. The perception is that immigrants increase the supply of laborers. As a result, unemployment increases and wages decrease. This results in a decline in prosperity for all members, or at least for those members who regularly engage in labor.

In contrast, immigration is sometimes viewed as a boon to prosperity. Many areas have tight labor supplies. As a consequence, prosperity is held back because labor costs too much. Immigration increases the labor supply and therefore reduces the cost of labor. Another advantage of immigration is that it allows a region to acquire sophisticated talent from other areas of the world. In this regard, certain successful alliances are often in need of workers knowledgeable in mathematics, engineering, computer programming, and science. Immigration allows these alliances to augment the collective knowledge and skillsets of their workforces.

As noted in Chapter 3, increasing the size of the membership of an alliance can have positive, negative, or neutral effects upon the current members. In the future, alliances will likely review and assess their specific situations to determine whether immigration is advantageous to the current membership. This analysis will be complex and difficult. The real inquiry will be whether immigration is a benefit to the members. Alliances might find that immigration is advantageous to some members but not to others. These differences will likely result in heated debates. A secondary question is whether the alliance will allow the immigrants to become members of the alliance. An alliance might allow individuals into the alliance's geographic region only to work. These individuals will not constitute members of the alliance. If the individuals become unable to work, they will be required to depart.

Social Insurance

Recall that the objective of Social Insurance is a subset of the objective of Mitigation of Catastrophe. Most successful governmental alliances have elaborate Social

Insurance programs. These programs are intended to provide monetary benefits, housing, food, education, health care, and other benefits to members down on their luck.

Immigrants are often seen as over-burdening these programs. Government alliances that have allowed immigrants to partake in Social Insurance programs often become swamped with claims.

Allowing immigrants to participate in Social Insurance can be inconsistent with the underlying scheme of Social Insurance. As discussed in Chapter 19, an assumption underlying Social Insurance is that members have contributed resources towards the program that are sufficient only to meet the needs of the current membership. In this regard, the governmental alliance has predicted how many claims will be made by current members in a given period of time. The governmental alliance then collects contribution of resources from the members sufficient to cover these predicted claims. If immigrants are allowed to make claims, this situation increases the number of individuals making claims on the resources that have been set aside. Furthermore, this situation will tend to throw off the government's predictions and jeopardize the viability of the Social Insurance program.

Current members might balk at allowing immigrants to participate in Social Insurance. These members have contributed resources towards the Social Insurance program over the course of their lives. Allowing immigrants to partake in the benefits of the program without having engaged in similar lifetimes of contribution is often viewed as being unfair. Furthermore, the situation can jeopardize the viability of Social Insurance because individuals will tend to immigrate only when they need the benefits. As a result, a large portion of the claims will be made by those who never contributed resources to the program.[1]

There are no easy answers to these problems and it will be interesting to see how they are addressed in the future. One possible solution is to stagger over time the Social Insurance benefits that are available to immigrants. In this situation, an immigrant admitted to membership will initially receive few Social Insurance benefits. As the immigrant resides in the new governmental alliance and contributes

---

[1]This problem is faced by many insurance companies. Insurance companies strive to keep from insuring individuals who intend to make immediate claims on a newly issued policy. The principles underlying the concept are complex and beyond the scope of this book. The point, however, is that insurance is not viable if most participants intend to make immediate claims once they receive coverage.

resources, the immigrant will gradually become eligible for more and more benefits offered by the Social Insurance programs. This arrangement might provide a fair and equitable compromise that serves the legitimate concerns of both long-term and new members.

Defense against Aggressors

After September 11, 2001, many successful governmental alliances have grown fearful of immigration. The concern is that terrorists will sneak into the country disguised as immigrants and attack alliance members and institutions.

To date, this concern has not resulted in governmental alliances ending immigration. Governmental alliances, however, have responded to terrorist concerns with heightened screening of new immigrants.

Nationalism

Although few will expressly admit it, most members tend to disfavor the immigration of individuals from cultures that differ substantially from the members' culture. The reasons for this tendency are usually dismissed as simple prejudice and intolerance. The true reasons seem more complex.

One reason seems to lie in the concept of nationalism. As noted earlier, nationalism is usually a combination of the forces of association glory and esprit de corps. Nationalism is typically fueled by a common culture such as a shared language, literature, traditions, music, art, science, food, and so on. Immigrants from foreign cultures are seen as not sharing in this common culture. As a consequence, members of a governmental alliance tend to not identify with such immigrants and do not want them in the alliance. The reasoning underlying the preference seems to be that such immigrants do not fit in and are contrary to the common culture of the alliance. Further, members often have perceptions that immigrants will disrupt this common culture and the association glory and esprit de corps associated with it.

A somewhat related reason appears to be the customs prevailing among the members of a governmental alliance. As discussed earlier, customs can be viewed using alliance concepts. In this regard, most customs are based upon implied accords and an implicit recognition that adherence to certain practices benefits all members (such as a custom of automatically forming lines and not cutting in lines reduces chaos and conflict). Immigrants are often new to these customs and might unwittingly fail to adhere to them. As a result, existing members tend to become displeased with immigrants and not inclined to extend them membership in the alliance.

Another reason appears to be a concern with the objectives pursued by the governmental alliance. Many members perceive that immigrants admitted to the alliance will attempt to change the objectives of the alliance. This change would be effected through membership vote. The new objectives would be those desired by the immigrants but not the current members.

Alliances are facing the question of Nationalism in different manners. One approach is to question whether the new immigrants are actually having a substantial effect upon the culture of the governmental alliance. Often, one might find that the perceptions of changes are much greater than reality. Another approach is to ask whether the changes in culture are undesirable. One might find that some changes are positive. Another avenue is to undertake efforts to inculcate the prevailing culture in the new immigrants. This approach focuses upon communicating to the immigrants the benefits of the prevailing culture. Instead of being fearful of immigrants and their different cultures, this approach embraces the immigrants and seeks to have the immigrants accept key components of the prevailing culture. Although the immigrants might retain many aspects of their original culture, they will tend to accept much of the prevailing culture and integrate it into their lives and families.

Charity & Justice

A final issue relating to membership and immigration is the extent to which the governmental alliance intends to pursue the objective of Charity & Justice. As a general rule, a governmental alliance will allow immigration only to the extent that it benefits the members of the alliance. The exception to this generalization is the objective of Charity & Justice. Recall that Charity & Justice yields no palpable benefit to the members of the alliance. Instead, members pursue an endeavor solely because they believe it is the right thing to do.

Often a governmental alliance will seek to aid immigrants due to Charity & Justice motivations, rather than due to a belief that immigration will benefit the alliance. Typically, a governmental alliance will identify a particular region of the World that is favored by its members. The governmental alliance will then allow individuals from that region to immigrate on favorable terms. For instance, the United States has usually afforded preferential treatment to individuals immigrating from communist countries.

There are limits to such charitable endeavors. It can be costly for governmental alliances to embrace Charity & Justice in their immigration policies. These costs are born by the members of the alliances in the form of higher taxes, overburdened Social Insurance programs, reduced prosperity, and so on. As such, Charity & Justice concerns must be weighed against these costs to attain a suitable balance.

Because there is essentially an endless supply of individuals desiring to immigrate to a successful alliance, difficult decisions will have to be made and many deserving individuals will have to be denied entry.

Summary

Immigration and membership poses, and will continue to pose, troublesome issues for governmental alliances for the foreseeable future. Members will have to determine whether allowing in new members constitutes a benefit to the alliance as a whole. Further, if members desire to further the objective of Charity & Justice through immigration policy, they will have to determine the extent to which they are willing to contribute resources towards that end.

GENERATION OF PROSPERITY

The objective of Generation of Prosperity carries enormous weight in the United States and most other governmental alliances. Most alliance members focus a great deal of attention on generating their own personal wealth and accumulating material items. In this regard, a typical member's primary goal in life is to be wealthy.

As a result of this emphasis, a great deal of attention is focused upon means that are thought to increase the prosperity of the alliance and its members. Debates constantly rage over which type of policy is the best for increasing prosperity. Examples of proposed means include tariffs and protectionist legislation, stimulus spending, manipulation of interest rates, broad-based tax cuts, targeted tax cuts for certain industries, reduction of payroll withholding rates, and so on.

In addition, almost any governmental action regardless of its nature is assessed for its effect upon an alliance's prosperity.

Illustration—A new sports stadium is proposed. Supporters assert that its construction will substantially increase economic prosperity in the area.

Illustration—A military base is targeted for elimination. Opponents contend that the base is vital to the local economy.

Illustration—An environmental Law-Compelled Objective is criticized for having a negative effect upon prosperity.

As time passes, it will be interesting to see if alliance members continue to place such a high degree of weight upon the generation of prosperity. A review of history indicates that the interest of individuals in comfort and material items has waxed and waned to some degree. While it seems quite clear that members will always be interested in maintaining a comfortable degree of prosperity, it is entirely possible that the current emphasis on prosperity will decline in the future.[1]

MORALITY

As discussed earlier, the objective of Morality can be subdivided into Religious concerns and Bolstering concerns. These will be discussed separately.

Religious Concerns

At present, Religious concerns have largely faded into the shadows. Governmental alliances rarely pursue any endeavor directly tied to a Religious concern. Most governmental actions are purely secular and are grounded in utilitarian notions associated with materialistic gains and losses, rather than spiritual affairs. There are exceptions, however, such as in Islamic countries.

The reason for this decline in Religious-based objectives appears to be the lack of consensus on the topic of religion. As more and more time passes, differences of opinion regarding religious topics have increased. Because there is little common ground regarding any religious viewpoint, pursuit of a Religious concern by a governmental alliance is largely not viable.

In the future, this trend will likely continue. While some event could occur that might unify religious viewpoints and make action by governmental alliances on Religious concerns a plausible action, it is more likely that individuals will continue to pursue Religious concerns through non-governmental alliances such as churches, synagogues, mosques, and temples.

Bolstering Concerns

Bolstering concerns currently play a large role in many governmental endeavors. Recall that the underlying concept is that a governmental alliance should strive to foster certain traits in the members, because such traits are believed to strengthen the ability of the members to achieve some other objective pursued by the alliance. For instance, a government alliance should attempt to make members healthy, because healthy members are able to generate more resources for the alliance.

Most current Bolstering endeavors of today focus on mandatory education for minors and encouragement of healthy lifestyles (such as government programs

---

[1]For instance, the current prominence of wealth accumulation might be replaced by religious devotion, education and learning, travel and exploration, communing with the environment, family experiences, and so on.

supporting exercise, diet, safe-sexual practices). The "War on Drugs" can be viewed as a Bolstering undertaking. Although the drug laws do have Paternalistic elements, the laws are often justified as furthering the public interest in having healthy citizens. Citizens under the disabling influence of narcotics are thought to be unable "to contribute to society" or, in other words, to contribute resources to the alliance.

In the future, it will be interesting to see how Bolstering endeavors change. For instance, the drug laws could be changed markedly in the future. While a very large portion of members of governmental alliances believe that drug usage is bad for both the user and the alliances, there is an increasing trend towards viewing the drug laws as being too expensive. The mental process being employed here is the same one described earlier in the book. The contribution required (such as money, loss of liberty, and so on) is not worth the value of decreasing drug use. Further, because the drug laws seem to be doing little to reduce drug usage, the sizeable contribution of resources towards the War on Drugs appears to be attaining little value and might even be counterproductive. As a result, the drug laws can be seen as quite costly and attaining few results.

Another topic to watch out for is the concept of virtue. In the past, many governmental alliances focused upon developing virtue in the members. Traits of virtue included courage, honesty, moderation, wisdom, honor, charity, and so on. At present, governmental alliances seem to not focus upon fostering such traits in the members. Instead, today's prevailing equivalent for what might be called virtue seems to be an extreme emphasis upon self-interestedness. Individuals of all politics and beliefs seem to focus upon individual fulfillment as the fundamental goal in life. For instance, if a particular action makes one more wealthy, famous, or powerful and is not forbidden by the law, the prevailing view is that such an action should be undertaken and others have largely no standing to criticize the action in any fashion. It will be interesting to see if this situation changes over time and older concepts of virtue arise again.

PATERNALISM

Paternalism seems to be largely out of vogue. The prevailing viewpoint is that individuals can best fend for themselves. This notion is typically framed as the freedom to do as one pleases.

There are exceptions where Paternalism arises in today's world. Examples include:

- Safety laws such as mandatory seatbelt and motorcycle helmet requirements

- Prohibitions on the use of narcotics

- Baseline employment terms that are not negotiable such as payday rules, overtime, minimum wage, child labor, and workplace safety rules

- Mandatory education for minors

- Bans on certain types of unhealthy foods

- Restrictions on tobacco usage[1]

Will Paternalism decrease, increase, or stay the same in the future? The answer is that it will probably decrease for several reasons. One reason for the likely decrease is that individuals will continue to see little or no benefit in a Paternalistic decision maker making decisions on their behalves. In the past, many individuals were very poorly educated and could not fend for themselves in many areas of life. Individuals in such circumstances often welcomed a Paternalistic entity looking out for their interests and controlling their actions. With the modern spread of knowledge and education, however, many individuals tend to feel much more comfortable acting on their own and without Paternalistic oversight. A second reason for the likely decline of Paternalism is the potential for decision-maker abuse. A sizeable concern with Paternalism is that it usually vests enormous power in the hands of decision makers. Because all decision makers are subject to the three limitations (motivational, ability, and fidelity), most members tend to fear conveying substantial liberty to less-than-perfect decision makers. The worry over a corrupt decision maker abusing such power to further his own ends is particularly troubling. Further, the historical association of the objective with tyrannies will likely serve to continue the decline in Paternalism.[2]

The topic of abortion is particularly difficult to set within any particular Objective. The prevailing view is that abortion is an issue best left to the pregnant mother to resolve, instead of the government. This viewpoint is effectively framed

---

[1]The rationale underlying these endeavors is not limited to Paternalism. Some are composite objectives. For instance, prohibition on the usage of narcotics can be seen as furthering both Paternalistic and Morality-Bolstering concerns. Seatbelt and motorcycle laws can be seen as furthering Paternalism and Social Insurance (that is, keeping the costs of health insurance down).

[2]Tyrants tend to employ Paternalistic rationales to conceal usage of the Tools of Tyranny. For instance, a tyrant will assert that individuals opposing the tyranny must be imprisoned and "reeducated" because they have embraced ideas that are not in their best interests. The real reason for the imprisonment is not to educate the opposition. Rather, the purpose is to eliminate the opposition and protect the power of the tyrant.

as a rejection of Paternalism.[1] Interestingly, opponents of abortion do not see the issue as one of Paternalism. Instead, the opponents are concerned with the fetus itself and desire to protect it from harm. This interest is probably best classified as Charity & Justice. The result of these widely differing perspectives is predictably messy and volatile arguments. In effect, the proponents and opponents are not speaking the same language and their arguments rarely mesh together. The future of the abortion debate remains unclear.

Another area of possible developments in the area of Paternalism is pornography. The currently prevailing view is that a decision to view pornography is one best left to the individual. This viewpoint appears to have developed in an era when access to pornography was rather limited and it was difficult to immerse oneself in the subject. With the expansive development of the internet and take-home videos, the landscape might have changed to a degree where there might be more calls for Paternalistic regulation of pornography. The rationale would be that pornography is currently prevalent to such a degree that it overwhelms a typical person's ability to look out for his best interests. As such, everyone will benefit by having governmental alliances regulate the subject of pornography to protect individuals from, in effect, themselves.

LEVELING

Recall that Leveling is an internal objective that focuses on restraining or limiting something associated with the members. The idea is that members might be prone to accumulating an item in excess and that this result is undesirable. As a consequence, the alliance imposes rules on the members setting some type of limits on what can be accumulated.

Leveling appears to influence certain governmental actions including tax policy and objectives like Social Insurance and Charity & Justice. Consider the following with regard to tax policy:

Illustration—The federal government has an estate tax, which taxes a dead person's surviving assets above a certain threshold. For instance, if one dies with $10 million in the bank, the federal government will tax a large portion of that sum. Ostensibly, the purpose of the estate tax is to collect contribution

---

[1] Proponents of abortion (or of the right to choose to have an abortion) tend to reference a right to "privacy." This terminology might be confusing, because privacy is generally understood as an interest in secrecy or confidentiality. It has been suggested that the subject should instead be termed a right to "personal autonomy" or a right to make an important decision affecting oneself without governmental intervention.

of resources. The true purpose, however, appears to be Leveling, whereby the goal is to reduce the wealth that can be passed by one to his or her heirs.

Although Leveling appears in governmental action from time to time, its influence is rarely acknowledged. The fact that Leveling seems to be a hidden objective suggests that it is not widely accepted. In the future, it will be interesting to see if Leveling actions become more transparent or if the objective declines over time.

LEGAL SYSTEM

Protection of the Person

Most governmental alliances employ two different means to attain the objective of Protection of the Person Civil law is one means and it consists of creating an arena for a member to use individual effort to protect his person. This arena is the civil courts system and the individual effort is a lawsuit. The member can use a lawsuit to obtain a court order intended to prevent an injury from occurring or the lawsuit can be used to recover compensatory damages for a past injury. The other means is criminal law which employs police, prosecutors, fines, and jails to prevent and deter injuries to the person.

Civil Law—There seems to be a general trend against the civil law. In recent years, members have had less and less enthusiasm for lawsuits. There appears to be two reasons for this development. The first is the contribution cost. The expenses of lawsuits and the costs of the new standards of conduct and prohibitions are felt by members in the form of increased contribution. This contribution consists of higher prices for goods and services that have been the subject of substantial litigation. Another type of contribution is the effective contribution of freedom to not engage in certain activities that are no longer viable due to fears of lawsuits. For instance, most members identify at least one leisure activity that has been effectively shut down due to an inability to acquire liability insurance or due to other concerns with legal liability. The second reason is effectiveness. When considering many of the new legal claims, most members appear to view individual effort as being a more effective means of attaining the desired result. The best example is the famous McDonalds coffee case. A typical member views placing legal blame on McDonalds for a hot-coffee burn as nonsensical. Instead, the best means of reducing such coffee burns is for individuals to be more careful. This is sometimes called "personal responsibility" or "taking responsibility for one's actions."[1] In the future,

---

[1] The concept of "personal responsibility" has roots in Alliance Theory. When it is argued that personal responsibility is applicable to a topic area, one is essentially stating that the area of concern is best suited for individual action and not an alliance effort. In

it is likely that civil-law efforts to attain the objective of Protection of the Person will stay level or decline.

Criminal Law—Most governmental alliances heavily utilize criminal laws to obtain the objective of Protection of the Person. Numerous laws exist criminalizing all types of assaults upon the person. Almost all criminal laws focus upon actual physical harm. In recent years, however, mental trauma caused by stalking has been criminalized. Further, there has been a trend to penalize offenders with more effective or serious punishments such as longer jail terms and capital punishment. It is likely that these various undertakings will stay at the same level in the future.

In many nations, debates have raged over individual possession and ownership of firearms. Although these debates are framed in many different ways, the true debate appears to be about whether individual effort or an alliance effort is the best means of attaining the objective of Protection of the Person. In this regard, possession of a firearm is the individual effort and relying upon police, prosecutors, and jail is the alliance effort. Opponents contend that individual firearm ownership is not an effective deterrent and also entails additional costs which effectively constitute a heavy contribution on the members (such as accidental shootings, vigilantism, and acquisition of the firearms by criminals). Due to these reasons, opponents argue that the goal of Protection of the Person should be attained by an alliance effort only (or at least without individual ownership of firearms). Proponents of individual firearm ownership contend that governmental alliances cannot adequately protect persons against criminal threats and that individual ownership of firearms significantly supplements the efforts of the governmental alliance and has a large effect on attaining the objective of Protection of the Person. Further, proponents argue that the costs associated with individual firearm ownership are overstated (that is, there are few accidental shootings, vigilantism is rare, and criminals will obtain firearms regardless of a ban on firearm ownership).

Protection of Property

There has been a recent trend towards reducing the Protection of Property objective. As noted earlier, this trend resulted from a belief that Protection of Property rules stood in the way of needed government actions to obtain other objectives

---

the case of the McDonalds coffee, the underlying theme was that protecting individuals from coffee burns is not an desirable objective for an alliance effort to pursue because individual effort is the best means of guarding against coffee burns. Individual effort in such a situation would consist of using due care in handling coffee and not taking risks with a hot cup of coffee.

such as Conservation, Generation of Prosperity, Charity & Justice, and certain other Law-Compelled Objectives. This downward trend has probably stabilized. In the future, it is probable that members will continue to recognize that the Protection of Property objective provides all members with a desirable benefit. Nonetheless, there likely will be numerous debates regarding the extent and breadth of the property-protection rules.

In the past, most non-western countries have not pursued the Protection-of-Protection objective with fervor. It appears that there is now a growing consensus that property rights in general are beneficial. As a result, more and more non-western governmental alliances will likely increase their pursuit of the Protection-of-Protection objective in the future.

Enforcement of Promises

Pursuit of this objective will continue into the foreseeable future. The specific measures used to attain the objective will change frequently to meet new needs that develop over time. For instance, it is likely that more gap-filler or background rules will be developed to reduce the need for substantial negotiations and due-diligence in transactions. In most situations, the parties to a promise will be able to opt out of the background rules if they choose to do so. If the parties are in a rush or otherwise do not desire to negotiate over each little topic, however, the background rules will provide a ready framework.

Globally, adherence to an enforcement-of-promises objective is increasing. Governmental alliances and other combined-effort entities are seeing the value of the objective and are striving to adhere to its requirements by supply the necessary contribution. This trend will probably continue into the future.

DEFENSE AGAINST AGGRESSORS

Pursuit of this objective by the United States declined markedly with the collapse of the Soviet Union and the end of the Cold War. The attacks of September 11, 2001, however, changed this trend downward. With the attacks, tremendous resources have been expended upon preventing further terrorist strikes.

At present, there is a debate regarding the proper means to be used to attain the objective of Defense against Aggressors. In the United States, for instance, the prevailing view has been that terrorism should be combated with force and with preemptive strikes at the terrorists' home bases. The alternative view, in contrast, is to change the terrorists' minds and attempt to eliminate their motivations for attacking the United States and other Western nations. This approach might be styled "appeasement," although reasonable minds could disagree over the use of that term.

In the War on Terrorism, a recurring controversy has been the treatment of captured terrorists and suspected terrorists. The prevailing view has been that the terrorists are not members (or "citizens") of the United States and, as a result, the Law-Compelled Objectives such as Protection of the Person have not been utilized to fight terrorism. Instead, the objective of Defense against Aggressors has controlled so far. As a consequence, the terrorists are viewed as non-members and are not afforded the rights typically given to the accused who are citizens of the United States. A related issue is how such captured individuals are to be treated under International Law. This topic has caused confusion because the terrorist organizations are not members of any international alliance and will not adhere to the provisions of the treaties that have been created regarding conflict, treatment of prisoners, and so on. That is, the terrorists are not party to any alliance with a Law-Compelled Objective governing their treatment so it is uncertain as to what protections they have, if any. Instead, the only thing protecting them might be a Charity & Justice concern that an alliance might choose to embrace. In this regard, an alliance might choose to afford substantial rights to terrorists because it is the "right thing" to do.

Aside from the War on Terrorism, another issue for the future will be the threat posed by other governmental alliances to the United States. Up until the collapse of the Soviet Union, the threat of a major war was seen as a realistic risk. At present, the risk remains unclear. China is viewed as the most likely candidate although the chances of a war between China and the United States appear slim at this time. A primary reason is the interrelated nature of the economies of the two nations. A war would devastate the economies of China and the United States. As such, because the objective of Generation of Prosperity is treasured, it is very un-likely that a war will occur.

CHARITY & JUSTICE

At present, the United States expends fair amounts of resources on the objective of Charity & Justice. Examples include aid to foreign nations, natural disaster relief for foreign regions, and programs styled as "Social Insurance" that appear more like Charity & Justice endeavors (that is, they target relatively discreet groups of members in dire straits instead of the entire membership).

This trend favoring the Charity & Justice objective is probably due to the sizeable prosperity that the United States has enjoyed since World War II ended. Another probable factor causing the trend is that a composite objective often seems to be present. For instance, a Charity & Justice action directed at a foreign region might generate goodwill towards the United States resulting in less conflict and therefore satisfy the Defense against Aggressors objective. Similarly, a Charity & Justice endeavor within the United States might reduce poverty which in turn might reduce crime and thus attain the Protection of Person objective.

In the future, Charity & Justice endeavors will probably stay about the same. Several factors, however, might cause this trend to decrease. First, as noted above, the United States' current strong interest in the objective appears to be directly related to the relatively high level of prosperity in the United States. If this prosperity declines, it is likely that the level of interest in the objective will decline as well.

Second, there has often been a debate over whether the government has a proper role in pursuing Charity & Justice objectives or whether they are best left to private alliances (for example, Goodwill, Red Cross, Salvation Army, and so on). The arguments against government action are twofold. One is that private alliances do a better job than the government. The second is that there is no consensus in the citizens of the United States regarding Charity & Justice objectives. As such, the best situation is for individuals to identify on their own which Charity & Justice endeavors they desire and they can then join private alliances to attain these specific objectives. The currently prevailing view appears to be a mix of governmental and non-governmental efforts. This trend could move towards favoring more non-governmental action.

A third factor is whether perceptions of certain Charity & Justice endeavors change and they start to be viewed as constituting objectives such as Leveling or Aggression against Nonmembers. In this regard, some critics today contend that many Charity & Justice programs constitute forced redistribution of resources whereby monetary assets are confiscated from the prosperous and given to the poor. Such efforts, the arguments go, constitute (i) Leveling if there is a universal rule limiting the amount of resources that might be possessed, or (ii) constitute Aggression against Nonmembers if the governmental entity is effectively being used to take resources from a minority and to give them to another group holding power. At this time, it is unclear whether these contentions will have an effect upon the perceptions of the Charity & Justice objective. They do have the potential, however, to reduce Charity & Justice endeavors in the future.

SOCIAL INSURANCE

It is likely that governmental alliances will pursue this objective in the future with less fervor. This trend will probably occur due to the current high costs associated with Social Insurance. Funding for Social Insurance programs takes up a very large portion of the spending of most governmental alliances. Further, individual effort will probably be viewed in the future as being more suitable to guard against many calamities, in comparison to governmental action. Nonetheless, Social Insurance will likely stay in place largely unchanged.

It is likely that there will continue to be two tiers of insurance. The first will be outsourced individual effort or, in other words, privately acquired insurance through either a mutual insurance company or a for-profit insurance company. This type of arrangement will tend to be effective in guarding members against most calamities. The second tier will be governmental Social Insurance. This arrangement will be less effective than the first tier of private insurance. Nonetheless, Social Insurance will serve as a "safety net" for those who fall through the gaps of the first tier.

Health insurance is currently a controversial topic. The costs of health care have risen markedly in recent years. At the same time, the quality of health care has increased substantially. The debates seem to focus upon the high costs and whether a free-market approach is the best mechanism for providing health care in the future. Many have suggested that the free market cannot work in health care and that a governmental actor is better suited to provide health care. Others have countered by contending that a free market does not exist in the health-care industry and its absence is the source of the problems. Further, these individual criticize governmental action as being inadequate and even detrimental. Much of the criticism of governmental action appears to lie in the capability limitations of decision makers. (That is, health care is so complex that decision makers cannot actively manage it; a free market approach under the "Rational Chaos" decision-making process is the only viable solution.)

At this point, it is unclear how the health-care debate will be resolved. A popular viewpoint proposes a strategy which appears to mix individual action with governmental-alliance action. The individual component is for the typical individual or family to pay directly for most routine health concerns such as doctor visits and minor illnesses and injuries. Insurance companies will no longer pay for these low-cost items. As a result, it is believed that individuals will shop around, question treatment plans, and look for the most cost-effective health care. This component is effectively an effort to institute a free market into routine health care decisions, and is premised upon the assumption that insurance coverage interferes with the market and results in costly decisions. The governmental-alliance component involves the government assisting low-income individuals who cannot afford to pay for low-cost treatments. Furthermore, the approach includes governmental facilitation (or outright provision) of health care for catastrophic injuries and illnesses such as cancer, heart attacks, strokes, and major accidents. The overall rationale for this strategy appears to be that an alliance approach (pursuing the Mitigation of Catastrophe / Social Insurance objective) is suited only for very serious injuries and illness and that an individual approach is more appropriate for routine illness and injuries.

TRENDS IN PRIVATE ALLIANCES

Corporations

Corporations are becoming immense in size. Many global corporations have assets and financial power that dwarf that of most countries. Such corporations are usually alliances whose members are shareholders. Because corporations are alliances, they are prone to all three limitations associated with delegated decision makers. Shareholders are currently viewing corporate management with skepticism. It is likely that this trend will continue into the future. In particular, shareholders might begin to see giant corporations in the same pessimistic light that most now see governmental alliances (that is, as indifferent and inefficient bureaucracies).

Labor Unions

Labor unions in the United States have been on the decline. In the past, unions were popular because they typically offered employees the only means of protection against employer abuse. A labor union is an alliance. By uniting together, union members were often able to prevent employer mistreatment and attain substantial gains in working conditions and compensation.

In today's world, most employees do not see a compelling need for such protection against their employers and therefore have little interest in joining a union. This decline appears to be the product of three factors. First, working conditions have improved markedly. One likely cause of this change is recent workplace regulation. Laws governing minimum wages, overtime pay, workplace safety, anti-discrimination, and benefit-plan protection have generally eliminated most abuses of workers. A second factor causing a decline in labor unions is a change in management attitudes. Most companies now find that a motivational, positive approach towards workers yields more productivity than a hard, tough approach (that is, the carrot instead the stick). As a result, most workplaces have become a more pleasant place to work over the past 30 years or so. Finally, union corruption appears to have caused a decline in interest in unions. Because a union is an alliance, its delegated decision makers are subject to all decision maker limitations. In particular, fidelity limitations have been prevalent in many unions. As a result, potential union members often decline to join a union because they perceive it as being corrupt and ineffective.

Another factor that seems to be reducing union interest is the upward mobility trend in the United States. A typical worker will tend to be interested in a union if he intends to work in the same job for the rest of his life. The reason is that the union will see that his job is protected and that he receives regular pay raises and better benefits. A worker who intends to be at a job for a few years or less, however, will not be so interested in a union. This worker intends to move on into a newer, better job and will not see a long-term need for the union.

In the future, it will be interesting to see if the trend against unions reverses and they become more popular. Such a trend reversal will likely occur only if working conditions decline or if more individuals start to work in jobs that they intend to hold for the rest of their lives.

Small Alliances

Small, non-governmental alliances such as small businesses (partnerships and corporations) and social groups such as clubs, organizations, and societies will continue to grow at significant rates for the foreseeable future. The reason is the internet and the resulting ability of individuals with atypical interests to find each other, communicate, and form alliances to attain their mutually desired objectives.

OPEN OBJECTIVE TRENDS AND SPECIAL INTERESTS

Over the past 75 years or so, the federal government and most other governmental alliances have trended towards embracing an open-objective framework. Before this topic can be discussed, it might be useful to review some concepts.

As noted in various earlier chapters, the most stable alliances pursue objectives that are desired by all of the members. Typically, such alliances have express or implied accords that limit the alliances to pursuing a specific objective or an indefinite objective. The difference between the two is that an indefinite objective is difficult to define with precision and therefore allows the alliance some degree of flexibility in the endeavors that it might pursue, unlike the constraining effect of a specific objective.

In contrast, an open objective has no parameters upon what an alliance might or might not pursue. The underlying rationale for an open objective is that the members see a benefit in having an alliance framework in place to act upon objectives that are well-suited for a combined effort. In the absence of an open objective, members must repeatedly form a new alliance for each new objective that they desire, or an existing alliance's accord must be constantly modified or amended to allow pursuit of the new objective.

The open-objective alliance offers a solution to these technical difficulties but it does have its downsides. It usually requires a delegated decision maker that holds sizeable power to determine both the specific objectives that the alliance will undertake and all other ancillary matters such as the means to be used, contribution required, allocation of benefits, and so on. When this substantial power is considered along with the typical limitations associated with decision makers, it is clear that there is a very large potential for failure and abuse. Such circumstances can result in a fairly predictable slide towards a tyranny.

In addition, an open objective allows the alliance to pursue specific objectives that are not necessarily desired by all members. The membership will tolerate the pursuit of specific objectives that they do not desire, so long as they perceive a net benefit from the alliance as a whole and its ability to pursue any objective well-suited for a combined effort. As an open-objective alliance begins to pursue more and more specific objectives not desired by large portions of members, the net perceived value of the alliance will tend to decline. If an open-objective alliance pursues too many such specific objectives, the net-perceived value will turn negative and the alliance will collapse.

The Twentieth Century saw a substantial growth in the scope of objectives pursued by both the federal government and state governments. As a result, most modern governmental alliances appear to operate with an open objective. For instance, the typical U.S. citizen seems to believe that the federal government is able to pursue any objective whatsoever, so long as it does not violate certain Bill-of-Rights protections such as freedom of speech. Similarly, the United States Congress seems to pass legislation, and the President seems to sign such legislation, with little regard as to whether the Constitution actually authorizes such legislation. Instead, these two parts of the federal government rely heavily upon the Supreme Court to decide whether the particular undertaking is permissible under the Constitution. Overall, while the federal government does not have an open objective, it operates at times as if it did have an open objective.

The trend towards embracing an open objective by the federal government and other governmental alliances appears to correspond largely to the desires of most citizens. Nonetheless, there have been repeated complaints regarding whether such governments are pursuing objectives that favor narrow "special interests" instead of the interests of all members. From a review of these complaints, it appears fairly evident that governmental alliances will, from time to time, undertake endeavors specifically designed to favor a special interest. In most situations, the delegated decision makers vote for special-interest projects through the "I'll scratch your back if you scratch my back" practice. In this regard, one group of delegated decision makers will agree to support a proposal favoring a special interest if another group will support their special-interest proposal.

This practice of governments favoring special interests is grudgingly tolerated by the citizens because they perceive a net value to such governmental alliances. The citizens will usually readily admit, however, that the special-interest endeavors cause them displeasure. Nonetheless, it appears clear that the citizens are not so turned off by the special interests at this time so as to terminate their membership in the alliances.

It will be interesting to see if this situation might change in the future. The current trend towards favoring special interests might grow to such a degree that members will no longer perceive net values in the governmental alliances and will terminate their memberships. It is possible that governmental alliances might act to stop the trend towards favoring special interests. At present, the focus is largely upon quid-pro-quo arrangements whereby alliances strive to prevent special interests from providing decision makers with some form of consideration. These measures criminalize providing most cash or gifts directly to the decision makers and strictly regulate the money that might be provided to decision makers' campaigns.

These efforts seem to have had some success but it appears that they cannot solve the problem. The only comprehensive solution might be to restrain the objective of the governmental alliances. This approach would require more specification and clarity in what the governmental alliances might and might not pursue (that is, specific or at least less indefinite objectives). It would also require a willingness by the decision makers to always review whether a particular action falls within the parameters of an agreed-upon objective. Finally, it would benefit greatly from an interwoven decision-making process (such as a strong court system) to review governmental actions and strike down any unauthorized undertaking. It seems unlikely at this time, however, that such a solution will be implemented.

DECISION-MAKING
PROCESS ISSUES

In comparison to the past, the decision-making processes currently in place for most governmental alliances seem to work fairly well. The future, however, could yield various developments.

Membership Vote

At present, citizens participate only to a small degree in governmental alliances. The typical participation is limited to electing delegated decision makers such as the President, Senators and Representatives, governors, state representatives, mayors, city council members, and so on. Some states such as California, however, allow citizens to vote on referendums which have the power to bind the state government and its decision makers. It is likely that there will be an increased trend towards the use of referendums in the future. These referendums will probably pertain to approval of objectives for the governmental alliance to pursue and similar matters. Notwithstanding a likely trend towards more referendums, members will probably continue to not participate extensively in the decision-making process.

Motivational Limitations

Many governmental decision makers seem to be subject to motivational limitations. Arguably, the problem lies in the relatively low rates of compensation, in comparison to what the decision makers could earn in other lines of employment. For instance, the President of the United States is the highest paid employee of the federal government at $400,000 per year and all other federal government employees are paid less. In contrast, large corporations typically pay their top executives millions of dollars in order to attract the best candidates and properly motivate them. If governmental decision makers are lacking in motivation, perhaps higher rates of compensation will offer at least a partial solution?

There is no clear answer at this time. The current prevailing view seems to be that delegated decision makers should not be well compensated as they are serving the public interest.[1] This view might change and there might be a trend towards increasing the compensation of delegated decision makers in order to attract more motivated candidates.

Capability Limitations

At times, the "magic-wand" concept seems to permeate views towards governmental alliances. If any major problem arises, questions are usually asked as to why a particular governmental alliance has not solved it. The assumption seems to be that a governmental alliance can solve any problem that might exist. As a result, governmental alliances often pursue objectives that are simply not attainable. These objectives are not attainable because no decision maker is intelligent or sufficiently talented to attain them.

The current prevalence of the magic-wand concept appears to be tied to substantial technological developments over the past decades and the marked abilities that they have given governmental alliances to attain new objectives. Members have taken note of these successes and tend to believe that governments can obtain any objective by in effect waving a magic wand at it.

As governmental alliances fail to attain more and more undertakings, it is likely that members will tend to appreciate the capability limitations of decision makers to a greater degree. As a result, members will develop more realistic views

---

[1] This "serve the public interest" rationale appears to be premised upon an assumption that low compensation will attract only those individuals truly interested in serving the best interests of the governmental alliance. This assumption might be flawed. Instead of attracting noble self-sacrificing decision makers, the low compensation might tend attract only those individuals who desire non-monetary rewards such as power, prestige, and fame.

towards what governments reasonably can be expected to attain and not attain. At present this trend has probably started as criticisms of the competency and ability of decision makers are commonplace. Nonetheless, the "magic wand" concept will likely continue on to some degree in the future.

Fidelity Limitations

Whenever a delegated decision maker is present, there is potential for fidelity limitations to be manifested. In the future, it is certain that fidelity limitations will continue to occur. All governmental alliances will need to accept this fact but also strive to reduce the occurrence of fidelity limitations as well. Vigilant scrutiny of decision makers is vital to reducing fidelity limitations.

Openness of the Decision-Making Process

There seems to be an increasing trend towards secrecy in the decision-making process. In the past, it appears that most legislation was crafted in an open forum such as the assembly halls of the governments' legislatures. In such halls, elected representatives would argue in favor or against particular laws and usually compromises would be struck in the presence of all attendees. Although there might have been some backroom deals outside of public scrutiny, most decisions seem to have been made in the open.

Nowadays, it seems that most legislation is drafted secretly and without any exposure to the public. Further, the laws are typically combined into massive bills such that no person could reasonably be expected to read the tomes and know what they contain before the legislature votes upon them. Such a system provides a fertile ground for fidelity limitations to prosper as the secrecy allows for the corrupt motivations to be concealed. In the future, it seems that this trend towards secret decision making will probably grow.

Resistance by Compromised Interests

It would be naïve to assume that decision-maker reform will take place without substantial resistance from corrupt decision makers and their beneficiaries. These individuals and entities gain from fidelity limitations and will always strive to see that these beneficial arrangements stay in place. It can be expected that they will form their own alliances to preserve the status quo and to prevent decision-maker reform.

Partisanship

Partisanship is difficult to define. Some use the term to define any situation where two or more parties conflict over a proposal. Perhaps the best definition is an undue emphasis upon the interests of a political party alliance over the interests of the greater governmental alliance. For instance, if the primary reason a political party advocates a position is to attract more voters, to damage the other party, or to otherwise strengthen its political power, such an action is partisan. The reason is that the motivating factor is not to further the interests of the governmental alliance. Instead, the motivation is to make the party stronger.

When is a party action not partisan? If a party acts to further the objective-based desires of its members, then it is acting in a non-partisan basis. Consider the following illustrations of partisan and non-partisan conduct:

Illustration—The party membership genuinely desires to increase road construction and believes that such a project is in the interest of the governmental alliance. As a result, the party advocates this proposal in the decision-making process. This action is non-partisan, because the motivation is to further the interests of the greater alliance.

Illustration—The party is indifferent towards road construction but the party leadership advocates the proposal simply to lure in more votes. This action is partisan. The reason is that the party leaders are focusing upon the party's interests instead of the interest of the alliance as a whole.

Illustration—The party opposes a proposal by a competing party, because it believes the proposal is bad policy. This conduct is non-partisan because the party is acting to further the interests of the greater alliance.

Illustration—The party opposes a proposal by a competing party, because it wishes to make the opposing party appear weak in the eyes of the voters. If the party is honest, it will concede that the proposal of the opposing party is of value to the alliance as whole. This action is partisan because the party is acting to weaken an opposing party.

Illustration—The party criticizes the leaders of the other party and contends that they are poor decision makers and that they embrace flawed ideologies. The party making these criticisms honestly believes them. This conduct is non-partisan, because the party's primary motivation is to further the interests of the alliance (and not to increase its political power).

Illustration—The party criticizes the leaders of the other party with arguments based upon false or distorted information. The party making these criticisms knows that its information is false or questionable. This conduct is partisan, because the party's primary motivation is to damage the political power of the other party and therefore increase its own power.

Partisanship is particularly troublesome in the context of association glory. It appears that members of political parties often take great pride in their affiliation with the party. If the party is not doing particularly well, some members will desire to mend the party and increase its authority and power. These efforts, however, are motivated solely to increase the association glory of the party rather than to pursue a particular policy-based objective. For instance, if a political party is failing, its members might go to extraordinary lengths to lure in new members and therefore radically alter the nature of the party. This outcome is peculiar because the party was presumably formed to pursue certain policy-base objectives. Over time, however, the party has been transformed into an entity whose primary focus is on securing political power in order to augment the association glory of the party. That is, the primary objective is now to make the party powerful so that its members might bask in its glory. The old policy-based objectives have fallen by the wayside.

Illustration—The party has lost substantial power over the span of about ten years. Party members decry this decline in power and influence and cite to the good old days when the party was powerful. In order to reverse this trend, the party members begin attacking the opposing party and criticizing every proposal advocated by the party. The party members, however, advocate few if any alternative proposals. This conduct suggests that the party's primary goal is to increase its association glory. The party is not attempting to have any particular legislation passed by the governmental alliance. Instead, the party seems to be focusing all of its energies solely upon increasing the association glory of the party.

The pitfalls of partisanship might be avoided if members deemphasize association glory and focus upon the real reasons they joined the political party. Further, the party decision makers should strive not to maximize the party's power as an end or, in other words, for the sake of holding power. Instead, the party should concentrate its efforts upon the policy-based objectives commonly held by the party members and endeavor to make them into law.

CONTRIBUTION

The primary means of funding governmental alliances is taxation of income. This mechanism has generated extraordinarily large sums of revenue. In recent years, the tax laws have been heavily criticized various reasons.

One criticism is that the tax laws are far too complex and result in massive inefficiencies and reductions in prosperity. Another criticism is that the purpose of the tax laws should be only to raise revenue. Nonetheless, the tax laws are commonly used to pursue various objectives such as Generation of Prosperity, Leveling, Charity & Justice, Morality, Conservation, and so on. These objectives are pursued through

(i) preferential tax treatment of certain activities like research and development, energy conservation, or charitable contributions, or (ii) disproportionate taxation of high-rates of income, luxury purchases, and so on. Critics contend that the pursuit of these objectives is largely covert (or through Objective Disguise), results in inefficiencies, and fosters fidelity limitations such as rewarding special interests. With regard to special interests, some critics go so far as to contend that the annual revisions in the tax code are primarily to serve accounting, legal, and consulting lobbies. Such professions profit immensely, the critics argue, by advising taxpayers how to comply with the most recent revisions to the tax laws. Thus, under this criticism, the primary reason for the constant tax code changes is to generate more business for accountants, lawyers, and consultants involved in tax preparation. In the future, it is likely that taxation methods will be revised to produce a result that is considered more equitable, less prone to fidelity limitations, and as having a less negative effective upon prosperity.

FUTURE GENERATIONS

At present, the United States is regularly requiring contribution from future members who, in many cases, are not even born yet. An evident example is the prevalent practice of deficit spending. Such practices will require future members to contribute resources towards objectives that were pursued before they became members. Such a situation might be justifiable if the future members will benefit from the objectives attained through deficit spending (for example, victories in World War II, the Cold War, the War on Terror, and so on). However, care should be taken to avoid saddling future members with too much contribution. If the contribution requirements are too great, future members might perceive no net value from the governmental alliance and refuse to join the alliance or contribute the required resources.

Another possible example of requiring contribution from future members is the practice of environmental pollution and degradation. If the current pollution and environmental practices will cause future members to suffer, such future members are effectively contributing resources like loss of health or nature enjoyment to allow current generations to enjoy certain activities such as convenient transport, or widely available electrical power.

CHAPTER 29

Individual Questions

The purpose of this chapter is to raise topics that an individual might wish to consider in assessing his surroundings. Because of the flexibility associated with alliance theory, a formula or decision tree cannot be set forward. Nonetheless, the following discussion has been organized in an effort to identify issues in a logical format that will allow most readers to assess alliances and other combined-effort entities with which they might be associated.

WHAT COMBINED-EFFORT ENTITIES
ARE YOU AFFILIATED WITH?

Unless you are a hermit completely isolated from all humans, it seems impossible for you not to be a member of several combined-effort entities. Recall that a combined-effort entity encompasses anything that combines resources held by individuals to achieve one or more objectives. Examples might include:

- National governmental entity

- City or local governmental entity

- Neighborhood association

- Religious institution

- Private educational institution

- Charitable association

- Business venture such as a corporation or a partnership

- Internet special interest group

- Carpool

- Country club

- Fan club

WHAT IS THE NATURE OF THE COMBINED-EFFORT ENTITIES?

For each combined-effort entity that you have identified, ask whether it is an alliance or some other form of a combined-effort entity. Recall that all alliances are combined-effort entities, but not all combined-effort entities are alliances. The combined-effort entities other than alliances include (i) semi-alliances, (ii) illusory alliances, and (iii) tyrannies.

At times, the determination of the nature of a combined-effort entity is simple. At other times, it is challenging and open to debate. Answers to the following questions might lead you in the correct direction.

WHAT ARE THE OBJECTIVES OF THE ENTITY?

An important part of the analysis is to identify the objectives pursued by the entity. Often, this analysis is straightforward. At other times, the analysis can be difficult and complicated.

Recall that anything can be an objective. General categories of objectives include:

External Objectives	Internal Objectives
Uniting against Natural Obstacles	Law-Compelled Objectives
Defense against Aggressors	Conservation
Offense against Non-Members	Morality
Cooperatives	Paternalism
Mitigation of Catastrophe	Leveling
Generation of Prosperity	Customs
Charity & Justice	Overlord

This list of categories is not exclusive. You should think openly in order to identify all possible objectives.

In addition, take care to not confuse (i) the *means* that an alliance employs to attain an objective with (ii) the *objective* of an alliance. Means are merely a mechanism for attaining the objective and should not be viewed as the objective underlying the alliance. Analysis of means is not always easy and sometimes you will have great difficulty ascertaining whether something should be classified as an objective, a means, or both. As noted earlier in the book, the objective and means can become blurred over time so that it might be impossible to ascertain whether something constitutes a means or an objective.

DO YOU DESIRE THE OBJECTIVE(S)?

When you have identified one or more objectives, seek to determine whether you desire them. And, if the entity pursues two or more objectives, ask how many of the objectives that you actually desire.

If you desire all of the objectives pursued, the entity is very likely a true alliance. If you desire none of the objectives, the entity is probably a tyranny. If you desire some but not all of the objectives, the entity is likely either a semi-alliance or an illusory alliance.

In addition, ponder whether the entity might be a tyrannical alliance. Recall that a tyrannical alliance is a true alliance that acts like a tyranny. The reason that it is a true alliance is because the members grudgingly tolerate the tyrannical aspects because they see no other feasible alternatives.

Further, consider whether the objectives pursued by the entity constitute an open objective. Recall that the rationale underlying an open objective is to have a decision-making process in place to attain objectives that are suited for a combined effort. As a result, it is very likely that a portion of the membership might never desire the attainment of a particular objective that is being pursued. Nonetheless, all members desire to have the decision-making process in place, even if it from time to time seeks to achieve objectives that they do not want.

Attitude towards the Objective(s)	Probable Combined-Effort Entity
Desire all or most of the objectives	True Alliance
Desire some but not many of the objectives	Semi-Alliance or Illusory Alliance
Desire few or none of the objectives	Tyranny

| Desire all or most the objectives but dislike or even despise the decision-making process | Tyrannical Alliance |
| Desire some but not all of the objectives but nonetheless highly value the existence of the decision-making process | Open-Objective Alliance |

ARE THERE ILLUSORY BENEFITS?

By now, you have analyzed the objectives that the entity pursues. Stop and reflect on whether you truly desire these objectives. Perhaps the objectives are in reality illusory benefits. Recall that illusory benefits are alliance undertakings that appear proper and legitimate but actually are inconsistent with the objective(s) underlying an alliance. Illusory benefits constitute the ruse that allows illusory alliances to exist.

The concept of illusory benefits encompasses several different situations which are sometimes interrelated. In these situations, the proposal is perceived as furthering the alliance objective but in reality the proposal: (i) does not further the objective; (ii) harms or otherwise impairs the objective; or (iii) furthers the objective only marginally (such that any actual value associated with it is outweighed by the value placed on the contribution necessary to achieve it). In determining whether illusory benefits exist, you should scrutinize the objectives and their underlying rationales to assess whether they are consistent with the definition of an alliance objective. For instance, is the objective one that you either (i) cannot attain through individual effort, or (ii) can attain more efficiently or effectively through a combined effort?

If illusory benefits are present, it suggests that the combined-effort entity is not a true alliance. You should study the decision-making process including the conduct of delegated decision makers and their interests. You should strive to see whether they (or special interests that reward them) are profiting from the illusory benefits. Attempt to seek out the motive or reason for the existence of the illusory benefits and you might find that the entity is in fact an illusory alliance.

If illusory benefits are present but not in a sizeable degree, an alliance might still be present. Nothing is perfect in the world. True alliances can exist in a less than perfect form.

IS THERE AN ACCORD?

An accord is a very important part of an alliance. If an accord is in place, it is a very strong indication that the entity is a true alliance. In looking for an accord, recall that accords can be express or implied and that express accords can be both spoken or in writing.

WHAT ARE THE PROVISIONS OF THE ACCORD?

If you identify an accord, examine its provisions. Does the accord place significant restrictions upon the objectives that might be pursued and the means that might be utilize? If so, that is a good sign that the entity is in fact an alliance.

IS THE ACCORD BEING FOLLOWED?

The fact that an accord exists means little if it is not followed. Many illusory alliances and tyrannies have accords but their provisions are ignored. Examine the surrounding circumstances to determine whether the accord's provisions are being adhered to by both the members and the elements of the decision-making process. A lack of substantial compliance suggests that an alliance is not present.

WHAT RESOURCES DO YOU CONTRIBUTE?

Often, the resources that you might contribute to an alliance are easy to identify. Examples of such readily apparent resources include money, physical material, and labor.

Other types of contributed resources might be difficult to ascertain at times. For example, are you contributing liberty to an alliance by agreeing to forego certain types of conduct and to adhere to one or more Law-Compelled Objectives? Are you contributing time to an alliance by agreeing to be present in an area or watch something for a certain period of time? Are you risking injury or death for an alliance effort?

If you are not contributing resources of any type or form, then you are not a member of an alliance, or an alliance does not exist. If you are contributing resources, however, an alliance is not necessarily present. Another type of combined-effort entity might be in existence.

ARE YOU A TRUE MEMBER?

Membership in an entity is usually obvious. Members are given designations such as citizen, participant, partner, member, constituent, and so on. Sometimes, however, things are not what they seem and individuals that appear to be members are in fact not members of the entity.

Do you participate in the decision-making process? If you do, that is a good sign that you are a bona-fide member of a true alliance. If you do not participate, however, that does not rule out membership in the alliance.

Although you might seem to be a member in an alliance, perhaps you are really being exploited by an illusory alliance or tyranny that has used illusory benefits and other tricks to deceive you? Maybe you are a second-class member not receiving the full range of benefits from the alliance?

Another possibility is forced membership. Do you really want to be a member of the alliance? Did you ostensibly "join" an alliance to fit in or for some other ulterior reason? Are you looking for a way to leave the alliance?

Are you a free rider? Recall that a free rider is a person who is not a member of an alliance but nonetheless enjoys the objective attained by the alliance. A free rider does not participate in the alliance's decision-making process and does not contribute resources. Free riders occur only when the nature of the objective is such that its benefits cannot be limited to the members themselves.

IS THERE A DECISION-MAKING PROCESS?

Not all alliances require decision-making processes. Further, some processes are so simple as to not be apparent. Recall that decision-making processes are first categorized into formal and nebulous processes. A formal process has structure and is identified as a decision-making process by the members. In contrast, a nebulous process is rarely recognized and is usually exemplified by decisions being made through an informal consensus. Formal processes are broken down into two sub-categories: membership vote and delegated decision maker. A membership vote is simply where the members make the decision through a vote of all members. A delegated decision maker occurs when the alliance delegates the decision to one of three possible decision makers: (i) executive, (ii) committee, and (iii) non-standard. These various processes can be interwoven or they can be staggered into tiered decision-making processes.

Can you identify a decision-making process for the entity? The presence of a membership vote is a very good sign that an alliance is present. Keep in mind, however, that membership votes can be used to deceive members into thinking that a true alliance is present when in reality an illusory alliance or tyranny is in effect. As such, you should inquire as to whether the membership vote has a true effect upon the decisions that are made by the alliance.

The presence of a single executive decision maker or a committee suggests strongly that an alliance is not present. It is possible, however, for an alliance to exist with such decision-making processes in place. A tyrannical alliance in particular is likely to use such processes.

WHAT LIMITATIONS DOES THE DECISION-MAKING PROCESS HAVE?

Scrutinize the decision-making process to see how susceptible it is to decision maker limitations. For example, is the process subject to motivational or capability limitations? Are fidelity limitations present? The latter is particularly problematic and suggests that an alliance might not be present.

If the entity is attaining objectives but at the same time is subject to one or more limitations, a semi-alliance might be present. The analysis, however, should be tempered with a dose of realism. Decision maker limitations are more or less an inherent condition and will almost always be present in some form or fashion. Thus, your focus should be upon the extent of the limitation and its effect upon the operation of the entity.

ARE THE TOOLS OF TYRANNY BEING UTILIZED?

If the tools of tyranny are present, it is a very good sign that a true alliance is not present. Recall that the tools of tyranny include:

- Stifling or distortion of information about alternatives to the combined-effort entity or its objectives;

- Suppression of dissent and criticism of the combined-effort entity;

- Preventing members from terminating their memberships; and

- Usage of illusory benefits to obscure fidelity limitations.

Some of these tools can be present and an alliance still can exist. There might be reasons for the tools to be utilized that are consistent with a particular alliance objective. For example, if an alliance is pursuing a Paternalistic objective regarding a particular lifestyle, one of the means might include squelching information about that lifestyle.

ARE SUSPECT ELEMENTS PRESENT?

You should review the circumstances to determine if suspect elements are present. Suspect elements are factors that can exist in a true alliance but their presence tends to suggest that the entity is in reality a semi-alliance, an illusory alliance, or a tyranny. Suspect elements include:

- *Indirect attainment*—This term describes the usage of a means that strives to attain the objective in a round-a-bout manner. Indirect attainment can be employed legitimately to attain objectives in numerous circumstances. The idea, however, holds great potential for abuse as it usually provides a good ruse for concealing corrupt undertakings.

- *Excessive contributions of liberty*—Most internal objectives are attained only through the contribution of liberty. As such, there is nothing suspect if an alliance structure requires a contribution of liberty to attain one or more objectives. Contributions of liberty, however, should be barely sufficient to attain the objective at hand. Surplus contributions of liberty are a sign that a tyranny might be present and that the additional contributions of liberty are utilized to prevent dissent, reform, and rebellions.

- *Domination by Association Glory*—Association glory is usually a by-product of an effective alliance and can increase the effectiveness of alliance efforts through the boost effect. Association glory, however, can take on a life of its own and become an objective of the alliance. In this situation, the alliance will seek to pursue ostensible objectives but, if the circumstances are reviewed, it will become apparent that the objectives constitute only means to refurbish, stabilize, or increase the association glory of the alliance. If an alliance becomes preoccupied with protecting and increasing its association glory, the alliance will tend to pursue means that are not desired by many of the members and the alliance will likely terminate.

WHAT IS THE RESULT?

You have considered all of the factors and surrounding circumstances and have identified the objective, the accord, the decision-making process, the resources contributed, the members, and any secondary considerations such as decision-maker limitations, tools of tyranny, and suspect factors. You now you need to finalize your analysis.

What is the result? Are you in an alliance or not? In some circumstances, the answer might be obvious. In other situations, it might be difficult to determine what type of combined-effort entity that you are dealing with. To aid you in reaching the answer, try subjectively valuing the resources that you contribute towards the entity. At the same time, subjectively value the benefit that your receive from the entity. If the subjective benefit outweighs the subjective costs, the entity is probably an alliance. If the subjective benefit is roughly equal to the subjective costs, you are probably in a semi-alliance. Finally, if the subjective benefit is less than the subjective costs, you are likely in an illusory alliance or a tyranny.

WHAT SHOULD YOU DO?

If you are in an alliance, that is good news. But you can improve that alliance if you want. Chapter 13 identifies the traits of successful alliances and should be consulted.

If you are not in an alliance, that is bad news. But it might not be that bad. Study the situation and seek to determine just how unfavorable the circumstances are for you. To do this, focus on the valuation analysis just discussed above. That is, try subjectively valuing the contribution that you are forced to give to the entity (semi-alliance, illusory alliance, tyranny). Then value the benefits, if any, that you receive from the entity. If the two valuations are roughly equal, you might wish to tolerate the combined-effort entity.[1]

If the valuation ratio is not acceptable, you have different options. In many situations, you can terminate your affiliation with the entity. And, if you desire one or more of the objectives that was ostensibly pursued by the entity, you can strive to attain those objectives through either (i) your own individual effort, or (ii) soliciting members and forming a brand new alliance.

In some circumstances, you might not be able to readily terminate your affiliation with the entity. For instance, you might be effectively imprisoned within a tyranny. Under such circumstances, your choices are usually either to submit to the tyranny or to form a counter-alliance and foment a rebellion.

THE MOST EFFECTIVE MECHANISM OF CHANGE

If you are not satisfied with an alliance that you belong to, what should you do? Should you instigate an inside revolution by attempting to seize control of the alliance's decision-making process and yoke the alliance structure to your viewpoint? Should you terminate your membership and launch an outside revolution through a new alliance that you create?

No doubt you are aware of other alliances and combined-effort entities that pursue objectives that you dislike or even abhor. If you desire to contest or combat these alliances or other combined-effort entities, how should you go about it?

---

[1] Recall that even a tyranny can be agreeable to exist under. For instance, if the tyrant fears a revolution, the tyranny might provide the subjugated individuals with desirable benefits to placate them and forestall a revolution.

Should you oppose them through individual effort? Should you strive to form counter-alliances to challenge them head on?

You certainly can attempt such direct, confrontational tactics. But these undertakings will fail in all likelihood. Why? The reason is that these head-to-head challenges typically require huge individual efforts or sizeable assemblies of combined resources. In most circumstances, the entity that you oppose will have the backing of a fair number of individual members and combined resources. You and your alliances might win these battles, but any victories will be costly and the chances of success will tend to be slim.

What if you desire to take a small scale approach? That is, instead of a head-on confrontation, you and perhaps a small counter-alliance strive to harass and hinder an opposing entity? This approach is certainly workable and could yield success in the long run. But if the opposing entity is strong, it is likely that your tactics will achieve no meaningful result.

Example 5 "Help the needy"—The alliance's decision-making process decides to aid the needy by providing them with contraceptives. Albert is a member of the alliance and opposes this undertaking. Albert believes that providing the needy with contraceptives is morally wrong. Albert and five other members terminate their membership in the alliance and form a competing alliance. The objective of this alliance is to interfere with and disrupt the purchase and distribution of contraceptives by Albert's former alliance. Albert and his fellow members engage in various acts of sabotage including stealing contraceptive shipments and deflating the tires of the charitable association's delivery trucks.

Example 4 "Wild West"—To bring order and decency to the community, the mercenary imprisons a number of non-member thieves in his jail. These non-members are in the jail indefinitely and are not treated particularly well. Joe is a member of the alliance. Joe and three other members are very concerned about the welfare of these imprisoned thieves. Joe and his cohorts believe that the thieves' misconduct was not severe and they should be given a second chance. Joe and his three cohorts form an alliance to secretly steal a key to the jail cell from the mercenary. After the key is stolen, Joe throws it through the outside window to the jail cell. The thieves find it and use it to escape.

Example 20 "Slavery"—The five enslaved individuals struggle under the circumstances that the tyranny that imposes upon them. They decide to form a counter-alliance to attack the tyrannical slave-owner (and his alliance with the other slave owners to combine resources to control and suppress the slaves). One night, the five slaves strike and succeed in severely injuring their slave owner and several other slave owners that come to his aid. The slave-owner alliance, however, was prepared for the rebellion and suppresses it in the end. Three of the revolting slaves are killed and the other two spend the rest of their lives working in chains. Further, in order to prevent a future rebellion, the other slave masters tighten the restrictions on their slaves and harden the conditions under which they toil.

In these examples, the counter-alliances attain some degree of success against the opposing entities. Nonetheless, the opposing entities survive the small-scale attacks and effectively nothing has changed. In the end, the undertakings of the counter-alliances are largely symbolic.

Aside from being ineffective, these counter-alliance undertakings are counterproductive. In the case of Example 5, the sabotage causes increased contributions to fund the contraceptive deliveries and a hardening of the alliance's resolve to deliver contraceptives to the needy. In Example 6, the escape of the thieves results in increased security in the jail and tougher and more restrictive conditions being imposed upon imprisoned thieves in the future. In Example 20, the rebellion results in death and a much more unpleasant life for the surviving slaves.

Does this discussion mean that head-on and indirect challenges to opposing combined-effort entities are doomed to failure? Does it mean that one should never strive to change an alliance that one belongs to or to combat a combined-effort entity that one dislikes or abhors? No. The foregoing discussion only underscores the difficulties that will be encountered with such tactics. If one opposes the undertakings of one's alliance or those of an opposing entity, one should always contemplate all available means to effect change including both individual efforts and counter-alliance efforts. At the same time, however, one should carefully examine the likelihood of such efforts actually succeeding.

Aside from head-on changes and indirect harassment, is there a more effective mechanism to attain your desired result? Yes. In many situations, there is a better alternative—to attack the intellectual or moral basis underlying the objective pursued by your alliance or the opposing combined-effort entity. As noted earlier, objectives are all ultimately driven by the world of ideas. The objective underlying an alliance, or any other combined-effort entity, is shaped by the wants, needs, and desires of individuals. As such, if you desire to attain a substantial and profound change, focus your attention and efforts upon the realm of ideas. If you employ this strategy against a particular objective, you can undermine and ultimately negate the subjective desire of others for the attainment of that objective. If you eliminate this desire within the minds of your fellow alliance members, your alliance will no longer desire to pursue the objective that you dislike or abhor. Similarly, if you eliminate the desire within the minds of the members of the opposing combined-effort entity, the entity will cease pursuing the objective and might even collapse if the objective in question is the primary basis of the entity's existence.

If you desire to employ this strategy, your primary tool should be the voice of reason. If you find that an objective is particularly compelling and should be pursued by an alliance, you should articulate the reasons for the alliance adopting that objective. If you find that an objective, or a means used to obtain an objective, is abhorrent, put your best case forward as to why such endeavors should be dropped. If your rationale is compelling, people will eventually start listening to it.

Although focusing in the world of ideas might not be particularly exciting, glamorous, or heroic and might take decades to produce any noticeable results, it is the most effective method for obtaining long-term change. History is replete with individuals who had profound changes upon the direction of the world simply through the ideas and concepts that they articulated to others. A few notable examples include:

- *Socrates*—During his day, Socrates was an irritating "gadfly" who mainly spent his time wandering around Athens picking intellectual fights with fellow Athenians. Ultimately, the Athenians grew weary of Socrates' incessant carping regarding seeking the truth in all things and executed him. Prior to his execution, Socrates was given a chance to defend himself and his way of life in a trial but the jury rejected his defense. Despite this ultimate rejection during Socrates' lifetime, the ideas and concepts articulated by Socrates persevered and were reduced to writing by his student Plato. These ideas continue to have a profound effect upon the world today and the underlying objectives sought to be attained by individuals.

- *Jesus*—Jesus was an impoverished wandering preacher who by and large criticized many prevailing religious practices and beliefs of Hebrews as being unnecessary. Moreover, Jesus contended that most Hebrew religious authorities of the day were hypocrites who failed to practice what they preached. Jesus was arrested and brought to trial. All of Jesus's disciples and supporters fled in terror and denied any ties to Jesus. The Roman authorities tried Jesus as a common criminal and executed him. It appeared that Jesus's movement was over and done with. Nonetheless, the ideas spread by Jesus took root and gave rise to the Christian religion which ultimately became the official religion of the Roman Empire and continues to shape the world today.

- *Mahatma Gandhi*—Gandhi was an Indian raised under British Colonial rule. Gandhi spoke English, integrated himself into British customs, and even became an attorney in the British legal system. In his middle ages, Gandhi concluded that the British Empire was morally wrong and sought to oppose it. Rather than forming revolutionary armies, Gandhi instead employed writings and spoken arguments to expose the failings and iniquities of the British Empire. Gandhi embraced non-violence and organized marches and boycotts to call attention to his arguments. To support his contentions, Gandhi often utilized Christian tents and Western legal concepts to expose hypocrisies in British rule. Ultimately, the British withdrew peacefully and left India to rule itself. This astonishing result was attained without warfare or violence. Instead, the result was due to the ideas and concepts set forward by Gandhi.

- *Martin Luther King*—King was a African American who lived under legally sponsored racial segregation. Although African Americans were "American" citizens and were required to pay taxes and serve in the military, they were denied equal rights by the state and local governments. Many African Americans were outraged by this situation and sought to form violent alliances to attack and overthrow the existing system of segregation. King rejected these efforts and embraced a non-violent approach which sought to expose the evils of state-sponsored segregation. Inspired by Gandhi's success, King repeatedly hammered away in speeches and in writings at the irrationality of prejudice and how state-sponsored segregation was fundamentally at odds with traditional American democratic tenets. Through fighting an unrelenting intellectual battle, King won the war of ideas and segregation collapsed.

- *The Cold War*—From approximately 1947 to 1991, the Soviet Union, the United States, and their respective allies prepared for a massive "End of the World" nuclear war. During this time period, the nations sparred indirectly in various regions such as Berlin, Korea, Cuba, Viet Nam, and Central America. Nonetheless, the war remained "cold" with no direct battles between the Superpowers. In December 1991, the implausible occurred. The Soviet Union voluntarily dissolved and the Cold War came to entirely unpredictable end. Arguably, this dissolution was a product of a realization by members of the Soviet Union that communism was unworkable, doomed to failure, and immoral. From the beginning of the Cold War, the Soviets and the Americans engaged in constant intellectual battles about the relative merits of communism and free-market democracies. For instance, U.S. Vice President Nixon and Soviet Premier Nikita Khrushchev famously argued about the two competing systems in their 1959 "Kitchen Debate." These intellectual battles were carried on by numerous individuals who attacked the political, economic, and moral foundations of Soviet communism. Notable examples include Russians such as Alexander Solzhenitsyn and Andrei Sakharov. By the late 1980s, the tide in this war of ideas turned in clearly against the Soviet Union. The United States and other Western democracies enjoyed relatively prosperous times. The Soviets and their allies, in contrast, were mired in a war in Afghanistan, shocked by the Chernobyl nuclear disaster, unable to compete with the military build up of the United States, suffering under a corrupt police state, and generally enduring widespread poverty and malaise. As a result, the Soviets appear to have concluded that communism had failed and that the Soviet Union would never succeed. The combined-effort entity, which was an alliance to some and a great tyranny to many, thus terminated.

These historical examples highlight the massive and profound effects that simple ideas can have upon changing alliances, combined-effort entities, and the world itself. If you strive to make similar changes, you should undertake your endeavors in the world of ideas.

CHAPTER 30

Closing

Having completed this book, the reader should have obtained useful tools to analyze various situations where humans engage in concerted conduct. These tools should allow the reader to assess his or her own circumstances as well as historical and present day events and happenings. Further, the reader should have a new language in which he or she can communicate regarding various situations where humans combine resources to attain mutually desired objectives. It is hoped that readers will be able to use alliance theory to find common ground with other humans on many points and then identify the true issues upon which they disagree.

As noted in the Introduction to this book, it appears that most public policy discussions of today are typified by insults, sophistry, and dirty-debating tricks. These tactics appear to be employed because the debaters lack a common framework for analyzing and discussing the topics at hand. With alliance theory, it is hoped that participants of all degrees of sophistication will be able to discard empty rhetoric and instead identify the true underlying issues at controversy and explore the strengths and weaknesses of both sides. Perhaps this is wishful thinking, but alliance theory might foster recognition by many that the differences they have with others are not so great and often can be discussed in rational, civil, and respectful manners.

MORALITY REVISITED

This book has come to an end but it has, by and large, neglected to raise a very important topic. This omitted issue is the topic of moral rights and wrongs, which also could be referred to as ethics, virtue, values, or a host of related terms. Instead of addressing these weighty matters, this book has adhered to an amoral approach. This tactic was chosen because the book pertains to the analysis of alliances and how they form, develop, evolve, and ultimately terminate. In order to study this topic as accurately and as precisely as possible, traditional concepts of morality were intentionally ignored (to the extent that one can ignore such matters). Morality entails judgment of right and wrong and that is not what this book is about.

The omission of morality from this book does not suggest that morality has no place in alliances or in the examination and study of alliance development. To the contrary, morality, ethics, virtue, and all related topics should have a controlling weight upon the formation, governance, and direction of all alliances. Anyone seeking to form an alliance or to make decisions within an alliance decision-making process should be guided by moral principles. When one studies alliances with an eye towards to improving them (as opposed to a focus upon how they grow, develop, and decline), one should engage in moral judgments of right and wrong. The subject of morality, however, is not a topic for this book.

A THOUGHT EXPERIMENT

Any reader who has completed the book and remains skeptical of alliance theory is invited to participate in a thought experiment. This experiment might appear somewhat peculiar to some but it should be useful.

Imagine the classic castaway scenario. You and ninety nine other adult individuals are shipwrecked on a desert island. There is no hope of rescue. Consistent with the castaway story, the civilized world believes that you are all dead and will not attempt to save you. You will spend the remainder of your life on the island.

The island has some fresh-water springs as well as coconut and fruit trees. The surrounding waters hold various forms of sea life. The island has a few caves and some trees that can be used to construct shelters.

What will your life be like on this desert island? Will you strive to live alone like a hermit, finding your own food and shelter? Will you instead join with other castaways to form something resembling a modern day government that has elected officers and strives to construct public works such as roads, wells, and bridges and to provide for police, firemen, courts, jails, and social welfare programs?

Stop and ponder these questions...

In all likelihood, your answers will be consistent with alliance theory. Specifically, you will rely largely upon individual effort to satisfy most of your wants and needs. You will find your own food and water and you will locate or construct your own shelter. Nonetheless, you will at times enter into alliance relationships with other individuals through both implied accords and express accords. These alliances will be single-objective alliances and will relate to objectives that either (i) you cannot attain with your own efforts, or (ii) can be attained more effectively or efficiently through a combined effort, in comparison to an individual effort. For instance, you might form single-objective alliances with a few other castaways to catch a large fish, to cut down a tree, to build a bridge across a stream, and so on. Further, you might also individually outsource efforts from time to time such as giving another castaway some fruit you collected in exchange for that castaway helping you to construct a shelter.

Will you enter multi-objective alliances? It depends upon whether there is a perceived need to do so. If one-hundred strangers are deposited upon a desert island, it seems likely that sporadic acts of violence and theft could break out. As a result, you and other castaways might form an alliance to pursue various Law-Compelled Objectives including Protection of the Person, Protection of Property, and possibly even Enforcement of Promises. Similarly, you all might fear tropical storms and pursue the objective of Mitigation against Catastrophe. If the fruit trees and water supplies are limited, you might strive to attain the objective of Conservation. Depending upon the circumstances presented and your needs and desires, a multi-objective alliance could be formed pursuing all of the categories of objectives identified in this book.

What about membership? Will all 100 castaways be members in the alliances that might form? It depends but it is likely that there will be some holdouts that refuse to join the various alliances that might spring up. These holdouts will be denied the benefits of membership. But the free-rider effect might allow them to benefit in the fruits of certain alliance efforts notwithstanding their lack of membership. Further, some castaways might join in an alliance only to fit in and not cause a controversy. These individuals will be forced members.

Will tyrannies or other combined-effort entities arise on the desert island? It is possible. For instance, a large group of castaways might ally together to subjugate the remaining castaways. And the subjugated castaways might form a counter-alliance to defend their interests and free themselves from the tyranny. Long-term warring alliances might result on this desert island.

Many other events could occur on this desert island, especially as time passes. All in all, as you ponder the questions of the desert island, alliance-theory concepts should greatly aid you in finding answers. And perhaps any skepticism that you may hold will be diminished.

Appendix A

The Declaration of Independence

July 4, 1776

When in the Course of human events, it becomes necessary for one people to dissolve the political bands which have connected them with another, and to assume, among the Powers of the earth, the separate and equal station to which the Laws of Nature and of Nature's God entitle them, a decent respect to the opinions of mankind requires that they should declare the causes which impel them to the separation.

We hold these truths to be self-evident, that all men are created equal, that they are endowed by their Creator with certain unalienable Rights, that among these are Life, Liberty, and the pursuit of Happiness. That to secure these rights, Governments are instituted among Men, deriving their just powers from the consent of the governed, That whenever any Form of Government becomes destructive of these ends, it is the Right of the People to alter or to abolish it, and to institute new Government, laying its foundation on such principles and organizing its powers in such form, as to them shall seem most likely to effect their Safety and Happiness. Prudence, indeed, will dictate that Governments long established should not be changed for light and transient causes; and accordingly all experience hath shown, that mankind are more disposed to suffer, while evils are sufferable, than to right themselves by abolishing the forms to which they are accustomed. But when a long train of abuses and usurpations, pursuing invariably the same Object evinces a design to reduce them under absolute Despotism, it is their right, it is their duty, to throw off such Government, and to provide new Guards for their future security. —Such has been the patient sufferance of these Colonies; and such is now the necessity which constrains them to alter their former Systems of Government. The history of the present King of Great Britain is a history of repeated injuries and usurpations, all having in direct object the establishment of an absolute Tyranny over these States. To prove this, let Facts be submitted to a candid world.

He has refused his Assent to Laws, the most wholesome and necessary for the public good.

He has forbidden his Governors to pass Laws of immediate and pressing importance, unless suspended in their operation till his Assent should be obtained; and when so suspended, he has utterly neglected to attend to them.

He has refused to pass other Laws for the accommodation of large districts of people, unless those people would relinquish the right of Representation in the Legislature, a right inestimable to them and formidable to tyrants only.

He has called together legislative bodies at places unusual, uncomfortable, and distant from the depository of their Public Records, for the sole purpose of fatiguing them into compliance with his measures.

He has dissolved Representative Houses repeatedly, for opposing with manly firmness his invasions on the rights of the people.

He has refused for a long time, after such dissolutions, to cause others to be elected; whereby the Legislative Powers, incapable of Annihilation, have returned to the People at large for their exercise; the State remaining in the mean time exposed to all the dangers of invasion from without, and convulsions within.

He has endeavoured to prevent the population of these States; for that purpose obstructing the Laws of Naturalization of Foreigners; refusing to pass others to encourage their migration hither, and raising the conditions of new Appropriations of Lands.

He has obstructed the Administration of Justice, by refusing his Assent to Laws for establishing Judiciary Powers.

He has made judges dependent on his Will alone, for the tenure of their offices, and the amount and payment of their salaries.

He has erected a multitude of New Offices, and sent hither swarms of Officers to harass our People, and eat out their substance.

He has kept among us, in times of peace, Standing Armies without the Consent of our legislatures.

He has affected to render the Military independent of and superior to the Civil Power.

He has combined with others to subject us to a jurisdiction foreign to our constitution, and unacknowledged by our laws; giving his Assent to their Acts of pretended legislation:

For quartering large bodies of armed troops among us:

For protecting them, by a mock Trial, from Punishment for any Murders which they should commit on the Inhabitants of these States:

For cutting off our Trade with all parts of the world:

For imposing taxes on us without our Consent:

For depriving us, in many cases, of the benefits of Trial by Jury:

For transporting us beyond Seas to be tried for pretended offences:

For abolishing the free System of English Laws in a neighbouring Province, establishing therein an Arbitrary government, and enlarging its Boundaries so as to render it at once an example and fit instrument for introducing the same absolute rule into these Colonies:

For taking away our Charters, abolishing our most valuable Laws, and altering fundamentally the Forms of our Governments:

For suspending our own Legislatures, and declaring themselves invested with Power to legislate for us in all cases whatsoever.

He has abdicated Government here, by declaring us out of his Protection and waging War against us.

He has plundered our seas, ravaged our Coasts, burnt our towns, and destroyed the lives of our people.

He is at this time transporting large armies of foreign mercenaries to compleat the works of death, desolation and tyranny, already begun with circumstances of Cruelty & perfidy scarcely paralleled in the most barbarous ages, and totally unworthy of the Head of a civilized nation.

He has constrained our fellow Citizens taken Captive on the high Seas to bear Arms against their Country, to become the executioners of their friends and Brethren, or to fall themselves by their Hands.

He has excited domestic insurrections amongst us, and has endeavoured to bring on the inhabitants of our frontiers, the merciless Indian Savages, whose known rule of warfare, is an undistinguished destruction of all ages, sexes and conditions.

In every stage of these Oppressions We have Petitioned for Redress in the most humble terms: Our repeated Petitions have been answered only by repeated injury. A Prince, whose character is thus marked by every act which might define a Tyrant, is unfit to be the ruler of a free People.

Nor have We been wanting in attention to our British brethren. We have warned them from time to time of attempts by their legislature to extend an unwarrantable jurisdiction over us. We have reminded them of the circumstances of our emigration and settlement here. We have appealed to their native justice and magnanimity, and we have conjured them by the ties of our common kindred to disavow these usurpations, which would inevitably interrupt our connections and correspondence. They too have been deaf to the voice of justice and of consanguinity. We must, therefore, acquiesce in the necessity, which denounces our Separation, and hold them, as we hold the rest of mankind, Enemies in War, in Peace Friends.

We, therefore, the Representatives of the United States of America, in General Congress, Assembled, appealing to the Supreme Judge of the world for the rectitude of our intentions, do, in the Name, and by the Authority of the good People of these Colonies, solemnly publish and declare, That these United Colonies are, and of Right ought to be Free and Independent States; that they are Absolved from all Allegiance to the British Crown, and that all political connection between them and the State of Great Britain, is and ought to be totally dissolved; and that as Free and Independent States, they have full Power to levy War, conclude Peace, contract Alliances, establish Commerce, and to do all other Acts and Things which Independent States might of right do. And for the support of this Declaration, with a firm reliance on the Protection of Divine Providence, we mutually pledge to each other our Lives, our Fortunes and our sacred Honor.

The Articles of Confederation

March 1, 1781

To all to whom these Presents shall come, we the under signed Delegates of the States affixed to our Names, send greeting.

Whereas the Delegates of the United States of America, in Congress assembled, did, on the 15th day of November, in the Year of Our Lord One thousand Seven Hundred and Seventy seven, and in the Second Year of the Independence of America, agree to certain articles of Confederation and perpetual Union between the States of New Hampshire, Massachusetts-bay, Rhode Island and Providence Plantations, Connecticut, New York, New Jersey, Pennsylvania, Delaware, Maryland, Virginia, North-Carolina, South-Carolina, and Georgia in the words following, viz. Articles of Confederation and perpetual Union between the states of New Hampshire, Massachusetts-bay, Rhode Island and Providence Plantations, Connecticut, New-York, New-Jersey, Pennsylvania, Delaware, Maryland, Virginia, North-Carolina, South-Carolina and Georgia.

Article I. The Stile of this confederacy shall be "The United States of America."

Article II. Each state retains its sovereignty, freedom, and independence, and every Power, Jurisdiction and right, which is not by this confederation expressly delegated to the United States, in Congress assembled.

Article III. The said states hereby severally enter into a firm league of friendship with each other, for their common defense, the security of their Liberties, and their mutual and general welfare, binding themselves to assist each other, against all force offered to, or attacks made upon them, or any of them, on account of religion, sovereignty, trade, or any other pretence whatever.

Article IV. The better to secure and perpetuate mutual friendship and intercourse among the people of the different states in this union, the free inhabitants of each of these states, paupers, vagabonds and fugitives from justice excepted, shall be entitled to all privileges and immunities of free citizens in the several states; and the people of each state shall have free ingress and regress to and from any other state, and shall enjoy therein all the privileges of trade and commerce, subject to the same duties, impositions and restrictions as the inhabitants thereof respectively, provided that such restriction shall not extend so far as to prevent the removal of property imported into any state, to any other state, of which the Owner is an inhabitant; provided also that no imposition, duties or restriction shall be laid by any state, on the property of the United States, or either of them.

If any Person guilty of, or charged with treason, felony, or other high misdemeanor in any state, shall flee from Justice, and be found in any of the United States, he shall, upon demand of the Governor or executive power, of the state from which he fled, be delivered up and removed to the state having jurisdiction of his offence. Full faith and credit shall be given in each of these states to the records, acts and judicial proceedings of the courts and magistrates of every other state.

Article V. For the more convenient management of the general interests of the United States, delegates shall be annually appointed in such manner as the legislature of each state shall direct, to meet in Congress on the first Monday in November, in every year, with a power reserved to each state, to recall its delegates, or any of them, at any time within the year, and to send others in their stead, for the remainder of the Year.

No state shall be represented in Congress by less than two, nor by more than seven Members; and no person shall be capable of being a delegate for more than three years in any term of six years; nor shall any person, being a delegate, be capable of holding any office under the United States, for which he, or another for his benefit receives any salary, fees or emolument of any kind.

Each state shall maintain its own delegates in a meeting of the states, and while they act as members of the committee of the states.

In determining questions in the United States in Congress assembled, each state shall have one vote.

Freedom of speech and debate in Congress shall not be impeached or questioned in any Court, or place out of Congress, and the members of congress shall be protected in their persons from arrests and imprisonments, during the time of their going to and from, and attendance on congress, except for treason, felony, or breach of the peace.

Article VI. No state, without the Consent of the United States in congress assembled, shall send any embassy to, or receive any embassy from, or enter into any conference, agreement, alliance or treaty with any King prince or state; nor shall any person holding any office of profit or trust under the United States, or any of them, accept of any present, emolument, office or title of any kind whatever from any king, prince or foreign state; nor shall the United States in congress assembled, or any of them, grant any title of nobility.

No two or more states shall enter into any treaty, confederation or alliance whatever between them, without the consent of the United States in congress assembled, specifying accurately the purposes for which the same is to be entered into, and how long it shall continue.

No state shall lay any imposts or duties, which might interfere with any stipulations in treaties, entered into by the United States in congress assembled, with any king, prince or state, in pursuance of any treaties already proposed by congress, to the courts of France and Spain.

No vessels of war shall be kept up in time of peace by any state, except such number only, as shall be deemed necessary by the United States in congress assembled, for the defense of such state, or its trade; nor shall any body of forces be kept up by any state, in time of peace, except such number only, as in the judgment of the United States, in congress assembled, shall be deemed requisite to garrison the forts necessary for the defense of such state; but every state shall always keep up a well regulated and disciplined militia, sufficiently armed and accoutered, and shall provide and constantly have ready for use, in public stores, a due number of field pieces and tents, and a proper quantity of arms, ammunition and camp equipage.

No state shall engage in any war without the consent of the United States in congress assembled, unless such state be actually invaded by enemies, or shall have received certain advice of a resolution being formed by some nation of Indians to invade such state, and the danger is so imminent as not to admit of a delay till the United States in congress assembled can be consulted: nor shall any state grant commissions to any ships or vessels of war, nor letters of marque or reprisal, except it be after a declaration of war by the United States in congress assembled, and then only against the kingdom or state and the subjects thereof, against which war has been so declared, and under such regulations as shall be established by the United States in congress assembled, unless such state be infested by pirates, in which case vessels of war might be fitted out for that occasion, and kept so long as the danger shall continue, or until the United States in congress assembled, shall determine otherwise.

Article VII. When land-forces are raised by any state for the common defense, all officers of or under the rank of colonel, shall be appointed by the legislature of each state respectively, by whom such forces shall be raised, or in such manner as such state shall direct, and all vacancies shall be filled up by the State which first made the appointment.

Article VIII. All charges of war, and all other expenses that shall be incurred for the common defense or general welfare, and allowed by the United States in congress assembled, shall be defrayed out of a common treasury, which shall be supplied by the several states in proportion to the value of all land within each state, granted to or surveyed for any Person, as such land and the buildings and improvements thereon shall be estimated according to such mode as the United States in congress assembled, shall from time to time direct and appoint.

The taxes for paying that proportion shall be laid and levied by the authority and direction of the legislatures of the several states within the time agreed upon by the United States in Congress assembled.

Article IX. The United States in congress assembled, shall have the sole and exclusive right and power of determining on peace and war, except in the cases mentioned in the sixth article—of sending and receiving ambassadors—entering into treaties and alliances, provided that no treaty of commerce shall be made whereby the legislative power of the respective states shall be restrained from imposing such imposts and duties on foreigners as their own people are subjected to, or from prohibiting the exportation or importation of any species of goods or commodities, whatsoever—of establishing rules for deciding in all cases, what captures on land or water shall be legal, and in what manner prizes taken by land or naval forces in the service of the United States shall be divided or appropriated—of granting letters of marque and reprisal in times of peace—appointing courts for the trial of piracies and felonies committed on the high seas and establishing courts for receiving and determining finally appeals in all cases of captures, provided that no member of congress shall be appointed a judge of any of the said courts.

The United States in congress assembled shall also be the last resort on appeal in all disputes and differences now subsisting or that hereafter might arise between two or more states concerning boundary, jurisdiction or any other cause whatever; which authority shall always be exercised in the manner following. Whenever the legislative or executive authority or lawful agent of any state in controversy with another shall present a petition to congress stating the matter in question and praying for a hearing, notice thereof shall be given by order of congress to the legislative or executive authority of the other state in controversy, and a day assigned for the appearance of the parties by their lawful agents, who shall then be directed to appoint by joint consent, commissioners or judges to constitute a court for hearing and determining the matter in question: but if they cannot agree, congress shall name three persons out of each of the United States, and from the list of such persons each party shall alternately strike out one, the petitioners beginning, until the number shall be reduced to thirteen; and from that number not less than seven, nor more than nine names as congress shall direct, shall in the presence of congress be drawn out by lot, and the persons whose names shall be so drawn or any five of them, shall be commissioners or judges, to hear and finally determine the controversy, so always as a major part of the judges who shall hear the cause shall agree in the determination: and if either party shall neglect to attend at the day appointed, without showing reasons, which congress shall judge sufficient, or being present shall refuse to strike, the congress shall proceed to nominate three persons out of each state, and the secretary of congress shall strike in behalf of such party absent or refusing; and the judgment and sentence of the court to be appointed, in the manner before prescribed, shall be final and conclusive; and if any of the parties shall refuse to submit to the authority of such court, or to appear or defend their claim or cause, the court shall nevertheless proceed to pronounce sentence, or judgment, which shall in like manner be final and decisive, the judgment or sentence and other proceedings being in either case transmitted to congress, and lodged among the acts of congress for the security of the parties concerned: provided that every commissioner, before he sits in judgment, shall take an oath to be administered by one of the judges of the supreme or superior court of the state, where the cause shall be tried, "well and truly to hear and determine the matter in question, according to the best of his judgment, without favor, affection or hope of reward:" provided also, that no state shall be deprived of territory for the benefit of the United States.

All controversies concerning the private right of soil claimed under different grants of two or more states, whose jurisdictions as they might respect such lands, and the states which passed such grants are adjusted, the said grants or either of them being at the same time claimed to have originated antecedent to such settlement of jurisdiction, shall on the petition of either party to the congress of the United States, be finally determined as near as might be in the same manner as is before prescribed for deciding disputes respecting territorial jurisdiction between different states.

The United States in congress assembled shall also have the sole and exclusive right and power of regulating the alloy and value of coin struck by their own authority, or by that of the respective states—fixing the standard of weights and measures throughout the United States—regulating the trade and managing all affairs with the Indians, not members of any of the states provided that the legislative right of any state within its own limits be not infringed or violated—establishing or regulating post-offices from one state to another, throughout all the United States, and exacting such postage on the papers passing thro' the same as might be requisite to defray the expenses of the said office—appointing all officers of the land forces, in the service of the United States, excepting regimental officers— appointing all the officers of the naval forces, and commissioning all officers whatever in the service of the United States—making rules for the government and regulation of the said land and naval forces, and directing their operations.

The United States in congress assembled shall have authority to appoint a committee, to sit in the recess of congress, to be denominated "A Committee of the States," and to consist of one delegate from each state; and to appoint such other committees and civil officers as might be necessary for managing the general affairs of the United States under their direction—to appoint one of their number to preside, provided that no person be allowed to serve in the office of president more than one year in any term of three years; to ascertain the necessary sums of money to be raised for the service of the United States, and to appropriate and apply the same for defraying the public expenses—to borrow money, or emit bills on the credit of the United States, transmitting every half year to the respective states an account of the sums of money so borrowed or emitted,—to build and equip a navy—to agree upon the number of land forces, and to make requisitions from each state for its quota, in proportion to the number of white inhabitants in such state; which requisition shall be binding, and thereupon the legislature of each state shall appoint the regimental officers, raise the men and clothe, arm and equip them in a soldier like manner, at the expense of the United States; and the officers and men so clothed, armed and equipped shall march to the place appointed, and within the time agreed on by the United States in congress assembled: But if the United States in congress assembled shall, on consideration of circumstances judge proper that any state should not raise men, or should raise a smaller number than its quota, and that any other state should raise a greater number of men than the quota thereof, such extra number shall be raised, officered, clothed, armed and equipped in the same manner as the quota of such state, unless the legislature of such state shall judge that such extra number cannot be safely spared out of the same, in which case they shall raise officer, clothe, arm and equip as many of such extra number as they judge can be safely spared. And the officers and men so clothed, armed and equipped, shall march to the place appointed, and within the time agreed on by the United States in congress assembled.

The United States in congress assembled shall never engage in a war, nor grant letters of marque and reprisal in time of peace, nor enter into any treaties or alliances, nor coin money, nor regulate the value thereof, nor ascertain the sums and expenses necessary for the defense and welfare of the United States, or any of them, nor emit bills, nor borrow money on the credit of the United States, nor appropriate money, nor agree upon the number of vessels of war, to be built or purchased, or the number of land or sea forces to be raised, nor appoint a commander in chief of the army or navy, unless nine states assent to the same: nor shall a question on any other point, except for adjourning from day to day be determined, unless by the votes of a majority of the United States in congress assembled.

The congress of the United States shall have power to adjourn to any time within the year, and to any place within the United States, so that no period of adjournment be for a longer duration than the space of six Months, and shall publish the Journal of their proceedings monthly, except such parts thereof relating to treaties, alliances or military operations, as in their judgment require secrecy; and the yeas and nays of the delegates of each state on any question shall be entered on the Journal, when it is desired by any delegate; and the delegates of a state, or any of them, at his or their request shall be furnished with a transcript of the said Journal, except such parts as are above excepted, to lay before the legislatures of the several states.

Article X. The committee of the states, or any nine of them, shall be authorized to execute, in the recess of congress, such of the powers of congress as the United States in congress assembled, by the consent of nine states, shall from time to time think expedient to vest them with; provided that no power be delegated to the said committee, for the exercise of which, by the articles of confederation, the voice of nine states in the congress of the United States assembled is requisite.

Article XI. Canada acceding to this confederation, and joining in the measures of the United States, shall be admitted into, and entitled to all the advantages of this union: but no other colony shall be admitted into the same, unless such admission be agreed to by nine states.

Article XII. All bills of credit emitted, monies borrowed and debt contracted by, or under the authority of congress, before the assembling of the United States, in pursuance of the present confederation, shall be deemed and considered as a charge against the United States, for payment and satisfaction whereof the said United States, and the public faith are hereby solemnly pledged.

Article XIII. Every state shall abide by the determinations of the United States in congress assembled, on all questions which by this confederation are submitted to them. And the Articles of this confederation shall be inviolably observed by every state, and the union shall be perpetual; nor shall any alteration at any time hereafter be made in any of them; unless such alteration be agreed to in a congress of the United States, and be afterwards confirmed by the legislatures of every state.

And Whereas it hath pleased the Great Governor of the World to incline the hearts of the legislatures we respectively represent in congress, to approve of, and to authorize us to ratify the said articles of confederation and perpetual union. Know Ye that we the undersigned delegates, by virtue of the power and authority to us given for that purpose, do by these presents, in the name and in behalf of our respective constituents, fully and entirely ratify and confirm each and every of the said articles of confederation and perpetual union, and all and singular the matters and things therein contained: And we do further solemnly plight and engage the faith of our respective constituents, that they shall abide by the determinations of the United States in congress assembled, on all questions, which by the said confederation are submitted to them. And that the articles thereof shall be inviolably observed by the states we respectively represent, and that the union shall be perpetual. In Witness whereof we have hereunto set our hands in Congress. Done at Philadelphia in the state of Pennsylvania the ninth day of July, in the Year of our Lord one Thousand seven Hundred and Seventy-eight, and in the third year of the independence of America.

The Constitution of the United States

September 17, 1787

PREAMBLE

We the people of the United States, in order to form a more perfect union, establish justice, insure domestic tranquility, provide for the common defense, promote the general welfare, and secure the blessings of liberty to ourselves and our posterity, do ordain and establish this constitution for the United States of America.

ARTICLE I

Section 1.

All legislative powers herein granted shall be vested in a congress of the United States, which shall consist of a senate and house of representatives.

Section 2.

The house of representatives shall be composed of members chosen every second year by the people of the several states, and the electors in each state shall have the qualifications requisite for electors of the most numerous branch of the state legislature.

No person shall be a representative who shall not have attained to the age of twenty-five years and been seven years a citizen of the United States, and who shall not, when elected, be an inhabitant of the state in which he shall be chosen.

Representatives and direct taxes shall be apportioned among the several states which might be included within this union, according to their respective numbers, which shall be determined by adding to the whole number of free persons, including those bound to service for a term of years, and excluding Indians not taxed, three-fifths of all other persons. The actual enumeration shall be made within three years after the first meeting of the congress of the United States, and within every subsequent term of ten years, in such manner as they shall by law direct. The number of representatives shall not exceed one for every thirty thousand, but each state shall have at least one representative; and until such enumeration shall be made, the state of New Hampshire shall be entitled to choose three, Massachusetts eight, Rhode Island and Providence Plantations one, Connecticut five,

New York six, New Jersey four Pennsylvania eight, Delaware one, Maryland six, Virginia ten North Carolina five, South Carolina five, and Georgia three.

When vacancies happen in the representation from any state the executive authority thereof shall issue writs of election to fill such vacancies.

The house of representatives shall choose their speaker and other officers; and shall have the sole power of impeachment.

Section 3.

The Senate of the United States shall be composed of two senators from each state, chosen by the legislature thereof, for six years; and each senator shall have one vote.

Immediately after they shall be assembled in consequence of the first election, they shall be divided as equally as might be into three classes. The seats of the senators of the first class shall be vacated at the expiration of the second year, of the second class at Constitution of the United States the expiration of the fourth year, and of the third class at the expiration of the sixth year, so that one-third might be chosen every second year; and if vacancies happen by resignation, or otherwise, during the recess of the legislature of any state, the executive thereof might make temporary appointments until the next meeting of the legislature, which shall then fill such vacancies.

No person shall be a Senator who shall not have attained to the age of thirty years, and been nine years a citizen of the United States, and who shall not, when elected, be an inhabitant of that state for which he shall be chosen.

The Vice President of the United States shall be president of the senate, but shall have no vote, unless they be equally divided.

The Senate shall choose their other officers, and also a president pro tempore, in the absence of the vice president, or when he shall exercise the office of president of the United States.

The Senate shall have the sole power to try all impeachments. When sitting for that purpose, they shall be on oath or affirmation. When the president of the United States is tried, the chief justice shall preside: And no person shall be convicted without the concurrence of two-thirds of the members present.

Judgment in cases of impeachment shall not extend further than to removal from office, and disqualification to hold and enjoy any office of honor, trust or profit under the United States: but the party convicted shall nevertheless be liable and subject to indictment, trial, judgment and punishment, according to law.

Section 4.

The times, places and manner of holding elections for Senators and representatives shall be prescribed in each state by the legislature thereof; but the congress might at any time by law make or alter such regulations, except as to the places of choosing senators.

The Congress shall assemble at least once in every year, and such meeting shall be on the first Monday in December, unless they shall by law appoint a different day.

Section 5.

Each house shall be the judge of the elections, returns and qualifications of its own members, and a majority of each shall constitute a quorum to do business; but a smaller number might adjourn from day to day, and might be authorized to compel the attendance of absent members, in such manner and under such penalties as each house might provide.

Each house might determine the rules of its proceedings, punish its members for disorderly behavior, and, with the concurrence of two-thirds, expel a member.

Each house shall keep a journal of its proceedings, and from time to time publish the same, excepting such parts as might in their judgment require secrecy; and the yeas and nays of the members of either house on any question shall, at the desire of one-fifth of those present, be entered on the journal.

Neither house, during the session of congress, shall, without the consent of the other, adjourn for more than three days, nor to any other place than that in which the two houses shall be sitting.

Section 6.

The Senators and representatives shall receive a compensation for their services, to be ascertained by law, and paid out of the treasury of the United States. They shall in all cases, except treason, felony and breach of the peace, be privileged from arrest during their attendance at the session of their respective houses, and in going to and returning from the same and for any speech or debate in either house they shall not be questioned in any other place.

No Senator or representative shall, during the time for which he was elected, be appointed to any civil office under the authority of the United States which shall have been created or the emoluments whereof shall have been increased during such time, and no person holding any office under the United States shall be a member of either house during his continuance in office.

Section 7.

All bills for raising revenue shall originate in the house of representatives; but the senate might propose or concur with amendments as on other bills.

Every bill which shall have passed the house of representatives and the senate shall, before it become a law, be presented to the president of the United States. If he approve, he shall sign it; but if not, he shall return it with his objections, to that house in which it shall have originated, who shall enter the objections at large on their journal, and proceed to reconsider it. If after such reconsideration two-thirds of that house shall agree to pass the bill, it shall be sent, together with the objections, to the other house by which it shall likewise be reconsidered, and if approved by two-thirds of that house, it shall become a law. But in all such cases the votes of both houses shall be determined by yeas and nays, and the names of the persons voting for and against the bill shall be entered on the journal of each house respectively. If any bill shall not be returned by the president within ten days (Sundays excepted) after it shall have been presented to him, the same shall be a law, in like manner as if he had signed it, unless the congress by their adjournment prevent its return, in which case it shall not be a law.

Every order, resolution, or vote to which the concurrence of the senate and house of representatives might be necessary (except on a question of adjournment) shall be presented to the president of the United States; and before the same shall take effect, shall be approved by him, or, being disapproved by him, shall be re-passed by two-thirds of the senate and house of representatives, according to the rules and limitations prescribed in the case of a bill.

Section 8.

The Congress shall have power

To lay and collect taxes, duties, imposts and excises, to pay the debts and provide for the common defense and general welfare of the United States, but all duties, imposts and excises shall be uniform throughout the United States;

To borrow money on the credit of the United States;

To regulate commerce with foreign nations, and among the several states, and with the Indian tribes; Constitution of the United States

To establish an uniform rule of naturalization, and uniform laws on the subject of bankruptcies throughout the United States;

To coin money, regulate the value thereof, and of foreign coin, and fix the standard of weights and measures;

To provide for the punishment of counterfeiting the securities and current coin of the United States;

To establish post offices and post roads;

To promote the progress of science and useful arts, by securing for limited times to authors and inventors the exclusive right to their respective writings and discoveries;

To constitute tribunals inferior to the supreme court;

To define and punish piracies and felonies committed on the high seas, and offence, against the law of nations;

To declare war, grant letters of marque and reprisal, and make rules concerning captures on land and water;

To raise and support armies, but no appropriation of money to that use shall be for a longer term than two years;

To provide and maintain a navy;

To make rules for the government and regulation of the land and naval forces;

To provide for calling forth the militia to execute the laws of the union, suppress insurrections and repel invasions;

To provide for organizing, arming, and disciplining the militia, and for governing such part of them as might be employed in the service of the United States, reserving to the states respectively the appointment of the officers and the authority of training the militia according to the discipline prescribed by congress;

To exercise exclusive legislation in all cases whatsoever, over such district (not exceeding ten miles square) as might, by cession of particular states, and the acceptance of congress, become the seat of the government of the United States, and to exercise like authority over all places purchased by the consent of the legislature of the state in which the same shall be, for the erection of forts, magazines, arsenals, dock-yards, and other needful buildings, and

To make all laws which shall be necessary and proper for carrying into execution the foregoing powers, and all other powers vested by this constitution in the government of the United States, or in any department or officer thereof.

Section 9.

The migration or importation of such persons as any of the states now existing shall think proper to admit shall not be prohibited by the congress prior to the year one thousand eight hundred and eight, but a tax or duty might be imposed on such importation, not exceeding ten dollars for each person.

The privilege of the writ of habeas corpus shall not be suspended, unless when in cases of rebellion or invasion the public safety might require it.

No bill of attainder or ex post facto law shall be passed.

No capitation or other direct tax shall be laid, unless in proportion to the census or enumeration here in before directed to be taken.

No tax or duty shall be laid on articles exported from any state.

No preference shall be given by any regulation of commerce or revenue to the ports of one state over those of another: nor shall vessels bound to, or from, one state, be obliged to enter, clear or pay duties in another.

No money shall be drawn from the treasury but in consequence of appropriations made by law, and a regular statement and account of the receipts and expenditures of all public money shall be published from time to time.

No title of nobility shall be granted by the United States: And no person holding any office of profit or trust under them shall, without the consent of the congress, accept of any present, emolument, office or title, of any kind whatever, from any king, prince, or foreign state.

Section 10.

No state shall enter into any treaty, alliance, or confederation; grant letters of marque and reprisal; coin money, emit bills of credit; make anything but gold and silver coin a tender in payment of debts, pass any bill of attainder, ex post facto law, or law impairing the obligations of contracts, or grant any title of nobility.

No state shall, without the consent of congress, lay any imposts or duties on imports or exports, except what might be absolutely necessary for executing its inspection laws, and the net produce of all duties and imposts laid by any state on imports or exports shall be for the use of the treasury of the United States; and all such laws shall be subject to the revision and control of the congress.

No state shall, without the consent of congress, lay any duty of tonnage, keep troops, or ships of war in time of peace, enter into any agreement or compact with another state, or with a foreign power, or engage in war, unless actually invaded, or in such imminent danger as will not admit of delay.

ARTICLE II

Section 1.

The executive power shall be vested in a president of the United States of America. He shall hold his office during the term of four years, and, together with the vice president, chosen for the same term, be elected, as follows:

Each state shall appoint, in such manner as the legislature thereof might direct, a number of electors, equal to the whole number Constitution of the United States of senators and representatives to which the state might be entitled in the congress: but no senator or representative, or person holding an office of trust or profit under the United States, shall be appointed an elector.

The electors shall meet in their respective states, and vote by ballot for two persons, of whom one at least shall not be an inhabitant of the same state with themselves. And they shall make a list of all the persons voted for, and of the number of votes for each; which list they shall sign and certify, and transmit sealed to the seat of the government of the United States, directed to the president of the senate. The president of the senate shall, in the presence of the senate and house of representatives open all the certificates, and the votes shall then be counted. The person having the greatest number of votes shall be the president, if such number be a majority of the whole number of electors appointed; and if there be more than one who have such majority, and have an equal number of votes then the house of representatives shall immediately choose by ballot one of them for president; and if no person have a majority, then from the five highest on the list the said house shall in like manner choose the president. But in choosing the president the votes shall be taken by states, the representation for each state having one vote; a quorum for this purpose shall consist of a member or members from two-thirds of the states, and a majority of all the states shall be necessary to a choice. In every case, after the choice of the president, the person having the greatest number of votes of the electors shall be the vice president. But if there should remain two or more who have equal votes, the senate shall choose from them by ballot the vice president.

The congress might determine the time of choosing the electors and the day on which they shall give their votes; which day shall be the same throughout the United States.

No person except a natural born citizen, or a citizen of the United States at the time of the adoption of this constitution, shall be eligible to the office of president; neither shall any person be eligible to that office who shall not have attained to the age of thirty-five years, and been fourteen years a resident within the United States.

In case of the removal of the president from office, or of his death, resignation, or inability to discharge the powers and duties of the said office, the same shall devolve on the vice president, and the congress might by law provide for the case of removal, death, resignation, or inability, both of the president and vice president, declaring what officer shall then act as president, and such officer shall act accordingly, until the disability be removed, or a president shall be elected.

The president shall, at stated times, receive for his services a compensation, which shall neither be increased nor diminished during the period for which he shall have been elected, and he shall not receive within that period any other emolument from the United States, or any of them.

Before he enter on the execution of his office, he shall take the following oath or affirmation:—"I do solemnly swear (or affirm) that I will faithfully execute the office of president of the United Constitution of the United States, and will to the best of my ability preserve, protect and defend the constitution of the United States."

Section 2.

The President shall be commander in chief of the army and navy of the United States, and of the militia of the several states, when called into the actual service of the United States; he might require the opinion, in writing, of the principal officer in each of the executive departments, upon any subject relating to the duties of their respective offices, and he shall have power to grant reprieves and pardons for offences against the United States, except in cases of impeachment.

He shall have power, by and with the advice and consent of the senate to make treaties, provided two-thirds of the senators present concur; and he shall nominate, and by and with the advice and consent of the senate, shall appoint ambassadors, other public ministers and consuls, judges of the supreme court, and all other officers of the United States whose appointments are not herein otherwise provided for, and which shall be established by law: but the congress might by law vest the appointment of such inferior officers, as they think proper, in the president alone, in the courts of law, or in the heads of departments.

The president shall have power to fill up all vacancies that might happen during the recess of the senate, by granting commissions which shall expire at the end of their next session.

Section 3.

He shall from time to time give to the congress information of the state of the union, and recommend to their consideration such measures as he shall judge necessary and expedient; he may, on extraordinary occasions, convene both houses, or either of them, and in case of disagreement between them, with respect to the time of adjournment, he might adjourn them to such time as he shall think proper; he shall receive ambassadors and other public ministers; he shall take care that the laws be faithfully executed, and shall commission all the officers of the United States.

Section 4.

The president, vice president and all civil officers of the United States shall be removed from office on impeachment for, and conviction of, treason, bribery, or other high crimes and misdemeanors.

ARTICLE III

Section 1.

The judicial power of the United States shall be vested in one supreme court, and in such inferior courts as the congress might from time to time ordain and establish. The judges, both of the supreme and inferior courts, shall hold their offices during good behavior, and shall, at stated times, receive for their services a compensation which shall not be diminished during their continuance in office.

Section 2.

The judicial power shall extend to all cases, in law and equity, arising under this constitution, the laws of the United States, and treaties made, or which shall be made, under their authority;—to all cases affecting ambassadors, other public ministers and consuls;—to all cases of admiralty and maritime jurisdiction;—to controversies to which the United States shall be a party;—to controversies between two or more states;—between a state and citizens of another state;—between citizens of different states;—between citizens of the same state claiming lands under grants of different states, and between a state, or the citizens thereof, and foreign states, citizens or subjects.

In all cases affecting ambassadors, other public ministers and consuls, and those in which a state shall be a party, the supreme court shall have original jurisdiction. In all the other cases before mentioned, the supreme court shall have appellate jurisdiction, both as to law and fact, with such exceptions and under such regulations as the congress shall make.

The trial of all crimes, except in cases of impeachment, shall be by jury; and such trial shall be held in the state where the said crimes shall have been committed; but when not committed within any state, the trial shall be at such place or places as the congress might by law have directed.

Section 3.

Treason against the United States shall consist only in levying war against them, or in adhering to their enemies, giving them aid and comfort. No person shall be convicted of treason unless on the testimony of two witnesses to the same overt act, or on confession in open court.

The congress shall have power to declare the punishment of treason, but no attainder of treason shall work corruption of blood, or forfeiture, except during the life of the person attainted.

ARTICLE IV
Section 1.

Full faith and credit shall be given in each state to the public acts, records, and judicial proceedings of every other state. And the congress might by general laws prescribe the manner in which such acts, records and proceedings shall be proved, and the effect thereof.

Section 2.

The citizens of each state shall be entitled to all privileges and immunities of citizens in the several states.

A person charged in any state with treason, felony, or other crime, who shall flee from justice, and be found in another state, shall, on demand of the executive authority of the state from which he fled, be delivered up, to be removed to the state having jurisdiction of the crime.

No person held to service or labor in one state, under the laws thereof, escaping into another, shall, in consequence of any law or regulation therein, be discharged from such service or labor, but shall be delivered up on claim of the party to whom such service or labor might be due.

Section 3.

New states might be admitted by the congress into this union; but no new state shall be formed or erected within the jurisdiction of any other state; nor any state be formed by the junction of two or more states, or parts of states, without the consent of the legislatures of the states concerned as well as of the congress.

The congress shall have power to dispose of and make all needful rules and regulations respecting the territory or other property belonging to the United States; and nothing in this constitution shall be so construed as to prejudice any claims of the United States, or of any particular state.

Section 4.

The United States shall guarantee to every state in this union a republican form of government, and shall protect each of them against invasion; and on application of the legislature, or of the executive (when the legislature cannot be convened), against domestic violence.

ARTICLE V

The congress, whenever two-thirds of both houses shall deem it necessary, shall propose amendments to this constitution, or, on the application of the legislatures of two-thirds of the several states, shall call a convention for proposing amendments, which, either case, shall be valid to all intents and purposes, as part of this constitution, when ratified by the legislatures of three-fourths of the several states, or by conventions in three-fourths thereof, as the one or the other mode of ratification might be proposed by the congress: Provided, that no amendment which might be made prior to the year one thousand eight hundred and eight shall in any manner affect the first and fourth clauses in the ninth section of the first article; and that no state, without its consent, shall be deprived of its equal suffrage in the senate.

ARTICLE VI

All debts contracted and engagements entered into, before the adoption of this constitution, shall be as valid against the United States under this constitution as under the confederation.

This constitution, and the laws of the United States which shall be made in pursuance thereof, and all treaties made, or which shall be made, under the authority of the United States, shall be the supreme law of the land; and the judges in every state shall be bound thereby, anything in the constitution or laws of any state to the contrary notwithstanding.

The senators and representatives before mentioned, and the members of the several state legislatures, and all executive and judicial officers, both of the United States and of the several states, shall be bound by oath or affirmation, to support this constitution but no religious test shall ever be required as a qualification to any office or public trust under the United States.

ARTICLE VII

The ratification of the conventions of nine states shall be sufficient for the establishment of this constitution between the states so ratifying the same.

AMENDMENTS

AMENDMENT 1

Congress shall make no law respecting an establishment of religion, or prohibiting the free exercise thereof; or abridging the freedom of speech or of the press; or the right of the people peaceably to assemble, and to petition the government for a redress of grievances.

AMENDMENT 2

A well regulated militia, being necessary to the security of a free state, the right of the people to keep and bear arms shall not be infringed.

AMENDMENT 3

No soldier shall, in time of peace, be quartered in any house without the consent of the owner, nor in time of war but in a manner to be prescribed by law.

AMENDMENT 4

The right of the people to be secure in their persons, houses, papers, and effects, against unreasonable searches and seizures shall not be violated, and no warrants shall issue but upon probable cause, supported by oath or affirmation and particularly describing the place to be searched and the persons or things to be seized.

AMENDMENT 5

No person shall be held to answer for a capital or otherwise infamous crime, unless on a presentment or indictment of a grand jury, except in cases arising in the land or naval forces, or in the militia, when in actual service in time of war or public danger, nor shall any person be subject for the same offense to be twice put in jeopardy of life or limb; nor shall be compelled in any criminal case to be a witness against himself, nor be deprived of life, liberty, or property, without due process of law; nor shall private property be taken for public use without just compensation.

AMENDMENT 6

In all criminal prosecutions the accused shall enjoy the right to a speedy and public trial, by an impartial jury of the state and district wherein the crime shall have been committed, which district shall have been previously ascertained by law, and to be informed of the nature and caused of the accusation, to be confronted with the witnesses against him; to have compulsory process for obtaining witnesses in his favor, and to have the assistance of counsel for his defense.

AMENDMENT 7

In suits at common law, where the value in controversy shall exceed twenty dollars, the right of trial by jury shall be preserved, and no fact tried by a jury shall be otherwise reexamined in any court of the United States than according to the rules of the common law.

AMENDMENT 8

Excessive bail shall not be required, nor excessive fines imposed, nor cruel and unusual punishments inflicted.

AMENDMENT 9

The enumeration in the constitution of certain rights shall not be construed to deny or disparage others retained by the people.

AMENDMENT 10

The powers not delegated to the United States by the constitution, nor prohibited by it to the states, are reserved to the states, respectively, or to the people.

AMENDMENT 11

The judicial power of the United States shall not be construed to extend to any suit in law or equity, commenced or prosecuted against one of the United States by citizens of another state, or by citizens or subjects of any foreign state.

AMENDMENT 12

The electors shall meet in their respective states, and vote by ballot for president and vice president, one of whom, at least, shall not be an inhabitant of the same state with themselves; they shall name in their ballots the person voted for as president, and in distinct ballots the person voted for as vice president, and they shall make distinct lists of all persons voted for as president, and of all persons voted for as vice president, and of the number of votes for each, which lists they shall sign and certify, and transmit sealed to the seat of the government of the United States, directed to the president of the senate;—the president to the senate shall, in the presence of the senate and house of representatives, open all the certificates and the votes shall then be counted,—the person having the greatest number of votes for president shall be the president, if such number be a majority of the whole number of electors appointed; and if no person have such majority, then from the persons having the highest numbers not exceeding three on the list of those voted for as president the house of representatives shall choose immediately, by ballot, the president. But in choosing the president, the votes shall he taken by states, the representation from each state having one vote; a quorum for this purpose shall consist of a member or members from two-thirds of the states, and a majority of all the states shall be necessary to a choice. And if the house of representatives shall not choose a president whenever the right of choice shall devolve upon them before the fourth day of March next following, then the vice president shall act as president, as in the case of the death or other constitutional disability of the president. The person having the greatest number involves as vice president shall be the vice president, if such number he a majority of the whole number of electors appointed, and if no person have a majority, then from the two highest numbers on the list the senate shall choose the vice president; a quorum for the purpose shall consist of two-thirds of the whole number of senators, and a majority of the whole number shall be necessary to a choice. But no person constitutionally ineligible to the office of president shall he eligible to that of vice president of the United States.

AMENDMENT 13

1. Neither slavery nor involuntary servitude, except as a punishment for crime whereof the party shall have been duly convicted shall exist within the United States, or any place subject to their jurisdiction.

2. Congress shall have power to enforce this article by appropriate legislation.

AMENDMENT 14

1. All persons born or naturalized in the United States, and subject to the jurisdiction thereof; are citizens of the United States and of the state wherein they reside. No state shall make or enforce any law which shall abridge the privileges or immunities of citizens of the United States; nor shall any state deprive any person of life liberty, or property, without due process of law, nor deny to any person within its jurisdiction the equal protection of the laws.

2. Representatives Shall be apportioned among the several states according to their respective numbers, counting the whole number of persons in each state, excluding Indians not taxed. But when the right to vote at any election for the choice of electors for president and vice president of the United States, representatives in congress, the executive and judicial officers of a state, or the members of the legislature thereof, is denied to any of the male inhabitants of such state, being twenty-one years of age, and citizens of the United States, or in any way abridged except for participation in rebellion, or other crime, the basis of representation therein shall be reduced in the proportion which the number of such male citizens shall bear to the whole number of male citizens twenty-one years of age in such state.

3. No person shall be a senator or representative in congress, or elector of president and vice president, or hold any office, civil or military, under the United States, or under any state, who, having previously taken an oath, as a member of congress, or as an officer of the United States, or as a member of any state legislature, or as an executive or judicial officer of any state, to support the constitution of the United States, shall have engaged in insurrection or rebellion against the same, or given aid or comfort to the enemies thereof. But congress might by a vote of two-thirds of each house remove such disability.

4. The validity of the public debt of the United States, authorized by law, including debts incurred for payment of pensions and bounties for services in suppressing insurrection or rebellion, shall not be questioned. But neither the United States nor any state shall assume or pay any debt or obligation incurred in aid of insurrection or rebellion against the United States, or any claim for the loss or emancipation of any slave; but all such debts, obligations and claims shall be held illegal and void.

5. The congress shall have power to enforce, by appropriate legislation, the provisions of this article.

AMENDMENT 15

1. The right of citizens of the United States to vote shall not be denied or abridged by the United States or by any state on account of race, color, or previous condition of servitude.

2. The congress shall have power to enforce this article by appropriate legislation.

AMENDMENT 16

The congress shall have power to lay and collect taxes on incomes, from whatever source derived, without apportionment among the several states, and without regard to any census or enumeration.

AMENDMENT 17

The senate of the United States shall be composed of two senators from each state, elected by the people thereof, for six years; and each senator shall have one vote. The electors in each state shall have the qualifications requisite for electors of the most numerous branch of the state legislatures. When vacancies happen in the representation of any state in the senate, the executive authority of such state shall issue writs of election to fill such vacancies: Provided, that the legislature of any state might empower the executive thereof to make temporary appointments until the people fill the vacancies by election as the legislature might direct. This amendment shall not be so construed as to affect the election or term of any senator chosen before it becomes valid as part of the constitution.

AMENDMENT 18

1. After one year from the ratification of this article, the manufacture, sale, or transportation of intoxicating liquors within, the importation thereof into, or the exportation thereof from the United States and all territory subject to the jurisdiction thereof, for beverage purposes, is hereby prohibited.

2. The congress and the several states shall have concurrent power to enforce this article by appropriate legislation.

3. This article shall be inoperative unless it shall have been ratified as an amendment to the constitution by the legislatures of the several states, as provided in the constitution, within seven years from the date of the submission hereof to the states by the congress.

AMENDMENT 19

1. The right of citizens of the United States to vote shall not be denied or abridged by the United States or by any state on account of sex.

2. Congress shall have power to enforce this article by appropriate legislation.

AMENDMENT 20

1. The terms of the president and vice president shall end at noon on the 20th day of January, and the terms of senators and representatives at noon on the 3d day of January, of the years in which such terms would have ended if this article had not been ratified; and the terms of their successors shall then begin.

2. The Congress shall assemble at least once in every year, and such meeting shall begin at noon on the 3d day of January, unless they shall by law appoint a different day.

3. If, at the time fixed for the beginning of the term of the president, the president elect shall have died, the vice president elect shall become president. If a president shall not have been chosen before the time fixed for the beginning of his term, or if the president elect shall have failed to qualify, then the vice president elect shall act as president until a president shall have qualified; and the congress might by law provide for the case wherein neither a president elect nor a vice president elect shall have qualified, declaring who shall then act as president, or the manner in which one who is to act shall be selected, and such person shall act accordingly until a president or vice president shall have qualified.

4. The congress might by law provide for the case of the death of any of the persons from whom the house of representatives might choose a president whenever the right of choice shall have devolved upon them, and for the case of the death of any of the persons from whom the senate might choose a vice president whenever the right of choice shall have devolved upon them.

5. Sections 1 and 2 shall take effect on the 15th day of October following the ratification of this article.

6. This article shall be inoperative unless it shall have been ratified as an amendment to the constitution by the legislatures of three-fourths of the several States within seven years from the date of its submission.

AMENDMENT 21

1. The eighteenth article of amendment to the constitution of the United States is hereby repealed.

2. The transportation or importation into any state, territory, or possession of the United States for delivery or use therein of intoxicating liquors, in violation of the laws thereof, is hereby prohibited.

3. This article shall be inoperative unless it shall have been ratified as an amendment to the constitution by conventions in the several states, as provided in the constitution, within seven years from the date of the submission hereof to the states by the congress.

AMENDMENT 22

1. No person shall be elected to the office of the president more than twice, and no person who has held the office of president, or acted as president, for more than two years of a term to which some other person was elected president shall be elected to the office of the president more than once. But this article shall not apply to any person holding the office of president when this article was proposed by the Congress, and shall not prevent any person who might be holding the office of president, or acting as president, during the term within which this article becomes operative from holding the office of president or acting as president during the remainder of such term.

2. This article shall be inoperative unless it shall have been ratified as an amendment to the constitution by the legislatures of three-fourths of the several States within seven years from the date of its submission to the States by the congress.

AMENDMENT 23

1. The District constituting the seat of Government of the United States shall appoint in such manner as the Congress might direct: A number of electors of President and Vice President equal to the whole number of Senators and Representatives in Congress to which the District would be entitled if it were a State, but in no event more than the least populous State; they shall be in addition to those appointed by the States, but they shall be considered, for the purpose of the election of President and Vice President, to be electors appointed by a State; and they shall meet in the District and perform such duties as provided by the twelfth article of amendment.

2. The Congress shall have power to enforce this article by appropriate legislation.

AMENDMENT 24

1. The right of citizens of the United States to vote in any primary or other election for President or Vice President, for electors for President or Vice President, or for Senator or Representative in Congress, shall not be denied or abridged by the United States or any State by reason of failure to pay any poll tax or other tax.

2. The Congress shall have power to enforce this article by appropriate legislation.

AMENDMENT 25

1. In case of the removal of the President from office or of his death or resignation, the Vice President shall become President.

2. Whenever there is a vacancy in the office of the Vice President, the President shall nominate a Vice President who shall take office upon confirmation by a majority vote of both Houses of Congress.

3. Whenever the President transmits to the President pro tempore of the Senate and the Speaker of the House of Representatives his written declaration that he is unable to discharge the powers and duties of his office, and until he transmits to them a written declaration to the contrary, such powers and duties shall be discharged by the Vice President as Acting President.

4. Whenever the Vice President and a majority of either the principal officers of the executive departments or of such other body as Congress might by law provide, transmit to the President pro tempore of the Senate and the Speaker of the House of Representatives their written declaration that the President is unable to discharge the powers and duties of his office, the Vice President shall immediately assume the powers and duties of the office as Acting President. Thereafter, when the President transmits to the President pro tempore of the Senate and the Speaker of the House of Representatives his written declaration that no inability exists, he shall resume the powers and duties of his office unless the Vice President and a majority of either the principal officers of the executive department or of such other body as Congress might by law provide, transmit within four days to the President pro tempore of the Senate and the Speaker of the House of Representatives their written declaration that the President is unable to discharge the powers and duties of his office. Thereupon Congress shall decide the issue, assembling within forty-eight hours for that purpose if not in session. If the Congress, within twenty-one days after receipt of the latter written declaration, or, if Congress is not in session, within twenty-one days after Congress is required to assemble, determines by two-thirds vote of both Houses that the President is unable to discharge the powers and duties of his office, the Vice President shall continue to discharge the same as Acting President; otherwise, the President shall resume the powers and duties of his office.

AMENDMENT 26

1. The right of citizens of the United States, who are eighteen years of age or older, to vote shall not be denied or abridged by the United States or by any State on account of age.

2. The Congress shall have power to enforce this article by appropriate legislation.

AMENDMENT 27

No law, varying the compensation for the services of the Senators and Representatives, shall take effect, until an election of Representatives shall have intervened.

Index

Catellus
Publishing

Interested in purchasing more copies?

Alliances—A Theory of Concerted Human Behavior
is available for sale from internet book sellers.

Or visit Catellus Publishing Website at:

http://www.catelluspublishing.com

If you have any questions, please:

Email: *questions@catelluspublishing.com*

Mail: Catellus Publishing
P.O. Box 550409
Houston, Texas 77255-0409